INTERNATIONAL COURTS AND TRIBUNALS SERIES

General Editors: Philippe Sands, Ruth Mackenzie, and Cesare Romano

REGULATING JURISDICTIONAL RELATIONS BETWEEN NATIONAL AND INTERNATIONAL COURTS

INTERNATIONAL COURTS AND TRIBUNALS SERIES

A distinctive feature of modern international society is the increase in the number of international judicial bodies and dispute settlement and implementation control bodies; in their case-loads; and in the range and importance of the issues that they are called upon to address. These factors reflect a new stage in the delivery of international justice. The International Courts and Tribunals series has been established to encourage the publication of independent and scholarly works which address, in critical and analytical fashion, the legal and policy aspects of the functioning of international courts and tribunals, including their institutional, substantive and procedural aspects.

REGULATING JURISDICTIONAL RELATIONS BETWEEN NATIONAL AND INTERNATIONAL COURTS

YUVAL SHANY

The Project on PiCT
International Courts and Tribunals

This series has been developed in cooperation with the Project on International Courts and Tribunals

OXFORD
UNIVERSITY PRESS

OXFORD
UNIVERSITY PRESS

Great Clarendon Street, Oxford, OX2 6DP,
United Kingdom

Oxford University Press is a department of the University of Oxford.
It furthers the University's objective of excellence in research, scholarship,
and education by publishing worldwide. Oxford is a registered trade mark of
Oxford University Press in the UK and in certain other countries

First published 2007

Published in the United States of America by Oxford University Press
198 Madison Avenue, New York, NY 10016, United States of America

British Library Cataloguing in Publication Data
Data available

ISBN 978–0–19–921179–1

SHANY
Regulating Jurisdictional Relations Between
National and International Courts
Shany

'All quest for scientific knowledge is motivated by an endeavor to find unity in the apparent multiplicity of phenomena.'

Hans Kelsen, *Principles of International Law* (1952) 426

General Editors' Preface

Dr Yuval Shany's previous book, *The Competing Jurisdictions of International Courts and Tribunals*, was the first book published in the *International Courts and Tribunals* series. It was deservedly awarded the American Society of International Law Certificate of Merit for creative scholarship in 2004, and has become a primary reference on jurisdictional relations between international courts. The present book addresses a related issue, the jurisdictional relations between international and national courts.

The topics explored in this book are becoming increasingly important in practice, as jurisdictional interactions between international and national courts become more frequent. Perhaps most notably, the proper jurisdictional relations between domestic courts and arbitral tribunals, established by bilateral investment treaties, have been called into question in a series of recent cases in which the treatment of contract and treaty claims, arising out of foreign investments, has been at issue. However, as Dr Shany makes clear, similar questions have arisen, or might arise, in other contexts including human rights, the law of the sea, humanitarian law and trade law, in cases where national and international courts are called upon to address essentially the same dispute.

The treatment of international law by national courts, and the relationship between national and international courts in specific cases and contexts, have attracted significant academic attention. However, Dr Shany is among the first to seek to analyse in a more general and comprehensive fashion the ways in which rules of international law might regulate the growing jurisdictional interactions between international and national courts. The analysis is forward-looking, and addresses the theoretical dimensions and implications of the topic while offering pragmatic solutions. As such this book offers a significant academic and practical contribution, and we are delighted that it is published in the *International Courts and Tribunals* series.

Ruth Mackenzie
Centre for International Courts and Tribunals
University College London
19 June 2007

Acknowledgements

The idea for this book was born in 2004, when the Amsterdam Center for International Law (ACIL) invited me to conduct research on the jurisdictional relations between national and international courts as part of their PIONEER project. During my short stay in Amsterdam, I was able to lay the groundwork for four separate law review articles on the topic and to start contemplating the idea of tackling the questions they addressed in the form of a book from a more general perspective. I am grateful to my friends and colleagues in ACIL, particularly Prof. André Nollkaemper, Prof. Erika De Wet, and Dr Nicholaos Lavranos, for inviting me to Amsterdam, providing me with a stimulating and encouraging research environment, and for keeping track of my progress long after I left Amsterdam.

My friends at the Project on International Courts and Tribunals (PICT) have been another source of support and encouragement for this project in the last three years. For this reason, I am proud that this book (like its predecessor on the competing jurisdictions of international courts and tribunals) appears in the joint OUP-PICT series on international courts and tribunals. I wish to thank Prof. Philippe Sands, Ms Ruth Mackenzie and Prof. Cesare Romano in particular.

The third and last professional group to which I am indebted is the Hebrew University International Law Forum, which served as a discussion group for many of the ideas raised here. I am especially grateful to the following forum members: Prof. Ruth Lapidoth, Prof. Moshe Hirsch, Dr Tomer Broude, Dr Guy Harpaz, and Mr Gil-Ad Noam.

This book would not have materialized without the support of several persons and institutions to whom I am immensely grateful: My publishers at OUP—predominantly Mr John Louth; Prof. Vaughan Lowe, who invited me to spend some research time in Oxford; Ms Natalie Rosen, Ms Adva Cohen and Ms Efrat Hakak my diligent research assistants; Ms Nina Reshef, who provided me with invaluable assistance in editing; numerous librarians at the Hebrew University of Jerusalem, the College of Management in Rishon Le Zion, the University of Amsterdam, the Peace Palace in The Hague, Georgetown Law Center in Washington DC, the Institute for Advanced Legal Studies in London and Oxford Law Library, who helped me in identifying and locating (sometimes obscure) research resources; and the Israel Science Foundation, which provided generous financial support for the research underlying the book.

I cannot close without thanking Merav, my wife, and Maya and Gali, my two daughters, for enduring my solo research excursions to different countries and for putting up with many lost weekends and long nights spent reading and writing throughout the last three years. I especially wish to thank my parents, Geula and Shraga, for their constant support (which included hosting me at their home while I was in Oxford). This book is dedicated to them.

Contents

II. REGULATING RELATIONS BETWEEN NATIONAL AND INTERNATIONAL COURTS

Table of Cases

Table of Treaties

Table of International Instruments

Table of Domestic Legislation

MISCELLANEOUS

List of Abbreviations

BIT(s)	Bilateral Investment Treaty(ies)
CAFTA	Central American Free Trade Agreement
CIT	Court of International Trade
EC	European Community
ECC	Extraordinary Challenge Committee
ECHR	European Convention on Human Rights
ECJ	European Court of Justice
EEC	European Economic Community
EU	European Union
Eur. Comm'n on H.R.	European Commission on Human Rights
ECtHR	European Court of Human Rights
FYROM	Former Yugoslav Republic of Macedonia
GATT	General Agreement on Tariffs and Trade
HCJ	High Court of Justice (Israel)
ICANN	Internet Corporation for Assigned Names and Numbers
ICC	International Criminal Court
ICJ	International Court of Justice
ICSID	International Centre for Settlement of Investment Disputes
ICTR	International Criminal Tribunal for Rwanda
ICTY	International Criminal Tribunal for Yugoslavia
IDF	Israeli Defense Forces
ILA	International Law Association
ILC	International Law Commission
I/A CtHR	The Inter-American Court of Human Rights
ITLOS	International Tribunal for the Law of the Sea
NAFTA	North American Free Trade Agreement
PCA	Permanent Court of Arbitration
PCIJ	Permanent Court of International Justice

SCSL	Special Court for Sierra Leone
UNCITRAL	United Nations Commission on International Trade Law
UNCLOS	United Nations Convention on the Law of the Sea
WTO	World Trade Organization
WTO DSB	WTO Dispute Settlement Body

Introduction

I. Doctrinal Implications of Increased Jurisdictional Interaction

1.1 The phenomenon of increased interaction

Jurisdictional interactions between national and international courts seem to have become more prominent and more frequent:[1] for instance, the International Court of Justice and the Inter-American Court of Human Rights have addressed a number of cases in recent years concerning the manner in which domestic courts in the US have addressed alleged violations of the duty to notify detained foreign nationals of their right to receive consular assistance pursuant to the 1963 Vienna Convention on Consular Relations.[2] The legal effect of some of the interim decisions and judgments issued by these international judicial bodies has been subsequently discussed by some US courts, including the Supreme Court.[3]

Another group of proceedings before US and international courts recently took place in the context of the *Zeroing* and *Softwood Lumber* disputes between Canadian and other exporters and US Trade Authorities. Here, too, the interplay between domestic and international proceedings and the effects of international decisions on proceedings pending before domestic courts were discussed at length.[4]

A further example may be drawn from the field of international humanitarian law. On 9 July 2004, the ICJ issued an advisory opinion on the lawfulness of Israel's controversial West Bank separation barrier[5]—ten days after Israel's Supreme Court had addressed essentially the same legal question.[6] The legal effect of the ICJ's opinion was considered in a subsequent Supreme Court judgment relating to another segment of the barrier.[7]

1 Jenny S. Martinez, 'Towards an International Judicial System', 56 *Stan. L. Rev.* (2003) 429, 441–2; Philippe Sands, 'After Pinochet: The Proper Relationship between National and International Courts', *The International Legal System in Quest of Equity and Universality—Liber Amicorum Georges Abi-Saab*, (Laurence Boisson de Chazournes and Vera Gowland-Debbas, eds, 2001) 699, 704.

2 *Vienna Convention on Consular Relations* (Paraguay v US), 1998 ICJ 248 (Provisional Measures); *LaGrand* (Germany v US), 2001 ICJ 466; *Avena* (Mexico v US), 43 ILM 581 (2004); *The Right to Information on Consular Assistance in the Framework of the Guarantees of the Due Process of Law*, Advisory Opinion of 1 Oct 1999, Inter-Am Ct HR (Ser A) No 16, at (1999).

3 See eg, *Breard v Greene*, 523 US 371 (1998); *Sanchez-Llamas v Oregon*, 126 S Ct 2669 (2006).

4 See eg, *Certain Softwood Lumber Products from Canada: Final Affirmative Antidumping Determination*, decision of 9 June 2005 (NAFTA Chapter 19 binational panel); *Ontario Forest Industries Assoc v US*, 444 F Supp 2d 1309 (2006) (US Court of International Trade).

5 *Legal Consequences of the Construction of a Wall in the Occupied Palestinian Territory*, 43 ILM 1009 (2004).

6 HCJ 2056/04 *Beit Sourik Village Council v Gov't of Israel*, 58(4) PD 807.

7 See eg, HCJ 7957/04 *Mara'abe v Prime Minister of Israel*, Judgment of 15 Sept 2005.

Finally, as of 2000, a growing number of arbitration cases adjudicated under the auspices of the International Centre for the Settlement of Investment Disputes (ICSID) have raised difficult problems of regulation between treaty claims (these claims, based on international investment protection treaties—typically bilateral investment treaties (BITs)—often provide for the adjudication of disputes before international judicial fora) and contract claims (claims based on private investment contracts that may refer disputes to domestic courts or local arbitration panels).[8] Significantly, these ICSID cases suggest that the delineation of the legal relations between treaty and contract claims affects the jurisdictional relationship between international arbitration and domestic proceedings stemming from the same investment disputes.

These and other incidents of jurisdictional interaction between national and international courts raise complicated legal problems,[9] pertaining to the division of labour between national and international courts, their ability (or duty) to consider their counterparts' judicial decisions, and their potential for cooperation and coordination. Furthermore, such jurisdictional interaction gives rise to a series of difficult theoretical issues that are woven into the long-standing debates over the nature of the intricate relationship between national and international law.

The present book explores the need to regulate jurisdictional overlaps between national and international courts—ie, jurisdictional interactions taking place between national and international courts with respect to disputes between the same parties (or, closely related sets of parties) over essentially identical issues, potentially or actually brought, simultaneously or consecutively, before national and international courts. In addition, the book aims to identify any rules of *international law* that could—or perhaps should—govern such interactions and, as a result, regulate forum-selection or multiple proceedings involving these courts. Finally, the book examines the standards of review that should be employed by international courts vis-à-vis the decisions of their domestic counterparts and vice versa.

1.2 Dualism as a conceptual obstacle to regulation

Yet, the very formulation of the research questions mentioned in the preceding paragraph may raise significant objections as the conditions of inducing jurisdictional interaction or overlap are controversial: as I explain in Part I below, national

[8] See eg, *Compania de Aquas del Aconquija SA v Argentina*, 40 ILM 426, 428–9 (2001) (hereinafter *Vivendi I*); *Compania de Aquas del Aconquija SA v Argentina*, 41 ILM 1135, 1154 (2002) (hereinafter *Vivendi II*); *Société Générale de Sureveillance SA (SGS) v Pakistan*, 42 ILM 1290, 1298 (2003); *Société Générale de Surveillance SA (SGS) v Philippines*, decision of 29 Jan, 2004, <http://www.worldbank.org/icsid/cases/SGSvPhil-final.pdf>.

[9] For example, challenges to the due process standards applied by international criminal courts have been raised in domestic proceedings, particularly regarding attempts to enforce international criminal court orders before domestic fora. See eg, *Milosevic v The Netherlands*, Hague District Court, decision of 31 Aug 2001, summarized in XLVIII *Netherlands International Law Review* 357 (2001); *Egbuna v Taylor*, Decision of 1 Nov 2005 (Federal High Court, Abuja, Nigeria), ILDC 163 (NG 2005) (domestic

and international courts are often perceived as courts of a different order altogether that apply different sets of laws and fulfil different social functions.[10] It is questionable whether claims presented in such different institutional contexts, invoking legal standards anchored in different legal systems, can ever be described as similar claims for the purpose of identifying jurisdictional overlaps. In other words, the question pertains to whether these claims possess the required degree of similarity to apply most jurisdiction-regulating rules. Hence, the existence of jurisdictional interaction between national and international courts per se and the need for regulating their jurisdictions might be disputed.

Regulation of jurisdictional interactions between national and international courts may ultimately depend on the identification of the paradigm that governs the relationship between the said institutions: do they operate in complete normative isolation from one another, or within more integrative frameworks of normative interaction. That act of identification (or selection) is informed to a considerable degree by competing visions of the relations between national and international law, which correspond to some extent to the classic monism/dualism debate.[11]

The two traditional schools of thought that address the framework of relations between national law and international law—monism and dualism—are well known. A third approach to these relations—legal pluralism—has also been suggested.[12] According to the traditional dualistic point of view, a doctrinal wall

courts have jurisdiction to review petition to revoke asylum of individual indicted by the Special Court in Sierra Leone). See also *Naletilić v Croatia*, decision of 4 May 2000, 2000-V Eur Ct HR 489 (review of decision by Croatian courts to extradite an individual to the ICTY). Cf *Melchers & Co v Germany*, App 13258/87, 1990 YB Eur Conv on HR 138 (Eur Comm'n on HR) (review of a German court decision not to contest an ECJ competition law judgment).

[10] Indeed, the traditional position of the PCIJ had been that national and international courts operate in different legal spheres and cannot, as a result, compete with one another. *Certain German Interests in Polish Upper Silesia* (Germany v Poland), 1925 PCIJ (Ser A), No 6, at 20 (Jurisdiction) (PCIJ, mixed arbitral tribunals and Polish civil tribunals—'are not courts of the same character'). See also *SGS v* Pakistan, 42 ILM at 1307, n 131 (citing the *Selwyn, Socaciu and Caire* cases); Christoph C Schreuer, *Decisions of International Institutions before Domestic Courts* (1981) 330–1.

[11] For a discussion of monism and dualism, Robert Jennings and Arthur Watts, 1 *Oppenheim's International Law* (9th ed, 1992) 53; J G Starke, 'Monism and Dualism in the Theory of International Law', 17 *Brit YB Int'l L* (1936) 66; Hannu Klami, 'Monism and Dualism in Law: National Versus International or Supranational Law', *Coherence and Conflict in Law* (Bob Brouwer et al, eds 1992) 139, 139–48; George Slyz, 'International Law in National Courts', 28 *NYUJ Int'l L & Pol* 65, 67 (1996); Giorgio Gaja, *Dualism—A Review*, a paper presented in an Amsterdam Center for International Law Seminar on Theoretical Approaches to the Relationship between International and National Law (2003) 2 (copy with author).

[12] Klaus Günther, 'Legal Pluralism and the Universal Code of Legality: Globalisation as a Problem of Legal Theory' (2003), <http://www.law.nyu.edu/clppt/program2003/readings/gunther.pdf>; Gunther Teubner, 'Global Bukowina: Legal Pluralism in the World Society', *Global Law Without a State* (Gunther Teubner, ed, 1997) 3, 11–15; Gunther Teubner, 'Breaking Frames: The Global Interplay of Legal and Social Systems', 45 *Am J Comp L* (1997) 149, 157. Although the terms pluralism and dualism were once used interchangeably, it is nowadays common to associate pluralism with the notion that decision makers (including courts) can apply norms derived from a multitude of sources. The invitation extended to courts to consider norms originating outside their own legal system brings modern pluralism closer to traditional monism than to traditional dualism.

separates national and international law: national and international law constitute two distinct legal orders that govern, separately and independently, the operation of national and international courts, provide them with distinct normative sources (endowed with autonomous bases of legitimacy), and dictate their idiosyncratic social functions. At the same time, monism posits that national and international law are, in truth, part of the same normative (and also, arguably, institutional) whole, and that the operation of one legal order may be governed and legitimized by the other.

Historical developments, especially the emergence of the European Community (EC)[13] and the European Convention on Human Rights (ECHR),[14] as well as the increased tendency to attribute non-self-executing status to international treaties in the US,[15] have taken the edge off much of the monism/dualism debate. It now appears that most national legal systems adopt a pragmatic approach influenced by political considerations towards the question of whether to incorporate international law into national law and to what extent.[16] Such an approach may range from full incorporation of all international law norms into the domestic legal system (eg, through direct effect rules)[17] to partial incorporation of some norms of international law (eg, through interpretative constructions).[18]

Still, as far as regulation of the relationship between national and international courts is concerned, the monism/dualism debate continues to have considerable influence over conceptualization of this jurisdictional relationship.[19] International courts in particular have continued, by and large, to maintain a dualistic attitude towards domestic courts, viewing the application of national law by the latter as normatively irrelevant.[20] Furthermore, it looks as if some of the pragmatism employed in the inter-normative context is absent from the debate over the jurisdictional relations between courts operating in the respective legal systems.

[13] Treaty Establishing the European Community (Consolidated Version), 24 Dec 2002, art 77, 2002 OJ (C325) 33 (hereinafter EC Treaty). The EC currently constitutes part of the European Union (EU), established by the Treaty on European Union, 7 Feb 1992, OJ (C 224) 1.

[14] European Convention for the Protection of Human Rights and Fundamental Freedoms, 4 Nov 1950, ETS 5 (hereinafter ECHR).

[15] See eg, Carlos Manuel Vazquez, 'The Four Doctrines of Self-Executing Treaties', 89 *AJIL* 695 (1995); Thomas Buergenthal, 'Self-Executing and Non-Self-Executing Treaties in National and International Law', 235 *Recueil des cours* 303 (1992-IV).

[16] Gaja, above, n 11, at 3.

[17] The direct effect of EC law in the EC member states was pronounced in a landmark ECJ decision. Case 26/62, *Van Gend & Loos v Netherlands Inland Revenue Administration* [1963] ECR 1.

[18] See eg, Restatement of the Law (3rd), Foreign Relations Law of the United States, § 114; Bruno Simma et al, 'The Role of German Courts in the Enforcement of International Human Rights', *Enforcing International Human Rights in Domestic Courts* (Benedetto Conforti and Francesco Francioni, eds, 1997) 71; *J H Rayner (Mincing Lane) Ltd v Department of Trade* [1990] 2 AC 418, 500–1 (hereinafter *Tin Council*).

[19] This conceptual dichotomy is further reinforced by traditional distinctions between private and public law. While domestic courts are well versed in resolving private disputes, international courts have traditionally operated in the public law domain. See eg, Christine Chinkin, 'A Critique of the Public/Private Dimension', 10 *EJIL* 387, 389 (1999).

[20] See eg, *'Monte Confurco'* (Seychelles v France), ITLOS Judgment of 18 Dec 2000, at para 72, <http://www.itlos.org/case_documents/2001/document_en_115.pdf>.

Arguably, precise normative and institutional distinctions could undercut possibilities for jurisdictional overlap. In fact, the embrace of dualism may provide a convenient methodology for determining the outcome of potential jurisdictional interactions: it dismisses the relevance of proceedings grounded in a different legal system, thus obviating, in effect, any need for regulation. In Chapter 3, I argue that this conceptual move is not fundamentally different from other disintegrative methodologies applied to protect specific (or self-contained) international legal regimes from the disruptive effects of norms derived from other legal regimes.

Still, notwithstanding the doctrinal clarity it provides, dualism does not present an exclusive conceptual framework for ascertaining the relations between national and international courts (nor for the relations between national and international laws). On the contrary, some jurists have been willing to acknowledge some degree of co-application of national and international law by the same judicial institutions and to facilitate the cross-application of judicial decisions from one legal order to the other. This position might derive from non-dualistic visions of the relations between national and international courts that regard these two sets of institutions—national and international courts—as potentially engaged in common functional and normative enterprises, specifically, the settlement of disputes together with development and enforcement of the rule of law in general, and international law in particular. According to this line of thinking, national and international law may serve as jurisdictional alternatives to one another;[21] hence, their jurisdictions ought to be coordinated. So, although national courts have no doubt many responsibilities under their respective domestic legal system, they can also be viewed as playing a part in the international system, at least when they apply its norms.

This last position was captured to some degree by Scelle's *dédoublement fonctionnel* theory.[22] It also finds indirect support from contemporary American process-oriented jurisprudence theories—most influentially Anne-Marie Slaughter's work on the emergence of an epistemological community of national and international courts.[23] The common denominator to these and other relevant monist or pluralist theories[24] is rejection of the notion that a clear dichotomy holds between national and international judicial bodies and their legal environments. Ultimately, this position lacks the doctrinal elegance of dualism; still, by acknowledging some jurisdictional or functional overlap, it promotes important pragmatic interests by improving coordination between national and international proceedings.

[21] This possibility is underscored by instruments that explicitly facilitate a choice between national and international courts. For a discussion of the complementarity principle and *electa una via* clauses, see below, Chapter 1.

[22] Georges Scelle, 'La phénomène juridique du dédoublement fonctionnel', *Rechtsfragen der Internationalen Organisation: Festschrift für Hans Wehberg* (1956) 324.

[23] See eg, Anne-Marie Slaughter, 'A Global Community of Courts', 44 *Harv Int'l LJ* (2003) 191.

[24] See eg, Hans Kelsen, *General Theory of Law and State* (Anders Wedberg trans, 1999)(1945) 363–388; Teubner, 'Global Bukowina', above n 12.

1.3 Hierarchy as a substitute for regulation

The need for regulating the jurisdictional relations between national and international courts is mired in another unsettled conceptual issue—the hierarchical relationships between the two sets of judicial institutions. Monist and even pluralist jurists often insist on a hierarchical configuration between national and international courts: since national law can never justify non-compliance with international law,[25] domestic court decisions, formally grounded in domestic law, in full or in part, are subject to international supervision. Hence, international lawyers often expect international courts to exercise vertical judicial control over the performance of international law obligations by state organs, including state courts (whose willingness and capacity to apply international law are sometimes questionable).[26] At the same time, many municipal lawyers regard national constitutions as the ultimate source of authority of the law applicable in any given national polity and expect national courts to reject international decisions that are inconsistent with fundamental domestic principles.[27]

These influential yet incompatible vertical narratives establish normative and/or institutional hierarchy by conferring supremacy over their counterparts to either national or international courts, leading to a perception of national and international courts as belonging to different orders (in the sense that their jurisdictions are hierarchically ranked). Such vertical conceptualization of the relationships holding between national and international courts minimizes the need to regulate jurisdictional overlaps because hierarchical jurisdictional regimes tolerate multiple proceedings and inconsistent decisions—decisions of an inferior court can always be overruled by the superior court.[28] While courts situated in hierarchical relations may interact with one another, they cannot conceivably *compete* with one another.

It is important to realize that hierarchy, in itself, constitutes a form of jurisdictional regulation. Indeed, important regional legal frameworks, such as the EC

[25] Vienna Convention on the Law of Treaties, 23 May 1969, art 27, 1155 UNTS 331; Draft Articles on Responsibility of States for Internationally Wrongful Acts, art 3, 32, UN GAOR 56th Sess, Supp No 10, UN Doc A/56/10, Ch IV.E.1 (2001). See also *Certain German Interests*, 1925 PCIJ (Ser A), No 7, at p 19 ('From the standpoint of International Law and of the Court which is its organ, municipal laws are merely facts which express the will and constitute the activities of States, in the same manner as do legal decisions or administrative measures'). Cf *Tin Council*, [1990] 2 AC at p 500 ('It must be borne in mind, furthermore, that the conclusion of an international treaty and its terms are as much matters of fact as any other fact').

[26] See eg, *The M/V 'Saiga'* (No 2), ITLOS judgment of 1 July 1999, at paras 120–1 (merits), <http://www.itlos.org/case_documents/2001/document_en_68.doc>. Cf Gaja, above, n 11, at 12.

[27] See eg, *Internationale Handelsgesellschaft mbH v Einfuhr- und Vorratsstelle für Getreide und Futtermittel*, 37 BVerfGE 271 (1974), translated in [1974] 2 CMLR 540, 552–4 (1974); *Sanchez-Llamas*, 126 S Ct 2669.

[28] One should also note that national courts sometime question the binding nature of international decisions. See eg, *Breard*, 523 US at 375; *Mara'abe*, above n 7, at para 56.

and ECHR, ultimately accept the superiority of international courts over national courts, and coordinate between the jurisdictions of these judicial bodies in accordance with the applicable hierarchical configuration. Still, in situations where national and international courts present incompatible claims of superiority vis-à-vis their counterparts, application of a hierarchical jurisdiction-regulating rule could cause more problems than it purports to resolve. This is because hierarchy might serve as a justification for the lack of coordination between proceedings: like dualism, vertical hierarchy downplays the relevance of the other set of proceedings and offers courts a clear and simple method to resolve potential jurisdictional conflicts. This approach, however, neither provides a method for the pragmatic resolution of incompatible claims of judicial supremacy nor offers the parties to the conflict a way out of such institutional 'locking of horns'. It is therefore not surprising that some commentators emphasize some of the horizontal features that characterize relations between national and international proceedings, and advocate inter-institutional deference and improved coordination between the involved courts. Some of the treaty provisions, judicial practice and theoretical writing that lend support to this latter horizontal vision are described in Part I of this treatise.

1.4 Disintegrationism v integrationism

The debate surrounding the role of national courts under international law could also be linked, in my mind, to the broader contemporary debate regarding the structure of international law and the challenge to its coherence posed by its fragmentation into specific regimes.[29] Here too, international law is in a state of a flux: some international courts and tribunals have embraced interpretations of jurisdictional provisions that emphasize their independence from other legal regimes (thereby confirming the 'self-contained' nature of the specific regimes).[30] For example, the International Tribunal for the Law of the Sea (ITLOS) has sometimes taken the position that claims based on different legal instruments are always distinct claims, even if the instruments in question contain identical language.[31] Such an approach necessarily negates jurisdictional competition between different international courts in the vast majority of cases: by disintegrating a dispute into separate disputes arising under different bodies of law, this approach emphasizes the formal differences between the competing claims (notwithstanding their normative comparability) and the impossibility of harmonizing their outcomes.

[29] International Law Commission Study Group, 'Fragmentation of International Law: Difficulties arising from the Diversification and Expansion of International Law', UN Doc A/CN.4/L.682 (2006), at 26–7 (prepared by Martti Koskenniemi).

[30] For a discussion of the possible existence of 'self-contained regimes', see Bruno Simma, 'Self-Contained Regimes', XVI *NYBIL* (1985) 111; Bruno Simma and Dirk Pulkowski, 'Of Planets and the Universe: Self-contained Regimes in International Law', 17 *EJIL* (2006) 483.

[31] *MOX Plant* (Ireland v UK), 41 ILM 405 (2002); *Southern Bluefin Tuna* (Australia and New Zealand v Japan), 38 ILM 1624 (1999).

At the same time, other international tribunals have attempted to adopt more flexible positions that are consistent with the notion that specific treaty regimes should be harmonized with other international law norms and regimes. For example, two United Nations Convention on the Law of the Sea (UNCLOS) arbitral panels—*Southern Bluefin Tuna* (2000)[32] and *MOX Plant* (2003)[33]—were ready to consider the proceedings brought under UNCLOS before each, as alternatives to those taking place under other legal regimes (a regional fisheries convention and EC law, respectively) and to embrace jurisdiction-regulating measures (dismissal of the claim or stay of the proceedings on the basis of comity). This approach integrates, in effect, a claim before one international court with other factually related claims pending before other international courts, into one multi-faceted dispute.

Arguably, parallels may be drawn between the choice of disintegrative or integrative strategies in the context of the relations between different international courts and the choices presented in our context. Here too, a choice may be available between applying clear-cut exclusionary rules that disintegrate a single factual dispute into separate claims under national and international law and denying possibility of any jurisdictional interaction between national and international courts, on the one hand, or applying more integrative methods of coordination that acknowledge the close links between the competing sets of proceedings, on the other hand. Indeed, some of the cases of jurisdictional interaction between national and international courts discussed in Chapter 3 reveal choices of language and interpretive methodology that closely resembles the choices applied in decisions regulating the jurisdictions of different international courts. They likewise reveal a tendency to alternate between disintegrative and integrative regulation strategies.

II. The Internationalization of the National

The conceptual moves that potentially determine the scope and nature of jurisdictional interactions between national and international proceedings—dualism, hierarchy, disintegrationism and their policy underpinnings—will be further discussed in Part I. My preliminary contention on the actual interplay between national and international adjudication circumvents, for the time being, the need to provide a definitive theoretical conceptualization of the relations that hold between national and international norms and institutions and focuses instead on their de facto relationship. In this context, I contend that a number of related developments at the national and international level have brought about the approximation of national and international legal systems, which has increased the potential for jurisdictional interaction between the respective courts.

[32] *Southern Bluefin Tuna* (Australia and NZ v Japan), Award of 4 Aug 2000 (Jurisdiction and admissibility), 39 ILM 1359 (2000).

[33] *MOX Plant* (Ireland v UK), order no 3 of 24 July 2003, <http://www.pca-cpa.org/PDF/MOX%20Order%20no3.pdf>.

Hence, one may refer to the internationalization of the national, ie, the extension of international norms and institutions over situations and disputes traditionally characterized as having an exclusively domestic character. At the same time, national norms and institutions are increasingly asserting their authority over situations and disputes traditionally belonging to the international realm. While one may question the desirability of these processes—since internationalization of the national and the parallel nationalization of the international entail various costs (eg, exacerbation of the 'deficit' in democratic decision-making and accountability at the international level, advancement of 'one-size-fits-all' international solutions to complicated problems, encouragement of unilateralist extensions of power by one state over another etc),[34] it seems that these developments are unquestionably taking place,[35] with the legal boundaries between national and international law becoming more and more ambiguous in consequence.

2.1 Extension of the international into the national

International law, as it developed from the 17th to the early 20th century, primarily regulated external relations between the states comprising the international community. It consequently had little to do with events taking place within a state's sovereign territories (with a few notable exceptions, such as the treatment of diplomats or alien nationals). International law's abstention from regulating the internal affairs of states meant, by and large, the existence of limited contact points between international law and domestic legal systems; with the latter focusing their attention, quite naturally, on the regulation of internal situations.[36]

There is little question that international law has undergone significant transformations in the second half of the 20th century that have affected the traditional division of labour between the national and the international. First, an increasing number of issues formerly deemed to fall exclusively within the domestic jurisdiction of states and the exclusive authority of their domestic courts have been made the subject of international regulation—ie, they have been internationalized.[37]

[34] See eg, Andrew P Cortell and James W Davis, 'When Norms Clash: International Norms, Domestic Practices, and Japan's Internalisation of the GATT/WTO', 31 *Rev Int'l Studies* (2005) 3–25; Daniel Bodansky, 'The Legitimacy of International Governance: A Coming Challenge for International Environmental Law?', 93 *AJIL* (1999) 596, 606–11.

[35] The trend of internationalization is not new in itself. See eg, Hans Kelsen, *Principles of International Law* (1952) 202 ('We may characterize this phenomenon as the increasing inclination to internationalize the law'). One may also link between the increased reach of international law and the more general phenomenon of social 'juridification'. See eg, Ariel L Bendor, 'Are There Any Limits to Justiciability? The Jurisprudential and Constitutional Controversy in Light of the Israeli and American Experience', 7 *Ind Int'l & Comp L Rev* (1997) 311.

[36] See eg, St George Tucker, 1 *Blackstone's Commentaries: With Notes of Reference, to the Constitution and Laws, of the Federal Government of the United States; and of the Commonwealth of Virginia* (1803) 43–4.

[37] The methodology under which domestic issues can be internationalized was described by the PCIJ in the following terms: 'The question whether a certain matter is or is not solely within the jurisdiction of

New or reinvigorated international law branches—such as international human rights law, international investment law, international criminal law and international environmental law—have made significant headway into regulating activities taking place within national territories; as a result, a considerable number of areas of human activity are now subject to parallel regulation at the national and the international level.

Significantly, this normative development has gone hand in hand with institutional expansion. The last decades of the 20th century in particular have witnessed a sharp increase in the number of functioning international courts and tribunals (a phenomenon sometimes referred to as the 'proliferation of international courts')[38] and a significant extension of their judicial powers; most notably the strengthening of the compulsory nature of their jurisdictional bases.[39] In addition, limitations upon the right of access of individuals to international judicial bodies have been significantly relaxed. Individual claimants may now bring suits before several international courts in procedures that tend to emulate considerably proceedings before national courts.[40]

The result of all of these developments is that a growing number of events and issues can be regulated by national and international law, and that disputes concerning these 'regulated-in-parallel' topics may also be increasingly referred to national judicial bodies and/or international judicial bodies for adjudication.[41] So, for example, international human rights courts (such as the European Court of Human Rights (ECtHR) or the Inter-American Court of Human Rights (I/A CtHR)) routinely examine domestic measures adopted by national governments under international human rights standards,[42] while national courts may examine those same measures from the perspective of domestic constitutional or administrative law. In addition, international criminal tribunals investigate criminal

a State is an essentially relative question; it depends upon the development of international relations... [I]t may well happen that, in a matter which like that of nationality, is not, in principle, regulated by international law, the rights of a State to use its discretion is nevertheless restricted by obligations which it may have undertaken towards other States... [T]he dispute as to the question whether a State has or has not the right to take certain measures becomes in these circumstances a dispute of an international character.' *Nationality Decrees Issued in Tunis and Morocco*, 1923 PCIJ (Ser B), No 4, at 24 (1923). For a similar view, see Kelsen (1952), above n 35, at 191–2.

[38] See eg, Benedict Kingsbury, 'Is the Proliferation of International Courts and Tribunals a Systematic Problem?', 31 *NYU JILP* (1999) 679; Shane Spelliscy, 'The Proliferation of International Tribunals: A Chink in the Armor', 40 *Colum J Transnat'l L* (2001) 143.

[39] For a discussion, see Yuval Shany, *The Competing Jurisdictions of International Courts and Tribunals* (2003) 3–7.

[40] Slaughter, above n 23, at 192; Laurence R Helfer and Anne-Marie Slaughter, 'Towards a Theory of Effective Supranational Adjudication', 107 *Yale LJ* (1997) 273, 288.

[41] For support, see Slaughter, above n 23, at 192.

[42] See eg, *The Sunday Times v UK*, 30 Eur Ct HR (Ser A)(1979); *Handyside v UK*, 24 Eur Ct HR (Ser A)(1976). The *ratione materiae* mandates of the different regional human rights courts are described in—ECHR, art 32; American Convention on Human Rights, 22 Nov 1969, art 62(3), OAS TS 36, 9 ILM 673 (1970); Protocol to the African Charter on Human and People's Rights on the Establishment of an African Court on Human and People's Rights, 9 June 1998, art 3, OAU Doc OAU/LEG/EXP/AFCHPR/PROT (III).

activities that are characterized under international law as war crimes, crimes against humanity or genocide,[43] while the same offences can also be prosecuted before a number of national courts pursuant to national criminal law norms (which often mirror international standards).[44] In the field of economic law, the dispute settlement panels of the World Trade Organization (WTO) or NAFTA may examine the lawfulness of national agency investigations and determinations pertaining to traded goods.[45] These same official acts are concurrently subject to legal challenges before domestic courts on the basis of national administrative law.[46] In like manner, the European Court of Justice (ECJ) routinely examines the compatibility of measures adopted by EU members with their obligations under EU law,[47] notwithstanding the existence of parallel constitutional law, administrative law, or other legal forms of challenge under the domestic laws of these same states.

Another important consequence of the normative and institutional expansion of international law in the last half of the century has been the increased direct application of international law by national courts. Although international law has long been, formally speaking, part of the law of the land of many countries,[48] its application by national courts used to be rather limited. This could have been attributed in part to the perceived irrelevance of classic international law, which focused on regulating foreign relations, to day-to-day issues pending before national judicial

[43] See Statute of the International Criminal Court, 17 July 1998, arts 5–8, 2187 UNTS 90 (hereinafter ICC Statute); Statute of the International Criminal Tribunal for the Former Yugoslavia, 25 May 1993, arts 1–5, 32 ILM 1192 (1993); Statute of the International Tribunal for Rwanda, arts 1–4, SC Res. 955, UN SCOR, 49th Sess, 3453d mtg at 3, 33 ILM 1600 (1994).

[44] See eg, *Prosecution v Sarić*, Danish High Court, Third Chamber, Eastern Division, Judgment of 25 Nov 1994; *Public Prosecutor v Jorgić*, Oberlandesgericht Düsseldorf, Judgment of 26 Sep 1997; *Public Prosecutor v Djajić*, Supreme Court of Bavaria, 3d Strafsenat, 23 May 1997, reported in 92 *AJIL* (1998) 528–32; CrC 40/61, *Attorney General v Adolf Eichmann*, District Court of Jerusalem, 36 ILR 5 (1961). But see *Prosecutor v Bagaragaza*, Decision on Rule 11*bis* Appeal of 30 Aug 2006, at paras 16–18 (International Criminal Tribunal for Rwanda—Appeals Chamber).

[45] See eg, *US—Laws, Regulations and Methodology for Calculating Dumping Margins (Zeroing)*, WTO Doc. WT/DS294/AB/R (2006); *US—Investigation of the International Trade Commission in Softwood Lumber from Canada*, WTO Doc. WT/DS277/R (2004). See also Benedict Kingsbury, Nico Krisch and Richard B Stewart, 'The Emergence of Global Administrative Law', 68 *Law & Contemp Prob* (2005) 15, 36–7.

[46] See eg, Lawrence R Walders, 'Citation by US Courts to Decisions of International Tribunals in International Trade Cases', 69 *Alb L Rev* (2006) 817, 820–1; David A Gantz, 'A Post-Uruguay Round Introduction to International Trade Law in the United States', 12 *Ariz J Int'l & Comp Law* (1995) 7, 120–8; Ernst-Ulrich Petersmann, 'Justice as Conflict Resolution: Proliferation, Fragmentation and Decentralization of Dispute Settlement in International Trade', 27 *U Pa J Int'l Econ L* (2006) 273, 334–5; Lawrence R Walders and Neil C Pratt, 'Trade Remedy Litigation—Choice of Forum and Choice of Law', 18 *St John's JL Comm* (2003) 51, 52–3.

[47] See eg, Case C-446/03, *Marks and Spencer plc v Halsey*, [2005] ECR I-10837 (review of tax determinations by local authorities); Case C-217/97 *Commission v Germany*, 1999 ECR I-5087 (review of regulations governing access to environmental information).

[48] In monist countries such as France or the US, international treaties constitute part of the law of the land. French Constitution, art 55; US Constitution, art VI. Even dualist countries, such as the UK, often incorporate customary international law into their domestic legal systems, without the need for specific acts of transformation. See *Trendtex Trading Corp v Central Bank of Nigeria* [1977] QB 529, 554.

bodies and to the ensuing lack of familiarity with the extraordinary norms and methodology of international law on the part of domestic judges.

Furthermore, even in those uncommon cases where specific rules of international law were relevant to issues adjudicated before national courts, the application of such rules was sometimes viewed as politically undesirable. National courts consequently developed a variety of judicial tactics designed to circumvent the need to enforce international norms. These tactics, which included a variety of 'avoidance techniques' (such as the, 'political question' and 'act of state' doctrines, and rules on standing, immunity and justiciability),[49] acknowledging the overriding nature of national over international law, had helped national judges to 'protect' their domestic legal systems from the unfavourable legal, political and, possibly, economic implications of applying international law.[50]

Still, over time, the continued penetration of international legal standards into the domestic realm and the growing influence of international norms and institutions on domestic decision makers and broader constituencies[51] have rendered the separation of international law from domestic law less and less tenable (in fact, some international norms explicitly require the incorporation of specific international law arrangements into domestic law).[52] As a result, some parliaments have moved to incorporate important international law instruments into their domestic laws[53] (in some unique contexts, incorporation has resulted in the granting of constitutional or quasi-constitutional status to international legal standards);[54] several governments have dropped their resistance to the application of international standards by national courts, with they themselves relying at times on such standards in order to justify their conduct during domestic litigation;[55] and a good number of

[49] Eyal Benvenisti, 'Judicial Misgivings Regarding the Application of International Law: An Analysis of Attitudes of National Courts', 4 *EJIL* (1993) 159, 169–73. See also August Reinisch, *International Organizations before National Courts* (2000), 35–168 (discussing avoidance techniques, through which national courts abstain from exercising jurisdiction over international organizations).

[50] Benvenisti, above n 49, at 173–5.

[51] The influence of this process has been captured by Harold Koh's famous 'transnational legal process' theory. See eg, Harold H Koh, 'Transnational Legal Process', 75 *Neb L Rev* (1994) 181, 184.

[52] See eg, *Jurisdiction of the Courts of Danzig*, 1928 PCIJ (Ser B), No 15, at 17–18 ('the very object of an international agreement, according to the intention of the contracting Parties, may be the adoption by the parties of some definite rules creating individual rights and obligations and enforceable by the national courts'). See also Yuval Shany, 'How Supreme is the Supreme Law of the Land? A Comparative Analysis of the Influence of International Human Rights Conventions upon the Interpretation of Constitutional Texts by Domestic Courts', 31 *Brooklyn J Int'l L* (2006) 341, 352–5.

[53] See eg, Human Rights Act, 1998 (UK); 28 USC 1350 (Torture Victims Protection Act of 1991); The International Criminal Court Bill, 2005 (Trinidad and Tobago), <http://www.iccnow.org/documents/TrinidadTobago_ICCBill_24Feb06.pdf>.

[54] See eg, European Communities Act, 1972, sec 2(4)(UK); Czech Constitution, art 10.

[55] See eg, HCJ 393/82, *Jam'iat Iscan Elma'almoon v Commander of the IDF Forces*, 37(4) PD 785 (invocation of the 1907 Hague Regulations by the IDF in order to justify land development measures in occupied territories); *R (on the application of Al-Jedda) v Secretary of State for Defence* [2006] EWCA Civ 327 (CA, Civil Division) (reliance of the UK on a Security Council resolution and the Hague Regulations as the legal basis for the detention of a British citizen in Iraq).

national judges have accepted a more prominent role for international law within domestic judicial proceedings and decisions.[56]

Indeed, in recent years, traditional barriers to domestic litigation involving international actors, such as the state immunity or 'non-justiciability' or 'act of state' doctrines, have been removed or considerably relaxed in numerous jurisdictions.[57] As a result, many domestic courts now routinely entertain claims against their own governments, public officials, foreign states, and even international organizations.[58] This, too, has enhanced the ability of national courts to process some claims formerly considered justiciable only on the international plane.

As a matter of fact, one can identify a positive link between the direct or indirect legal pressures applied by international courts on those national institutions whose conduct they monitor, and the willingness of national courts to apply international norms.[59] Some writers have even observed that national courts can strategically utilize international judicial supervision to form epistemological and professional alliances with international judicial bodies in order to improve their own standing vis-à-vis domestic branches of government (including other domestic courts).[60]

The result of the increased application of international law by national courts is the further narrowing of the distinctions between national and international adjudication: not only are the two procedures now capable of addressing the same factual issues affecting the same legal relations between the same parties, they may also increasingly do so in accordance with the same international legal standards. Indeed, one can identify in recent years an increase in the number of cases in which national courts have applied international norms in proceedings parallel to those pending before international courts.[61] Some of these cases are discussed in Chapter 1.

2.2 Other causes for the blurring of the distinction

It is perhaps interesting to note that the overlap in subject matter between national and international law has been further encouraged by the increasing extra-territorial reach of certain pieces of national legislation, such as long-arm anti-trust and tort

[56] See Francesco Francioni, 'International Law as a Common Language for National Courts', 36 *Tex Int'l LJ* (2001) 587, 587–8.

[57] See eg, 28 USCS § 1605; State Immunity Act, 1978, sec 2 (UK). See also *Occidental Exploration and Production Co v Ecuador*, 45 ILM 249, 266 (2006)(UK Court of Appeal).

[58] August Reinisch, *International Organizations before National Courts* (2000) 169.

[59] See eg, Amichai Cohen, 'Administrating the Territories: An Inquiry into the Application of International Humanitarian Law by the IDF in the Occupied Territories', 38 *Isr L Rev* (2005) 24, 62–5, 72–5.

[60] Anne-Marie Slaughter, 'Judicial Globalization', 40 *Virginia J Int'l L* (2000) 1103, 1105–8; Anthony Arnull, *The European Union and its Court of Justice* (2nd edn, 2006) 99.

[61] See eg, *Sanchez-Llamas*, 126 S Ct 2669; *Beit Sourik*, above n 6; *Mara'abe*, above n 7; *Occidental*, 45 ILM 249; *Ecuador* v *Occidental Exploration & Production Co*, [2005] EWHC 774 (QB).

statutes,[62] as well as universal jurisdiction laws,[63] which extended the reach of national law to issues traditionally regulated only by international law.[64] Hence, the normative expansion of international law coincides with the normative expansion of many domestic laws, which may offer norms similar in their contents to the parallel international standards.[65]

The increasing fusion of national and international norms and institutions is perhaps demonstrated most vividly in the creation and operation of hybrid judicial bodies that apply both national and international law.[66] For example, arbitration tribunals operating under ICSID may arbitrate disputes on the basis of any body of norms selected by the parties—contractual obligations, national law, international law or a combination thereof. In the absence of such choice, the tribunals ought to decide cases on the basis of the law of the host state (which include its rules on conflict of laws) and 'such rules of international law as may be applicable'.[67] 'Umbrella clauses' in BITs, which authorize arbitral tribunals to examine compliance on the part of host states with all obligations taken upon themselves vis-à-vis the covered investment project might be of particular importance in this regard. These clauses introduce the possibility that the relevant international norms could cover some or all of the parties' obligations under the investment contract in question, and, perhaps, under the domestic law of the host State too.[68]

Other examples of hybrid judicial bodies are the mixed criminal tribunals that have been established under the domestic law of several states (eg, Sierra Leone,

[62] See eg, Sherman Act, 15 USC §6a; Alien Tort Claims Act, 28 USC §1350; The Torture Victim Protection Act of 1991, 106 Stat 73 (1992).

[63] See eg, Act to Introduce the Code of Crimes Against International Law of 26 June 2002 (Germany), 42 ILM 998 (2003); Geneva Conventions Act, RS, 1985, c G-3 (Canada).

[64] For a recent evaluation of this development, see Hannah L Buxbaum, 'Transnational Regulatory Litigation', 46 *Virginia J Int'l L* (2006) 251.

[65] Still, Kelsen aptly posited that there are limits to the ability of national law to regulate extra-territorial matters and questions relating to the creation and application of international law itself. Kelsen (1952), above n 35, at 202.

[66] It is perhaps worth noting that the PCIJ deemed itself competent to apply national law when the circumstances so required. *Payment of Various Serbian Loans Issued in France* (France v Serb-Croat-Slovene), 1929 PCIJ (Ser A), No 20/21, at 19; *Payment in Gold of the Brazilian Federal Loans Issued in France* (France v Brazil), 1929 PCIJ (Ser A), No 20/21, at 124.

[67] Convention on the Settlement of Investment Disputes between States and Nationals of Other States, 18 March 1965, art 42, 575 UNTS 159. For a discussion, see Christoph H Schreuer, *The ICSID Convention: A Commentary* (2001) 558–631. Cf David D Caron, 'The Nature of the Iran-United States Claims Tribunal and the Evolving Structure of International Dispute Resolution', 84 *AJIL* (1990) 104, 121–6.

[68] For a discussion on the meaning and scope of umbrella clauses, see *SGS v Pakistan*, 42 ILM 1290; *SGS v Philippines*, above n 8; *Joy Mining Machinery Ltd v Egypt*, Award on jurisdiction of 6 Aug 2004, <http://www.investmentclaims.com/decisions/JoyMining-Egypt-Jurisdiction-30Jul2004.pdf>; *Salini Costruttori SpA v Jordan*, decision on jurisdiction of 9 Nov 2004, <http://www.investmentclaims.com/decisions/35a%20-%20salini-decision_000.pdf>; *Noble Ventures v Romania*, Award of 12 Oct 2005, <http://www.investmentclaims.com/decisions/Noble-Ventures-Final-Award.pdf>; *El Paso Energy International Co v Argentina*, decision on jurisdiction of 27 April 2006, <http://www.investmentclaims.com/decisions/El_Paso_Energy-Argentina-Jurisdictional_Decision.pdf>.

East Timor, Cambodia), pursuant to international instruments.[69] Mixed criminal tribunals typically apply a combination of national and international law norms;[70] they also entail the participation of national and international judges, prosecutors and defense lawyers, thus further obfuscating the tribunal's precise nature: hence, they may remain separate from the domestic judicial system[71] even though their ties to domestic law can be far more intensive than those of 'ordinary' international tribunals.[72]

While these normative and institutional developments do not negate the conceptual distinction between national and international law, they do seem to diminish its practical significance. This de facto convergence of judicial functions raises the question of whether the parallel exercise of judicial power by national and international courts merits regulation. This is the question explored in Section III of this Introduction.

III. The Need for Regulation

3.1 The lessons of existing regulation

The notion that jurisdictional relations between national and international proceedings may merit some form of regulation is hardly revolutionary. In fact, many international instruments contain provisions precisely designed to regulate this relationship in the context of disputes amenable to both jurisdictions. Their objective is to determine the order of proceedings, limit multiple proceedings and control the respective effects of the decisions issued by those judicial bodies.

69 See eg, William Burke-White 'A Community of Courts: Towards a System of International Criminal Law Enforcement', 24 *Mich J Int'l L* (2002) 1, 23–4; Suzanne Katzenstein, 'Hybrid Tribunals: Searching for Justice in East Timor', 16 *Harv Hum Rts J* (2003) 245, 245–8; Jenia I. Turner, 'Nationalizing International Criminal Law', 41 *Stan J Int'l L* (2005) 1, 36–9.

70 See eg, Statute for the Special Court in Sierra Leone, 16 Jan 2002, arts 2–5, <http://www.pict-pcti.org/courts/pdf/SL/SpecialCourtStatute2002.pdf>; Regulation No 2000/15 on the Establishment of Panels with Exclusive Jurisdiction over Serious Criminal Offences, s 1.3, UN Doc UNTAET/REG/2000/15 (2000); Establishment of Extraordinary Chambers in the Courts of Cambodia for the Prosecution of Crimes Committed During the Period of Democratic Kampuchea, 10 Aug 2001, art 1 <http://www.derechos.org/human-rights/seasia/doc/krlaw.html>. For a discussion, see Bert Swart, 'Internationalized Courts and Substantive Criminal Law', *Internationalized Criminal Courts—Sierra Leone, East Timor, Kosovo, and Cambodia* (Cesare PR Romano et al, eds., 2004) 291, 295–304.

71 See *Prosecutor v Brima*, SCSL ruling on *habeas corpus* application of 22 July 2003 (holding that the operation of the SCSL is not governed by the Constitution of Sierra Leone).

72 See *Prosecutor v Stanković*, decision of 17 May 2005 on referral of case under Rule 11*bis*, at para 25 ('The inclusion of some non-nationals among the judges of the State Court does that make that court any less a "national court" of Bosnia and Herzegovina'). But see, *Prosecutor v Taylor*, Special Court for Sierra Leone, decision of 31 May 2004, at paras 37–42, available through <http://www.sc-sl.org/taylor-decisions.html>.

For example, Article 35 of the ECHR provides that claims may be brought before the ECtHR only after domestic proceedings had been exhausted. This arrangement, which mirrors the customary 'exhaustion of local remedies' rule, also serves as a jurisdiction-regulation rule controlling the order of national and international proceedings.[73] It should be noted that the new Protocol 14 to the ECHR goes beyond the traditional exhaustion of local remedies rule and adds new grounds of admissibility: where it appears that the applicant has not suffered a significant disadvantage, the Court may dismiss the petition if it was 'duly considered by a domestic tribunal'[74] Hence, the Protocol introduces a new rule facilitating the substantive division of labour between national and international courts—minor human rights infringements are to be addressed, as a rule, by national courts, whereas more serious violations are to be handled by national and international courts, in consecutive order.

Another prominent example of an existing jurisdiction-regulating regime, exceptional in its judicial socializing force, is the preliminary ruling procedure under Article 234 of the EC Treaty.[75] The article introduces a sophisticated regime of coordination between the national courts of the EU Member States and the ECJ with respect to domestic disputes that raise questions of EC law. Article 234 sets the order of the proceedings (national and international/supra-national) and regulates the weight to be assigned to ECJ decisions in subsequent stages of domestic litigation.

One could also mention in this regard other regulatory principles to be discussed in Chapter 1, such as complimentarity and *ne bis in idem* introduced by the International Criminal Court (ICC) Statute[76] and specific forum-selection clauses found in international investment-related instruments.[77] Arguably, the very existence of a variety of jurisdiction-regulation provisions in different legal instruments supports the proposition of the need to regulate national and international proceedings, at least in some institutional or jurisdictional settings. One can assume that it is highly unlikely that many lawmakers would have troubled themselves to introduce time and time again complex divisions of labour or coordination regimes to address a non-existent problem. It is more reasonable to assume that the aforementioned provisions do respond to real needs for coordination between national and international jurisdictions.

[73] CF Amerasinghe, *Local Remedies in International Law* (2nd edn, 2004) 417–18.

[74] Protocol No 14 to the Convention for the Protection of Human Rights and Fundamental Freedoms, 13 May 2004, ETS 194.

[75] EC Treaty, art 234. See Helfer and Slaughter, above n 40, at 291–2.

[76] ICC Statute, arts 17, 20.

[77] See eg, Agreement on the Promotion and Protection of Investments (Austria/FYROM), 28 March 2001, art 12, 2195 UNTS 192; Agreement on the Reciprocal Promotion and Protection of Investments (France/Argentina), 3 July 1991, art 8(2), 1728 UNTS 297; Agreement on the Promotion and Protection of Investments (Australia/Philippines), 25 Jan 1995, art 13, 1945 UNTS 144; Treaty concerning the Encouragement and Reciprocal Protection of Investment (US/Jordan), 2 July 1997, art IX, 1997 UST Lexis 119. See also Declaration of the Government of the Democratic and Popular Republic of Algeria concerning the Settlement of Claims by Iran and the United States, 19 Jan 1981, art II(1), 20 ILM 230 (1981).

3.2 The costs of unregulated interactions

But if regulation is suggestive of a need to regulate, what does failure to regulate suggest? As Chapter 1 demonstrates, several important and recurring interactions between national and international courts are regulated unsatisfactorily or unregulated altogether. For example, ICJ proceedings seem to converge with related domestic proceedings with growing frequency. As these jurisdictional interactions remain largely unregulated, uncoordinated multiple proceedings could take place concurrently or consecutively. The consular notification cases brought against the US[78] and the advisory opinion regarding the separation wall (or barrier) in the Occupied Territories, which were conducted alongside judicial proceedings in the US and Israel, exemplify this claim. Similarly, in the field of international investment law, one encounters difficult yet sparsely regulated questions relating to the potential or actual interplay between jurisdictional provisions found in private investment contracts and those appearing in inter-state BITs. As a result, the relationships holding between national and international proceedings pursued on the basis of such uncoordinated provisions appear to be unsatisfactorily regulated.[79]

Can one submit that the inadequate regulation in these cases as in other cases discussed in Chapter 1 indicates redundancy of regulation or the mundane nature of the problem? To my mind, such a position is implausible since even a rudimentary analysis of unregulated or insufficiently regulated interactions between national and international proceedings leads to the conclusion that this situation raises potentially serious practical and theoretical problems.

First, the existence of parallel proceedings relating to the same transactions may be wasteful[80] due to the considerable expenditures incurred by the disputing parties who may be forced to maintain two separate litigation teams (or shuttle a single team from one forum to the other) and duplicate submission of arguments and evidence before two separate tribunals (the tribunals' parallel operation also entails considerable costs for the parties, especially in situations where the parties fund all expenses, including the arbitrators' salaries).[81] The risk of prohibitively high expenditures could potentially restrict access to justice for some parties (especially non-state parties). The raising of jurisdictional arguments pertaining to the

[78] *Vienna Convention on Consular Relations (Breard)* (Paraguay v US), 1998 ICJ 266 (provisional measures); *LaGrand* (Germany v US), 2001 ICJ 466; *Avena* (Mexico v US), 43 ILM 581 (2004).

[79] See eg, *SGS v Pakistan*, 42 ILM at 1293–8 (2003) (describing the existence of multiple proceedings relating to a single investment before an ICSID arbitral panel, a Pakistani arbitrator, and the domestic courts of Switzerland and Pakistan).

[80] Cf *SGS v Pakistan*, Procedural Order no 2, 16 Oct 2002, <http://www.worldbank.org/icsid/cases/SGS-order.pdf> ('The Tribunal, however, also believes that normally it would be wasteful of resources for two proceedings relating to the same or substantially the same matter to unfold separately while the jurisdiction of one tribunal awaits determination').

[81] See eg, Jack J Coe, Jr, 'Toward a Complementary Use of Conciliation in Investor-State Disputes—A Preliminary Sketch', 12 *UC Davis J Int'l L & Pol'y* (2005) 7, 9.

putative effects of one set of proceedings on the other exacerbates the aforementioned problems. In addition, uncoordinated multiple proceedings might also result in counter-productive 'battle of injunctions', further complicating the legal situation of the litigants (while multiplying costs and delays).[82]

Uncoordinated multiple litigation might also be deemed inefficient from an institutional perspective, since it could cause more than one tribunal to perform essentially the same judicial task. This in turn leads to suboptimal utilization of the scarce judicial resources existing at both the national and international level[83] and restricts, in effect, the availability of courts to other potential litigants.

Crucially, parallel proceedings might lead to inconsistent or even conflicting judgments by national and international courts. To the degree that these judgments are formally anchored in international law, they increase the uncertainty of the contents of international norms and challenge the coherence and perceived fairness of the international legal system (ie, the expectation that similar cases will be treated alike).[84]

In all events, even if one were to disregard the theoretic dimensions of this problem and the possible doctrinal solutions thereto (eg, whether or not the conflicting judicial prescriptions validly exist in the context of a common normative universe), it is difficult to contest the proposition that multiple judgments generate serious practical problems: faced with conflicting judgments, the parties might

[82] For example, in *SGS v Pakistan*, the Pakistani courts issued an injunction against the continuation of the ICSID proceedings, whereas the ICSID panel recommended stay of arbitral proceedings in Pakistan, pending the determination of its own scope of jurisdiction. *SGS v Pakistan* (Order no 2), above n 80. This recommendation was eventually accepted by the Pakistani arbitrator. *SGS v Pakistan*, 42 ILM at 1298. For another example of the issuance of an anti-suit injunction—this time directed by an international tribunal against a domestic court, see *Tokios Tokeles v Ukraine*, ICSID Decision on Jurisdiction of 29 April 2004, at para 12 <http://www.worldbank.org/icsid/cases/tokios-decision.pdf> (noting previous decision by the arbitral tribunal to order the suspension of local court proceedings in the Ukraine). But see *Waste Management Inc v Mexico*, 40 ILM 56, 63 (2002) (ICSID Additional Facility) ('This Tribunal . . . lacks the necessary authority to bar the Claimant from initiating other proceedings in fora other than the present one'). For a comprehensive discussion of the problems related to the issuance of anti-suit injunctions vis-à-vis international arbitration proceedings, see Emmanuel Gaillard (ed), *Anti-Suit Injunctions in International Arbitration* (2005).

[83] Cf Council of Europe, Explanatory Report to Protocol No 14 to the Convention for the Protection of Human Rights and Fundamental Freedoms, amending the control system of the Convention (CETS No 194), at para 77, <http://conventions.coe.int/Treaty/EN/Reports/Html/194.htm> ('the purpose of this amendment is to provide the Court with an additional tool which should assist it in its filtering work and allow it to devote more time to cases which warrant examination on the merit').

[84] See Report of the International Law Commission Working Group on Long-term Programme of Work, 'Risks Ensuing from the Fragmentation of International Law', UN Doc. ILC(LII)/WG/LT/L.1.Add.1 (2000), at 26, 35 (prepared by Gerard Hafner); Gerard Hafner, 'Pros and Cons Ensuing from Fragmentation of International Law', 25 *Mich J Int'l L* (2004) 849, 856–8; Karin Oellers-Frahm, 'Multiplication of International Courts and Tribunals and Conflicting Jurisdiction—Problems and Possible Solutions', 5 *Max Planck Yearbook of United Nations Law* (2001) 67, 70–3; Shany, above n 39, at 117–20 (arguing that international law's need for coherence is particularly acute given its decentralized structures, lack of binding conflict resolution procedures, voluntary nature of its enforcement mechanisms, and its fragile basis of legitimacy).

find themselves in the untenable position of being compelled to disobey one or more of the judgments issued and face the consequences thereof.[85] Furthermore, even parallel proceedings which give rise to consistent judgments may raise practical problems of coordination to prevent double recovery on the part of the prevailing party.[86]

Finally, failure to coordinate between national and international proceedings taking place simultaneously may deprive all judicial bodies involved in the multiple litigation the benefits of improved coordination. Most prominently, lack of synchronization restricts the ability of one court to draw upon the comparative advantages of its counterpart through inter-fora cooperation. For example, it is arguable that the quality of international judgments could be improved if international courts were to have before them a complete record of evidence and fact analysis prepared by national courts. This is because national courts normally have better fact-finding capabilities than their international counterparts.[87] At the same time, a domestic court judgment might benefit from a preliminary legal analysis of complicated international law issues offered by an international court invested with greater professional expertise on the matter.[88]

The possible benefits of such coordination have led the PCIJ to declare in the 1933 *Prince von Pless* case that:

> [I]t will certainly be an advantage to the Court, as regards the points which have to be established in the case, to be acquainted with the final decisions of the Supreme Polish Administrative Tribunal upon the appeals brought by Prince von Pless and now pending before that Tribunal; and as the Court must therefore arrange its procedure so as to ensure that this will be possible.[89]

In the same vein, an ICSID arbitral tribunal recently held in *SGS v Philippines* that:

> [J]ustice would be best served if the Tribunal were to stay the present proceedings pending determination of the amount payable, either by agreement by the parties or by the Philippine courts in accordance with Article 12 of the CISS Agreement (emphasis added).[90]

[85] ILC Study Group, above n 29, at 26–7. Such considerations have led the PCIJ to hesitate in pronouncing on the contents of national law in ways that contradict legal pronouncements issued by local courts. *Serbian Loans*, 1929 PCIJ (Ser A), No 20/21, at 46.

[86] See eg, *Occidental Exploration & Production Co v Ecuador*, Final Award of 1 July 2004, at para 209, <http://www.asil.org/ilib/OEPC-Ecuador.pdf> (ordering the claimant to cease proceedings before national courts and decreeing that such proceedings will carry no legal effect).

[87] See Yuval Shany, 'Toward a General Margin of Appreciation Doctrine', 16 *EJIL* (2005) 907, 919; Paulo G Carozza, 'Subsidiarity as a Structural Principle of International Human Rights Law', 97 *AJIL*(2003) 38, 73. Steven P Croley and John H Jackson, 'WTO Procedures, Standard of Review, and Deference to National Governments', 90 *AJIL* (1996) 193, 208.

[88] For a discussion, see Yuval Shany, 'Capacities and Inadequacies: A Look at the Two Separation Barrier Case', 38 *Isr L Rev* (2005) 230, 240–5.

[89] *Prince von Pless Administration* (Germany v Poland), 1933 PCIJ (Ser A/B), No 52, at 16 (interim order).

[90] *SGS v Philippines*, above n 8, at para 175.

In short, many of the policy considerations which militate against uncoordinated multiple proceedings at the national level (between domestic courts) and at the international level (between international courts),[91] could also support the regulation of multiple proceedings taking place at the national and international level. This does not mean, however, that regulation is cost-free. Indeed, Part II of this treatise, which examines various regulatory methods, will discuss the adverse consequences of introducing specific forms of regulation, such as *res judicata* or judicial comity, to relations between national and international courts. Among these costs one may note at this stage, the doctrinal confusion generated by the rejection of dualism and/or hierarchy as conceptual frameworks and the concerns over the legitimacy of deferring to national or international judicial institutions whose democratic or international law credentials might be open to question.

IV. Structure of the Treatise and Research Methodology

4.1 Theory and law

So, this book aims to respond to a growing complex reality in which national and international courts increasingly interact with one another, under circumstances in which their jurisdictional relations may be conceptualized in different ways—either as detached or linked to one another, as having vertical or horizontal features, or as displaying a combination of such features—a situation that has already generated inconsistent case law.[92] My primary objective is to situate the various relational models in a broader framework of analysis, informed by general theoretical debates over the fragmented or unified nature of international law and its relation to domestic law. Through this exercise I plan to challenge some traditional distinctions between the national and the international that may provide doctrinal clarity yet are often blind to an increasingly ambiguous reality. My secondary purpose is to examine critically the jurisdiction-regulating 'tools' that could, under some or all relational models, regulate the jurisdictional interactions between national and international courts.

Despite the practical nature of some of the research questions I pose, the treatise is built around a significant theoretical component. Indeed, my hypothesis is that

[91] See Shany, above n 39, at 284–5. Cf *MOX Plant* (Ireland v UK), Order No 3 of 24 July 2003, at para 28, <http://www.pca-cpa.org/PDF/MOX%20Order%20no3.pdf> (hereinafter *MOX Plant* (UNCLOS)) ('a procedure that might result in two conflicting decisions on the same issue would not be helpful to the resolution of the dispute between the Parties').

[92] See *SGS v Pakistan*, 42 ILM 1290; *SGS v Philippines*, above n 8 (conflicting decisions by ICSID tribunals on the need to stay proceedings in the face of parallel domestic proceedings). See also *LaGrand*, 2001 ICJ 466; *Oil Platforms* (Iran v US), 42 ILM 1334 (2004) (divergent judgments on the latitude to be afforded to national authorities in implementing their international obligations).

identification of suitable rules of international law for governing jurisdictional interactions between national and international courts may ultimately hinge upon the conceptualization of the systemic nature of the relations maintained between the two groups of judicial bodies. For example, the choice between more or less intensive levels of regulation depends on the strength of the systemic links that exist—or should exist—between national and international courts.[93] At the same time, delineation of the law governing jurisdictional relations helps ascertain the systemic nature of the interaction between national and international courts. Similarly, the question of whether the practice of specific national and international courts (eg, ICSID or ITLOS) can be applied across the international legal 'system' may ultimately depend on a preconceived idea of the system's (dis)unity and its boundaries.

We are thus faced with essentially circular arguments—what is the law determines what should be the law, and vice versa.[94] At the end of the day, normative arguments pertaining to the need to augment or curb the coherence and effectiveness of law-based dispute settlement procedures and competing visions of the role of judges in promoting this end (shaped inevitably by one's political and ideological preferences) must prevail. While this author believes that judges ought to be equipped with flexible problem-solving powers that should harmonize different normative orders, other positions are also possible.[95] Indeed, the recourse to an indeterminate *lex ferenda* highlights the existence of alternative discourses and the limits of a political legal doctrines in modelling legal institutions given such quintessential dilemmas. In any event, these methodological limits must be acknowledged up front.

At the same time, the approach I propose in Chapter 6 seeks to bypass, to a considerable degree, some of the long-running disputes concerning the nature of the relations between national and international courts and to offer a pragmatic methodology, applicable across the board to all international dispute settlement procedures. In particular, I posit that flexible jurisdiction-regulating principles, especially those suitable for coordination between *related* proceedings—comity and *abus de droit*—ought to be resorted to in all jurisdictional interaction cases involving national and international courts, even when the formal conditions of jurisdictional competition (same parties, same issues) are not met. The application of these principles by all international-law-applying courts—national and international—offers a pragmatic yet flexible way to promote comprehensive and harmonious dispute settlement and to mitigate many of the problems associated with the jurisdictional conflicts that the current disorder invites.

[93] For a discussion of the distinction between inter- and intra-systematic interactions and its relevance to the choice of jurisdiction-regulating regimes, see Shany, n 39, at 81–3.

[94] For a comparable phenomenon, see Teubner, 'Breaking Frames', above n 12, at 153.

[95] Cf David Kennedy, 'When Renewal Repeats: Thinking Against the Box', 32 *NYU J Int'l L & Pol* 335, 356–7 (2000).

4.2 Structure

The structure of the book strives to correspond to the linkage and de-linkage between theories and norms. Part I of the book offers an analytical and theoretical description of current jurisdictional relations between national and international courts. Chapter 1 maps some of the most prominent regulated and unregulated forms of interaction between national and international courts. It posits that no single model of regulation does or should exist, and that different types of regulation can comport to different possible relationship models. Chapter 2 links the categorization of interactions to a number of theories on the dualistic, monistic, or pluralistic nature of the relations between national and international law, and to a number of functional theories on the role of national courts in developing and applying international law. Chapter 3 then discusses the contributions of the debate over the fragmentation of international law to our understanding of some of the dilemmas of regulating relations between national and international courts. In sum, Part I examines the interrelated practice of national and international courts in light of the relevant theoretical, ideological, and methodological discourses.

Part II then explores the application in theory and practice of various measures designed to mitigate or circumvent altogether tensions between the two groups of judicial bodies: Chapter 4 examines the possibility of conceptualizing disputes between national and international courts as 'the same disputes' for the purpose of applying a variety of jurisdiction-regulating rules. Chapter 5 proceeds to investigate the potential or actual applicability of several strict jurisdiction-regulating measures, developed in the context of intra-regime regulation (eg, *lis alibi pendens* and *res judicata*) to jurisdictional interactions between national and international courts. Chapter 6 then examines the possible utilization of comity-based measures and doctrines, such as discretionary stay of proceedings and margin of appreciation-type judicial review to hierarchically and non-hierarchically configured jurisdictional interactions. It also considers the potential application of the *abus de droit* principle to such interactions. Arguably, some, though certainly not all of these potential measures offer pragmatic solutions to the problems plaguing relations between national and international courts. These could likely circumvent the need to select a governing theoretical paradigm of the relationship.

4.3 Scope of the research

The greatest challenge posed by this research project has been determination of its scope—ie, how to discipline the vast number of legal authorities touched by the present project, particularly, the almost indefinite number of national and international judicial proceedings where some degree of actual or potential jurisdictional interaction can be identified (eg, all exhaustion of local remedies cases; all decisions on the recognition and enforcement of international arbitral awards). Efficiency considerations dictate that I focus on selected categories of cases and use a limited number of case studies per category. In other words, this book does not purport to survey comprehensively the case law of national and international courts but, rather, to propose some ideas on possible ways to conceptualize their relationships and to indicate possible jurisdiction-regulating measures to govern them.

In addition, time and space considerations have determined that the scope of the present research be limited to situations where essentially *the same case* is pending or can be potentially brought before both national and international judicial bodies, ie, when both courts exercise jurisdiction over essentially identical disputes, involving the same or sufficiently related parties. I do not purport, however, to cover the entire spectrum of options by which national and international courts exert normative influence over one another's jurisprudence (eg, interpretation of similar norms in unrelated cases or pronouncements of international customary law). Of course, interaction in specific cases is informed by the status of national or international case law generally in the parallel legal system. Hence, I address the general context of the normative relations between national and international courts to the degree that it affects jurisdictional overlaps.

So, for example, denial of justice situations—where domestic judicial action allegedly constitutes an internationally wrongful act—fall outside the scope of the research question and will be mentioned only peripherally. This is because the legal controversy addressed in the international proceedings (eg, did national courts abuse international standards on judicial conduct) is qualitatively different from the substantive question originally addressed by the national court (eg, whether the rights of aliens been infringed). Hence, the two proceedings do not exercise jurisdiction over the same case. Still, some relevant lessons may be drawn from this form of interaction (especially with respect to the extension of judicial comity).

Finally, it should be clarified that in light of the book's goal of identifying *international* rules that may govern jurisdictional interactions between national and international courts, my research places greater emphasis on the practice of international law-applying bodies, ie, international courts, than on the parallel practices of national courts. While the latter may also encounter the need to regulate their jurisdictional relations with international judicial bodies, they often invoke domestic law notions and principles[96] that are not easily transferred to other legal contexts. Hence, only relatively few examples of domestic court practice will be discussed.

[96] See eg, *Sanchez-Llamas*, 126 S Ct at 2684; *Timken Co v US*, 354 F 3d 1334 (2004) (domestic principles of interpretation bar reliance on international judicial decisions); *Turtle Island Restoration Network v Evans*, 284 F 3d 1282 (2002) (clear statutory language obviates the need to consider the effect of international decisions); *Occidental*, 45 ILM 249 (discussing whether domestic doctrines of non-justiciability bar review of an international arbitral award).

Although similar arguments may be raised with relation to the transposable qualities of specific international court holdings—eg, whether jurisdictional decisions of ICSID have relevance in other international fora—it would seem that as long as these holdings are ostensibly based exclusively or predominantly on international law, they merit close review by all international bodies. While one should be sensitive to nuances and context-based distinctions, exaggerated focus on the differences between the 'trees' might cause one to lose sight of the 'forest'—in the present case, the common cross-regime challenge of jurisdictional interactions between national and international courts.

My working hypothesis in this regard is that the jurisdiction-regulating practices of courts, be they national or international, invoking international law norms and principles are relevant to the present study. Indeed, as Chapter 3 shows, there are close parallels in language and methodology between decisions of ICSID arbitral tribunals and decisions of 'purely' international bodies, such as ITLOS or UNCLOS arbitration panels. Furthermore, I posit that some parallels may even be drawn between domestic and international court decisions on the same jurisdictional topic.

In all events, this treatise should not, by any means, be regarded as a call for uniform standards to govern all cases of jurisdictional interactions. Quite the opposite: it may be more appropriate to 'tailor' specific jurisdiction-regulating norms to specific fields of law and specific treaty regimes. My purpose in this work is to expose the common dilemmas and the potentially common choices faced by national and international courts. The actual choices made can—and perhaps should—differ in different normative contexts.

PART I

COMPETING PARADIGMS FOR DELINEATING RELATIONS BETWEEN NATIONAL AND INTERNATIONAL COURTS

1

Categorizing Vertical and Horizontal Jurisdictional Interactions

1.1 Stating the Obvious: Regulated Interactions between National and International Courts

There is nothing remarkable in the proposition that the jurisdictions of national and international courts may interact. In fact, some of the most entrenched legal doctrines in international law acknowledge and regulate such interactions. The international rule on exhaustion of local remedies prior to initiation of some international law proceedings, the preliminary ruling procedure under the EC treaty, the rule of complementarity under the Rome Statute establishing the International Criminal Court (ICC) and certain treaties containing *electa una via* (or 'fork in the road') provisions introducing a choice between national and international courts, all support the existence of jurisdictional interaction and the need for its regulation. Another type of arrangements designed to govern jurisdictional interactions may be found in legal instruments such as the New York Convention that provide for the recognition of international arbitral agreements and awards by national courts.[1]

The following section reviews five examples of jurisdiction-regulating norms and will attempt to assess their implications for the nature of the relations between the governed national and international courts. This survey will not only promote better understanding of the specific legal regimes in question; it may also suggest possible modes for regulating the jurisdictional interactions discussed in the second half of this chapter, which are not fully governed by explicit jurisdiction-regulating norms.

1.1.1 Exhaustion of local remedies

Under customary international law, international claims relating to the treatment of individuals (traditionally, the treatment of alien nationals according to 'international minimal standards' or 'national standards'[2] and, more recently, the treatment of all

[1] Convention on the Recognition and Enforcement of Foreign Arbitral Awards, 10 June 1958, 330 UNTS 38 (hereinafter New York Convention).

[2] C F Amerasinghe, *Local Remedies in International Law* (2nd edn, 2004) 84–92; Special Rapporteur of the International Law Commission (John Dugard), 7th Report on Diplomatic Protection, UN Doc A/CN.4/567 (2006), at 5–11.

individuals in accordance with international human rights standards) must normally be preceded by the exhaustion of all local remedies, ie, referral of the case to domestic courts and exhaustion of all reasonable domestic avenues of appeal.[3] The exhaustion of local remedies rule serves, in fact, as a jurisdiction-regulating rule, primarily governing the order of national and international proceedings. In addition, as I explain below, the exhaustion rule is a 'hierarchy signifier'—it facilitates the exercise of judicial supervision by international courts over their national counterparts, thereby establishing vertical jurisdictional relations between them.

As is the case with other jurisdiction-regulating rules, several policy considerations may underlie the adoption of the exhaustion rule: The exhaustion rule delays activation of international procedures and encourages deliberation of disputes amenable to the parallel jurisdiction of both courts in national courts. This, in turn, may reflect a belief in the greater effectiveness of national courts in resolving disputes,[4] especially in light of the chronic gap in the enforcement capabilities of international tribunals,[5] or in the desirability of litigating on the international level *after* a judicial process has already been completed at the national level. Given the comparative advantages that national courts may have over international courts in collecting evidence and establishing facts (eg, national courts may compel the submission of evidence by the disputing parties or third parties, and they are typically situated closer to the facts underlying the dispute—a position that facilitates greater familiarity with background conditions),[6] their involvement at the first stage of the proceedings could improve the quality of the international judgment rendered at the second stage. Of course, additional policy considerations such as the need to protect the sovereignty of the host state in which the alleged violation occurred by affording it the opportunity of reversing the alleged violation through its own judicial organs (as opposed to intervention by external judicial bodies),[7] and aversion to excessive litigation on the international plane may also account for the exhaustion rule. Indeed, when these background circumstances are absent—as when there is no credible domestic judicial alternative[8] or when there is a specific interest in delivering prompt international justice[9]—the rule may be

[3] See eg, *Finnish Ships Arbitration* (Fin v UK), 3 RIAA 1479 (1934); *Interhandel* (Switz v US) 1959 ICJ 6; Amerasinghe, above n 2; A Cancado Trindade, *Exhaustion of Local Remedies in International Law* (1983); Edwin M Borchard, *The Diplomatic Protection of Citizens Abroad: The Law of International Claims* (1915).

[4] See eg, Ian Brownlie, *Principles of Public International Law* (6th edn, 2003) 473.

[5] See eg, Colter Paulson 'Compliance with Final Judgments of the International Court of Justice since 1987', 98 *AJIL* (2004) 434, 436–52.

[6] See eg, Yuval Shany, 'Capacities and Inadequacies: A Look at the Two Separation Barrier Cases', 38 *Isr L Rev* (2005) 230, 240–1.

[7] See eg, William S Dodge, 'Loewen v United States: Trials and Errors Under NAFTA Chapter Eleven', 52 *DePaul L Rev* (2002) 563, 573; Andrea K Bjorklund, 'Reconciling State Sovereignty and Investor Protection in Denial of Justice Claims', 45 *Va J Int'l L* (2005) 809, 877.

[8] Amerasinghe, above n 2, at 58.

[9] See eg, *Camouco* (Panama v France), 39 ILM 666, 678 (2000).

waived or modified. As a result, different courts, operating in different areas of the law, may apply a unique exhaustion rule or refrain from applying it altogether.

For example, the European Convention for Human Rights (ECHR) applies the exhaustion of local remedies rule as a precondition for referring cases to the European Court of Human Rights (ECtHR).[10] The application of the rule is subject, however, to some additional requirements: The ECtHR action must be initiated within six months from the date of exhaustion of local remedies (a provision which operates like a statute of limitations);[11] more importantly, pursuant to the not yet in force 14th Protocol to the ECHR, the ECtHR may dismiss claims duly considered by domestic courts when it appears that the applicant has not suffered a significant disadvantage.[12] This last provision goes beyond regulating the temporal order of the proceedings; it introduces a substantive test designed to allocate the labour between national courts and the ECtHR, thereby directing the focus of the ECtHR's vertical monitoring function over national courts to cases suggestive of serious human rights violations.[13] Arguably, this reform underscores the need to consider differences in the case-handling capacities of national and international courts when designing jurisdiction-regulation rules.[14]

At the same time, article 26 of the Washington Convention establishing the International Centre for the Settlement of Investment Disputes (ICSID)[15] clearly does away with the exhaustion of local remedies rule in most cases. It permits investors to initiate ICSID proceedings without the need for seizing national courts (unless the host State has explicitly required the retention of the exhaustion rule or if another relevant norm has reintroduced an exhaustion of remedies requirement).[16] This provision conforms to the Convention's general objective of simplifying dispute settlement procedures and providing investors with a litigation

[10] European Convention for the Protection of Human Rights and Fundamental Freedoms, 4 Nov 1950 (hereinafter ECHR), art 35(1), ETS 5. For similar exhaustion rules, see eg, American Convention on Human Rights, 22 Nov 1969, art 62(3), OAS TS 36, 9 ILM 673 (1970)(hereinafter I/A CHR); African Charter on Human and People's Rights, 27 June 1981, art 50, 21 ILM 58 (1982); Optional Protocol to the International Covenant on Civil and Political Rights, 16 Dec 1966, art 5(2)(b), 999 UNTS 302.

[11] See Clare Ovey and Robin White, *European Convention on Human Rights* (3rd edn, 2002) 411.

[12] Protocol No 14 to the Convention for the Protection of Human Rights and Fundamental Freedoms, 13 May 2004, ETS 194.

[13] But see Allan Rosas, 'With a Little Help from My Friends: International Case-Law as a Source of Reference for the EU Courts', 5 *The Global Community: Yearbook of International Law and Jurisprudence* (2005) 203, 205 (relations between national courts and the ECtHR are 'semi-vertical', because national courts could refuse to give effect to ECtHR judgments).

[14] Council of Europe, Explanatory Report to Protocol No 14 to the Convention for the Protection of Human Rights and Fundamental Freedoms, amending the control system of the Convention (CETS 194), 13 May 2004, at para 15, <http://www.conventions.coe.int/Treaty/EN/Reports/Html/194.htm>.

[15] Convention on the Settlement of Disputes between States and Nationals of Other States, 18 March 1965, 575 UNTS 159 (hereinafter ICSID Convention).

[16] Christoph H Schreuer, *The ICSID Convention: A Commentary* (2001) 346–8. See also *Compania de Aquas del Aconquija, SA v Argentina*, 40 ILM 426, 444 (2001)(hereinafter *Vivendi I*) (exhaustion of local remedies is required by virtue of the terms of the contract between the parties).

forum other than the domestic courts of the host state (which might be viewed as biased in favour of their own state).[17] This last explanation accounts, in all probability, for the implicit waiver of the exhaustion rule under the Algiers Declaration establishing the Iran–US Claims Tribunal.[18]

It should be appreciated that the exhaustion of local remedies rule represents an informal jurisdiction-regulating rule in the sense that it does not condition its application on any formal similarity between the law governing the regulated proceedings. Instead, it suffices to identify a good, albeit imperfect match between the substantive contents of national and international law and the remedies they offer.[19] This point will be discussed further in Chapter 4, which examines the formal conditions for regulating jurisdictional interactions between national and international courts.

The NAFTA 'No U-turn' Rule

While some legal regimes have explicitly adopted or rejected the exhaustion of local remedies rule, the situation under some legal regimes, such as NAFTA, is less certain. This is, perhaps, indicative of the unclear state of relations between national and international courts within such regimes.

Article 1121(1)(b) of NAFTA, which is sometimes dubbed the 'no U-turn provision' requires investors, before initiating a Chapter 11 NAFTA Claim to:

> Waive their right to initiate or continue before any administrative tribunal or court under the law of any Party, or other dispute settlement procedures, any proceedings with respect to the measure of the disputing Party that is alleged to be a breach referred to in Article 1117, except for proceedings for injunctive, declaratory or other extraordinary relief, not involving the payment of damages, before an administrative tribunal or court under the law of the disputing Party.[20]

Although this provision appears to endow NAFTA, once selected as the appropriate forum, with exclusive competence vis-à-vis domestic courts, irrespective of whether domestic proceeding were exhausted, a Chapter 11 arbitral tribunal held in *Loewen* that it is unlikely that the parties to NAFTA had intended to encourage litigation at

[17] Report of the Executive Directors on the Convention on the Settlement of Investment Disputes Between States and Nationals of Other States, International Bank for Reconstruction and Development March 18, 1965, section III, para 11, <http://www.worldbank.org/icsid/basicdoc/partB-section03.htm>.

[18] Declaration of the Government of the Democratic and Popular Republic of Algeria Concerning the Settlement of Claims by the Government of the United States of America and the Government of the Islamic Republic of Iran, art II(1), 20 ILM 230 (1981). For a discussion, see Ted L Stein, 'Jurisprudence and Jurists' Prudence: The Iranian-Forum Clause Decisions of the Iran–U.S. Claims Tribunal', 78 *AJIL* (1984) 1.

[19] See eg, *Guzzardi v Italy*, 39 Eur Ct HR (Ser A), at 26 (application of the exhaustion of local remedies rules undertaken 'with a certain degree of flexibility and without excessive regard for matters of form'); *Akdivar v Turkey*, 1996-IV EHRR 1210, 1211; Amerasinghe, above n 2, at 198.

[20] North American Free Trade Agreement, 17 Dec 1992, art 1121(1)(b)(2), 32 ILM 289 and 605 (1993) (hereinafter NAFTA). For a discussion of exhaustion of local remedies under NAFTA, see William S Dodge, 'National Courts and International Arbitration: Exhaustion of Remedies and Res Judicata under Chapter Eleven of NAFTA', 23 *Hastings Int'l & Comp L Rev* (2000) 357, 370–83.

the international level before all avenues of recourse to local remedies have been exhausted. Hence, in the absence of explicit language to this effect, the tribunal was unwilling to presume that the parties to NAFTA had intended to dispense with such an important principle of international law as the exhaustion rule.[21]

The position taken in *Loewen* has attracted considerable criticism; hence, the propriety and breadth of the holding remains controversial.[22] This controversy may be attributed in part to the tribunal's failure to explain clearly the differences in the application of the exhaustion rule with respect to denial of justice claims and claims alleging other violations of the rights assigned to foreign investors. Whereas the latter category of claims may or may not be subject to the exhaustion rule—a law-making or law-interpreting decision influenced, no doubt, by the policy considerations enumerated above—denial of justice claims cannot be established prior to the scrutiny of lower level judicial decisions by domestic appellate procedures. This is because as long as the domestic legal system is still reviewing the case (within a reasonable timeframe), justice cannot yet be deemed as denied. In other words, 'exhaustion' constitutes one of the substantive elements of the claim in denial-of-justice cases, and not a mere procedural condition.[23]

Still, the controversy surrounding *Loewen* may ultimately be related to a question of legal theory: the existence of a rule of exhaustion, or the lack of such a rule, might depend on the paradigm governing the relations between national and international courts. Since the exhaustion rule constitutes a 'hierarchy signifier', insistence on its retention implies that international courts are competent to exercise powers of review over national courts.[24] At the same time, dispensing with the rule may

[21] *The Loewen Group, Inc v US*, 42 ILM 811, 837 (2003). In questioning the intent of the parties to dispense with important international law rules, The tribunal appears to have followed the approach taken by the ICJ in the *ELSI* case. *Elettronica Sicula SpA (ELSI)* (US v Italy), 1989 ICJ 15, 50 ('the Chamber finds itself unable to accept that an important principle of customary international law [ie, the need to exhaust local remedies] should be held to have been tacitly dispensed with, in the absence of any words making clear an intention to do so'). However, other approaches are also possible. For example, the Iran–US Claims Tribunal has construed the silence of the Algiers Settlement of Claims Declaration as indicative of the absence of an exhaustion of local remedies requirement. *Amoco International Finance Corp v Iran*, 15 Iran–US CTR 189, 197 (1987).

[22] See eg, Bradford K. Gathright, 'A Step in the Wrong Direction: The Loewen Finality Requirement and the Local Remedies Rule in NAFTA Chapter Eleven', 54 *Emory LJ* (2005) 1093; Andrea K Bjorklund, 'Waiver and the Exhaustion of Local Remedies Rule in NAFTA Jurisprudence', *NAFTA Investment Law and Arbitration: Past Issues, Current Practice, Future Prospects* (Todd Weiler, ed, 2004) 253, 278–9.

[23] Jan Paulsson, *Denial of Justice in International Law* (2005) 107–12. Cf *Avena* (Mexico v US), 43 ILM 581, 613 (2004) (it would be premature to conclude that the US had failed to provide a remedy for its violation of the Vienna Convention on Consular Relations with relation to those individuals whose cases are still pending before US courts); *El Oro Mining and Railway Co (Ltd)*(GB v Mexico), 5 RIAA 191, 195–8 (1931); *Mexican Union Railway (Ltd)*(GB v Mexico), 5 RIAA 115, 122 (1930) (denial of justice claims can be brought only if it is shown that all effective remedies had been reasonably exhausted).

[24] Interestingly enough, the *Loewen* tribunal suggested that it did not purport to replace domestic appellate courts. *Loewen*, 42 ILM at 837 ('it is unlikely that the Parties to NAFTA would have wished to encourage recourse to NAFTA arbitration at the expense of domestic appeal or review when, in the general run of cases, domestic appeal or review would offer more wide-ranging review as they are not

suggest a more horizontal relationship in which international courts act in lieu of national courts, without superimposing international judicial authority over national judicial authority.

This question of hierarchical configuration was indirectly addressed in another NAFTA Chapter 11 decision—*Azinian*—which addressed the weight to be granted to a domestic court judgment issued in relation to the same dispute. In its 1999 award, the arbitral tribunal suggested that decisions of a national court should generally be respected:

> The possibility of holding a State internationally liable for judicial decisions does not, however, entitle a claimant to seek international review of the national court decisions as though the international jurisdiction seized has plenary appellate jurisdiction. This is not true generally, and it is not true for NAFTA. What must be shown is that the court decision itself constitutes a violation of the treaty. Even if the Claimants were to convince this Arbitral Tribunal that the Mexican courts were wrong with respect to the invalidity of the Concession Contract, this would not per se be conclusive as to a violation of NAFTA. More is required; the Claimants must show either a denial of justice, or a pretence of form to achieve an internationally unlawful end.[25]

Hence, according to the *Azinian* tribunal, the existence of prior review in domestic courts shifts the emphasis of the case at hand from the question of whether the host government has breached its substantive international obligations under Chapter 11, to a more limited question, ie, whether domestic courts have acted in good faith or engaged in denial of justice. This standard of review is not dissimilar to the model applicable in cases involving the recognition of foreign awards (discussed below); a model that implies a largely horizontal framework of relations between national and international courts (with some vertical safeguards designed to prevent abusive exercise of jurisdiction).

It has been remarked, however, that the deferential approach adopted by the *Azinian* tribunal may be problematic from a policy perspective. This is because excessive deference to national judgments may discourage investors from seizing national courts in the first place.[26] While the *Azinian* tribunal acknowledged this policy concern with regard to the need to deny national court decisions a *res judicata* status vis-à-vis Chapter 11 arbitrations,[27] it failed to appreciate that the considerable

confined to breaches of international law'). See also *Mondev Int'l Ltd v US*, 42 ILM (2003) 85, 109 ('it is not the function of NAFTA tribunals to act as courts of appeal'). However, in effect, these NAFTA Chapter 11 tribunals seemed to have been conducting appellate-type review of national courts. See Benjamin Klafter, 'International Commercial Arbitration as Appellate Review: NAFTA's Chapter 11, Exhaustion of Local Remedies and Res Judicata', 12 *UC Davis J Int'l L & Pol'y* (2005) 409, 427; Bjorklund, above n 7, at 871.

[25] *Azinian v Mexico*, 39 ILM 537, 552 (1999).

[26] William S Dodge and David D Caron, 'Loewen Group, Inc. v. United States', 98 *AJIL* (2004) 155, 163; Klafter, above n 24, at 435–6.

[27] See *Azinian*, 39 ILM at 550 ('it would be unfortunate if potential claimants under NAFTA were dissuaded from seeking relief under domestic law from national courts, because such actions might have the salutary effect of resolving the dispute without resorting to investor–state arbitration under NAFTA').

deference with which it treated the outcome of the proceedings before Mexican courts may entail similar consequences. So, the introduction of horizontal features into the relations between national and international courts may affect the inclination to utilize both groups of tribunals when adjudicating the same dispute.[28]

1.1.2 Preliminary ruling

A unique regime of regulated interaction between national and international courts exists under Article 234 of the EC Treaty,[29] which institutes a preliminary ruling procedure. According to this procedure, when questions of EC law arise in the course of domestic litigation, domestic courts may or, if they are courts of last instance, must refer the question to the Court of Justice of the European Communities (ECJ) for a ruling.[30] During the period of reference, domestic proceedings are discontinued; the domestic court is required subsequently to apply the preliminary ruling to the facts of the case before it. Hence, the ECJ does not purport to dispose of the case pending before the national forum—a power that remains with the national court—but merely authoritatively to determine the EC law aspects of the case.[31]

The preliminary ruling procedure constitutes an important legal tool designed to ensure the proper application of EC law, in a harmonized manner, throughout the EU.[32] For our purposes, it is important to note the hierarchical attributes of the procedure: It requires the courts of the member states to subject determinations pertaining to EC law to judicial control by the ECJ. By forming a vertical jurisdictional relationship between national courts and the ECJ, the preliminary ruling procedure reinforces the normative supremacy of EC law over national law.[33] At the same time, the 'division of labour' attributes of the procedure—in particular, retention of exclusive fact-finding and implementation powers by domestic courts—may be described as horizontal in nature.

[28] See *Loewen*, 42 ILM at 837 (adherence to the exhaustion rule would encourage litigation before domestic fora).

[29] Treaty Establishing the European Economic Community, 25 March 1957, 298 UNTS 3, as revised on 24 Dec 2002, 2002 OJ (C325) 33 (hereinafter EC Treaty).

[30] In some exceptional circumstances, national courts may, however, decide not to refer a case to a preliminary ruling before the ECJ: if the questions arising under EC law are irrelevant to the final outcome of the domestic proceedings, if they were already decided by the ECJ or if an obvious answer to these questions exists (the *'acte claire'* doctrine). See Case 283/81, *CILFIT v Ministry of Health* [1982] ECR 3415; Kevin Andrew Swartz, 'Powerful, Unique, and Anonymous: The European Court of Justice and Its Continuing Impact on the Formation of the European Community', 3 *S Cal Interdisc LJ* (1994) 687, 697–8.

[31] See Anthony Arnull, *The European Union and its Court of Justice* (2nd edn, 2006), 95–125; Yvonne N Gierczyk, 'The Evolution of the European Legal System: The European Court of Justice's Role in the Harmonization of Laws', 12 *ILSA J Int'l & Comp L* (2005) 153.

[32] Francis G Jacobs. 'Judicial Dialogue and the Cross-Fertilization of Legal Systems: The European Court of Justice', 38 *Tex Int'l LJ* (2003) 547, 549; Joseph R Wetzel, 'Improving Fundamental Rights Protection in the European Union: Resolving the Conflict and Confusion Between the Luxemburg and Strasbourg Courts', 71 *Fordham L Rev* (2003) 2823, 2829.

[33] See Rosas, above n 13, at 204.

In all events, it may be noted that the scope of the jurisdictional interaction under the preliminary ruling procedure is more limited than under the traditional exhaustion of local remedies rule. Whereas the latter rule is indifferent to the normative source producing the requested remedy in domestic adjudication—as the parties are expected to invoke the entire gamut of rights and remedies available to them under both national law and international law before national courts—the preliminary ruling procedure only regulates jurisdictional interaction pertaining to the application of EC law in the specific proceedings at hand. It is therefore a more formalized jurisdiction-regulating rule, whose application depends on the parallel authority of national courts and the ECJ to address identical legal questions.

1.1.3 Complementarity

A third example of regulated interaction between national and international courts is the complementarity rule introduced by Article 17 of the Rome Statute on the ICC.[34] The complementarity rule provides that the ICC refrain from exercising its authority over criminal acts falling within the scope of its jurisdiction if a national court is willing and able to prosecute these acts. Hence, the ICC should exercise its jurisdiction as a last resort only in the absence of a credible judicial alternative at the national level. This rule is arguably, also reflective of idiosyncratic policy considerations, eg, the limited resources of the ICC, and the political reluctance of states to commit, in advance, to the substitution of national with international prosecution.[35]

Indeed, by introducing the complementarity rule, the Rome Statute deviates from the rule of supremacy adopted in the Statutes of the international ad hoc criminal tribunals for the Former Yugoslavia and Rwanda and some hybrid criminal tribunals that authorize international or internationalized courts to assume exclusive jurisdiction over cases pending before national courts.[36] The International

[34] Statute of the International Criminal Court, 17 July 1998, art 17, 2187 UNTS 90 (hereinafter ICC Statute).

[35] See eg, Statement made by Mr. Luis Moreno-Ocampo (ICC Chief Prosecutor), 16 June 2003, at 2, <http://www.icc-cpi.int/library/organs/otp/030616_moreno_ocampo_english_final.pdf> ('the absence of trials before this Court, as a consequence of the regular functioning of national institutions, would be a major success').

[36] Statute of the International Criminal Tribunal for the Former Yugoslavia, 25 May 1993, art 9(2), 32 ILM (1993) 1192 (hereinafter ICTY Statute); Statute of the International Tribunal for Rwanda, art 8(2), SC Res 955, UN SCOR, 49th Sess., 3453d mtg. at 3, 33 ILM 1600 (1994) (hereinafter ICTR Statute). See also Statute for the Special Court in Sierra Leone, 16 Jan 2002, art 8, <http://www.pict-pcti.org/courts/pdf/SL/SpecialCourtStatute2002.pdf>. For a discussion, see Jann K Kleffner and André Nollkaemper, 'The Relationship Between Internationalized Courts and National Courts', *Internationalized Criminal Courts—Sierra Leone, East Timor, Kosovo, and Cambodia* (Cesare PR Romano et al, eds, 2004) 359, 365, 367–8.

The jurisdictional regime adopted by the other hybrid tribunals is more difficult to understand. The East Timorese Panels have been endowed with exclusive jurisdiction over serious offences (if committed from 1 Jan 1999 to 25 Oct 1999), but it is unclear whether this was intended to block proceedings outside East Timor (eg, in Indonesia) (Regulation No 2000/15 on the Establishment of Panels with Exclusive Jurisdiction over Serious Criminal Offences, s 1.1, UN Doc UNTAET/REG/2000/15

Criminal Tribunal for Yugoslavia (ICTY) and International Criminal Tribunal for Rwanda (ICTR) have recently modified this rule so to accommodate referral of criminal cases from some international courts to national courts.[37]

Unlike some of the instances of regulated interaction just discussed, the complementarity rule appears to establish a horizontal relationship between national and international courts: they constitute jurisdictional alternatives to one another with right of way normally given to national courts. This perception is reinforced by Article 20 of the Rome Statute—the *ne bis in idem* (double jeopardy) clause—which precludes the ICC from reopening criminal convictions or acquittals reached in domestic courts and, similarly, precludes national courts of member states from reopening ICC judgments. In other words, the decisions of the ICC and national courts are equally non-reviewable and carry a preclusive effect vis-à-vis each other.

A limited exception to the horizontal paradigm introduced by the Rome Statute can be found in the power of the ICC to deviate from the terms of articles 17 and 20 if it believes that national proceedings were not conducted in good faith (eg, were merely designed to shield the accused from ICC jurisdiction) or otherwise ineffective and thus not entitled to 'full faith and credit'.[38] This suggests, perhaps, that the horizontal structuring of relations between national and international courts may need to be supplemented by some vertical features of supervision to accommodate fears of abuse.[39]

(2000); Kleffner and Nollkaemper, above, at 365, 362–4. The Cambodian law establishing special chambers for prosecuting international crimes does not regulate jurisdictional relations with other courts. Law on the Establishment of Extraordinary Chambers in the Courts of Cambodia for the Prosecution of Crimes Committed During the Period of Democratic Kampuchea, 10 Aug 2001, art 5 <http://www.derechos.org/human-rights/seasia/doc/krlaw.html>. Still, it is highly unlikely that other Cambodian courts would exercise jurisdiction over crimes covered by the 2001 Law. Kleffner and Nollkaemper, above, at 364–5. This also seems to be the situation in Kosovo (in actuality, all cases relating to the 1998–1999 conflict were dealt with by the internationalized courts operating in Kosovo). Kleffner and Nollkaemper, above, at 361.

[37] See *Prosecutor v Ljubičić*, ICTY Case No IT-00-41-AR-11*bis*1, decision of 4 July 2006 <http://www.un.org/icty/ljubicic/appeal/decision-e/acdec040606e.pdf>; *Prosecutor v Ademi*, ICTY Case No: IT-04-78-PT, decision of 14 Sept 2005, <http://www.un.org/icty/ademi/trialc/decision-e/050914.htm>; *Prosecutor v Milošević*, ICTY Case No: IT-98-29/1-PT, decision of 8 July 2005 <http://www.un.org/icty/milosevic-d/trialc/decision-e/050708.htm>; *Prosecution v Stanković*, ICTY Case No IT-96-23/2-PT, decision of 17 May 2005, <http://www.un.org/icty/stankovic/trialc/decision-e/050517.htm>; *Prosecution v Stanković*, ICTY Case No IT-96-23/2-AR11*bis*.1, decision of 1 Sept 2005, <http://www.un.org/icty/stankovic/appeal/decision-e/050901.htm>; *Prosecutor v Janković*, ICTY Case No IT-96-23/2-PT, decision of 22 July 2005, <http://www.un.org/icty/stankovic/trialc/decision-e/050722.htm>; *Prosecutor v Janković*, ICTY Case No IT-96-23/2-AR11*bis*.2, decision of 15 Nov 2005, <http://www.un.org/icty/stankovic/appeal/decision-e/051115.htm>.

According to Rule 11*bis* of the ICTY Rules of Procedure and Evidence, the ICTY should consider, while reviewing a motion for referral, the gravity of the crime, the responsibility of the accused and the fairness of the procedure before the national court. ICTY Rules of Procedure and Evidence (revised version), 30 May 2006, UN Doc IT/32/Rev 38 (2006).

[38] Cf US Constitution, art 4(1).

[39] A recent example of such an abuse may be the newly founded special courts established by the government of Sudan in an apparent attempt to invoke the rule of complementary against ICC proceedings concerning Darfur. International human rights groups have questioned the credibility of such special courts. See eg, BBC News, 'Sudan Sets up War Crimes Tribunal', 14 June 2005, <http://news.bbc.co.uk/2/hi/africa/4091146.stm>.

It should also be noted that the complementarity rule, as reflected in the Rome Statute, does not explicitly condition its relations with national courts on application of *international* legal standards in domestic proceedings. Hence, this jurisdiction-regulating regime may potentially encompass interactions between national and international courts that address the same criminal acts but are governed by different bodies of law.[40] At the same time, the conditions for jurisdictional overlap between national courts and ad hoc international criminal tribunals may be more restrictive. Indeed, the ICTR has recently rejected a prosecutorial motion to refer a genocide case from the ICTR to Norway, citing the absence of a crime of genocide under Norwegian criminal law.[41] Since, the ICTR Statute—unlike the Rome Statute—excludes the application of the *ne bis in idem* rule to national judgments that characterize the acts of the accused as ordinary crimes, the ICTR was of the view that proceedings in Norway could not represent an alternative jurisdiction for adjudication of serious international crimes, as required by article 8 of its Statute.[42]

1.1.4 *Electa una via* or 'Fork in the Road'

A fourth example of existing jurisdictional regulation may be found in the form of some legal arrangements, especially in the field of investment law, that contain *electa una via* (ie, the principle of election) or 'fork in the road' provisions. Such provisions typically grant potential claimants a choice among several alternative procedures, including national and international courts. Normally, selection of one tribunal excludes the right of reference to all other competent tribunals.

Electa una via provisions can be found, for example, in several BITs and trade liberalization instruments,[43] and in the Energy Charter Treaty (with respect to claims against the contracting states listed in Annex ID to the Treaty).[44] For instance, the Central American Free Trade Agreement (CAFTA) requires US investors to choose between national and international adjudication in accordance with the following terms: article 10.18 (which mirrors article 1121(1)(b) of NAFTA) stipulates that initiation of international arbitration proceedings must be accompanied by a written waiver of 'any right to initiate or continue before any administrative tribunal or court under the law of any Party'.[45]

[40] See eg, Jann K Kleffner, 'The Impact of Complementarity on National Implementation of Substantive International Criminal Law', 1 *J Int'l. Crim J* (2003) 86, 95–9.

[41] *Prosecutor v Bagaragaza*, Decision on Rule 11*bis* Appeal of 30 Aug 2006 (ICTR AC).

[42] ICTR Statute, arts 8–9.

[43] See eg, Treaty Concerning the Encouragement and Reciprocal Protection of Investment (US/Uruguay), 25 Oct 2004, Annex C, para 2, 44 ILM 268 (2005); Free Trade Agreement (US/Chile), 6 June 2003, Annex 10-E, <http://www.ustr.gov/Trade_Agreements/Bilateral/Chile_FTA/Final_Texts/Section_Index.html>.

[44] Energy Charter Treaty, 17 Dec 1994, art 26(3)(b), 33 ILM 360 (1994).

[45] The Central America–Dominican Republic–United States Free Trade Agreement (CAFTA), 5 Aug 2004, art 10.18 <http://www.ustr.gov/Trade_Agreements/Bilateral/CAFTA/CAFTA-DR_Final_Texts/Section_Index.html>.

At the same time, Annex 10-E provides that:

> [I]f an investor of the United States elects to submit a claim of the type described in paragraph 1 to a court or administrative tribunal of a Central American Party or the Dominican Republic, that election shall be definitive, and the investor may not thereafter submit the claim to arbitration under Section B.[46]

The ability to seize, at will, either national or international courts, and the preclusion of multiple proceedings that prevents, in turn, challenging the findings of the seized court before other courts, would seem to suggest a belief that national and international courts can represent judicial alternatives to one another of relatively equal status—in other words, the absence of hierarchy from the relationship holding between them.

In contrast, the 'no U-turn' jurisdictional rule adopted in Chapter 11 of NAFTA only requires investors who seize NAFTA tribunals to waive recourse to national proceedings; it does not preclude consecutive resort to national courts first and to international arbitration later. Hence, article 1121(1)(b) of NAFTA, which only bars recourse to national courts after the initiation of Chapter 11 arbitral proceedings, operates in a more limited manner than do full-fledged *electa una via* provisions.[47] Indeed, it has already been noted that NAFTA Chapter 11 tribunals may probably operate vis-à-vis national courts in accordance with a vertical, not horizontal, relationship paradigm.[48]

1.1.5 Recognition of international arbitral agreements and awards

The final example of a regulated form of interaction between national and international tribunals to be discussed in the present chapter is the regime governing the recognition and enforcement of international arbitral agreements and awards found in the field of international commercial arbitration. According to the New York Convention on the Recognition and Enforcement of Foreign Awards and analogous instruments,[49] which cover mainly private commercial arbitrations conducted in foreign territory but also some international arbitration procedures involving international actors and subject to international legal standards (eg, the Iran–US Claims Tribunal, NAFTA Chapter 11 arbitrations and ICSID Additional

[46] Ibid, at Annex 10-E, para 2.

[47] See eg, David A Gantz, 'The Evolution of FTA Investment Provisions: From NAFTA to the United States—Chile Free Trade Agreement', 19 *Am U Int'l L Rev* (2004) 679, 754; Mark Clodfelter, 'U.S. State Department Participation in International Economic Dispute Resolution', 42 *S Tex L Rev* (2001) 1273, 1279. Similar jurisdictional arrangements based on the NAFTA 'no U-turn' model can also be found in the US and Canadian Model BITs. US Model BIT 2004, art 26(2)(b), <http://www.ustr.gov/assets/Trade_Sectors/Investment/Model_BIT/asset_upload_file847_6897.pdf>; Canadian Model BIT 2004, art. 26(1)(e), <http://ita.law.uvic.ca/documents/Canadian2004-FIPA-model-en.pdf>.

[48] See Klafter, above n 24, at 416–17.

[49] See eg, Inter-American Convention on International Commercial Arbitration, 30 Jan 1975, 14 ILM 336 (1975); NAFTA, art 1136(6).

Facility arbitrations),[50] national courts are required to recognize agreements to arbitrate outside their territory and to give effect to arbitral awards rendered in such proceedings.[51]

The duty to recognize agreements to arbitrate imposed on national courts sustains the actual jurisdictional choice made by the parties to the dispute and applies the *electa una via* rule vis-à-vis the agreement to arbitrate. This same duty precludes the authority of national judicial fora over the same dispute. The rule establishes international (or foreign) arbitration proceedings as jurisdictional alternatives to domestic litigation and thus constitutes an essentially horizontal form of regulation. In addition, under the terms of the New York Convention, the arbitral tribunal's findings on the *merits* are, by and large, non-reviewable by the national courts of the jurisdiction in which recognition and enforcement are sought.[52] This rule, which is designed to encourage utilization of international arbitration, suggests as well that the relationship between national courts and international arbitration tribunals has conspicuous horizontal features.

Still, as is the case with the complementarity rule discussed above, national courts do preserve some degree of oversight over the propriety of the arbitral agreement and the conduct of the arbitral proceedings. As a result, they may refuse to recognize agreements to arbitrate or arbitral awards which run contrary to important public policies of the forum state or contravene domestic judicial pronouncements in the same case.[53] Significantly, national courts may also refuse to enforce awards that were rendered through a seriously irregular process. This power of judicial oversight introduces a vertical element into the otherwise horizontal relations between national courts and international arbitral tribunals dealing with international commercial disputes.

[50] See also Commercial Arbitration Act, RS 1985, sec 5(4) (Canada) (applying the Commercial Arbitration Act to NAFTA arbitrations); *Occidental Exploration and Production Co v Ecuador*, 45 ILM 249, 263 (UK Court of Appeal, 2006) (applying the Arbitration Act 1996 to a UNCITRAL arbitral award); *Dallal v Bank Mellat* [1986] QB 441 (general principles of comity provide basis for enforcing a Iran–US Claims Tribunal award). This outcome is sometimes facilitated by rules on the seat of the arbitration designed to ensure that the proceedings take place in the territory of parties to the New York Convention. See eg, NAFTA, art 1130; Additional Facility Rules, Schedule C—Arbitration (Additional Facility) Rules, Rule 19, <http://www.worldbank.org/icsid/facility/partA.htm>; Ibrahim F I Shihata & Antonio R Parra, 'The Experience of the International Centre for Settlement of Investment Disputes', 14 *ICSID Rev—FILJ* (1999) 299, 344–55.

One may note that a special legal regime governs ICSID arbitrations (as opposed to ICSID Additional Facility arbitrations). ICSID Convention, art 54(1) ('Each Contracting State shall recognize an award rendered pursuant to this Convention as binding and enforce the pecuniary obligations imposed by that award within its territories as if it were a final judgment of a court in that State'). Domestic courts are required not to review the merits of the ICSID award whose recognition and enforcement is sought. *Marine International Nominees Establishment (MINE) v Guinea*, 4 ICSID Rep 84, 85, 88 (1989)(ad hoc annulment committee); Schreuer, above n 16, at 1127.

[51] New York Convention, art II, III. See Gary B Born, *International Arbitration and Forum Selection Agreements: Drafting and Enforcing* (3rd edn, 2006) 9–11.

[52] See Albert Jan van den Berg, *The New York Arbitration Convention of 1958: Towards a Uniform Judicial Interpretation* (1981) (reprinted in 1994) 265.

[53] New York Convention, art V.

In practice, international awards were refused recognition by domestic courts, in whole or in part, on some occasions.[54] In Chapter 6 below, I discuss the policy considerations militating for and against interference in the outcome of international judgments or awards—a discussion that is relevant for ascertaining the degree of deference owed to the international arbitral tribunal by the reviewing domestic courts.

Finally, it should be noted that the regulatory regime introduced by the New York Convention is informal in nature—it is not conditioned on any formal identity between the sources of law applied in the arbitration proceedings in question and the law of the reviewing jurisdiction. In fact, in most cases of jurisdictional interaction covered by the New York Convention, the applicable law in the arbitration differs from the domestic law of the forum state where recognition and enforcement is sought. This does not, however, release the forum state from the obligation to give effect to arbitration agreements and awards which appertain to the same 'action', ie, the same factual dispute over the same transaction between the same parties.[55]

1.2 Uncharted Territory: Unregulated Interactions between National and International Courts

The previous section established the proposition that jurisdictional interaction between national and international courts is feasible but also amenable to international regulation. However, no uniform model of regulation exists: some regulatory regimes are horizontal in nature, whereas others have vertical features (establishing the supremacy of international courts vis-à-vis national courts or vice versa); some jurisdiction-regulating rules limit themselves to interactions between proceedings based on the same formal legal standards, whereas other rules are broader in scope and encompass all interactions relating to the same fact patterns and/or remedies pursued.

The difficult question arising is what, if any, legal regime governs unregulated interactions between national and international courts, ie, situations of jurisdictional interaction not fully covered by any specific *international law* instrument governing the interplay between the relevant international courts and their national counterparts. This section examines a number of case studies indicative of the incoherent practice of national and international courts in configuring their relations vis-à-vis each other in the absence of clear guidance in treaty law or custom. These include some early precedents involving jurisdictional interactions between international and national proceedings, more recent cases involving the ICJ and national

[54] See eg, *Mexico v Metalclad Inc*, [2001] BCTC 664 (British Columbia Supreme Court) (setting aside in part a NAFTA Chapter 11 award); *Iran Aircraft Industries v Avco Corp*, 980 F 2d 141 (1994).

[55] Born, above n 51, at 9–11.

courts, such as the Consular Notification and Separation Barrier/Wall cases, national and international case law on the effects of trade-related determinations adopted by domestic agencies, prompt release of vessel cases under UNCLOS and the ICSID contract/treaty claims cases, which potentially entail litigation of investment disputes before national and international fora.

1.2.1 Early interactions between international and national proceedings

Legal problems relating to jurisdictional interplay between proceedings conducted on the international and national level have arisen in the context of some early 20th century arbitrations during which it was alleged by the respondent party that national courts constitute the proper forum for adjudication of the dispute due to Calvo Clause-type contractual provisions.[56] Typically, the legal question discussed in these cases was whether the private contract providing for the exclusive jurisdiction of domestic courts over the dispute prevented mixed claims commissions from adjudicating claims for damages brought by the foreign investors' states of nationality against the relevant host states.

In the *Mexican Union Railway* case, a British–Mexican Claims Commission adjudicated a claim made by a British corporation, operating a railroad in Mexico, for damages it sustained during insurgency and counter-insurgency operations that took place in Mexico between 1910–1920.[57] The majority on the commission held that a Calvo Clause undertaking by the foreign company, waiving the right to diplomatic protection and confirming the exclusive jurisdiction of domestic Mexican courts, should be given effect.[58] Furthermore, it held that the presentation of claims before the commission by the British government itself did not transform the nature of the claims into inter-state claims.[59] Still, it was held that the British government could present, in due time, denial of justice or undue delay of justice claims against Mexico because such claims would be qualitatively different from the claims covered by the contractual clause.

Similarly, in *North American Dredging*, the American–Mexican Claims Commission held that a contractual Calvo Clause, which invests the domestic courts of Mexico with exclusive jurisdiction over contractual disputes between the foreign investor and Mexico, is generally enforceable:

> [W]here a claimant has expressly agreed in writing, attested by his signature, that in all matters pertaining to the execution, fulfillment, and interpretation of the contract he will have resort to local tribunals, remedies and authorities and then willfully ignores them by

[56] The Calvo Clauses invested national courts with exclusive jurisdiction over contractual disputes between foreign investors and the host state. See F V García-Amador, 'Calvo Doctrine, Calvo Clause', I *Encyclopedia of Public International Law* (Rudholf Bernhardt, ed, 1997) 521.

[57] *Mexican Union Railway*, 5 RIAA 115. [58] Ibid, at 120. [59] Ibid.

applying in such matters to his Government, he will be held bound by his contract and the Commission will not take jurisdiction.[60]

However, this commission too qualified its holding by noting that the investor's right to request and receive diplomatic protection would re-emerge if the judicial proceedings conducted before the courts of the host state amounted to denial or delay of justice.[61] This is because such conduct would give rise to an independent breach of international law, not covered by the contractual undertaking.[62]

Finally, in *Woodruff*, the American–Venezuelan Claims Commission accepted that a contractual undertaking not to bring claims before judicial fora other than local courts in Venezuela bars a private party from bringing a claim alleging breach of the same contract before the commission.[63] The commission did note, however, that the state of nationality's right to bring an international claim is not impaired by the private contractual undertaking.[64]

In sum, the three commissions were willing to acknowledge the binding force of exclusive jurisdictional clauses inserted in private contracts between states and foreign investors.[65] Yet, the independent claims of the investors' state of nationality or new claims arising from the adjudicative process itself were not necessarily subsumed in the contractual forum-selection clause, and may have remained subject to the jurisdiction of international fora.

It should be noted, however, that other authorities from the same period of time do seem to pull in the other direction. In the *Martini* case, the Italian–Venezuelan Mixed Commission reviewed a claim brought by an Italian company whose property had suffered considerable material injury in the course of a revolutionary uprising in Venezuela (1902–1903). As a preliminary matter, it was argued on behalf of Venezuela that the jurisdiction of the mixed commission was excluded by article 16 of the concession contract, which provided for the exclusive jurisdiction of local Venezuelan courts over contractual questions and controversies. In rejecting this argument, Umpire Ralston held that the right of the Italian and Venezuelan governments to refer the grievances against Venezuela of an Italian national to the Mixed Commission 'is entirely superior to that of the subject to contract it away'.[66]

60 *North American Dredging Company of Texas* (US v Mexico), 4 RIAA 26, 33 (1926).

61 *North American Dredging*, 4 RIAA at 32.

62 See also *El Oro*, 5 RIAA at 195–8

63 *Woodruff* (US v Venezuela), 9 RIAA 213, 222 (1903) ('Whereas certainly a contract between a sovereign and a citizen of a foreign country can never impede the right of the Government of that citizen to make international reclamation, wherever according to international law it has the right or even the duty to do so, as its rights and obligations can not be affected by any precedent agreement to which it is not a party; But whereas this does not interfere with the right of a citizen to pledge to any other party that he, the contractor, in disputes upon certain matters will never appeal to other judges than to those designated by the agreement, nor with his obligation to keep this promise when pledged').

64 Ibid. The Commission also noted that the private claimant would be entitled to request diplomatic protection in the event of denial of justice by local courts.

65 For a similar decision by the US–Venezuela claims commission, see *Flannagan, Bradley, Clarke & Co* (US v Venezuela), excerpts in John Bassett, Moore, IV *History and Digest of the International Arbitrations to Which the US Has Been a Party* 3564 (1898).

66 *Martini & Co v Venezuela* (Italy v Venezuela), 10 RIAA 644, 663 (1903).

The Umpire also found no indication in the text of the Protocol establishing the mixed commission[67] that the parties intended to limit its powers to claims governed by pre-existing forum-selection clauses.[68] Similarly, in *Greece v Yulkan Werke*, a mixed arbitral tribunal held that considerations of public order dictate that an inter-state jurisdictional agreement (the Treaty of Versailles) overrides any private contractual arrangement reached by the parties to the dispute.[69]

The proposition that private contractual undertakings do not bar the litigation of independent inter-state claims (which some of the claims commissions accepted) was confirmed by the PCIJ in two leading cases dealing with the jurisdictional relationship between PCIJ proceedings and proceedings before national courts or mixed arbitral tribunals. In the *Certain German Interests* case, the PCIJ dealt with claims presented by the German government alleging infringement by the Polish government of the property rights of some German corporations and individuals with respect to assets located in Upper Silesia. Since some of the dispossessed German proprietors had also challenged the liquidation of their property rights before the Germano–Polish Mixed Arbitral Tribunal in Paris (and also before domestic courts in Poland), the Polish government asked for suspension of the PCIJ proceedings until the conclusion of the arbitral proceedings by reason of litispendence.[70] Although the case primarily focused on jurisdictional competition between two international courts—the PCIJ and the mixed arbitral tribunal (which was authorized to apply both national and international law)[71]—the approach taken by the PCIJ would equally seem to apply to regulation of the relationship between its jurisdiction and that of Polish local courts.

In its decision on jurisdiction of 1925, the PCIJ dismissed Poland's objection and noted that no *lis alibi pendens* claim was possible in the circumstances of the case. This is because the proceedings before the PCIJ and mixed arbitral tribunal involved different objects (interpretation of an international instrument and return of property rights, respectively) and different claimants (German individuals and corporations and the German state, respectively). In addition, the Court held that the PCIJ and the mixed arbitral tribunal 'are not courts of the same character'

[67] Protocol (Italy/Venezuela), 13 Feb 1903, 10 RIAA 479.

[68] *Martini*, 10 RIAA at 663–4.

[69] *Greece v Vulkan Werke*, 5 *Décisions des tribunaux arbitraux mixtes* (1926) 887, 896–7. But see *Eigher v Germany*, 5 *Décisions des tribunaux arbitraux mixtes* (1926) 604, 609 (the jurisdictional provisions of the Treaty of Versailles referring disputes to the Romano–German Mixed Arbitral tribunal do not establish 'public order' and may be deviated from by way of explicit or implicit agreement).

[70] *Certain German Interests in Polish Upper Silesia* (Germany v Poland), 1925 PCIJ (Ser C), No 9/1, at 52–6 (discours prononcé par Limburg (Poland)).

[71] Mixed arbitral tribunals are arbitral bodies invested with authority to adjudicate large numbers of claims brought by individuals against foreign governments. Such tribunals have been typically established in the aftermath of wars and other large-scale catastrophes (most notably in the inter-war period). Norbert Wühler, 'Mixed Arbitral Tribunals', III *Encyclopedia of Public International Law* (Rudholf Bernhardt, ed, 1997) 433. Since the mixed tribunals applied a combination of national and international law, it is difficult to determine their precise nature. Rudolf Blühdorn, 'Le fonctionnement et la jurisprudence des tribunaux arbitraux mixtes créés par les traités de paris' 41 *Recueil des cours* (1932-III) 141, 144–6.

(this also applied, *a fortiori*, to relations between the PCIJ and the local Polish court).[72] The different legal context in which the PCIJ and the mixed arbitral tribunal (or national courts) operated thus served as grounds for the Court's refusal to regulate the parallel exercise of their jurisdictions.[73] Indeed, the *Certain German Interests* case is often cited for its endorsement of a related proposition that, from an international law viewpoint, national laws and national courts decisions are merely facts,[74] ie, national judicial pronouncements have no normative import for international adjudication and thus cannot compete with international courts.

The division of labour between the PCIJ and the Germano–Polish Mixed Arbitral Tribunal was also discussed by the PCIJ in the *Chorzów Factory* case, a case dealing with the German government's demand for compensation on behalf of two German companies whose property rights over a factory in Upper Silesia were liquidated by the Polish government (the international unlawfulness of the confiscation was already established by the PCIJ in its *Certain German Interests* judgment). Once again, Poland requested the Court to decline jurisdiction in favour of the mixed arbitral tribunal, arguing that the explicit provisions of the Geneva Convention concerning Upper Silesia,[75] which provided for a system for settling disputes over expropriation of property (including two mixed arbitral tribunals—Upper Silesian and Germano–Polish—and national courts), constitute *lex specialis*, which ought to divest the PCIJ of jurisdiction over the case.[76]

The Court held that there can be no overlap between the jurisdiction of the PCIJ and ordinary Polish courts since the latter apply the same domestic laws that the PCIJ had already decreed to be internationally unlawful.[77] With regard to the mixed arbitral tribunal, the PCIJ acknowledged the existence of some overlap between the remedies available before the two judicial institutions, but ultimately held that there was no clear treaty provision that excluded its jurisdiction over the German claims (especially because the claims brought by Germany before the PCIJ were broader in scope than the claims brought by the German company before the mixed arbitral tribunal).[78]

In its subsequent judgment on the merits of the *Chorzów Factory* case, the PCIJ held that a decision issued by a domestic Polish court, which held that the relevant

[72] *Certain German Interests*, 1925 PCIJ (Ser A), No 6, at 20.

[73] But see, *Certain German Interests*, 1925 PCIJ (Ser A), No 7, at 38 (dissenting opinion of Judge Rostworowski) (matters falling under the jurisdiction of the Mixed Arbitral Tribunal are excluded from the jurisdiction of the PCIJ).

[74] *Certain German Interests*, 1925 PCIJ (Ser A), No 7, at 19. See also *Payment of Various Serbian Loans Issued in France* (France v Serb-Croat-Slovene), 1929 PCIJ (Ser A), No 20/21, at 19; *Frontier Dispute* (Benin/Niger), Judgment of 12 July 2005, at para 28 ('when reference is made to domestic law in such a context, that law is applicable not in itself (as if there were a sort of *continuum juris*, a legal relay between such law and international law), but only as one factual element among others, or as evidence indicative of . . . the "colonial heritage" ').

[75] Convention concerning Upper Silesia (Germany/Poland), 15 May 1922, 9 LNTS 465.

[76] *Factory at Chorzów* (Germany v Poland), 1927 PCIJ (Ser C) No 13/1, at 154–6 (preliminary objections of Poland).

[77] *Chorzów Factory*, 1927 PCIJ (Ser A) No 9, at 26.

[78] Ibid, at 30.

German corporations did not have valid property rights in the disputed factory, cannot affect the conclusions reached by the PCIJ in the *Certain German Interests* case. This is because such an outcome 'would be attributing to a judgment of a municipal court power indirectly to invalidate a judgment of an international court, which is impossible'.[79]

In sum, these two PCIJ cases on the rights of German individuals in Poland seem to embrace a sharp distinction between the jurisdiction of the World Court, on the one hand, and the jurisdictions of other judicial bodies implicated in the litigation of the same transactions—national courts and the mixed arbitral tribunals—on the other hand. The differences in the applicable law and in the identity of the parties in the separate sets of proceedings, as well as the perception that the judicial bodies involved belong to different orders, facilitated the Court's reluctance to regulate jurisdictional relations between itself and its counterparts, expressed in its anti-regulatory stance (ie, the Court would exercise its jurisdiction unless faced with a sufficiently precise clause that grants jurisdiction over the same issues to a different tribunal).

Still, another PCIJ decision relating to the situation in Upper Silesia—the *Von Pless Administration* case—suggests the possibility of adopting a more nuanced approach to the relationship between national and international proceedings. This case involved allegations on the part of the German government that the treatment of a German individual living in Upper Silesia by the Polish tax authorities ran afoul of Poland's obligations under the aforementioned 1922 Geneva Convention. However, since proceedings were still pending before the Polish Supreme Administrative Court, the PCIJ accepted two Polish requests to delay the proceedings, noting that irrespective of any question relating to the formal requirement that the relevant private individual should exhaust the local remedies available in Poland:

> [I]t will certainly be an advantage to the Court, as regards the points which have to be established in the case, to be acquainted with the final decisions of the Supreme Polish Administrative Tribunal upon the appeals brought by Prince von Pless and now pending before that Tribunal; and as the Court must therefore arrange its procedure so as to ensure that this will be possible.[80]

This position, arguably, accepts the practical—if not normative—value of domestic adjudication for international courts, and is perhaps indicative of appreciation by the Court of the utility of coordination between the outcomes of national and international proceedings. Because no decision on the merits of the case was ever rendered by the Court, one can only speculate what effect the PCIJ would have given the domestic court decision.

[79] *Chorzów Factory*, 1927 PCIJ (Ser A), No 12, at 33.

[80] *Prince von Pless Administration* (Germany v Poland), 1933 PCIJ (Ser A/B), No 52, at 16 (interim order). See also *Prince von Pless Administration* (Germany v Poland), 1933 PCIJ (Ser A/B), No 57 (prorogation).

1.2.2 Jurisdictional interactions between the ICJ and national courts

I now turn to examine two other, more recent, categories of jurisdictional interaction between an international court—this time, the ICJ—and national courts. The first sub-section will discuss the various Consular Notification cases, which gave rise to litigation before the ICJ and domestic US courts (some of these cases were also brought before the Inter-American Court and the Inter-American Commission of Human Rights). The following sub-section examines the interaction between the ICJ and the Israeli Supreme Court in respect of the *Separation Barrier/Wall* case. Whereas the discussion in the previous section focused on the reaction of international courts to instances of jurisdictional competition, this section places greater stress on the positions taken by domestic courts with regard to the authority of legal pronouncements issued by international courts on the same questions of fact and law. As will be shown, some of the positions adopted by domestic courts on jurisdictional interaction can be perceived as mirror images of some of the positions taken by international courts on the same matter.

The Consular Notification *cases*

The repeated failure of US law enforcement authorities to notify detained foreign nationals of their right to seek assistance from the consular officials that represent their country in the US, as is required by article 36(1))(b) of the 1963 Vienna Convention on Consular Relations,[81] has generated a significant number of legal proceedings before national and international courts. These cases have arisen mainly in the context of legal challenges to death penalties imposed on foreign nationals who were not notified at the time of their arrest of their right to seek consular assistance, an omission that allegedly compromised their ability to present a proper legal defense. Still, the procedural default doctrine that US federal and state law apply,[82] has barred many individuals sentenced to death from raising procedural arguments that were not made at the first instance trial in the course of their appellate proceedings—including challenges based on the omission to provide them with timely consular notification. The specific question addressed in the Consular Notification cases therefore relates to second-order international law obligations: what is the proper remedy that the US ought to provide as a result of this failure pursuant to the Vienna Convention, and to whom is this remedy due (the individual or her state of nationality)?

In the first of this series of cases—*Breard*—a Paraguayan national, who was sentenced to death in Virginia for committing murder, challenged his sentence before

[81] Vienna Convention on Consular Relations, 24 April 1963, 596 UNTS 261.

[82] See *Massaro v US*, 538 US 500, 504 (2003). For a legislative endorsement of the doctrine, see 28 USCS § 2254(e)(2). For a discussion of the history of the procedural default rule in the US, see Carole C Cooke, 'Procedural Defaults at the Appellate Stage and Federal Habeas Corpus Review', 38 *Stan L Rev* (1986) 463; Alan W Clarke, 'Procedural Labyrinths and the Injustice of Death: A Critique of Death Penalty Habeas Corpus (Part Two)', 30 *U Rich L Rev* (1996) 303, 328–8.

domestic US courts, all the way to the Supreme Court, on the grounds that the authorities failed to provide him with timely consular notification following his arrest. In parallel, Paraguay brought proceedings before US courts, alleging violation of its own rights under the Vienna Consular Relations Convention. Following dismissal of the suit for lack of jurisdiction by lower federal courts,[83] Paraguay brought a claim against the US before the ICJ. Although the US had urged the ICJ to reject Paraguay's request for provisional measures because such a remedy might lead to 'serious disruption of the criminal justice systems of the parties to the Vienna Convention',[84] the Court accepted the provisional measures motion and requested that the US refrain from executing Breard while the case was still pending before the ICJ.[85]

Breard and Paraguay then petitioned the Supreme Court for *habeas corpus* and stay of execution, pursuant to the provisional measures indicated by the ICJ. Still, the Supreme Court, sitting only five days after the date of the ICJ decision, rejected the petition and authorized execution for that same night. According to the Supreme Court, although it 'should give respectful consideration to the interpretation of an international treaty rendered by an international court with jurisdiction to interpret such', the procedural rules of the forum state regarding the implementation of such a treaty—including the procedural default doctrine—enjoy legal precedence under US law and the terms of the Vienna Convention itself.[86] In addition, the Supreme Court opined that in all likelihood, prompt consular notification would not have changed the outcome of Breard's trial. The Court also dismissed Paraguay's claim because of its failure to identify an independent right of action under the Vienna Convention and by reason of the immunity from claims by foreign sovereigns afforded to the US under existing Eleventh Amendment jurisprudence.[87]

Although not explicitly pronounced, the majority in the Supreme Court seemed to be of the view that the ICJ proceedings should have little, if any impact on US

[83] *Republic of Paraguay v Allen*, 949 F Supp 1269 (ED Va 1996); *Paraguay v Allen*, 134 F 3d 622 (1998).

[84] Vienna Convention on Consular Relations (Paraguay v US), oral pleadings of 7 April 1998, at para 45 (M J Matheson (US), <http://www.icj-cij.org/icjwww/idocket/ipaus/ipauscr980407/ipaus_icr9807.html>. A similar argument was made by the US in the course of the advisory proceedings initiated by Mexico before the Inter-American Court of Human Rights. *The Right to Information on Consular Assistance in the Framework of the Guarantees of the Due Process of Law*, brief of the United States of 1 June 1998, excerpts in *The Right to Information on Consular Assistance in the Framework of the Guarantees of the Due Process of Law*, Advisory Opinion of 1 Oct 1999, Inter-Am Ct HR (Ser A) No 16, at para 26 (1999) ('Any decision by the Court, even of an advisory nature, would gravely affect the cases still pending before the respective judicial systems and seriously compromise the rights of the individuals and governments involved, including the victims of the crimes committed, who have not had the opportunity to participate in these proceedings').

[85] *Vienna Convention on Consular Relations* (Paraguay v US), 1998 ICJ 248.

[86] *Breard v Greene*, 523 US 371, 375 (1998).

[87] US Constitution, 11th Amendment. Although the 11th Amendment only bars explicitly claims made by foreign citizens against the US, it has been construed so as to also exclude inter-state claims. US Courts, *Principality of Monaco v Mississippi*, 292 US 313 (1934).

proceedings. In part, this stance might have resulted from the position taken by the US government in the *amicus* brief, submitted to the Supreme Court, questioning the binding force of ICJ provisional measures on the international plane,[88] a position taken more forcefully during the *LaGrand* litigation before the ICJ.[89]

Still, the reluctance to give effect to the ICJ provisional measures may be explained by reference to a more fundamental point: according to the Supreme Court, any interpretation of international law pronounced by the ICJ would have been subject to the overriding requirements of domestic law. Hence, if domestic law applies the procedural default rule to all claims of error in a criminal trial, then—'Breard's ability to obtain relief based on violations of the Vienna Convention is subject to this subsequently-enacted rule, just as any claim arising under the United States Constitution would be'.[90] In other words, the weight afforded to the ICJ position on the Vienna Convention is circumscribed by the subordination of international treaties to domestic constitutional and procedural principles.[91]

The refusal of US courts to accommodate the provisional measures indicated by the ICJ was discussed by the latter jurisdiction not in *Breard*, which was eventually settled out of court, but in the subsequent *LaGrand* case. Like *Breard*, the *LaGrand* case involved a failure on the part of US authorities to notify foreign nationals (this time, two brothers holding German nationality), suspected of a crime and eventually sentenced to death, of their right to consular notification. Similarly, the case concerned the application of the procedural default rule by federal courts against attempts to rely on the authorities' failure as grounds for challenging the propriety of the State proceedings (this time, the State of Arizona). Following the execution of Karl LaGrand on 24 February 1999, Germany initiated ICJ proceedings against the US for violating the Vienna Convention on Consular Relations and obtained a provisional measures order requiring the US to abstain from executing his brother, Walter LaGrand, while the case was still pending before the ICJ.[92]

Yet, the US again refused to comply with the provisional measures order and authorized Walter LaGrand's execution: the Supreme Court dismissed an eleventh-hour-motion by Germany to enforce the ICJ's order, citing various jurisdictional concerns related to Germany's right of standing and the tardiness with which

[88] *Breard v Greene*, *amicus* brief submitted to the Supreme Court by the US, cited in *LaGrand* (Germany v US), 2001 ICJ 466, 507.

[89] *LaGrand*, counter-memorial of the US (27 March 2000), at Part VI, Ch 4, <http://www.icj-cij.org/icjwww/idocket/igus/iguspleadings/iGUS_ipleading_CounterMemorial_US_20000327.htm>.

[90] *Breard*, 523 US at 376.

[91] In addition, it would seem that constitutional principles require lower US courts to prefer the Supreme Court's decision in *Breard* to the position of the ICJ on the proper relations between the procedural default rule and the Vienna Convention. See *Valdez v State*, 2002 OK CR 20, 23 ('For this Court to decide the ICJ's ruling overrules a binding decision of the United States Supreme Court and affords a judicial remedy to an individual for a violation of the Convention would interfere with the nation's foreign affairs and run afoul of the U.S. Constitution'); *Ex parte Medellin*, 2006 Tex Crim App LEXIS 2236, at 36 ('we are bound by the Supreme Court's determination that ICJ decisions are not binding on United States courts').

[92] *LaGrand*, 1999 ICJ 9 (provisional measures).

Germany had handled the case.[93] It might be assumed that this decision, too, was influenced to some degree by the position of the US Solicitor General, who disputed the binding authority of ICJ provisional measures in a letter submitted to the Court.[94] At the same time, the dissenting judges—Breyer and Stevens—took the position that the fact that the ICJ and a sovereign State have asked for a stay was sufficient reason to accede to the request in order to consider the jurisdictional and international issues at stake.[95] This dissent was noted with approval by the ICJ in its decision on the merits of the *LaGrand* case, in which it held that the position taken by the majority of judges of the US Supreme Court failed to give effect to the provisional measures order issued by the ICJ (which the ICJ held to be of a legally binding nature).[96] Still, as discussed in Chapter 6 below, the ICJ refrained in its judgment from prescribing the precise manner in which the violation of the Vienna Convention on Consular Relations ought to be remedied and left the choice of the remedial procedure to US authorities.[97]

The jurisdictional juggling between US and international courts continued in a number of cases involving Mexican citizens sentenced to death in the US without being afforded timely consular notification. Several Mexican nationals have lodged complaints against the US with the Inter-American Commission on Human Rights, alleging that the failure to provide them with consular notification constitutes a violation of their human rights. In addition, the Mexican government has requested that the Inter-American Court (I/A CtHR) issue an advisory opinion on the same subject. Perhaps not surprisingly, both inter-American human rights bodies have opined that the decision of US judicial authorities to execute foreign nationals without remedying the failure to provide them with timely consular notification constitutes a violation of the 1948 Inter-American Declaration of the Rights and Duties of Man.[98] These decisions, however, have had no noticeable impact on litigation within the US[99]—an outcome partly explained by their non-binding nature (I/A Commission reports and I/A CtHR advisory opinions are non-binding; the precise legal status of the entire 1948 Declaration may also be open to question).[100]

93 *Germany v US*, 526 US 111 (1999)

94 The US Solicitor-General's letter is referred to in Justice Breyer's dissent. *Germany*, 525 US at 113.

95 *Germany*, 525 US at 113.

96 *LaGrand*, 2001 ICJ at 508.

97 Ibid, at 514.

98 See Case 11.753, *Martinez Villareal v US*, Inter-Am CHR, Doc 5 rev 1 at 821 (2002); Case 11.331, *Cesar Fierro v United States*, Report No 99/03, Inter-Am CHR, OEA/Ser./L/V/II.114 Doc. 70 rev. 1 at 769 (2003); Advisory Opinion OC-16/99, *The Right to Information on Consular Assistance in the Framework of Guarantees of the Due Process of Law*, Opinion of 1 Oct 1999, at paras 54–65, <http://www.corteidh.or.cr/serieapdf/seriea_16_esp.pdf>. For the text of the American Declaration, see American Declaration of the Rights and Duties of Man, OAS Res XXX, adopted by the Ninth International Conference of American States (1948), *reprinted in* Basic Documents Pertaining to Human Rights in the Inter-American System, OEA/Ser.L.V/II.82 doc.6 rev.1 at 17 (1992).

99 Those decisions were invoked only in some exceptional instances. See eg, *Illinois v Madej*, 739 N.E.2d 423, 430–31 (2000) (dissenting opinion of Judge McMorrow)(citing the I/A CtHR opinion in support of a Polish defendant's application for re-sentencing).

100 See eg, *Garza v Lappin*, 253 F 3d 918, 924–5 (2001).

In contrast, the litigation before the ICJ in *Avena*—a case brought by Mexico against the US pertaining to the conviction and sentencing of 54 Mexican nationals by American courts—did have somewhat greater impact. In 2003, the ICJ issued provisional measures barring the execution of three Mexican nationals with impending execution dates;[101] in 2004, the ICJ issued its judgment on the merits, requiring the US to review and reconsider (by means of its own choosing) the convictions and sentences of 51 Mexican nationals.[102] The effect of these decisions on the US legal system has been discussed in several US Supreme Court opinions (which are discussed below), including cases decided pursuant to proceedings brought by some of the individuals whose cases were addressed by the ICJ in its *Avena* provisional measures order and final judgment.

In the 2003 *Torres* case, the US Supreme Court refused, in an unmotivated decision, to issue a *certiorari* in a death penalty case involving one of the three Mexican citizens to whom the ICJ provisional measures ordered in *Avena* applied (*Torres* was decided by the Supreme Court before the ICJ ruled on the merits of the case).[103] In his dissent, Justice Breyer noted the position taken by the US government in two related cases. This position had challenged the domestic legal effect of ICJ provisional measures orders while asserting that 'the ICJ does not exercise any judicial power of the United States, which is vested exclusively by the Constitution in the United States federal courts'.[104] Breyer questioned the correctness of this legal position in light of US acceptance of the ICJ's jurisdiction to adjudicate disputes over the interpretation of the Vienna Convention on Consular Relations.[105] In the same vein, Justice Stevens opined that rejecting the ICJ position in *LaGrand*, amounted to a violation of the Vienna Convention—an outcome incompatible with the status of international treaties as the 'supreme law of the land' under article VI of the US Constitution.[106] Hence, the dissenting judges were of the view that ICJ decisions may have normative value in the American legal system by virtue of the US membership in the Vienna Convention in general, and its Optional Protocol, which invested the ICJ with jurisdiction to settle disputes over the interpretation and application of the Vienna Convention, in particular.[107]

Following publication of the ICJ *Avena* judgment, President Bush issued a memorandum in which he officially declared 'that the United States will discharge its international obligations under the decision of the International Court of Justice in [*Avena*], by having state courts give effect to the decision in accordance with general principles of comity in cases filed by the 51 Mexican nationals addressed in

[101] *Avena*, 42 ILM 309 (provisional measures).

[102] *Avena*, 43 ILM 581.

[103] *Torres v Mulin*, 540 US 1035 (2003).

[104] The briefs were filed in *Ortiz v US* and *Sinesterra v US*, and cited in *Torres v Mulin*, 540 US 1035, 1041 (2003).

[105] *Torres*, 540 US at 1041.

[106] *Torres*, 540 US at 1036–7.

[107] Optional Protocol concerning the Compulsory Settlement of Disputes, accompanying the Vienna Convention on Consular Relations, 24 April 1963, 596 UNTS 261.

that decision'.[108] The effects of this statement, as well as that of the *Avena* judgment, were discussed by the Supreme Court in the subsequent *Medellin* and *Sanchez-Llamaz* cases.

In *Medellin*, the Supreme Court revoked a *certiorari* it had previously granted in order to review a death penalty case involving one of the 51 Mexicans covered by the final *Avena* judgment. The revocation was explained by the fact that new proceedings for reviewing and reconsidering the sentence were now available to the petitioner (in Texas) in light of the President's statement.[109] Still, the majority indicated that had the Supreme Court reviewed the merits of the case, it would probably refrain from interfering with the State's sentencing judgment. This is because of the effect of constitutional law principles that limit federal review over alleged errors made by State courts in non-constitutional matters as well as a perceived lack of proof that Medellin was in fact adversely affected by the failure of notification.[110] This opinion seems to confirm once more the dominance of domestic law doctrines in the eyes of the US Supreme Court over implementation of international obligations, including binding ICJ judgments.

Notably, several Supreme Court justices appended dissenting opinions to the majority's opinion advocating greater deference to the ICJ judgment. Justice O'Connor opined that the Vienna Convention was a self-executing treaty, which invested the petitioner with substantive rights enforceable in US courts. Although she accepted that there might be more than one plausible interpretation of the relationship between the Convention's rights and the procedural default rule, she believed that '[e]ven if *Avena* is not itself a binding rule of decision in this case, it may at least be occasion to return to the question of Article 36(2)'s implications for procedural default'.[111] This is particularly so given the interest in promoting uniform interpretations of a treaty among treaty partners.[112] Furthermore, Justice Breyer suggested that Medellin could argue before the local courts in Texas that they were obligated to abide by the *Avena* judgment by virtue of the Presidential undertaking to enforce the judgment, the self-executing nature of the Vienna Convention, the jurisdiction conferred to the ICJ by the Optional Protocol to the Vienna Convention and the duty to comply with ICJ judgments assumed by the

[108] George W Bush, Memorandum for the Attorney General, 28 Feb 2005, <http://www.whitehouse.gov/news/releases/2005/02/20050228-18.html>. For analysis of the memorandum, see Frederic L Kirgis, 'President Bush's Determination Regarding Mexican Nationals and Consular Convention Rights', *ASIL Insights* (March 2005) <http://www.asil.org/insights/2005/03/insights050309.html#author#author>; A Mark Weisburd, 'International Judicial Decisions, Domestic Courts, and the Foreign Affairs Power', *CATO Supreme Court Review 2004–2005* (Mark K Moller, ed, 2005) 287, 305–20. Still, a Texas State court has recently held that the President has exceeded his constitutional authority by issuing instructions to the judiciary. *Ex parte Medellin*, 2006 Tex Crim App. LEXIS 2236, at 45–6.

[109] Eventually, the Texas State court refused, however, to review the sentence. *Ex parte Medellin*, 2006 Tex Crim App LEXIS 2236.

[110] *Medellin v Dretke* 544 US 660 (2005).

[111] *Medellin*, 544 US, at 689–90. Justices Stevens, Souter, and Breyer joined Justice O'Connor's dissenting opinion.

[112] Ibid, at 684.

US when joining the UN Charter.[113] In light of these and other considerations, the dissenting judges voted in favour of retaining the *certiorari* issued in the case.

The latest word on the legal import for the US legal system of ICJ decisions in Consular Notification cases has been rendered by the US Supreme Court in the recent *Sanchez-Llamas* judgment. The case addressed two challenges to prolonged imprisonment sentences issued by State courts in Oregon and Virginia in cases involving Mexican and Honduran nationals whose right to timely consular notification had been violated by State authorities. Significantly, none of the petitioners in *Sanchez-Llamas* were mentioned in any of the Consular Notification cases before the ICJ.

In rejecting the claim that the Supreme Court is bound to follow the interpretation of article 36 of the Vienna Convention on Consular Relations as adopted by the ICJ in *Avena* and *LaGrand*, President Roberts, writing for the majority held:

> Under our Constitution, 'the judicial Power of the United States' is 'vested in one supreme Court, and in such inferior Courts as the Congress may from time to time ordain and establish.' Art. III, § 1. That 'judicial Power... extends to... Treaties.' *Id.*, § 2. And, as Chief Justice Marshall famously explained, that judicial power includes the duty 'to say what the law is.' *Marbury* v. *Madison*, 5 US 137, 1 Cranch 137, 177, 2 L. Ed. 60 (1803). If treaties are to be given effect as federal law under our legal system, determining their meaning as a matter of federal law 'is emphatically the province and duty of the judicial department,' headed by the 'one supreme Court' established by the Constitution. *Ibid*... Nothing in the structure or purpose of the ICJ suggests that its interpretations were intended to be conclusive on our courts.[114]

As a result, the majority affirmed the applicability of the procedural default rule to allegations that the Vienna Convention had been violated; the case was consequently dismissed.

While the decision of the majority in *Sanchez-Llamas* does not directly address the question discussed in the earlier Consular Notification cases—the effect of ICJ decisions on the same dispute when pending before the Supreme Court—the explanation provided by the majority for rejecting the interpretation of the Vienna Convention on Consular Relations as offered by the ICJ in analogous cases would probably control cases of jurisdictional overlap as well. By emphasizing the Supreme Court's constitutional role of providing authoritative interpretation of federal law and international law, as applicable in the US, the majority implied that it cannot be bound by ICJ decisions on the contents of those laws. In other words, the US constitution might prevent the Supreme Court from abdicating its duty to determine the contents of applicable US and international law and defer to

[113] Ibid, at 693–4. The UN Charter requires member states 'to comply with the decision of the International Court of Justice in any case to which it is a party'. Charter of the United Nations, 26 June 1945, art 94, XV UNCIO Doc 355 (hereinafter UN Charter).

[114] *Sanchez-Llamas v Oregon*, 126 S Ct 2669, 2684 (2006).

other non-constitutionally empowered courts, including the ICJ.[115] In addition, the majority alluded to the inter-state nature of ICJ proceedings and enforcement procedures,[116] possibly as indications of the non-self-executing nature of ICJ decisions.[117] These elements of the decision, together with the majority's reference to the limited history of US court reliance on ICJ judgments[118] and the tradition of attributing great weight to executive branch interpretations of the treaties it negotiates,[119] cast serious doubt on whether the Supreme Court would have been willing to apply an ICJ judgment (ie, accord it a *res judicata* effect) in the event that such a judgment was issued in the very same case pending before the Supreme Court.

Still, it should be noted that a minority of judges were of the view (expressed by the dissenting opinion of Justice Breyer, to which Justices Stevens and Souter fully joined and Justice Ginsburg joined in part) that ICJ judgments, while not formally binding on the Supreme Court in cases involving different parties, were persuasive evidence of what international law is—a proposition supported by the interest in promoting uniform treaty interpretation and recognition of the unique expertise of the ICJ in the field.[120] Moreover, the minority saw no conflict between the ICJ judgments—if properly understood—and any US constitutional law principle. Thus, the minority advocated the carving out of an exception to the procedural default rule in those cases where acts or omissions of State authorities had caused defendants to default in pursuing their claims under the Vienna Convention.

In sum, the *Consular Notification* cases demonstrate the potential for irreconcilable jurisdictional conflicts between national and international courts over the same disputes. In the absence of clear jurisdictional regulation, both the ICJ and the US Supreme Court seem to have taken the position that they each possess the ultimate right to pronounce an interpretation of the Vienna Convention.[121] While formulations such as 'respectful consideration', used by the US Supreme Court, or the

[115] For a discussion of a similar argument, see Mark Tushnet, 'Transnational/Domestic Constitutional Law', 37 *Loy LA L Rev* (2003) 239, 251–7.

[116] *Sanchez-Llamas*, 126 S Ct, at 2684–5.

[117] For a discussion, see Weisburd, above n 108, at 298–305; for a similar position, which rejects the direct effect of ICJ/PCIJ judgments in the domestic legal system, see *Socobel v Greece*, 18 ILR 3, 4–5 (Belg, Trib Civ de Bruxelles 1951). For a discussion of other incidents of refusal by national courts to enforce international decisions, see A Mark Weisburd, 'International Courts and American Courts', 21 *Mich J Int'l L* (2000) 877, 886–7.

[118] *Sanchez-Llamas*, 126 S Ct, at 2684, n 5.

[119] Ibid, at 2685. The majority also noted that the US had just revoked its ratification of the Optional Protocol to the Vienna Convention on Consular Assistance that invested the ICJ with jurisdiction to adjudicate disputes over the interpretation and application of the Convention. According to the majority, this provided another reason why the ICJ interpretations of the Convention are not controlling. Ibid.

[120] Ibid, at 2700–15.

[121] Indeed, the US has argued in both *LaGrand* and *Avena* that exercise of jurisdiction by the ICJ over these cases would transform it into a court of appeals over domestic court decisions. *LaGrand* (Germany v US), verbatim record of oral pleadings of 14 Nov 2000, ICJ Doc CR 2003/26, at para 1.19, <http://www.icj-cij.org/icjwww/idocket/igus/iguscr/igus_icr2000-28.html>; *Avena* (Mexico v US), verbatim record of oral pleadings of 16 Dec 2003, ICJ Doc CR 2003/26, at para 2.9, <http://www.icj-cij.org/icjwww/idocket/imus/imuscr/imus_icr2003-26_20031216.PDF>.

freedom afforded by the ICJ to the US authorities to introduce 'means of their own choosing'[122] in order to remedy their violations of the Vienna Convention may be flexible enough to avert a full-scale conflict, it is questionable whether their actual application by the interacting courts have such an aim or effect. This criticism may be particularly relevant with respect to the US Supreme Court, whose decisions reveal limited willingness to harmonize its decisions with those of the ICJ.

The Separation Barrier/Wall *cases*

Another recent example of jurisdictional interaction between the ICJ and national courts can be found in the *Separation Barrier* or *Wall* cases addressed by the ICJ and the Supreme Court of Israel. Litigation in both fora involved legal challenges to the controversial West Bank separation barrier project, initiated by the Israeli government in 2002 in the midst of the second Palestinian *intifada*. The barrier, comprised of hundreds of kilometers of physical obstacles, including barbed wire fences, concrete walls, ditches, and sand roads, was officially designed to curb attacks by Palestinian terrorists against Israeli population centres. It proved, however, to be highly disruptive of the lives of Palestinians residing in towns and villages situated in proximity to its route (which sometimes cut right through Palestinian settlements or agricultural land). The barrier was also perceived by many inside and outside the West Bank as a political measure designed to punish collectively the Palestinian population for its support of the *intifada* as well as a means to consolidate Israel's control over parts of the West Bank.[123]

Opposition to the separation barrier project in general, but especially to its route, has generated more than a hundred petitions to the Supreme Court of Israel since 2002. Some have challenged the lawfulness of specific segments of the barrier under Israeli and international law; many of these petitions also challenged the legality of the entire project under international law. In addition, the General Assembly of the UN requested in December 2003 that the ICJ render an advisory opinion on the legal consequences of the separation barrier's construction (referred to by the General Assembly as a 'Wall').[124]

The first Israeli Supreme Court case that directly addressed both sets of challenges to the lawfulness of the separation barrier was the *Beit Sourik* decision, which pertained to a 40 km segment situated Northwest of Jerusalem.[125] In a detailed decision, based primarily on international law (which constitutes under

[122] *LaGrand*, 2001 ICJ at 516; *Avena*, 43 ILM at 617.

[123] See eg, Zaha Hassan, 'Building Walls and Burning Bridges: Legal Obligations of the United States with respect to Israel's Construction of the Wall of Separation in Occupied Palestinian Territory', 13 *Willamette J Int'l L & Dispute Res* (2005) 197, 212–18; Chris McGreal, 'Israelis Hasten Land Grab in Shadow of Wall', *Guardian*, 14 Dec 2004, at 12, <http://www.guardian.co.uk/international/story/0,1372918,00.html>.

[124] GA Res A/RES/ES-10/14 , 3 Dec 2003, UN Doc A/ES-10.L.16 (2003).

[125] HCJ 2056/04 *Beit Sourik Village Council v Gov't of Israel*, 58 PD 806 (an English translation is available at ILDC 16 (IL 2004)).

Israeli law a binding source for assessing the lawfulness of measures adopted by the Israeli military and other administrative agencies),[126] the Court held that the Israeli Defense Forces (IDF) were authorized to construct a separation barrier in the Occupied Territories to the extent that the route reflected genuine security needs. However, it also held that some 30 km of the reviewed segment caused disproportionate harm to the local Palestinian residents and must therefore be rerouted.

The ICJ rendered its advisory opinion on the legal consequences of the separation barrier only ten days after the Supreme Court published its judgment in *Beit Sourik*.[127] Perhaps because of this short interim, the advisory opinion contains no mention whatsoever of the Israeli proceedings.[128] On the substance of the case, the ICJ opinion differs from the Israeli Supreme Court decision in some crucial respects. Most significantly, the ICJ was not persuaded that the barrier's construction was at all necessary from a military perspective, and suspected that it was designed, in truth, to serve Israel's unlawful annexationist policies vis-à-vis some parts of the West Bank.[129] Hence, it declared the entire project to be unlawful.

So, the domestic court in *Beit Sourik* and the ICJ in *Separation Wall* conducted their proceedings in apparent disregard of one another. This attitude might be indicative of a perceived lack of jurisdictional interaction: although the two courts examined many similar issues under the same body of law—ie, international law—their refusal to coordinate their proceedings in a meaningful way could imply a common belief that the decisions are normatively irrelevant to one another. A possible explanation for such mutual disregard may be the differences in the nature of the two proceedings, which involved different parties, distinct issues and varied institutional contexts. Whereas the domestic proceedings in *Beit Sourik* involved a petition by Palestinian village councils against the Israeli government challenging the legality of a particular segment of the barrier, the ICJ proceedings were of an advisory (ie, non-contentious) nature and addressed the lawfulness of the entire project; Palestinian interests were represented in the ICJ proceedings by the Palestinian Authority (referred to in the ICJ proceedings as Palestine), not the affected villages themselves. Furthermore, whereas the Israeli Supreme Court judgment was final and binding, the ICJ advisory opinion did not enjoy a similar status.[130] As a result, it would seem that the traditional tests for identifying jurisdictional overlap for the purpose of introducing jurisdiction-regulating rules, such

[126] See eg, HCJ 7015/02 *Ajuri v IDF Commander in West Bank*, 56(6) PD 352 (an English translation is available at ILDC 14 (IL 2002)).

[127] *Legal Consequences of the Construction of a Wall in the Occupied Palestinian Territory*, 43 ILM 1009 (2004).

[128] It can be speculated that the timing of the *Beit Sourik* decision's publication may have been influenced by the pendency of the ICJ advisory proceedings. However, one may also assume that the Israeli decision was made public just too late—after the ICJ opinion was already finalized and sent out for translation. This might explain why the advisory opinion failed even to mention the closely related Israeli Supreme Court judgment.

[129] *Wall*, 43 ILM at 1042.

[130] See eg, Shabtai Rosenne, *The Perplexities of Modern International Law* 122 (2002) 122. But see Richard A Falk, 'Toward Authoritativeness: The ICJ Ruling on Israel's Security Wall', 99 *AJIL* (2005) 42.

as *lis alibi pendens* or *res judicata*,[131] were clearly not met in the case at hand; hence, the two courts were not legally barred from conducting parallel proceedings.

However, as I argue in Chapter 6 below, the absence of full jurisdictional overlap should not have absolved the courts from the duty of applying other coordinating principles, particularly the principle of judicial comity. Moreover, the two cases had some obvious similarities—they addressed the same factual issues in proceedings involving parties representing essentially the same sets of interests and pursuant to international law. The reluctance to coordinate the proceedings might thus have derived from conceptual or policy considerations: the presumed rush on the part of Israel's Supreme Court to preempt the ICJ opinion may be explained by its interest in underscoring the availability of robust local judicial review over the separation barrier project, thus suggesting the redundancy of international supervision over the same matter. At the same time, the ICJ's failure to coordinate the proceedings and to make the necessary procedural arrangements to facilitate such coordination (in deviation from the sprit and language used by the PCIJ in the *Prince von Pless* case)[132] might suggest a mistrust of local courts or a belief in jurisdictional hierarchy—a view that renders local court decisions powerless to affect international judgments.[133] Another possible explanation for the ICJ's failure to coordinate might have been the General Assembly Resolution,[134] which required the Court to issue an opinion as soon as possible—arguably, even at the price of poorer coordination with national courts.

In any event, Israel's Supreme Court did have another chance to harmonize its own analysis of the legality of the separation barrier and that offered by the ICJ. In the *Mara'abe* case (dealing with another segment of the barrier in the Northern Samaria area)[135]—the first major Israeli separation barrier judgment rendered after the ICJ advisory opinion—the Supreme Court explained what normative weight, if any, should be given to the ICJ opinion on the barrier's lawfulness:

> The opinion of the ICJ—as its title testifies, and in contrast to a judgment by the same court—is an Advisory Opinion. It does not bind the party who requested it. As the ICJ itself noted in its opinion (paragraph 31), it does not bind the states. It is not *res judicata*. However, the opinion of the International Court of Justice is an interpretation of international law, performed by the highest judicial body in international law. The ICJ's interpretation of international law should be given its full appropriate weight (cites omitted).[136]

So, although Israel's Supreme Court was of the view that the opinion had no binding effect, it was willing to acknowledge, like its US counterpart in *Breard* and

131 See below Chapter 5.

132 *Prince von Pless Administration* (Germany v Poland), 1933 PCIJ (Ser A/B), No 52, at 16 (interim order).

133 *Chorzów Factory*, 1927 PCIJ (Ser A), No 12, at 33 (changing an international judgment by virtue of a municipal court judgment 'would be attributing to a judgment of a municipal court power indirectly to invalidate a judgment of an international court, which is impossible').

134 GA Res A/RES/ES-10/14, above n 124, at 3 (the GA requested the ICJ to 'urgently render an advisory opinion').

135 HCJ 7957/04 *Mara'abe v Prime Minister of Israel*, Judgment of 15 Sept 2005 (an English translation is available at ILDC 157 (IL 2005)).

136 Ibid, at para 56.

Sanchez-Llamas, the potential persuasiveness of ICJ opinions and the need to afford them 'appropriate weight' (or 'respectful consideration'). Still, it is interesting to note that in the *Mara'abe* judgment, the Israeli Supreme Court, like the US Supreme Court, ultimately rejected the legal conclusions offered by the ICJ. According to Israel's Supreme Court, the ICJ opinion on the barrier's legality was deficient, mainly in its factual analysis: the ICJ did not receive pertinent information on the security needs motivating the barrier; and did not engage in a rigorous analysis of the humanitarian impact of its different segments. Hence, the Supreme Court developed a dichotomy between law and facts—whereas the ICJ's analysis of the law should attract 'full appropriate weight', its appreciation of the facts was not compelling.[137]

1.2.3 Review of Trade-Related Determinations before National and International Courts

Another incident of jurisdictional interaction only partly regulated by international instruments can be identified in the field of trade law, where the same domestic administrative determinations can be challenged before national and international courts. Indeed, a number of cases involving US trade determinations have been litigated before domestic US courts and several international judicial bodies in recent years.

One example of such jurisdictional interaction is the protracted line of cases involving the practice of 'zeroing' in US Department of Commerce anti-dumping investigations and determinations.[138] The lawfulness of this practice has been challenged by private importers before domestic courts in the US and a NAFTA Chapter 19 arbitral tribunal (Chapter 19 bi-national panels are competent to review the lawfulness of determinations made by trade authorities in anti-dumping and countervailing duties cases involving exporters from one of the NAFTA countries; review by a panel is conducted in accordance with the domestic law of the importing state)[139] At the same time, the WTO Dispute Settlement Body (DSB) has reviewed several inter-state challenges to the legality of zeroing under WTO law (particularly, the Anti-Dumping Agreement)[140] and pronounced the unlawfulness of US practices in this regard on several occasions.[141]

[137] Ibid, at para 74.

[138] 'Zeroing' is a calculation method that discounts the impact of imports sold above normal market value. Used to identify a 'weighted-average dumping margin', it serves as a basis for calculating anti-dumping duties.

[139] NAFTA, arts 1901–11. For an up-to-date discussion of the effectiveness of such mechanisms, see Juscelino F Colares, 'Alternative Methods of Appellate Review in Trade Remedy Cases: Examining Results of US Judicial and NAFTA Binational Review of U.S. Agency Decisions from 1989 to 2005' (2006), available at <http://papers.ssrn.com/sol3/papers.cfm?abstract_id=920144>.

[140] Anti-Dumping Agreement, 30 June 1967, 6 ILM 920 (1967).

[141] *US–Sunset Review of Antidumping Duties on Corrosion-Resistant Carbon Steel Flat Products from Japan*, WTO Doc WT/DS244/AB/R (2003) (AB Report); *US–Final Dumping Determination*

In the leading domestic case on the legality of zeroing—*Corus Staal*[142]—the US Court of Appeals for the Federal Circuit affirmed in 2005 a decision of the Court of International Trade (CIT) rejecting a challenge brought by Dutch steel importers regarding the lawfulness of zeroing under US and international law. The Court of Appeals dismissed the relevance of two WTO DSB reports invoked by the appellants, which criticized US zeroing practices,[143] the first by reason of the obiter dicta nature of the reference to US zeroing found in the report, and the second because no action had been taken by the Executive branch to give this decision effect under US law in accordance with the Uruguay Round agreements incorporating legislation.[144] Hence, the Court held that:

> WTO decisions are 'not binding on the United States, much less this court.' ... Congress has enacted legislation to deal with the conflict presented here. It has authorized the United States Trade Representative, an arm of the executive branch, in consultation with various congressional and executive bodies and agencies, to determine whether or not to implement WTO reports and determinations and, if so implemented, the extent of implementation...
>
> We will not attempt to perform duties that fall within the exclusive province of the political branches, and we therefore refuse to overturn Commerce's zeroing practice based on any ruling by the WTO or other international body unless and until such ruling has been adopted pursuant to the specified statutory scheme.[145]

An essentially identical position was taken by the same US Court of Appeals in the *Timken* case decided a year earlier, in 2004,[146] which addressed an appeal brought by Japanese importers of tapered roller bearings (cone-shaped rings used as machine parts for rotary applications) against a CIT judgment confirming the permissibility of zeroing in Department of Commerce investigations and determinations. The Court of Appeals rejected an attempt by the appellants to rely on a WTO DSB report criticizing analogous EC policies as persuasive authority for proper interpretation of the Anti-Dumping Agreement:[147] it held that the DSB conclusions were distinguishable from the case before the Court of Appeals, which involved somewhat different US practices and that in any event, these conclusions were not 'sufficiently persuasive to find Commerce's practice unreasonable'.[148]

The approach taken by the Court of Appeals in *Corus Staal* and *Timken* may thus be summarized as follows: DSB reports are not binding on US Courts because

on Softwood Lumber from Canada, WTO Doc WT/DS264/AB/R (2004) (AB Report); *US–Laws, Regulations, and Methodology for Calculating Dumping Margins*, WTO Doc WT/DS294/AB/R (2006) (AB report); *US–Measures Relating to Zeroing and Sunset Reviews*, WTO Doc WT/DS322/R (2006) (Panel Report).

142 *Corus Staal BV v Dept of Commerce*, 395 F 3d 1343 (2005).

143 *Carbon Steel*, above n 141; *Softwood Lumber (Final Determination)*, above, n 141.

144 19 USC §3533.

145 *Corus Staal*, 395 F 3d, at 1348–9.

146 *Timken Co v US*, 354 F 3d 1334 (2004).

147 *EC–Antidumping Duties on Imports of Cotton-Type Bed Linen from India*, WTO Doc WT/DS/141/AB/R (2001) (AB Report).

148 *Timken*, 354 F 3d at 1344.

they are not self-executing and, arguably, not binding per se;[149] furthermore, their persuasive influence is limited and does not override other canons of interpretation regarding the discretion exercised by administrative agencies (most notably the *Chevron* doctrine).[150]

A recent attempt to contest this position was made in a case brought before the CIT by one of the Japanese importers involved in *Timken* (this time challenging a Department of Commerce determination regarding the import of ball bearings). The plaintiff sought to amend its original challenge of the determination and to rely upon a new DSB report proclaiming the unlawfulness of US zeroing practices.[151] Still, the CIT rejected the motion, holding that: '[the Plaintiff's] wish to amend its Complaint and challenge US law based upon a WTO ruling is futile given that it is not controlling precedent and is immaterial to the court's examination of the administrative decisions issued by Defendant'.[152]

It is interesting to note that a NAFTA Chapter 19 bi-national panel has taken a different approach to the matter when it examined the application of zeroing to Canadian softwood lumber imports. According to the panel, which applies US law *in lieu* of US domestic courts, DSB reports help clarify WTO law; WTO law should, in turn, be granted effect in US law pursuant to the *Charming Betsy* canon of interpretation[153] (this canon requires courts to construe domestic legislation in conformity to international law).[154] Since the US Trade Representative instructed in 2004 the Department of Commerce to issue a new anti-dumping determination that would conform to the respective DSB report,[155] the panel held that pre-existing agency determinations, whose continued validity is not regulated by the Uruguay Round Agreements implementing legislation, are also governed by the *Charming Betsy* rule. Hence, in light of the DSB ruling and US acceptance thereof, it is unlawful under US law for the US Department of Commerce to continue to apply zeroing in its investigations.

The decision of the Chapter 19 panel seems to throw new light on the previously discussed Court of Appeal and CIT decisions. It suggests that harmonizing measures between domestic and international proceedings may after all be available to US Courts. Hence, the decision of whether to employ them may in fact be linked to policy considerations relating to the appropriate division of labour between

[149] For the position that DSB reports are non-binding, see eg, Judith H Bello, 'The WTO Dispute Settlement Understanding: Less Is More', 90 *AJIL* (1996) 416. For a different position, see John H Jackson, 'The WTO Dispute Settlement Understanding—Misunderstandings on the Nature of Legal Obligation', 91 *AJIL* (1997) 60.

[150] *Chevron, USA, Inc v Natural Resource Defense Council Inc*, 467 US 837, 843–4 (1985).

[151] *Dumping Margins*, above, n 141. Since then, another DSB report has been rendered, directly relating to zeroing as applied to the import of mechanical parts from Japan (*Zeroing and Sunset Reviews*, above, n 141).

[152] *Koyo Seiko Co v US*, 442 F Supp 2d 1360.

[153] *Murray v The Schooner Charming Betsy*, 6 US 64 (1804).

[154] *Certain Softwood Lumber Products from Canada: Final Affirmative Antidumping Determination*, decision of 9 June 2005 (NAFTA Chapter 19 bi-national Panel).

[155] *Softwood Lumber (Final Determination)*, above, n 141.

the judiciary and other branches of government. It is perhaps not coincidental that a NAFTA panel—an international tribunal that applies national law and is less immersed in inter-branch politics—demonstrated greater willingness to give effect to DSB rulings than did domestic US courts.

A final example of an attempt to regulate the jurisdictional relations holding between national and international proceedings over trade-related issues can be found in a recent CIT decision relating to one stage of the protracted and multi-fora *Softwood Lumber* litigation saga between Canadian lumber manufacturers and exporters and US international trade agencies.[156] In principle, relations between the CIT and NAFTA Chapter 19 bi-national panels are regulated in the US legislation that incorporated NAFTA: Section 1516a of the revised US Tariff Act[157] provides that domestic proceedings can take place only if the affected parties fail, within 30 days of the issuance of the challenged agency determination, to invoke the jurisdiction of a bi-national panel, if the bi-national refuses jurisdiction or terminates its proceedings, or if the challenge raises US constitutional issues. Hence, the Section provides for an essentially horizontal division of labour between the CIT and Chapter 19 bi-national panels that grants parties interested in challenging anti-dumping determinations or countervailing duties a choice between seizing national or international fora, yet preserves the superiority of domestic courts with relation to constitutional issues (even then, US proceedings should be initiated only after the bi-national panels conclude their proceedings).[158]

Still, there are some gaps in this regulatory scheme, with some interactions between national courts and Chapter 19 panels unsatisfactorily regulated. This was

[156] See eg, *In re Certain Softwood Lumber Products from Canada*, File No USA-92-1904-01, FTA Chapter 19 Panel decision of 6 March 1993; *In re Softwood Lumber from Canada*, File No USA-92-1904-04, FTA Chapter 19 Panel decision of 26 July 1993; *In re Certain Softwood Lumber Products from Canada*, File No USA-92-1904-01, FTA Chapter 19 Panel decision of 17 Dec 1993 (on remand); USA-CDA-2002-1904-07, Panel decision of 5 Sept 2003; *In re Certain Softwood Lumber Products from Canada*, File No USA-CDA-2002-1904-07, Panel decision of 5 Sept 2003; *In re Certain Softwood Lumber Products from Canada*, File No USA-CDA-2002-1904-07, Panel decision of 19 Apr 2004; *In re Certain Softwood Lumber Products from Canada*, File No USA-CDA-2002-1904-07, Panel decision of 31 Aug 2004; *In re Certain Softwood Lumber Products from Canada: Final Affirmative Countervailing Duty Determination*, File No USA-CDA-2002-1904-03, Panel decision of 17 March 2006 (decision on the fifth remand determination); US–Investigation of the International Trade Commission in Softwood Lumber from Canada, WTO Doc WT/DS277/R (2004)(Panel Report); US–Preliminary Determinations with Respect to Certain Softwood Lumber from Canada, WTO Doc WT/DS236/R (2002)(Panel Report); *Canfor Corp v US*, decision of 6 June 2006, <http://www.state.gov/documents/organization/67753.pdf> (UNCITRAL).

[157] 19 USC Ch. IV.

[158] For a recent challenge to the constitutionality of Chapter 19 bi-national panels, see *Coalition for Fair Lumber Imports, Executive Committee v US*, petitioners' brief filed in DC Circuit Court on 13 Sept 2005, <http://www.fairlumbercoalition.org/origdocs/const_challenge_brief.pdf>. For an earlier challenge, see *American Coalition for Competitive Trade v Clinton*, 128 F 3d 761, 763 (DC Cir 1997). For an analogous challenge made in Canada, see *Council of Canadians v Canada*, 2005 ACWSJ 11501 (Superior Court of Justice, Ontario). For a discussion, see Patricia Kelmar, 'Binational Panels of the Canada-United States Free Trade Agreement in Action: The Constitutional Challenge Continues', 27 *GWJ Int'l L & Econ* (1993) 173.

demonstrated in the *Ontario Forest* case,[159] which involved a motion by a group of Canadian lumber exporters to compel the US government actively to nominate its members to an Extraordinary Challenge Committee (ECC), whose establishment had been requested by the US itself (the ECC was asked to review a bi-national panel ruling rendered several weeks before).[160] The CIT was of the opinion that its jurisdiction to review the motion was not negated by any specific legislative provision. Still, it held that it had the power to dismiss, on the basis of 'abstention principles', motions for equitable or discretionary relief.[161] Given the circumstances of the case, the Court was of the view that considerations of international comity militate against its intrusion into NAFTA procedures, especially in light of the settlement negotiations taking place between Canada and the US regarding the *Softwood Lumber* claims.

The CIT opinion may indicate the delicate balance it perceives between national and international courts. This perspective cautions against unwarranted intrusions on the part of national courts in the conduct of international procedures, even in circumstances where they may be formally competent to do so. One possible explanation for the deferential position of the CIT vis-à-vis NAFTA procedures in this context is the US government's clear interest in conducting international trade negotiations with minimal judicial interference. Unlike the *Consular Notification* or *Zeroing* cases, where deference to the ICJ or DSB might have been perceived as a court challenge to the power of the executive and legislative branches to control the penetration of international law into domestic US law, CIT abstention here met executive branch interests by minimizing judicial intervention in ongoing negotiations.

1.2.4 Prompt Release of Vessel Cases before ITLOS and National Courts

A very different example of an only partially regulated interaction between national and international courts can be found in relation to prompt release of vessel cases arising under UNCLOS. Article 292 of UNCLOS provides that:

1. Where the authorities of a State Party have detained a vessel flying the flag of another State Party and it is alleged that the detaining State has not complied with the provisions of this Convention for the prompt release of the vessel or its crew upon the posting of a reasonable bond or other financial security, the question of release from detention may be

[159] *Ontario Forest Industries Assoc v US*, 444 F Supp. 2d 1309 (2006)(US CIT). Another example of a legislative gap may be found in *Tembec v US*, 441 F Supp. 2d 1302 (2006) (US CIT) (the jurisdictional rule governing relations between NAFTA bi-national panels and US courts covers the substance of anti-dumping and countervailing trade determinations but not challenges to the administration and enforcement of such determinations on the basis of US administrative law).

[160] See Rules of Procedure for NAFTA Article 1904 Extraordinary Challenge Committees, 59 Fed Reg 8702 (1994).

[161] *Ontario Forest*, 444 F Supp. 2d at 1239–330.

submitted to any court or tribunal agreed upon by the parties or, failing such agreement within 10 days from the time of detention, to a court or tribunal accepted by the detaining State under article 287 or to the International Tribunal for the Law of the Sea, unless the parties otherwise agree . . . 3. The court or tribunal shall deal without delay with the application for release and shall deal only with the question of release, without prejudice to the merits of any case before the appropriate domestic forum against the vessel, its owner or its crew. The authorities of the detaining State remain competent to release the vessel or its crew at any time.[162]

The provision seems to accord ITLOS right of way over petitions for the prompt release of a vessel while preserving the residual competence of national fora to address the merits of the case underlying the vessel's detention. The text provides limited guidance, however, as to whether the vessel's owner can present parallel release applications before national and international courts[163] and what weight, if any, should ITLOS accord to findings reached by a national court that had already reviewed the same case and vice versa. Particularly unclear is whether final decisions on the merits of the case by national courts (eg, in expedited proceedings) would be binding on ITLOS.[164]

Some of these issues have been explicitly discussed in three ITLOS prompt release case *M/V Saiga*, *Camouco*, and *Monte Confurco*. In *M/V Saiga*, a case dealing with the arrest of a tanker flying the flag of Saint Vincent and the Grenadines by authorities in Guinea, the Tribunal confirmed that while its decision to order the prompt release of the foreign vessel was binding upon the national authorities in Guinea, it could not prejudge the merits of the claim pending before the national courts of Guinea. Hence, national courts are not bound by any finding of law or fact reached by ITLOS (they are obliged, however, to comply with ITLOS provisional orders).[165] The disconnect between the parallel national and international proceedings was further emphasized in the ITLOS judgment on the merits of the case. ITLOS rejected the Guinean attempt to rely on a decision reached by its local courts, before which criminal proceedings against the Master of the *Saiga* had taken place, and cited with approval the dicta used by the PCIJ in the *Certain*

[162] United Nations Convention on the Law of the Sea, 10 Dec 1982, art 292, 21 ILM 1261 (1982) (hereinafter UNCLOS).

[163] It would seem reasonable, however, to construe the text of art 292 in a way that permits successive applications to national courts and ITLOS in cases where national courts fail to set promptly a bond or set an unreasonable bond. See Myron H Nordquist et al (ed), V *United Nations Convention on the Law of the Sea 1982: A Commentary* (1989) 69–70.

[164] The question of the proper relations between domestic courts and ITLOS did arise to some extent in the '*Grand Prince*' and '*Juno Trader*' cases. In both cases, domestic courts had issued final decisions ordering confiscation of the vessels in question prior to the adjudication of the prompt release of vessel cases before ITLOS. However, in both cases, the prompt release applications were decided on other grounds. '*Grand Prince*' (Belize v France), ITLOS Judgment of 20 April 2001, <http://www.itlos.org/case_documents/2001/document_en_88.pdf>; '*Juno Trader*' (St Vincent and the Grenadines v Guinea-Bissau), 44 ILM 498 (2005). For a discussion, see Jillaine Seymour, 'The International Tribunal for the Law of the Sea: A Great Mistake?', 13 *Ind J Global Leg Stud* (2006) 1, 23.

[165] '*M/V Saiga*' (Saint Vincent and the Grenadines v Guinea), 37 ILM (2000) 360, 370 (prompt release of vessel).

German Interests case that from an international perspective, municipal laws are merely facts.[166]

The *Camouco* case—another prompt release of vessel case before ITLOS—arose from the arrest of a Panamanian vessel and its Master for allegedly fishing without a permit in the Exclusive Economic Zone of the French Crozet Islands (located in the Indian Ocean). Since ITLOS proceedings were initiated after a French Court of First Instance had already issued a decision setting out bond requirements and while an appeal was pending before a French Court of Appeal, France had alleged inadmissibility of the claim, arguing that a situation of *lis pendens* has been created. It further insinuated that in circumstances where domestic proceedings were actually invoked, exhaustion of local remedies would be required[167] or that, alternatively, the claimant should be estopped, by reason of choice of a local forum, from pursuing proceedings before ITLOS. In rejecting such arguments, the Tribunal construed article 292 as providing for an international remedy that is independent of any remedy that has been or can be provided in national fora:

> Article 292 provides for an independent remedy and not an appeal against a decision of a national court. No limitation should be read into article 292 that would have the effect of defeating its very object and purpose. Indeed, article 292 permits the making of an application within a short period from the date of detention and it is not normally the case that local remedies could be exhausted in such a short period.[168]

On this basis, the Tribunal proceeded to engage in a *de novo* assessment of the bond set by the French Court, concluding that it was unreasonable in the circumstances of the case.

A similar outcome was reached in *Monte Confurco*—another case arising out of the detention of a foreign vessel (this time flying a Seychellois flag) allegedly engaged in fishing without a license in the Exclusive Economic Zone of a French Indian Ocean island (Kerguelen Island). Although the tribunal declared that it was not sitting as a court of appeal over the decision of the French Court of First Instance, which had imposed the initial bond, ITLOS ultimately found that determination to be unreasonable.[169]

Significantly, however, some of the individual judges in *Camouco* and *Monte Confurco* appended dissenting opinions to the judgments, which offer a different view of the relations between the national and international proceedings.[170] In *Camouco*, Judge Anderson was of the view that the decision of the Court of First

[166] '*M/V Saiga*', Judgment of 1 July 1999, at para 120 (merits), <http://www.itlos.org/case_documents/2001/document_en_68.doc>.

[167] UNCLOS, art 295 introduces a general exhaustion of local remedies provision. However, that provision requires exhaustion only 'where this is required by international law'.

[168] *Camouco*, 39 ILM at 678.

[169] '*Monte Confurco*' (Seychelles v France), ITLOS Judgment of 18 Dec 2000, at para 72, <http://www.itlos.org/case_documents/2001/document_115_en.pdf>.

[170] At the same time, some individual judges offered support to the majority's position on the matter. See eg, *Camouco*, 39 ILM at 688 (separate opinion of Judge Nelson).

Instance on the release bond's amount and the pendency of appellate proceedings were relevant factors in deciding whether ITLOS should grant relief.[171] More specifically, in both the *Camouco* and *Monte Confurco* cases, he believed that the Court of First Instance decisions should be generally deferred to and that in the particular circumstances of *Camouco*, local proceedings should have been exhausted.[172] In addition, Judge Vukas, in *Camouco*, was of the view that initiating ITLOS proceedings in the circumstances of that case ran contrary to the principle of litispendence, and that parallel proceedings were unjustified.[173]

Arguably, the majority position in all three prompt release of vessel cases discussed here may be understood in terms of legal dualism: the Tribunal treated the decisions of the local courts as *facts* and emphasized that it did not sit as a court of appeal over their decisions.[174] In truth, however, the Tribunal did revisit the various elements underlying the fixing of bonds by domestic courts and did reverse their findings—exercising *de facto* powers of *de novo* review over interim domestic decisions.[175]

At the same time, some of the individual judges sitting on ITLOS seem to have embraced a more integrative vision that perceives the roles of ITLOS and national courts as parallel or even complementary in nature. Indeed, as Judge Laing wrote in *Monte Confurco*, 'the Tribunal's complex function is that of the helpmate of the authorities of the detained vessel or crew and, at the same time, the presumptive alter ego, but also the guide, of the national bond setting judge'.[176]

1.2.5 The ICSID Cases

The final and, arguably, most controversial example of unregulated interaction between national and international fora comes from the world of international investment law. The three ICSID cases discussed below—*Vivendi*, *SGS v Pakistan* and *SGS v Philippines*—are more than indicative of the growing interaction between national and international courts; they also demonstrate the level of doctrinal and practical confusion surrounding attempts to regulate the complicated relations woven between parallel procedures involving formally different, yet

171 Ibid, 39 ILM at 690 (dissenting opinion of Judge Anderson); *Monte Confurco*, above n 169, 1–2 of the dissenting opinion of Judge Anderson).

172 *Camouco*, 39 ILM at 690 (dissenting opinion of Judge Anderson).

173 Ibid, at 696–7 (dissenting opinion of Judge Vukas). Judge Vukas accepted, however, the appeal of the argument that international judgments should trump national judgments in the event of a conflict. Ibid, at 697.

174 *Monte Confurco*, above, n 169, at para 72 ('The Tribunal, however, wishes to make it clear that, under article 292 of the Convention, it is not an appellate forum against a decision of a national court').

175 See ibid, separate opinion of Judge Nelson ('It must be acknowledged that the power given this Tribunal, under article 292, to order the prompt release of vessels and crews upon the posting of a reasonable bond constitutes to a certain extent "an interference" with the coastal State's judicial authorities.'). See also Erik Franckx, '"Reasonable Bond" in the Practice of the International Tribunal for the Law of the Sea', 32 *Cal W Int'l LJ* (2002) 303, 332.

176 *Monte Confurco*, above, n 169, at para 8 of the dissenting opinion of Judge Laing.

substantially similar applicable laws: the four principal decisions issued in these three cases are fundamentally incompatible and reveal conflicting approaches to the very need to regulate jurisdictional interactions as well as the method of regulation. In addition, the ICSID cases discussed below, which pertain to complex business disputes, demonstrate some of the unsatisfactory outcomes potentially emerging from the application of traditional concepts of legal dualism and hierarchy to the contemporary interplay of national and international dispute settlement proceedings.

The growing prominence of ICSID as a focal point for discussions on the jurisdictional relations holding between national and international courts is not coincidental and may well derive from the very object and nature of ICSID arbitration: first, ICSID was created as a jurisdictional alternative to national courts, ie, to offer a neutral forum in which investment claims previously subject to the jurisdiction of the domestic courts of the host state could be adjudicated.[177] Hence, ICSID tribunals may supplant national courts and exercise powers in their stead. Second, article 42 of the ICSID Convention requires ICSID arbitral tribunals to apply the law selected by the parties; but in the absence of such selection, it should apply the domestic law of the host state and the applicable rules of international law.[178] As a result, the jurisdiction of ICSID tribunals may encompass, at least in theory, claims formulated under either national or international law. In other words, the functions of ICSID and its jurisdictional powers have national and international law features. This renders ICSID a natural venue for normative contacts between national and international law and for jurisdictional interactions between national and international courts over disputes arising from such bodies of law. One should recall however, that although this section focuses on ICSID cases, parallel issues may also arise in relation to international investment arbitration proceeding outside the ICSID framework.[179]

Vivendi I

The proceedings in *Vivendi* arose from a 1995 investment contract between an Argentinean corporation—Compania de Aguas del Aconquija, SA (CAA)—which was controlled in the respective period by a French corporation, Compagnie Générale des Eaux (CGE, subsequently, 'Vivendi Universal'), on the one hand, and the Argentinean Province of Tucumán on the other hand. Under the contract, CAA was granted a concession to operate Tucumán's water and sewage systems. However, when a dispute arose between the parties in late 1996 over the project's execution, the investing corporations, CAA and CGE, chose not to invoke article

177 Report of the Executive Directors, above, n 17, at section III, para 11.

178 Schreuer, above, n 16, at 558–631.

179 See eg, *Occidental Exploration and Production Co v Ecuador*, Award of 1 July, 2004, <http://www.asil.org/ilib/OEPC-Ecuador.pdf> (UNCITRAL); *Eureko BV v Poland*, Partial Award, 19 August 2005, <http://www.investmentclaims.com/decisions/Eureko-Poland-LiabilityAward.pdf> (ad hoc arbitration).

16.4 of the investment contract, which referred contractual disputes to the exclusive jurisdiction of Tucumán's administrative tribunals. Instead, the French investor requested establishment of an ICSID arbitral tribunal pursuant to article 8 of the 1991 Argentina-France BIT,[180] which provided that foreign investors of French or Argentinean nationality may refer their investment disputes with the other party (ie, the host state) to the latter's domestic courts or to international arbitration (ICSID or UNCITRAL arbitrations). The relationship between the BIT choice of forum provision and the contractual exclusive jurisdiction clause were at the heart of the *Vivendi* litigation (and at the heart of the other cases discussed in this section as well).

During the ICSID proceedings, the respondent—Argentina—alleged that the arbitral tribunal should refuse to entertain the case since the submission to ICSID violated the contractual jurisdictional clause which the parties to the contract had freely undertaken. In its 2000 award, the ICSID arbitral tribunal accepted this jurisdictional objection and rejected the investor's claim in its entirety.[181] According to the tribunal, CAA and CGE had two analytically separate claims—1) the Tucumán claim—that the provincial government (for whose conduct Argentina carried international responsibility) was acting to destroy the concession; and (2) the federal claim—that Argentina had independently failed to protect adequately the investment, as required by the Argentina–France BIT.

With regard to the Tucumán claim, the tribunal was of the opinion that under the BIT, the claim was 'crucially connected' with the investor's claim under the contract: all specific allegations arising from the acts and omissions of the Province of Tucumán under the BIT would also be available to the investor in domestic proceedings brought under the investment contract. As a result, review of the Tucumán claim by the ICSID tribunal would necessarily require it to interpret and apply contractual provisions as well[182]—ie, to exercise jurisdiction over legal questions that were, according to the contractual forum-selection clause, subject to the exclusive jurisdiction of local Tucumán courts.[183] Since, the tribunal viewed the contractual clause as a specific agreement between the parties that overrode the more general provision of the BIT, it declined jurisdiction over the Tucumán claim.[184] At the same time, the tribunal held that the investor's federal claim was not established prima facie.[185] Hence, it dismissed the claim.

Interestingly enough, the tribunal did suggest that recourse to ICSID under the BIT would have been possible if it could be shown that the proceedings before the

[180] Agreement for the Promotion and Reciprocal Protection of Investments (Argentina/France), 3 July 1991, 1728 UNTS 298.

[181] *Vivendi I*, 40 ILM 426.

[182] Ibid, at 428–9 ('the nature of the facts supporting most of the claims presented in this case make it impossible for the Tribunal to distinguish or separate violations of the BIT from breaches of the Concession Contract without first interpreting and applying the detailed provisions of that agreement').

[183] Ibid, at 443.

[184] Presumably, the tribunal could have also regarded the contract as a valid of choice of forum under the BIT or a legal obligation governing such a choice.

[185] *Vivendi I*, 40 ILM at 446.

local courts of Tucumán had failed to meet international standards of justice (echoing the allusion to 'denial of justice' in the early 20th century mixed commission cases).[186] However, since the investor had completely refrained from bringing the case to the local courts, no denial of justice claim was possible.[187]

The decision in *Vivendi I* implies the following: (1) jurisdictional interaction between national and international proceedings is feasible and amenable to regulation—even if the parallel claims before national and international courts are formally based on different bodies of law (an investment contract or BIT)—to the degree that the substantive facts and norms in the two proceedings are 'crucially connected' to one another; (2) a specific contractual forum-selection clause can govern some or all claims raised in international proceedings that are based on a more general jurisdiction conferring instrument. Thus, the arbitral tribunal construed the jurisdictional relations established by the contract and the BIT as a horizontal regime in which national and international jurisdictions serve as legal alternatives to one another.

It is perhaps interesting to note that the regulatory regime introduced by the *Vivendi I* arbitral tribunal constitutes a mirror image of the jurisdictional regime adopted in the New York Convention:[188] whereas under that Convention an agreement to arbitrate a dispute before an international arbitral body excludes the authority of national courts, under *Vivendi I*, an agreement to invest a domestic forum with exclusive jurisdiction excludes the authority of an international arbitration tribunal over all claims either covered by the forum-selection clause or crucially connected thereto. Similarly, under *Vivendi I*, ICSID tribunals maintain a residual power to review the proper conduct of domestic tribunals (in denial of justice cases) that is analogous to the power of domestic courts to review the propriety of international arbitration proceedings under the New York Convention.

Vivendi II

The decision of the arbitral tribunal in *Vivendi I* to dismiss the investor's claims did not, however, end litigation in that case. The investor challenged the validity of the award before an ad hoc ICSID annulment committee, and the committee nullified the first tribunal's award in 2002.[189] According to the committee, the first tribunal's refusal to review the investor's Tucumán claim under the BIT constituted an excess of power, which requires nullification of the award.[190] In reaching

[186] Ibid, at 445. Cf *North American Dredging*, 4 RIAA at 32; *Mexican Union Railway*, 5 RIAA at 120.

[187] Paulsson, above, n 23, at 108.

[188] See above, section 1.1.4.

[189] *Compania de Aquas del Aconquija, SA v Argentina*, 41 ILM 1135, 1154 (2002) (hereinafter *Vivendi II*).

[190] According to ICSID Convention, art 52: '(1) Either party may request annulment of the award by an application in writing addressed to the Secretary-General on one or more of the following grounds... (b) that the Tribunal has manifestly exceeded its powers... (3) The Committee shall have the authority to annul the award or any part thereof on any of the grounds set forth in paragraph (1).' For a discussion, see Aron Broches, 'Observations on the Finality of ICSID Awards', 6 *ICSID*

this conclusion, the committee emphasized the separate and independent existence of the contract and the treaty claims:

[W]hether there has been a breach of the BIT and whether there has been a breach of contract are different questions. Each of these claims will be determined by reference to its own proper or applicable law—in the case of the BIT by international law; in the case of the Concession Contract, by the proper law of the contract, in other words, the law of Tucumán. [191]

As a result, the committee believed that Argentina 'cannot rely on an exclusive jurisdiction clause in a contract to avoid the characterization of its conduct as internationally unlawful under a treaty'.[192] In other words, the committee adopted what seems to be a dualistic configuration of the relations holding between the law of the contract, which applies in the domestic forum, and the law of the BIT, which applies in the international procedure. This dualist perspecitve circumvented the need for jurisdictional regulation or for consideration of the effect of the contractual jurisdiction-regulating clause: if the contract and BIT claim exist on separate doctrinal levels, then the effect of a jurisdiction-regulating clause that operates on one level cannot carry over to the other level.

Still, the committee did not foreclose all possibilities of jurisdictional interaction between national and international proceedings. It suggested that reliance on a contractual forum-selection clause may be permissible in cases 'where the *essential basis* of a claim brought before an international tribunal is a breach of contract' (emphasis added).[193] Apparently, the committee was of the view that this caveat was not applicable to the *Vivendi* case and that neither the Tucumán nor the federal claim were essentially based on the contract but rather on the BIT. It follows that the ICSID arbitral tribunal should have litigated the case regardless of the contractual forum-selection clause.[194]

Rev FILJ (1991) 321; Aron Broches, 'On the Finality of Awards: A Reply to Michael Reisman', 8 *ICSID Rev FILJ* (1993) 92; David D Caron, 'Reputation and Reality in the ICSID Annulment Process: Understanding the Distinction Between Annulment and Appeal', 7 *ICSID Rev. FILJ* (1992) 21; Carolyn B Lamm, 'Jurisdiction of the International Centre for Settlement of Investment Disputes', 6 *ICSID Rev FILJ* (1991) 462; Michael W Reisman, 'The Breakdown of the Control Mechanism in ICSID Arbitration', [1989] *Duke LJ* 739.

191 *Vivendi II*, 41 ILM at 1154. Cf *CMS Gas Transmission Co v Argentina*, 42 ILM 788, 800 (2003) (ICSID).

192 *Vivendi II*, 41 ILM at 1156.

193 Ibid, at 1155. The tribunal noted, however, that 'where "the fundamental basis of the claim" is a treaty laying down an independent standard by which the conduct of the parties is to be judged, the existence of an exclusive jurisdiction clause in a contract between the claimant and the respondent state or one of its subdivisions cannot operate as a bar to the application of the treaty standard'. Ibid, at 1156. For other applications of the 'essential basis' test, see *Joy Mining Machinery Ltd v Egypt*, 44 ILM 73, 86 (2005); *Siemens AG v Argentina*, 44 ILM 138, 167 (2005). It may be noted that the arbitral tribunal in *Occidental* affirmed the separate existence of contract and treaty claims (*Occidental*, above, n 179, at paras 50–2) and held that 'the objective fact is that the Contract is central to the [treaty] dispute'. Ibid, at para 73. Hence, its assertion that treaty-based claims form the *essential basis* of the case (ibid, at para 57) is questionable (still, it may be acknowledged that some of the investor's treaty claims—most notably the fair and equal treatment claim—could not have been subsumed in the contract claim).

194 *Vivendi II*, 41 ILM at 1155–6. See also *Occidental*, above, n 179, at para 57; *Joy Mining*, 44 ILM at 68.

Notably, even the *Vivendi II* decision supports the proposition that some degree of jurisdictional interaction between national and international courts is possible. However, the committee's proposed test for regulating such interactions—whenever the 'essential basis of the claim' before ICSID is contractual—is less than clear in some important aspects: first, it is unclear whether the 'essential basis of the claim' test is an objective or subjective test (ie, determined by an objective assessment of the claims of the parties, or by the way the parties formulate their claims).[195] Second, it is questionable whether any degree of substantive similarity between the contract and the treaty claims would enable an arbitral tribunal to conclude that the essential basis of the treaty claim is contractual. Instead, one might argue that the commission had in effect suggested that the contractual forum-selection clause would be relevant only in cases where the ICSID tribunal is *formally* authorized to apply the law of the contract to the exclusion, in effect, of any treaty standards. Finally, it remains uncertain what, if any, effect would be given to an 'umbrella clause', which imports contractual standards into the BIT,[196] upon determination of the essential basis of the claim (eg, would a BIT claim based on the umbrella clause be considered a treaty claim or a contract claim?).

SGS v Pakistan

The next important contract/treaty claims case—*SGS v Pakistan*—supports the dualistic tendencies of the *Vivendi II* decision. However, the case also illustrates some of the practical problems that refusal to regulate parallel proceedings before national and international adjudicatory bodies might entail.

The *SGS v Pakistan* dispute arose out of a 1994 contract between SGS, a Swiss corporation specializing in customs inspections, and Pakistan, according to which SGS was to perform pre-shipment inspections of goods imported to Pakistan from several foreign ports and recommend appropriate customs classifications. Similar to the contract discussed in *Vivendi*, the 1994 contract contained an exclusive jurisdiction clause referring any contractual disputes that the parties might have to arbitration in Pakistan, pursuant to the domestic Arbitration Act.

However, when a dispute broke out in 1996, SGS attempted to sue Pakistan before the domestic courts in Switzerland, an attempt that ultimately failed by reason of Pakistan's sovereign immunity.[197] In 2001, SGS initiated another set of

[195] Cf *Occidental*, above, n 179, at para 47; *Azurix Corp v Mexico*, 43 ILM 262, 277 (2004); *Société Générale de Surveillance SA (SGS) v Pakistan*, 42 ILM 1290, 1314 (2003); *El Paso Energy International Co v Argentina*, decision on jurisdiction of 27 April 2006, at para 109 <http://www.investmentclaims.com/decisions/El_Paso_Energy-Argentina-Jurisdictional_Decision.pdf>.

[196] See eg, Christoph H Schreuer, 'Traveling the BIT Route: of Waiting Periods, Umbrella clauses and Forks in The Road', 5 *J World Inv* (2004) 231; Anthony C Sinclair, 'The Origins of the Umbrella Clause in the International Law of Investment Protection', 20 *Arb Int'l* (2004) 411; Thomas Wälde, 'The Umbrella Clause in Investment Arbitration—A Comment on Original Intentions and Recent Cases', 6 *J World Invest & Trade* (2005) 183.

[197] The first-instance Swiss court that reviewed the case dismissed it by reason of the contractual forum-selection. Still, on appeal, the case was dismissed on the basis of Pakistan's sovereign immunity.

proceedings against Pakistan, this time invoking the terms of the Pakistani–Swiss BIT,[198] which entitled foreign investors to refer their investment disputes to an ICSID arbitral tribunal. In the meantime, Pakistan initiated, in 2001, arbitration proceedings in Pakistan before a single Pakistani arbitrator pursuant to the contractual forum-selection clause. While SGS objected to these arbitral proceedings, it presented the arbitrator with a counter-claim against Pakistan (without prejudicing its jurisdictional objections).

The parallel pendency of multiple proceedings gave rise to conflicting injunctions: In March 2002, Pakistan applied to its own Supreme Court and obtained an injunction against SGS, barring it from continuing the ICSID arbitral proceedings in parallel to the domestic arbitration proceedings. Shortly thereafter, SGS reacted by asking the ICSID arbitral tribunal for a parallel order against the Pakistani arbitration proceedings. Indeed, the ICSID tribunal recommended in October 2002 a stay of the arbitral proceedings in Pakistan until the ICSID tribunal had decided the jurisdictional issues related to the case.[199] The recommendation was eventually heeded by the Pakistani arbitrator who decided in November 2002 temporarily to stay the domestic arbitral proceedings.

In the course of the ICSID proceedings, Pakistan raised several jurisdictional objections, arguing, in particular, that ICSID was divested of jurisdiction over the case because of the contractual forum-selection clause; that the terms of the contract between SGS and Pakistan constitute the essential basis of the proceedings before ICSID (relying on the 'essential basis of the claim' test introduced by the *Vivendi* tribunal) and that, as a result, no independent treaty claim exists. In all events, Pakistan argued that the *lis pendens* rule bars the ICSID tribunal from adjudicating the case parallel to the Pakistani arbitrator. SGS responded to the last point by asserting that in the event of jurisdictional overlap, international dispute settlement procedures should prevail over their domestic counterparts.

In 2003, the ICSID arbitral tribunal issued its decision on jurisdiction, in which it rejected Pakistan's jurisdictional objections and accepted jurisdiction over SGS's treaty claims. In doing so it reaffirmed the dicta of the *Vivendi* ad hoc committee on the separate existence of contract and treaty claims:[200] since the causes of action in the two proceedings cannot be identical—one claim is presented under national law and the other under international law—no jurisdictional overlap exists. Hence no dismissal or stay of the international proceedings is warranted.[201]

[198] Agreement on the Promotion and Reciprocal Protection of Investment (Pakistan/Switz), 11 July 1995, art 9, *excerpts* in *SGS v Pakistan*, 42 ILM at 1303.

[199] *SGS v Pakistan*, Procedural Order no 2, Oct 16, 2002 <http://www.worldbank.org/icsid/cases/SGS-order.pdf>. Note that some controversy surrounds the authority of ICSID tribunals to issue binding and enforceable provisional measures. See Schreuer, above, n 16, at 757–62. It may be argued, however, that the comparable language used in article 47 of the ICSID Convention and article 41 of the ICJ Statute should render the ICJ *LaGrand* judgment relevant for the purpose of ICSID as well. *LaGrand*, 2001 ICJ at 506.

[200] *SGS v Pakistan*, 42 ILM at 1315–16.

[201] Ibid, at 1323.

The *SGS v Pakistan* decision thus stands for the position that the lack of normative overlap between the law applicable in the domestic proceedings (ie, law of the contract) and in the international proceedings (ie, BIT law) negates *ab initio* the conditions for jurisdictional overlap between the parallel tribunals.[202] Significantly, this approach offers greater doctrinal clarity and ease of application than the more nuanced tests offered in the two stages of the *Vivendi* litigation ('crucial connection' between contract and treaty claims in *Vivendi I*; and the 'essential basis of the claim' test introduced in *Vivendi II*): since the two jurisdiction-regulating clauses apply to parallel legal universes, the tribunal is released from the need to coordinate between them. In view of this simple and elegant outcome, it is perhaps not surprising that most of the international investment arbitrations that reviewed the jurisdictional relations between national and international courts to date have found the *SGS v Pakistan* approach to jurisdictional regulation appealing.[203]

However, the *SGS v Pakistan* case also illustrates some of the practical problems associated with legal dualism: it encourages parallel proceedings over the same factual issues before different judicial fora, which may involve the application of comparable legal standards (unlike its *Vivendi I* counterpart, the *SGS v Pakistan* did not engage in an analysis of the substantive allegations of the parties under the contract and the treaty). While the arbitral tribunal did acknowledge the wasteful nature of parallel proceedings over similar matters in one of its interim decisions,[204] its final jurisdictional decision did not offer any real solution to the practical difficulties that uncoordinated multiple proceedings, between the same parties, involving the same transaction and similar substantive norms, might entail (most significantly, the need to reconcile incompatible legal decisions).

Finally, one should note the interpretive methodology adopted by the *SGS v Pakistan* tribunal when construing its jurisdiction and applicable law: the tribunal adopted a narrow reading of its jurisdictional powers in ways that excluded contract claims, notwithstanding the open-ended language of article 9 of the BIT (which authorized the ICSID tribunal to settle disputes 'with respect to an investment between a Contracting Party and an investor of the other Contracting Party');[205] similarly, the tribunal held that article 11 of the Pakistani–Swiss BIT (the umbrella clause), which required each of the two signatory states to 'constantly guarantee the observance of the commitments it has entered into with respect to the investments of the investors of the other Contracting Party' could not be reasonably

[202] Ibid, at 1318.

[203] See eg, *Occidental*, above, n 179, at paras 50–2; *Wena Hotels Ltd v Egypt*, 41 ILM 933, 940 (2002); *Azurix*, 43 ILM at 277; *Vivendi I*, 40 ILM at 438–439; *Loewen*, 42 ILM at 819, 833; *Anaconda Iran Inc v Iran*, 13 Iran–US CTR 199, 224 (1988) (noting contractual forum-selection is overridden as a result of the 'supremacy of the rules of international character'); *Salini Costruttori SpA v Jordan*, 44 ILM 573, 589 (2005).

[204] *SGS v Pakistan*, Procedural Order no 2, 16 Oct 2002 <http://www.worldbank.org/icsid/cases/SGS-order.pdf> ('The Tribunal, however, also believes that normally it would be wasteful of resources for two proceedings relating to the same or substantially the same matter to unfold separately while the jurisdiction of one tribunal awaits determination').

[205] Ibid, at 1317–18.

construed as if it was designed to incorporate the contractual obligations of the parties into the BIT.[206] At the same time, the arbitral tribunal accepted SGS's submission that it would not be able to present its BIT claim before the Pakistani arbitrator.[207] These interpretive moves and findings accentuated the normative differences between national and international proceedings, and facilitated the separate application of contractual and treaty jurisdictional clauses to the respective types of procedures. In Chapter 3 of this book, I argue that analogies may be drawn between the disintegrationist methodology applied by the *SGS v Pakistan* tribunal (ie, the disaggregating of a single dispute into several disputes under different bodies of law) and the manner in which some international courts have addressed the relations between competing international legal regimes—a topic that falls within the current debate over the fragmentation of international law.

SGS v Philippines

The *SGS v Philippines* case possesses some striking similarities to the *SGS v Pakistan* case: Not only was the same claimant involved in another dispute over a contract for the provision of customs-related services, but the jurisdictional questions posed in the course of the proceedings were generally similar, ie, whether ICSID tribunals have jurisdiction over contract claims and whether an umbrella clause in the governing BIT transforms contract claims into treaty claims. Most significantly, both cases delved into the effect of a contractual forum-selection clause investing a domestic judicial forum with exclusive jurisdiction over an international arbitration tribunal and the effect of the parallel pendency of domestic and international proceedings. Hence, it is quite remarkable that the *SGS v Philippines* arbitral tribunal provided very different answers than its *SGS v Pakistan* predecessor to essentially the same questions.

This case involved a dispute over the implementation of a contract for pre-shipment inspection of imported goods between SGS and the government of the Philippines, originally signed in 1991 (the terms of the contract were, however, extended on a number of occasions until its final expiration in 2000). Under the contractual forum-selection clause, disputes 'in connection with the obligations of either party to this Agreement' were subject to the exclusive jurisdiction of local Philippine courts.[208]

[206] Ibid, at 1319–21. Despite the open-ended language of article 11 of the BIT, the tribunal held that the expansive construction advocated by SGS—incorporating the fulfillment of contractual obligations within the BIT—would result in the imposition of unreasonable procedural and substantive burdens upon host states. The tribunal was not willing to assume, without clearer textual guidance, that this was the meaning intended by the drafters. For support, see *Joy Mining*, 44 ILM at 85; *El Paso*, above, n 195, at para 76. According to the latter tribunal, the umbrella clause should be read narrowly, since it was designed mainly to protect investors from unilateral interference by the host state in their contractual rights. Ibid, at para 84.

[207] *SGS v Pakistan*, 42 ILM at 1308, 1316.

[208] Article 12 of the Agreement of 23 August 1991 between SGS and the Government of the Philippines regarding the provision of comprehensive import supervision services, cited in *Société Générale de Surveillance SA* (SGS) *v Philippines*, decision of Jan 29, 2004, at para 22 <http://www.worldbank.org/icsid/cases/SGSvPhil-final.pdf>.

In 2002, SGS brought a claim against the Philippines to an ICSID arbitral tribunal pursuant to article VIII of the Philippino–Swiss BIT,[209] alleging the existence of unpaid debts. Like Argentina in *Vivendi* and Pakistan in *SGS v Pakistan*, the Philippines objected to the jurisdiction of the ICSID tribunal and argued that the dispute at hand was purely contractual and governed by the contractual forum-selection clause. In addition, the Philippines argued that its local courts were better situated to adjudicate the contract claims in question and should therefore be granted right of way.[210]

SGS, in turn, contended that ICSID is competent to review both contract and treaty claims.[211] The latter contention was based on the language of the Philippino–Swiss BIT forum-selection clause (article VIII) which could be construed in a way that authorizes ICSID to adjudicate contract claims.[212] In addition, SGS argued that the BIT umbrella clause (article X(2)) had the effect of transforming SGS's contract claims into treaty claims.[213] Finally, SGS claimed that in situations of jurisdictional overlap, the jurisdiction of an international tribunal such as ICSID should supersede that of national courts.[214]

In its 2004 decision on jurisdiction, the *SGS v Philippines* arbitral tribunal accepted that the Philippino–Swiss BIT provided it with jurisdiction over contract and treaty claims. This is because the language of article VIII, which invested ICSID with the authority to adjudicate any dispute 'with respect to investments between a Contracting Party and an investor of the other Contracting Party' was sufficiently broad to encompass both contract and treaty claims.[215] In addition, the arbitral tribunal held that article X(2) (the umbrella clause), which provided that '[e]ach Contracting Party shall observe any obligation it has assumed with regard to specific investments in its territory by investors of the other Contracting Party', also encompasses the obligation to fulfil contractual obligations.

Significantly, the ICSID arbitral tribunal supported these interpretive moves, which facilitate the application of different sets of legal norms in one set of proceedings by reference to policy considerations. According to the tribunal, a disintegrative reading of its jurisdictional clauses would lead to unnecessary claim-splitting and jurisdictional uncertainties.[216] In addition, an expansive reading of the umbrella clause would better serve the BITs' goal of protecting investors while giving the clause substantive meaning.[217] It is also important to note that the *SGS v Philippines*

[209] Agreement on the Promotion and Reciprocal Protection of Investment (Philippines/Switz.), 31 March 1997, art VIII, *excerpts* in *SGS v Philippines*, above, n 208, at para 34. Article VIII of the BIT provided the investor with a right of choice between three dispute settlement procedures: national courts, an ICSID tribunal and an ad hoc UNCITRAL arbitral tribunal.

[210] *SGS v Philippines*, above, n 208, at para 52–6, 73–5.

[211] Ibid, at para 64, 85.

[212] Ibid, at para 66, 87.

[213] Ibid, at para 65, 86.

[214] Ibid, at para 60.

[215] Ibid, at para 130–5. For a similar holding, see *Salini Costrutorri SPA v Morocco*, Decision of July 23, 2001, 42 ILM 609, 623 (2003).

[216] For an analogous decision, which supports a broad reading of a jurisdictional clause in order to settle a dispute 'once and for all', see *Chorzów Factory*, 1927 PCIJ (ser A) No 9, at 25 (jurisdiction).

[217] *SGS v Philippines*, above, n 208, at para 116–28. The tribunal noted, however, that the obligation to respect contractual obligations does not transfer the obligations themselves onto the international

tribunal explicitly repudiated the interpretation given by the *SGS v Pakistan* arbitral tribunal to the Swiss–Pakistani compromissory clause (which contained virtually identical language to that used in the Swiss-Philippine BIT).[218] Similarly, the arbitral tribunal characterized the interpretive construction of the umbrella clause offered by the *SGS v Pakistan* tribunal as 'unconvincing'.[219] Hence, it seems that different perceptions of the *telos* of dispute settlement arrangements under investment protection instruments[220]—not the minor textual differences between the umbrella clauses of the Swiss–Philippine BIT and the Swiss–Pakistani BIT ('observe any obligation' v 'guarantee the observance of the commitments')—may explain the radically different interpretive outcomes in the two cases.[221]

The arbitral tribunal's findings on jurisdiction and applicable law created a direct jurisdictional conflict between the ICSID proceedings and the domestic proceedings in the Philippines, as contract claims fell under the concurrent jurisdiction of both judicial fora. This facilitated the possibility of applying the jurisdiction-regulating rule—the exclusive jurisdictional arrangement found in the contractual forum-selection clause (a question the *SGS v Philippines* tribunal regarded as a matter of admissibility)—to the parallel jurisdiction of the domestic court and ICSID over contract claims.[222]

Like its counterpart in *Vivendi I*, the majority on the tribunal was of the view that a contractual forum-selection clause constitutes *lex specialis* and should prevail over the more general jurisdictional arrangements found in the BIT.[223] As a result, it held that although the BIT invested the tribunal with authority to

plane. Ibid, at para 128. For support, see *Eureko*, above, n 179, at para 257; *Noble Ventures v Romania*, Award of 12 Oct 2005, at para 51, <http://www.investmentclaims.com/decisions/Noble-Ventures-Final-Award.pdf>. For criticism, see *El Paso*, above, note 195, at para 76.

218 *SGS v Philippines*, above, n 208, at para 134. The clauses discussed in both *SGS cases* invested the ICSID tribunal with jurisdiction over 'disputes with respect to investments'.

219 Ibid, at paras 125–6.

220 For a teleological discussion of the desirability of applying an interpretive presumption in favour of the host state or the private investor, see *Methanex Corp v US*, Partial Award of 7 August 2002, at paras 103–5, 137–9 <http://www.investmentclaims.com/decisions/Methanex-US-1stPartialAward-7Aug2002.pdf>; *El Paso* above, n 195, at paras 68–70; *Noble Ventures*, above, n 217, at para 52; *Pan American Energy LLC v Argentina*, decision on preliminary objections of 27 July 2006, at para 97–9 <http://ita.law.uvic.ca/documents/PanAmericanBPJurisdiction-eng.pdf>.

221 *SGS v Philippines*, above, n 208, at para 121 (referring, in passing, to some textual differences between the two clauses). But see *Salini*, 44 ILM at 593 ('The Tribunal notes that Article 2(4) of the BIT between Italy and Jordan is couched in terms that are appreciably different from the provisions applied in the arbitral decisions and awards cited by the Parties. Under Article 2(4), each Contracting Party committed itself to create and maintain in its territory a "legal framework" favourable to investments. This legal framework must be apt to guarantee to investors the continuity of legal treatment. It must in particular be such as to ensure compliance of all undertakings assumed under relevant contracts with respect to each specific investor. But under Article 2(4), each Contracting Party did not commit itself to "observe" any "obligation" it had previously assumed with regard to specific investments of investors of the other Contracting Party as did the Philippines. It did not even guarantee the observance of commitments it had entered into with respect to the investments of the investors of the other Contracting Parties as did Pakistan. It only committed itself to create and maintain a legal framework apt to guarantee the compliance of all undertakings assumed with regard to each specific investor').

222 *SGS v Philippines*, above, n 208, at para 154.

223 Ibid, at paras 139–43.

adjudicate SGS's contract claims, it 'should not exercise its jurisdiction over a contractual claim when the parties have already agreed on how such a claim is to be resolved, and have done so exclusively'. The dissenting arbitrator, Antonio Crivellaro, took another view on the matter: since he believed that the BIT constituted *lex posteriori*, Crivellaro posited that it was designed to expand upon the pre-existing jurisdictional avenues open to the investor in the event of a dispute.[224] Hence, the BIT arguably modified the contractual forum-selection clause and entitled investors to bring their contract claim before an ICSID tribunal, notwithstanding their contractual undertaking. So, while all three members of the tribunal were in agreement that a horizontal regulation of the parallel jurisdiction over contract claims was warranted, they conflicted over the question of which regulating scheme—the contractual or the BIT forum-selection clause—were to be given right of way.

Another point of contention between the majority and the minority related to the need to coordinate the exclusive jurisdiction of the arbitration proceedings over the investor's treaty claim with the exclusive jurisdiction of the domestic court over the contract claim. Since the contract and treaty claims were strongly interrelated, the majority believed that it would be 'inappropriate and premature' to address the treaty claim before the contract claim had been settled by domestic courts in the Philippines.[225] Hence, it stayed the ICSID arbitral proceedings until the final settlement of the contract claim.[226] This decision was criticized by Crivellaro, the minority arbitrator:[227] since Crivellaro was of the view that the tribunal should maintain jurisdiction over all of the investor's claims—contract and treaty claims—he thought that staying the proceedings was unnecessary, especially in view of the fact that the contract claims had really become treaty claims by virtue of the umbrella clause.[228]

The decision of the arbitral tribunal in *SGS v Philippines* is instructive: it illustrates the real potential for jurisdictional interaction between national and international courts when both sets of procedures address the same subject matter and/or apply the same law. In these circumstances, there is room for the operation of jurisdiction-regulating rules (eg, a contractual exclusive jurisdiction provision). Furthermore, even when the parallel proceedings involved claims founded in

224 Ibid, at paras 2–7 of Crivellaro's declaration (available at, <http://www.worldbank.org/icsid/cases/SGSvPhil-declaration.pdf>). Crivellaro opined that differences in the identities of the parties to the BIT and the contract rendered the *lex specialis* principle inapplicable. Still, the third-party rights conferred on SGS by the BIT enabled it to invoke the *lex posteriori* argument. Ibid, at paras 9–10. One may question, however, the usefulness of the *lex posteriori* principle in the particular facts of the case in light of the renewal of the contract following the conclusion of the BIT. Cf Joost Pauwelyn, 'Bridging Fragmentation and Unity: International Law as a Universe of Inter-Connected Islands', 25 *Mich J Int'l L* (2004) 903, 908.

225 *SGS v Philippines*, above, n 208, at paras 162–3.

226 Ibid, at para 175. The majority grounded its decision to stay proceedings in its general powers under the ICSID Arbitration Rules and the ICSID Convention to 'make orders required for the conduct of the proceeding'. Ibid, at para 173.

227 Ibid, at para 11 of Crivellaro's declaration.

228 Ibid, at para 11–13 of Crivellaro's declaration.

different laws—contract claims v treaty claims—the arbitral tribunal was willing to acknowledge the pragmatic need to coordinate between the findings in the two proceedings on the comparable factual and legal questions they involve: hence, the application of inter-judicial comity on the part of the ICSID tribunal, expressed in the willingness to arrange its own proceedings in order eventually to facilitate utilization of the Philippine domestic court's decision on related issues.

Significantly, the *SGS v Philippines* decision did not fully reject legal dualism: after all, it accepted as did its counterparts in *Vivendi II* and *SGS v Pakistan*, that a contractual forum-selection provision does not directly control treaty claims even if the two heads of claims are factually interrelated (or even inseparable) and did not follow the *Vivendi I* 'crucial connection' test for stretching the effect of a contractual clause to treaty claims. Still, it did deviate from the more dogmatic version of dualism applied in *SGS v Pakistan* in two important aspects: first, the arbitral tribunal was willing to give effect to the contractual forum-selection clause vis-à-vis some treaty claims, ie, the contract claims that were transformed, in effect, into treaty claims through the umbrella clause. So, although the tribunal accepted that the BIT also encompassed contract claims, it held that the contractual forum-selection clause had rendered these claims inadmissible, ie, that it would be inappropriate for the tribunal to address them by reason of the express agreement of the parties to adjudicate these issues before a domestic forum. The distinction between jurisdiction and admissibility enabled the tribunal to reconcile between the doctrinal division between contract claims and treaty claims and the legitimate expectations of the parties to address disputes arising under the contract before domestic courts in the Philippines.[229]

Second, the arbitral tribunal did not use legal dualism as an excuse for the lack of coordination between the parallel sets of proceedings. On the contrary, the tribunal applied principles of judicial comity to regulate the order of the national and international proceedings.[230] This seems to represent, in the circumstances of the case, acceptance on the part of the arbitral tribunal of the preferential status of the domestic proceedings by reason of the dominance of the specific contract claims (which were subject to the exclusive jurisdiction of the domestic court) and the explicit and direct nature of the parties' agreement to litigate before the domestic forum (note that the investor is not a party to the BIT that established ICSID's jurisdiction). As will be discussed in Chapter 6, the comparative advantages of national and international courts may also be taken into consideration in determining the proper order of the proceedings.

In all events, the decision in *SGS v Philippines* can be viewed as dismissive of the notion that an inherent hierarchy holds between national and international courts (as proposed by SGS). Instead, it applied horizontal rules to divide the labour

[229] For a distinction between jurisdiction and admissibility, see John Collier and Vaughan Lowe, *The Settlement of Disputes in International Law: Institutions and Procedures* (1999) 155–6.

[230] On the possibility of applying comity across legal regimes, see Rosas, above, n 13, at 205.

between itself and the national court in the Philippines with respect to the parallel contract claims (exclusive jurisdiction over pure contract claims and lack of admissibility over contract claims covered by the umbrella clause). These same horizontal rules were employed to coordinate between the non-overlapping aspects of the two proceedings through a deferential rule of comity. Such a method of regulation seems consistent with a view of national and international courts as judicial alternatives to one another or, at least, as counterparts who may benefit from some degree of coordination and cooperation.

Finally, *SGS v Philippines* demonstrates the links between jurisdictional regulation and application of integrationist methods of interpretation (ie, an approach that acknowledges that a multi-faceted dispute may constitute a single whole) in construing the respective tribunals' scope of jurisdiction and applicable law. As each tribunal—national and international—is assigned broader, more comprehensive competencies, normative overlaps become more likely and the need for regulation increases.[231] As a result, an interpretive methodology that authorizes courts to address the dispute as a whole encourages resort to jurisdiction-regulating rules; indeed, as Chapter 3 indicates, integrationism and jurisdictional regulation stem from a common pragmatic agenda that seeks to improve coordination between competing norms and procedures and to maximize the utility of adjudication.

In sum, the ICSID decisions in *Vivendi I, Vivendi II, SGS v Pakistan* and *SGS v Philippines* reveal major differences in their conceptual approaches towards relations between contract and treaty claims; as a result, they differ in their perspectives toward regulation of the jurisdictions of national and international courts. *Vivendi I* adopts a pragmatic problem-solving approach, which dismisses the importance of doctrinal differences between the two types of claims and consequently leans toward horizontal regulation of jurisdictional relations between national and international courts on the basis of a contractual forum-selection clause. *SGS v Pakistan* is situated at the opposite pole: it dismisses the legal significance of the actual interplay between the parallel proceedings while emphasizing their separate legal bases and circumventing, through invocation of legal dualism, the need to regulate the jurisdictions of national and international courts. *Vivendi II* and *SGS v Philippines* represent a more nuanced or middle ground approach: *Vivendi II* suggests that in exceptional cases (where the essential basis of the treaty claim is contractual), jurisdictional interaction is feasible and regulation necessary, whereas *SGS v Philippines* acknowledges some actual interactions between the claims and accepts the need for coordination between the courts' jurisdictions. The inconclusive nature of the jurisprudence on relations between national and international investment dispute-settlement proceedings perhaps suggests some confusion over

[231] For example, a broad interpretation of umbrella clauses may authorize international courts to apply national law in parallel to domestic courts. See eg, *Noble Ventures*, above, n 217, at para 55 ('an umbrella clause, when included in a bilateral investment treaty, introduces an exception to the general separation of States obligations under municipal and under international law').

the utility and effect of jurisdictional regulation in the absence of clear textual guidance in ICSID's constitutive instruments.

1.2.6 Interim conclusions

The survey of cases and categories of cases conducted in this chapter reveals grossly inconsistent approaches to the regulation of relations between national and international proceedings relating to the same disputes, across different legal regimes and even within the same regimes. Whereas some judges dismiss the normative relevance of legal proceedings conducted outside their own legal system (or, at least, dispute the binding effect of the legal pronouncements produced by external legal proceedings), other judges have adopted a more deferential attitude towards parallel proceedings and their outcomes. Furthermore, even the conditions for identifying jurisdictional overlap vary from one specific legal regime to the other, and sometimes within the same regime.

At the heart of the matter there appear to be different theories explaining relations between national law and international law, and different visions of the roles of the respective dispute settlement regimes. Whereas most judges tend to view national and international proceedings as distinctive procedures, separated by dualism in a way that bars jurisdictional interaction, several judges have shown a willingness to adopt a more integrative view of the relationship between national and international courts. Similarly, some legal regimes and individual judges situate national and international courts within a vertical paradigm, whereas other legal regimes and judges apply an essentially horizontal paradigm.

We must conclude then that the actual regulation of jurisdictional interactions between national and international courts appears to be influenced by the legal theory espoused by the relevant decision makers (judges, treaty or law makers, etc). The next chapter therefore investigates in greater depth the various theories that might explain the relationship holding between national and international courts. This discussion will lay the foundations for the identification, in Part II, of specific legal measures that ought to regulate jurisdictional interactions between national and international courts.

2

Conceptualizing the Relations between National and International Courts

2.1 Traditional Objections to Regulation: Dualism and Hierarchy

While the co-existence of parallel litigation before national and international courts raises a host of practical difficulties (briefly described in the Introduction to this book), the crucial issues that influence the manner in which many courts and jurists approach regulation of jurisdictional interactions between national and international proceedings are conceptual. The acknowledgement of jurisdictional interaction and the need to regulate it, as well as the choice of jurisdiction-regulating measures, derive to a large extent from the theoretical constructs defining the nature of the relationship between the respective courts.

As the discussion in Chapter 1 revealed, national and international judges have resorted, in the main, to two legal manoeuvres in order to evade introduction of jurisdiction-regulating measures vis-à-vis parallel proceedings: dualism and hierarchy. A third legal manoeuvre—questioning the binding effect of international decisions—has been applied by some national courts.[232] Finally, some national and international courts have stressed the differences between the case pending before each and the parallel case pending before the other court, thereby avoiding the need to apply jurisdiction-regulating measures.[233]

Acceptance of one or more of these legal moves either negates the conditions under which jurisdictional interaction between national and international courts can take place or strictly limits the need for introducing jurisdiction-regulating measures. Since dualism and hierarchy objections have significant theoretical implications, they will be discussed at some length. The other avoidance techniques—contesting the 'bindingness' of international decisions or 'sameness' of the two relevant proceedings—tend to be of a more practical or circumstance-dependent nature and will be addressed in the second part of this book.

After discussing the theoretical underpinnings of dualism and hierarchy, I will examine some alternative theoretical approaches to the nature of the relations

232 See eg, *Breard*, 523 US 371; *Mara'abe*, above, n 135; *Corus Staal*, 395 F 3d 1343.
233 See eg, *Certain German Interests*, 1925 PCIJ (Ser A), No 6, at 20.

between the two sets of courts. While I do not purport to settle definitively here this long-standing debate (which ultimately relates to basic theories on the nature of international law), I hope to cast some doubt on the deterministic contours of parts of the discussion on the conceptual feasibility of jurisdictional regulation. In other words, I posit that the espousal of dualism or hierarchy as overarching paradigms that bar or limit jurisdictional regulation is not always obligatory. Advocacy of a particular model may, in fact, signify a policy choice on the part of courts, which can be open to criticism.

2.1.1 Dualism

Dualism posits that national and international law are separate and independent legal systems that operate on different planes[234]—specifically, the intra-state and inter-state levels.[235] This separateness between the two bodies of law is characterized not by a 'legal continuum' (*continuum juris*)[236] but, rather, by a sharp division—a normative gulf. This is because national and international law originate in different legislative processes, fulfil different social functions, and enjoy distinct forms of legitimacy.

Hence, dualism is premised on the perceived ability of judges and lawyers to classify norms as either national or international, and to categorize legal claims based on the respective norms as either national law or international law claims. For example, in *Loewen*, a NAFTA Chapter 11 tribunal proposed the following distinction between private law claims, which draw their validity from domestic law, and NAFTA claims, which are valid under international law:

> Rights of action under private law arise from personal obligations (albeit they may be owed by or to a State) brought into existence by domestic law and enforceable through domestic tribunals and courts. NAFTA claims have a quite different character, stemming from a corner of public international law in which, by treaty, the power of States under that law to take international measures for the correction of wrongs done to its nationals has been replaced by an ad hoc definition of certain kinds of wrongs, coupled with specialist means

[234] See eg, *Council of Canadians v Canada*, 2005 ACWSJ 11501, at para 41 (Superior Court of Justice, Ontario) ('International law and domestic law are distinct legal systems that operate in different spheres').

[235] For a classic exposition of dualism and monism, see Robert Jennings and Arthur Watts, I *Oppenheim's International Law* (9th edn, 1992) 53; J G Starke, 'Monism and Dualism in the Theory of International Law', 17 *Brit YB Int'l L* (1936) 66; Hannu Klami, 'Monism and Dualism in Law: National Versus International or Supranational Law', *Coherence and Conflict in Law* (Bob Brouwer et al, eds, 1992) 139, 139–48; George Slyz, 'International Law in National Courts', 28 *NYU J Int'l L & Pol* 65, 67 (1996); Giorgio Gaja, 'Dualism—A Review', a paper presented in an Amsterdam Center for International Law Seminar on Theoretical Approaches to the Relationship between International and National Law (2003) at 2 (copy with author). See also *Jurisdiction of the Courts of Danzig*, 1928 PCIJ (Ser B), No 15, at 17; *J H Rayner (Mincing Lane) Ltd v Department of Trade* [1990] 2 AC 418, 476 (per Lord Templeman) and ibid, at 499–500 (per Lord Oliver of Aylmerton).

[236] *Frontier Dispute* (Burkina Faso/ Mali), 1986 ICJ 554, 568; *Frontier Dispute* (Benin/Niger), 2005 ICJ (forthcoming).

of compensation. These means are both distinct from and exclusive of the remedies for wrongful acts under private law.[237]

In the same vein, the *Vivendi II* ICSID ad hoc annulment committee distinguished between contract claims (governed by national law) and BIT claims (governed by international law) in the following terms:

[W]hether there has been a breach of the BIT and whether there has been a breach of contract are different questions. Each of these claims will be determined by reference to its own proper or applicable law—in the case of the BIT by international law; in the case of the Concession Contract, by the proper law of the contract, in other words, the law of Tucumán.[238]

Of course, acknowledging the distinction between national and international law does not negate, in itself, the possibility that some norms which originate in one legal system would have a legal effect in the other legal system. Still, dualism does not merely offer a descriptive analysis of the differences between national and international law, it also contains a normative component: dualism posits that the distinction between national and international law should carry a preclusive effect so as to prevent the application of norms derived from one legal system in a polity governed by a different legal system unless such norms have been positively incorporated among the latter system's norms. In the same vein, dualism prohibits justifying violations of norms derived from one body of law by reliance on the other body of law. In other words, the different systemic contexts in which national and international law operate bar the direct penetration of norms from one legal order to the other (in the same way that English law has no legal effect in France, unless and to the degree that French law ascribes such an effect).

The separateness of national and international law carries clear implications for the jurisdictional relations between the respective courts: if national and international courts derive their authority from totally different legal orders and apply the norms of these separate orders, then their jurisdictions, ie, the power to issue binding normative statements[239]—must exist independently of one another. Stated differently, dualism denies the existence of normative contact points between the two jurisdictions.[240] This, in turn, adversely affects the ability of courts to recognize the relevance of judicial proceedings grounded in different legal systems: if private law claims derive their legal validity from a domestic legal system, then their disposition by national courts or arbitrators can have no more an effect on the law applicable before an international court than a domestic statute, which does not normally constitute a permissible source of law in international proceedings.[241]

237 *Loewen*, 42 ILM at 848–9.

238 *Vivendi II*, 41 ILM at 1154. Cf *CMS Gas Transmission Co v Argentina*, 42 ILM 788, 800 (2003).

239 See eg, Malcolm N Shaw, *International Law* (5th edn, 2003) 572 ('Jurisdiction concerns the power of the state to affect people, property, and circumstances and reflects the basic principles of state sovereignty, equality of states, and non-interference in domestic affairs').

240 See eg, Brownlie, above, n 4, at 50–1.

241 Statute of the International Court of Justice, 26 June 1945, art 38, XV UNCIO Doc 355 (Annex to UN Charter).

Similarly, if a national legal system views WTO agreements as non-self-executing (or lacking in effect under domestic law for some other reason),[242] then DSB pronouncements will have no valid effect within that domestic jurisdiction.[243]

Since, according to dualist thinking, national and international courts apply distinct and not necessarily compatible bodies of law, they can never be regarded as judicial alternatives to one another. Moreover, conflicting decisions by national and international courts on related issues do not present doctrinal problems. The distinctiveness of national and international law means that any inconsistency between the two does not affect each legal order's internal coherence, legitimacy, or workability. While some practical coordination problems might persist, they are not essentially different than those arising in the legal relations between France and the US, where conflicting regulation of similar matters occurs from time to time.

Hence, dualism serves as a principal objection to regulating the jurisdictions of national and international courts. A short survey of the positions taken by international law and national legal systems illustrates the prevalence of dualism as a conceptual paradigm for configuring the relationship between these courts.

The international law perspective

International law has traditionally adopted a dualist attitude vis-à-vis national law:[244] since national law can never justify a failure on the part of the state to comply with its international law obligations,[245] domestic court decisions, formally grounded, in full or in part, in domestic law cannot influence the judicial outcomes of proceedings before international courts, which are based on international law. As a result, domestic court decisions are devoid of normative effect from an international perspective. In the words of the PCIJ in the *Certain German Interests* case:

> From the standpoint of International Law and of the Court which is its organ, municipal laws are merely *facts* which express the will and constitute the activities of States, *in the same manner as do legal decisions* or administrative measures[246] (emphasis added).

[242] The binding nature of DSB reports is controversial. See eg, Bello, above, n 149; Jackson, above, n 149. See also C-93/02 P, *Biret Int'l SA v Council*, 2003 ECR I-10497, at para 81 of Advocate-General Aber's opinion.

[243] For the mainstream EC view on the matter, see *Biret*, 2003 ECR I-10497, at para 52–3 (DSB reports normally do not create a directly effective obligation under EC law). For a different view of EC law, see ibid, para 114 of Advocate-General Aber's opinion. The DSB itself has not yet taken a firm position on the matter. See *US–Sections 301–310 of the Trade Act of 1974*, WTO Doc WT/DS152/R (1999) (Panel Report) ('Neither the GATT nor the WTO has so far been interpreted by GATT/WTO institutions as a legal order producing direct effect'). See generally, Alberto Alemanno, 'Judicial Enforcement of the WTO Hormones Ruling Within the European Community: Toward EC Liability for the Non-Implementation of WTO Dispute Settlement Decisions?', 45 *Harv Int'l LJ* (2004) 547.

[244] Cf, *Danzig*, 1928 PCIJ (Ser B), No 15, at 17 ('according to a well established principle of international law, the *Beamtenabkommen*, being an international agreement, cannot, as such, create direct rights and obligations for private individuals').

[245] Vienna Convention on the Law of Treaties, 23 May 1969, art 27, 1155 UNTS 331 (hereinafter VCLT); Draft Articles on the Responsibility of States for International Wrongful Acts, art 3, 32, UN GAOR 56th Sess, Supp No 10, UN Doc A/56/10, Ch IV.E.1 (2001) (hereinafter Draft Articles on State Responsibility).

[246] *Certain German Interests*, 1925 PCIJ (Ser A), No 7, at 19.

This treatment of domestic court decisions as facts, not norms, has been affirmed by other international court decisions as well. For example, in the 2000 '*Monte Confurco*' release of vessel case, ITLOS held that:

> When determining whether the assessment made by the detaining State in fixing the bond or other security is reasonable, the Tribunal will treat the laws of the detaining State and the *decisions of its courts* as relevant *facts*[247] (emphasis added).

One might have expected special international courts (or hybrid judicial bodies), such as ICSID—which are authorized to apply international, as well as national law—to embrace a less rigid dichotomy between the national and international. Still, several recent decisions of ICSID tribunals have explicitly highlighted the conceptual differences between national and international proceedings and used these as primary justifications for their refusal to coordinate between their own jurisdiction and the jurisdiction of domestic proceedings conducted in parallel.[248]

The national law perspective

From a national law point of view, the situation is more complicated. This is because the domestic effect of international judgments ultimately depends on the widely divergent ways in which domestic legal systems incorporate their international obligations into domestic law.

Generally speaking, the different approaches to that broader question are situated along a spectrum between wholesale rejection of the domestic effect of international law and full embrace of international norms. Hence, in some states, such as the Scandinavian countries, all international treaties depend on legislative incorporation into domestic law for their domestic legal effect.[249] In some countries, such as the UK, treaty norms require specific incorporation into domestic law unless they reflect customary international law (which constitutes part of the law of the

[247] *Monte Confurco*, above, n 169, at para 72. See also *Camouco*, 39 ILM at 689 (dissenting opinion of Judge Anderson)('The work of the national court, however, is an indispensable part of the factual background').

[248] See eg, *SGS v Pakistan*, 42 ILM 1290; *Wena*, 41 ILM at 940; *Azurix*, 43 ILM at 277; *Loewen*, 42 ILM at 819, 833; *Salini*, 44 ILM at 589; *Bayindir Insaat Turizm Ticaret ve Sanayi AŞ v Pakistan*, decision of 14 Nov 2005, at para 167 <http://www.worldbank.org/icsid/cases/ARB0329Decisionjurisdiction.pdf>; *Impregilo SpA v Pakistan*, decision of 22 April 2005, at para 258 <http://www.worldbank.org/icsid/cases/impregilo-decision.pdf>; *Occidental*, above, n 179, at paras 50–2; *Suez, Sociedad General de Aguas de Barcelona SA v Argentina*, decision on jurisdiction of 3 Aug 2005, para 43–5 (ICSID), <http://ita.law.uvic.ca/documents/SuezVivendiAWGjurisdiction.pdf>.

Note that even the tribunal in *SGS v Philippines* accepted the distinct nature of the investor's contract and treaty claims and refused to apply a contractual forum-selection clause to the latter set of claims (it did, however, coordinate between the two claims through application of admissibility rules and judicial comity). *SGS v Philippines*, above, n 208, at para 156–64.

[249] See eg, Core Document forming part of the Reports of the States Parties: Sweden, UN Doc HRI/CORE/1/Add.4/Rev.1 (Core Document)(2002), at paras 77–83; Core Document forming part of the Reports of the States Parties: Denmark, 29/06/95 HRI/CORE/1/Add.58. (Core Document)(1995), at para 103; Core Document forming part of the Reports of the States Parties: Iceland, 24/06/93 UN Doc HRI/CORE/1/Add.26. (Core Document) (1993), at para 54.

land);[250] in other countries, such as the US, treaties are, as a rule, part of the law of the land. Still, their self-executing nature, ie, the ability to rely directly on their provisions in domestic litigation, may be open to question.[251] Moreover, some countries, such as the Netherlands, give full effect to international law in their national legal systems[252] (even though international treaties are sometimes made subject to constitutional principles in these countries).[253] So, if an international treaty that is directly effective within the domestic legal system of one of the parties to the litigation confers upon an international court the power to settle a legal dispute, then the legal effects of that international court's judgment may enjoy a status under domestic law that is similar to that of the jurisdiction-conferring treaty in question. This idea was explained by an Oklahoma Court of Criminal Appeals judge with respect to the legal relevance of the ICJ judgment in *Avena*,[254] in the following terms:

> The United States voluntarily and legally entered into a treaty, a contract with over 100 countries. The United States is bound by the terms of the treaty and the State of Oklahoma is obligated by virtue of the Supremacy Clause to give effect to the treaty. As this Court is bound by the treaty itself, we are bound to give full faith and credit to the *Avena* decision...
>
> The Optional Protocol, an integral part of the treaty, provides that the International Court of Justice is the forum for resolution of disputes under the Vienna Convention... *Avena* is the product of the process set forth in the Optional Protocol, under which Mexico brought a suit against the United States for alleged treaty violations. This process is promulgated by the treaty itself and exists between states as a result of international law.[255]

An alternative doctrinal basis for recognizing the legal relevance of international judgments may be through linking their effect to the domestic status of the international legal norm, whose interpretation had been the subject of the international

[250] See eg, *A v Secretary of State for the Home Department (No 2)*[2006] 2 AC 221, at para 27 (per Lord Bingham of Conhill). The same rule applies in Israel. HCJ 785/87 *Affo v Commander of I.D.F. Forces in the Judea and Samaria Region*, 42(2) PD 4.

[251] See Carlos Manuel Vazquez, 'The Four Doctrines of Self-Executing Theories', 89 *AJIL* (1995) 695; Thomas Buergenthal, 'Self-Executing and Non-Self-Executing Treaties in National and International Law' 235 *Recueil des cours* (1992-IV) 303.

[252] See eg, Constitution of the Netherlands, art 93 ('Provisions of treaties and of resolutions by international institutions, which may be binding on all persons by virtue of their contents shall become binding after they have been published').

[253] See eg, Bruno Simma et al, 'The Role of German Courts in the Enforcement of International Human Rights', *Enforcing International Human Rights in Domestic Courts*, Benedetto Conforti and Francesco Francioni, eds, 1997) 71, 89–92 (discussing the constitutional status of treaties in Germany); Rett R Ludwikowski, 'Supreme Law or Basic Law? The Decline of the Concept of Constitutional Supremacy', 9 *Cardozo J Int'l & Comp L* (2001) 253, 283–4 (discussing the constitutional status of international law in France). But see Constitution of the Netherlands, art 91(3) ('Any provisions of a treaty that conflict with the Constitution or which lead to conflicts with it may be approved by the Chambers of the Parliament only if at least two-thirds of the votes cast are in favor').

[254] *Avena*, 43 ILM 581.

[255] *Torres v State*, order granting stay of execution and remanding case for evidentiary hearing of 13 May 2004, at 5–7 (concurring opinion of Judge Chapel) <http://www.debevoise.com/publications/pdf/StayofExecutionandRemandingCase.PDF>.

proceedings. If an international treaty provision or customary norm constitutes part of the law of the land,[256] its authoritative interpretation by an international court may entail—at least in some cases—a legal effect in the domestic legal system in question. This incorporation methodology was explained by a NAFTA Chapter 19 bi-national panel assigned to consider the permissibility of relying on a WTO DSB report, proclaiming the unlawfulness of Department of Commerce's use of zeroing in anti-dumping investigations and determinations in proceedings based on domestic US law:

> The Federal Circuit has found the WTO Agreements to be international obligations for purposes of *Charming Betsy* [the interpretive canon which requires courts to construe domestic legislation in a way which conforms to international law] . . . The United States has accepted, as a party to the WTO's Dispute Settlement Understanding, that the WTO dispute settlement process serves 'to clarify the existing provisions of the [WTO] agreements' Article 3(2), WTO Dispute Settlement Understanding. The WTO *Softwood Lumber* Decision has established that zeroing, as applied by the United States in this investigation, does violate the Antidumping Agreement . . . The obligations of the WTO Antidumping Agreement have been clarified in the WTO *Softwood Lumber* Decision, and that clarification was accepted by the United States in the Final Section 129 Determination.[257]

Hence, domestic courts operating in legal systems that incorporate international law may deem international judgments to be legally binding or, at least, influential sources of law.

However, in the US and in other non-dualist jurisdictions, one can often identify reluctance to grant full effect to international norms in the absence of specific incorporating legislation: international treaties are sometimes characterized as non-self-executing (a characterization that leads to treating the relevant treaty under a de facto dualist paradigm).[258] In these same jurisdictions, the persuasive effects of international judgments as a source for clarifying international law have been downplayed at times and made subject to general interpretive doctrines under domestic law.[259]

Indeed, in *Sanchez-Llamas*, the majority opinion of the US Supreme Court suggested that ICJ judgments are not self-executing—that is, not part of the law of the land:

> Nothing in the structure or purpose of the ICJ suggests that its interpretations were intended to be conclusive on our courts . . . The ICJ's principal purpose is to arbitrate particular

[256] See eg, Francesco Francioni, 'International Law as a Common Language for National Courts', 36 *Tex. Int'l LJ* (2001) 587, 588; (most modern constitutions incorporate customary international law in municipal law; in the UK and the US the same result is achieved by judicial doctrines).

[257] *Softwood Lumber (Final Determination)*(NAFTA), above, n 154, at 42–3.

[258] See eg, *Corus Staal*, 395 F 3d, at 1348–9.

[259] See eg, *Sanchez-Llamas*, 126 S Ct at 2685 ('the rule of procedural default—which applies even to claimed violations of our Constitution [cite omitted]—applies also to Vienna Convention claims'); *Timken*, 354 F 3d at 1344 ('In light of the fact that Commerce's "longstanding and consistent administrative interpretation is entitled to considerable weight," [cite omitted], we refuse to overturn the zeroing practice based on EC—Bed Linen').

disputes between national governments. *Id.*, at 1055 (ICJ is 'the principal judicial organ of the United Nations'); see also Art. 34, *id.*, at 1059 ('Only states [*ie*, countries] may be parties in cases before the Court'). While each member of the United Nations has agreed to comply with decisions of the ICJ 'in any case to which it is a party,' United Nations Charter, Art. 94(1), 59 Stat. 1051, T. S. No. 933 (1945), the Charter's procedure for noncompliance—referral to the Security Council by the aggrieved state—contemplates quintessentially *international* remedies, Art. 94(2), *ibid.*[260]

Furthermore, as indicated above, some jurisdictions reject monism altogether; they therefore apply a dualist paradigm to international law in general and, as a result, to international judicial decisions as well.

It is important to note that the dualistic objections to regulating relations between national and international proceedings cannot be overcome by reference to the actual interaction between the contents of each corpus of norms. Indeed, even ardent dualists agree that national courts sometimes interact with the international legal system: domestic legislation may sometimes require national courts to apply international law norms,[261] national courts play a modest part in the creation of international law norms[262] and their acts or omissions have some bearing on the state's ability to comply with its international obligations.[263] But those interactions do not transform the essential characterization of domestic courts as domestic institutions governed, formally speaking, only by national law. Indeed, even when national courts explicitly apply international law norms, they may do so only because national law authorizes them to do so (in the same way that domestic conflict of law rules sometimes authorize courts to apply foreign legal norms). So, conceptually speaking, under dualism, domestic court decisions always remain the product of the domestic legal system.[264]

Dualism and policy considerations

The dualistic objections to coordination between national and international proceedings are sometimes reinforced by observations on the actual differences in how national and international courts operate and decide cases that derive from the fields of political science and legal realism.[265] Arguably, national and international courts have important political functions within the legal and political system to

[260] *Sanchez-Llamas*, 126 S Ct at 2684.

[261] See eg, Human Rights Act 1998; Act to Introduce the Code of Crimes against International Law of 26 June 2002 (Germany), 42 ILM 998 (2003); Geneva Conventions Act, RS, 1985, c G-3 (Canada).

[262] See eg, Brownlie, above, n 4, at 6.

[263] See Eduardo Junenez de Aréchaga, 'International Law in the Past Third of a Century', 159 *Recueil des cours* (1978) 1, 278–82; *Azinian*, 39 ILM at 552.

[264] In the same manner, international court decisions remain the product of the international legal system, even when an international norm (such as an umbrella clause) refers courts to a domestic legal standard.

[265] See eg, Alex Mills and Tim Stephens, 'Challenging the Role of Judges in Slaughter's Liberal Theory of International Law', 18 *Leiden Journal of International Law* (2005) 1, 18–20.

which they belong, and their responsibilities and ultimate loyalties are to be found primarily with the overarching political and institutional frameworks which they serve.[266] This means that, even when they are applying what appears to be the same body of law (either in form or substance), the different political context of their operations can often lead to inconsistent outcomes. This, too, may encourage viewing national and international courts as courts of a totally different order, with limited potential for constituting real jurisdictional alternatives to one another.

Another factor supporting the conceptual dichotomy between national and international proceedings is the traditional distinction between private law and public law.[267] While domestic courts are well versed in the resolution of private law disputes, international courts have traditionally been perceived as institutions operating in the public law domain, empowered to adjudicate disputes relating to the application of governmental power by states in particular. This historic difference in the judicial 'centre of gravity' of these separate courts reinforces their image as being engaged in a qualitatively different judicial enterprise.

Finally, as discussed in Chapter 3, dualism (like other disintegrative methods for addressing jurisdictional interactions) offers the advantage of doctrinal clarity. It represents a clear-cut method to circumvent the inextricable complexity of coordinating between proceedings grounded in different legal environments. This, in turn, serves the important policy goals of predictability and legal certainty.[268]

As a result, dualism may not only be viewed as a theory endowed with significant explanatory power, but also as reflecting a desirable state of affairs, one which ought to be protected from pragmatic or integrationist tendencies. Indeed, some recent ICSID cases have cited the need to maintain the separation between national and international law as a factor in their disinclination to read BIT umbrella clauses covering contractual claims in an expansive manner: such an outcome, they argue, would blur the international nature of the proceedings before them and should be avoided if possible.[269]

[266] See eg, *Laker Airways Ltd v Sabena, Belgian World Airlines*, 731 F 2d 909, 951 (1984) ('Despite the real obligation of courts to apply international law and foster comity, domestic courts do not sit as internationally constituted tribunals. Domestic courts are created by national constitutions and statutes to enforce primarily national laws. The courts of most developed countries follow international law only to the extent it is not overridden by national law... When there is any doubt, national interests will tend to be favored over foreign interests').

[267] See eg, Christine Chinkin, 'A Critique of the Public/Private Dimension', 10 *EJIL* (1999) 387, 389.

[268] Gerard Brennan, 'The Rule and Role of Domestic Law in International Relations', Singapore Academy of Law Annual Lecture 1998, <http://www.sal.org.sg/media_speeches_al1998.htm#top>; Ludwikowski, above, n 253, at 262.

[269] *El Paso*, above, n 195, at para 77 ('the consequence [of reading the umbrella clause as encompassing contractual obligations] being that the division between the national legal order and the international legal order is completely blurred'); *Pan American*, above, n 220, at para 111 ('These far reaching consequences of a broad interpretation of the so-called umbrella clauses [are] quite destructive of the distinction between the national legal orders and the international legal order').

2.1.2 Hierarchy

Hierarchy and the need to regulate jurisdictional interactions

Another conceptual obstacle to the improved regulation of relations between national and international courts is the view that their institutional interaction is hierarchically configured. Since national courts constitute state actors under the laws of state responsibility, their acts and omissions may be subject, as any other state agency, to international monitoring on the basis of international legal norms.[270] Thus, even the application of international law by domestic courts—such as interpretations of an international treaty or pronouncements on the international lawfulness of specific governmental measures—may constitute official state acts, entailing international responsibility. The general principle against self-judging (*nemo judex in sua causa*)[271] further militates against absolving national courts that review their own state's compliance with international law from international supervision. Consequently, international courts have often viewed themselves as hierarchically superior to—or as exercising vertical judicial control—over national courts.[272]

At the same time, domestic courts have often reserved to themselves the ultimate power to determine what, if any, effect to grant within their domestic legal system to international judicial decision—a position likewise implying a hierarchical configuration of jurisdictional relations. Arguably, if domestic legal instruments (such as the national constitution) require national courts to identify and apply the law governing the relevant polity, then national courts cannot abdicate the responsibilities these instruments entail by deferring to international courts.[273] Such a position is, of course, anchored in important policy considerations that stress the structural superiority and enhanced legitimacy of political arrangements at the domestic level—eg, democratic accountability, proximity to the governed, enforceability, etc[274]—over those existing internationally.

As a result, even if national and international courts reject dualism and acknowledge the co-existence of their legal pronouncements in the same legal universe (be it national law, international law, or some pluralistic body of law amalgamated

[270] See *Difference Relating to Immunity from Legal Process of a Special Rapporteur of the Commission on Human Rights*, 1999 ICJ 62, 87. See also Paulsson, above, n 23, at 38–44; ILC Commentary to article 4 of the Draft Articles on State Responsibility for Internationally Unlawful Acts, GAOR 56th Sess, Supp No 10 (A/56/10), chp.IV.E.2 (2001), at 85–7; Jimenez de Aréchaga, above, n 263, at 278.

[271] See Bin Cheng, *General Principles of Law as Applied by International Courts and Tribunals* (1987) (originally published in 1953) 279–89, 357. See also Dodge, above, n 20, at 369–70.

[272] See eg, *Saiga*, above, n 166, at paras 120–1; *Chorzów Factory*, 1927 PCIJ (Ser A), No 12, at 33. Cf Gaja, above, n 2, at 12.

[273] See eg, *Sanchez-Llamas*, 126 S Ct at 2684; Carl Lebeck, 'National Constitutionalism, Openness to International Law and the Pragmatic Limits of European Integration—European Law in the German Constitutional Court from EEC to the PJCC', 7 *German Law Journal* (2006) 907, 941.

[274] For a discussion, see Yuval Shany, 'Toward a General Margin of Appreciation Doctrine', 16 *EJIL* (2005) 907, 919–22.

from multiple sources),[275] hierarchy presents another method to evade application of most jurisdiction-regulating measures. This is because the establishment of hierarchical relations negates the possibility of viewing parallel proceedings as judicial alternatives to one another. Furthermore, hierarchy implies that multiple proceedings before national and international courts, entailing inconsistent decisions, do not present a serious jurisdictional problem: since hierarchy (in ways not unlike dualism) confers ultimate validity only on the decisions of one set of institutions—the hierarchically superior court—normative inconsistencies are easily resolved. Such a situation is not significantly different from the one arising in the context of relations between a lower court and a court of appeal within a single legal system, where inconsistencies in decisions represent an almost daily occurrence.

Significantly, one may view hierarchy not as a way to *evade* the problems raised by unregulated jurisdictional interactions but, rather, as a solution to those problems. In other words, hierarchy may constitute a jurisdiction-regulating regime *in itself*: it ranks the authoritativeness of the respective courts' decisions and thereby settles the problem of inconsistent judicial decisions. Still, hierarchy alone may fail to resolve some of the practical problems of coordination that multiple proceedings entail (eg, procedural harassment of the parties, judicial economy concerns); furthermore, failure to synchronize the timing of the proceedings may deprive national and international courts of some of the benefits of cooperation, which a coordinated operation might offer.[276] Hence, hierarchy cannot purport to serve as an exhaustive jurisdiction-regulating rule.

Worse still, national and international courts sometimes present conflicting hierarchical claims—both judicial bodies may assert powers of review over their counterparts' decisions. In fact, this appears to be the typical mode of interaction between general international courts, such as the ICJ or the PCIJ, and national courts.[277] Hence, not only is it possible that incompatible judgments may be issued by national and international courts; it is also likely that each parallel court will profess the supremacy of its own legal pronouncements vis-à-vis its counterpart. In the same vein, the two sets of tribunals may be tempted to issue injunctive relief against the conduct of parallel proceedings in order to protect their allegedly superior authority.[278] The incompatibility of these claims for normative supremacy exacerbates the practical dilemmas posed before the parties to litigation as to which judgment to honour and which to breach. In other words—hierarchy may increase rather than decrease the need for jurisdictional regulation.

[275] Acceptance of dualism as a conceptual paradigm evades the need to reconcile incompatible normative supremacy claims made by national and international courts. This is because dualism recognizes the possibility that national law and international law would produce contradictory results, including incompatible assertions of hierarchical supremacy. Brownlie, above, n 4, at 33. However, adoption of some of the more disintegrative approaches to the relations between the systems discussed below may perpetuate the deadlock between competing claims of hierarchy.

[276] For a discussion of the tension between vertical review and the need to exercise inter-judicial deference, see Ernest A Young, 'Institutional Settlement in a Globalization Judicial System', 54 *Duke LJ* (2005) 1143, 1179–97.

[277] See above, section 1.2.2.

[278] See above, section 1.2.5 (discussion of the 'battle of injunctions' in *SGS v Pakistan*).

Hierarchy and non-hierarchy signifiers

While the question of how to identify hierarchical or non-hierarchical jurisdictional regimes will be discussed at some length in Chapter 4, some initial observations on the matter are appropriate. Jurisdictional hierarchy can be characterized by two main features: (a) legal relations that permit and even encourage multiple litigation of the same dispute before different courts; and (b) attribution of binding and conclusive status to the decisions of some (but not all) of the said courts. Crucially, the principle of finality (or 'bindingness') applies in vertical contexts in a unidirectional manner—the decisions of the some designated court are binding upon the other courts but not vice versa. Yet, although hierarchy often involves entrusting superior courts with the power of review over the decisions of lower courts,[279] judicial review does not seem to be a *sine qua non* for ascertaining inter-fora hierarchy.

The question of whether a particular set of relationships between national and international courts falls within these two parameters—permissible multiplicity and unidirectional bindingness—can be answered through the identification of hierarchy signifiers, ie, specific jurisdictional rules that facilitate fulfilment of these two conditions. Two clear examples of such hierarchy signifiers are the exhaustion of local remedies rule and the preliminary ruling procedure, both discussed in Chapter 1. The exhaustion of local remedies rule encourages multiple proceedings, channels the unidirectional application of the finality principle and confirms thereby the superior status of the decisions of international courts over national courts.[280] The preliminary ruling procedure existing under EC law[281] facilitates multiple litigation and accords authoritative status (supremacy) to the rulings of one designated court—the ECJ—vis-à-vis other competent courts (national courts).

Of course, non-hierarchy signifiers are also available. Principal among those are the *electa una via* (or 'fork in the road') provisions found in numerous BITs and comparable instruments that enable the parties to a dispute to choose between national and international courts. This arrangement is generally understood as instituting *horizontal* relations between national and international courts in a manner that bars multiple proceedings. One could also regard the rule of complementarity found in the Rome Statute[282] as a non-hierarchy signifier because it rejects the possibility of multiple criminal proceedings before national and international courts (except in the case of patently inappropriate national proceedings) and applies the principle of finality (*ne bis in idem*) in a *bi-directional* manner.

Configuration of relations in the absence of signifiers

The crucial issue before us lies in ascertaining the nature of the relations between national and international courts in the absence of clear hierarchy or non-hierarchy

[279] See Schreuer, above, n 16, at 27.

[280] See eg, ECHR, art 35, ETS 5; I/A CHR, art 46(a). See also Laurence R Helfer and Anne-Marie Slaughter, 'Towards a Theory of Effective Supranational Adjudication', 107 *Yale LJ* (1997) 282, 297.

[281] EC Treaty, art 234.

[282] ICC Statute, art 17, 20.

signifiers.[283] This is the context in which conceptual differences over the nature and structure of international law come into play. 'Internationalists' may posit that in the absence of a contrary indication, international courts ought to be deemed superior to national courts[284] whereas 'nationalists' may submit an opposite proposition—in the absence of a contrary indication, national courts are hierarchically superior to international courts. A third conceptual framework can also be discerned: since national and international courts often fulfil comparable dispute resolution functions (especially when national courts apply international law), there should arguably be no *a priori* hierarchy between them (unless a jurisdiction-conferring instrument has explicitly or implicitly provided for it).[285]

In effect, the choice between the alternative positions on hierarchy is informed not only by doctrinal considerations but also by more pragmatic policy considerations, which are sometimes applied on a case-by-case basis: the willingness on the part of national courts to grant deference or otherwise cooperate with their international counterparts often depends on an assessment of the propriety and fairness of the international proceedings[286] and on the perceived relative advantages and disadvantages of national versus international adjudication.[287] At the same time, international courts sometimes view domestic court decisions with some suspicion by reason of these courts' potential local bias and their limited international law expertise. Hence, international courts are, at times, disposed not to defer to decisions issued by national courts, which they deem to be untrustworthy.[288] These attitudes may explain the uneven treatment of international courts by the same domestic courts,[289] and variations in the willingness (or reluctance) of international courts to exercise supervisory powers over diverse national courts.[290]

[283] A related issue may be whether the establishment of an international procedure was designed to signify intent on the part of the parties to exclude the jurisdiction of national courts. For a discussion, see Christoph C Schreuer, *Decisions of International Institutions before Domestic Courts* (1981) 338–9.

[284] See eg, *SAIMI* (France v Italy), *excerpts* in 18 ILR 471 (1951); *Caire* (France v Mexico), 5 RIAA 516, 523–5 (1929); *Holiday Inns SA v Morocco, excerpts* in Pierre Lalive, 'The First "World Bank" Arbitration (Holiday Inns v Morocco)—Some Legal Problems', 1 ICSID Rep 645, 680–1 (1980). See also August Reinisch, 'The Use and Limits of Res Judicata and Lis Pendens as Procedural Tools to Avoid Conflicting Dispute Settlement Outcomes', 3 *The Law and Practice of International Courts and Tribunals* (2004) 37, 51 (arguing that the fact that domestic court judgments are reviewable by international courts negates the possibility of jurisdictional overlap).

[285] See Schreuer, above, n 283, at 328. Cf Gunther Teubner, 'Breaking Frames: The Global Interplay of Legal and Social Systems', 45 *Am J Comp L* (1997) 149, 158–9 (globalization results in the replacement of hierarchical with non-hierarchical legal frameworks).

[286] See eg, Laura Moranchek, 'Protecting National Security Evidence While Prosecuting War Crimes: Problems and Lessons for International Justice from the ICTY', 31 *Yale J Int'l L* (2006) 477, 500.

[287] See eg, *Mara'abe*, above, n 135, at paras 73–4. For a discussion of some of the comparative advantages and disadvantages of national and international courts, see Shany, above, n 6, at 243; Shany, above, n 274, at 919.

[288] See eg, Young, above, n 276, at 1187–8, 1193.

[289] See eg, ibid, at 1242–3; Helfer and Slaughter, above, n 286, at 316–7.

[290] See eg, Philip Alston & Joseph H H Weiler, 'An "Ever Closer Union" in Need of a Human Rights Policy: The European Union and Human Rights', *The EU and Human Rights* (Philip Alston, ed, 1999) 3; Andrew Williams, 'Enlargement of the Union and Human Rights Conditionality: A Policy of Distinction?', 25 *Eur L Rev* (2000) 601.

Judicial practice

As Chapter 1 revealed, the practice of national and international courts with respect to the residual nature of the hierarchy rule may be described, at best, as inconsistent. Some decisions do seem to confirm the hierarchical superiority of international over national courts in the absence of contrary regulation,[291] as seen in these international courts that have construed their jurisdictional instruments in a manner suggestive of a pro-hierarchy presumption. For example, the majority of ITLOS judges in the prompt release of vessel cases interpreted article 292 of UNCLOS so as to authorize ITLOS to overrule previous domestic court decisions on release bond, which demonstrates treatment of national courts under a *de facto* rule of hierarchy.[292] The award of the NAFTA Chapter 11 arbitral panel in *Loewen*, which held that the state parties to NAFTA could not have intended to do away with the exhaustion of local remedies rule as such a waiver would unduly expose them to international liability, is also consistent with a residual pro-hierarchy stance.[293] This is because the emphasis the decision places on the need to avert 'international liability' may be indicative of the arbitral tribunal's position that it ultimately oversees the work of national courts (and all other implicated state actors) through the application of international rules of state responsibility.

At the same time, US court decisions in the Consular Notification cases and US and Canadian recent constitutional challenges to NAFTA dispute settlement proceedings[294] seem to be premised on a general legal principle that grants supremacy to national over international courts. For example, in *Breard*, the US Supreme Court stressed that in the absence of a contrary domestic rule, domestic law principles—ultimately pronounced by domestic courts—govern implementation of international treaty law, notwithstanding the interpretation of the treaty in question offered by the ICJ:

> While we should give respectful consideration to the interpretation of an international treaty rendered by an international court with jurisdiction to interpret such, it has been recognized in international law that, absent a clear and express statement to the contrary, the procedural rules of the forum State govern the implementation of the treaty in that State.[295]

Similarly, the US Supreme Court in *Sanchez-Llamas* confirmed that in the absence of a contrary indication, the supremacy conferred to it under the US Constitution

[291] See eg, *Chorzów Factory*, 1927 PCIJ (Ser A), No 12, at 33.

[292] It is interesting to note, however, that the Tribunal asserted in a number of release of vessel cases that it does not purport to sit as a court of appeal over national courts. *Camouco*, 39 ILM at 678 ('Article 292 provides for an independent remedy and not an appeal against a decision of a national court'); *Monte Confurco*, above, n 169, at para 72; *Volga* (Russia v Australia), 42 ILM 159, 186 (2003) (separate opinion of Judge Cot).

[293] *Loewen*, 42 ILM at 837. It should be noted, however, that the *Loewen* case involved a denial of justice claim. In denial of justice cases, strong policy considerations militate in favour of providing domestic courts with the opportunity of correcting aberrations in their own legal system.

[294] *Sanchez-Llamas*, 126 S, Ct 2669; *Coalition for Fair Lumber*, above, n 158; *Council of Canadians*, above, n 158.

[295] *Breard*, 523 US at 375.

continues to apply vis-à-vis the ICJ:

> If treaties are to be given effect as federal law under our legal system, determining their meaning as a matter of federal law 'is emphatically the province and duty of the judicial department,' headed by the 'one supreme Court' established by the Constitution... Nothing in the structure or purpose of the ICJ suggests that its interpretations were intended to be conclusive on our courts.[296]

While the above national and international court decisions advocate a residual pro-hierarchy rule investing one or another court with superiority over its counterparts, two of the ICSID arbitral decisions discussed in Chapter 1—*Vivendi I* and *SGS v Philippines*—appear to apply a no-hierarchy presumption in the absence of any hierarchy signifiers.[297] These cases rejected the notion that relations between national and international courts are hierarchically configured and applied horizontal jurisdiction-regulating rules to govern interactions between the two judicial bodies.[298] Similarly, some of the opinions issued by US judges involved in the Consular Notification cases, which grant considerable deference to the position taken by the ICJ,[299] and that adopted by the CIT in the *Ontario Forest* case vis-à-vis NAFTA proceedings[300] seem to be more consistent with a non-hierarchy than with a pro-hierarchy presumption.

2.2 Alternative Relationship Theories

2.2.1 Dualism, hierarchy, and the continued need for regulation

Now, I do not intend to contest the relevance of dualism (or other doctrines emphasizing the separate or 'self-contained' nature of different legal regimes)[301] or hierarchy as theories that can explain and regulate relations between national and international proceedings. Still, the clear-cut solutions offered by dualist and hierarchical thinking, which systematically prefer one set of judicial decisions at the expense of others, may sometimes lead to undesirable results, at least from the perspective of the immediate parties to a dispute subject to multiple adjudication before national and international courts.[302] By seriously limiting the normative effects of parallel proceedings, dualism and hierarchy operate to dissuade some or all of the courts involved in jurisdictional interactions from attempting to provide

[296] *Sanchez-Llamas*, 126 S Ct at 2684.
[297] *Vivendi I*, 40 ILM 426; *Vivendi II*, 41 ILM 1135; *SGS v Philippines*, above, n 208.
[298] See *SGS v Philippines*, above, n 208, at para 12 of Crivellaro's declaration ('we are not a Court of Appeal in respect of domestic courts').
[299] *Torres*, 540 US at 1041; *Torres v State* (stay of execution), above, n 255, (concurring opinion of Judge Chapel); *Sanchez-Llamas*, 126 S Ct at 2700–02 (dissenting opinion of Justice Breyer).
[300] *Ontario Forest*, 444 F Supp 2d 1309.
[301] For a discussion of self-contained regimes, see below, Chapter 3.
[302] See eg, Schreuer, above, n 283, at 331.

a meaningful degree of coordination. Hence, under dualistic and hierarchical paradigms, multiple proceedings may still take place and the parties may still be compelled to litigate the same issues before two or more judicial bodies from beginning to end. This, as already suggested, may not only lead to procedural inconveniences, it may also create situations in which the parties are required to comply with two inconsistent, yet enforceable judicial decisions. In short, application of legal dualism and assertions of normative supremacy by both national and international courts can exacerbate—not mitigate—the need for coordination between their parallel jurisdictions.

In consideration of the preceding, it can be argued that dualism and hierarchy do not provide exclusive conceptual frameworks for understanding relations between national and international courts and that other legal and political theories, more conducive to better coordination between national and international proceedings, are also conceivable. Such alternative theories may also be more attuned to the internationalization of the national and the ensuing narrowing of the normative distinctions separating national from international law, described in the Introduction to this book.

For example, one may posit that national and international courts could, at least in some cases, be viewed as engaged in a common functional and normative enterprise: the settlement of disputes and the development and enforcement of comparable norms (sometimes even derived from the same normative sources). This position, which accepts the horizontal co-existence of national and international jurisdictions, was captured to some degree by Scelle's *dédoublement fonctionnel* theory.[303] Recent indirect support for this position is found in American process-oriented jurisprudence theories, most influentially, Ann-Marie Slaughter's work on the emerging epistemological community comprising national and international courts.[304] In addition, the classic Kelsenian exposition on legal monism[305] as well as Gunther Teubner's writings on legal pluralism, which involve rejection of a monolithic vision of law as created by institutionalized political processes,[306] also challenge the traditional dichotomy between the national and the international. It would seem that these theories, separately and jointly, may facilitate a more functional assessment of the parallel operation of national and international courts, together with their normative and institutional points of contact.

In all events, whether one accepts or rejects traditional dogma on the relations between national and international courts or the theoretical challenges thereto, an

303 Georges Scelle, 'La phénomène juridique du dédoublement fonctionnel', *Rechtsfragen der Internationalen Organisation: Festschrift für Hans Wehberg* (1956) 324.

304 See eg, Anne-Marie Slaughter, 'A Global Community of Courts', 44 *Harv Int'l LJ* (2003) 191.

305 See eg, Hans Kelsen, *General Theory of Law and State* (Anders Wedberg trans, 1999) (1945) 363–88.

306 Gunther Teubner, 'Global Bukowina: Legal Pluralism in the World Society', *Global Law Without a State* (Gunther Teubner, ed, 1997) 3, 11–15; Teubner, above, n 285, at 157. Although pluralism and dualism were once used interchangeably, it is nowadays common to associate modern pluralism with the notion that decision makers (including courts) can apply norms derived from a multitude of sources.

argument can be made that some of the rudimentary rules of coordination discussed in Part 2 of this treatise—such as comity or the *abus de droit* principles—should be applied under all relationship paradigms. Hence, acceptance of a dualist or hierarchical configuration should affect, at most, the manner—not the need—of regulation.

2.2.2 Other possible theories

The seeming failure of dualism and hierarchy in adequately regulating the interplay between national and international courts and, especially, prescribing workable outcomes for the parties to a dispute subject to multi-fora litigation validates the need for exploration of alternative explanatory and normative relationship theories. Such theories could, perhaps, lay down less rigid boundaries between jurisdictions and address, in a more nuanced manner, the potential effects of claims presented before each court on litigation before its counterpart.

However, it must be acknowledged in advance that there probably exists no single theory capable of enjoying universal acceptance and of definitively resolving problems arising from the relations between national and international fora. Koskenniemi seems to be correct in asserting that one's approach to the issue ultimately depends upon one's choice of argumentation technique: legal arguments on the nature of international law and its relationship to domestic legal orders can derive from descending or ascending authority premises,[307] a choice possibly dictated by normative considerations regarding the proceeding's desired end. Accordingly, domestic law could be described as either a method for implementing international obligations and, thus, part of the international legal order (ie, monism), or as an independent legal order (ie, dualism). An intermediate position may also be offered. Such a position suggests that domestic institutions sometimes assume functions under both domestic law and international law (ie, *dédoublement fonctionnel*).

The following section examines two influential theories on the structural relationship between national and international courts—monism and *dédoublement fonctionnel*); it also looks into two non-structural approaches—informal socialization and pluralism—which provide important insights on the aforementioned relationship. Finally, it offers some ideas on normative systemization as a half-way approach, one that accepts the informal nature of the institutional links between national and international courts but insists on the existence of some structured,

[307] See eg, Starke, above, n 235 (discussing the political nature of the choice between statal and international primacy); Martti Koskenniemi, *From Apology to Utopia: The Structure of International Legal Argument* (1989) 40–2; Martti Koskenniemi, 'The Politics of International Law', 1 *EJIL* 4, 28–9 (1990) (both a centralized and decentralized views of world order are sustainable). See also Hans Kelsen, *Principles of International Law* (1952) 437, 444–5 (accepting that the choice between the primacy of international law and the primacy of national law may ultimately depend on ethical or political preferences).

normative interaction between them. While other theories may also be relevant,[308] the five approaches discussed below appear to be most directly associated with our project: ascertaining the role of national courts within the international legal order for the purpose of considering the application of jurisdiction-regulating rules.

Monism

According to Kelsen, national and international laws constitute parts of the same multi-levelled normative whole and are linked to one another through hierarchical relations. While Kelsen took the view that international law provides the *grundnorm* from which the different national legal systems derive their validity, he conceded that from a theoretical point of view, a reverse pyramid of norms, conferring supremacy on national law, is also conceivable (though undesirable from a normative perspective).[309] In his extensive writing on the topic, Kelsen based his position on the relationship between national and international law upon an analysis of the very nature of international law and the logical impossibility of the proposition that different independent systems of norms can simultaneously enjoy validity over the same space and time.[310]

To Kelsen's mind, the nature of international law is that of an incomplete legal system whose effectiveness ultimately depends on the complementary functions performed by national legal systems:[311] domestic law provides international law with much needed normative contents and enforcement capabilities.[312] Furthermore, since the norms of international law clearly purport to govern the application of national law by states, the co-existence of the two legal systems must be presumed. Hence, Kelsen believed that it is possible to understand the nature of international law only by reference to a monist theory, which views states as 'organs' of international law subject to its legal norms.[313] Put differently, international law must

308 See eg, Yale's Policy-Oriented Jurisprudence theory that does not sharply distinguish between national and international decision-makers (Myres S McDougal, Harold D Lasswell, and James C Miller, *The Interpretation of International Agreements and World Public Order: Principles of Content and Procedure* (1994) 27–8), or Sir Gerald Fitzmaurice's theory on conflict of obligations. Gerald Fitzmaurice, 'The General Principles of International Law Considered from the Standpoint of the Rule of Law', 92 *Recueil des cours* (1957-II) 68–94.

309 For more on Kelsen's conception of states as organs of the international legal order, see Kelsen, above, n 305, at 351; Kelsen, above, n 307, at 415, 435–8.

310 See eg, Kelsen, above, n 307, at 403–4; Kelsen, above, n 305, at 363.

311 For a different view, see Vaughan Lowe, 'The Politics of Law-making: Are the Method and Character of Norm Creation Changing?', *The Role of Law in International Politics: Essays in International Relations and International Law* (Michael Byers, ed, 2000) 200, 201.

312 Kelsen, above, n 307, at 193–4. See Benedetto Conforti, *International Law and the Role of Domestic Legal Systems*, (1993) 8–10 (the practice of domestic courts provides the quality of 'law' to international law, or at least helps much to secure the *rule* of law). See also *Danzig*, 1928 PCIJ Ser B, No 15, at 17–18 ('it cannot be disputed that the very object of an international agreement, according to the intention of the contracting Parties, may be the adoption by the Parties of some definite rules creating individual rights and enforceable by the national courts. That there is such an intention in the present case can be established by reference to the terms of the *Beamtenabkommen*').

313 Kelsen, above, n 305, at 351. Another important 'organic' role conferred upon states is the promulgation of international law norms, mainly through conclusion of treaties.

have delegated the legal powers required for its implementation to domestic institutions, and the latter derive their validity from the former.

While Kelsen accepted that the constitutional law of some states applies dualism and requires the transformation of international law into national law as a condition for its application,[314] he stressed that from the perspective of international law such transformations are always unnecessary.[315]Furthermore, although Kelsen did not dispute the possibility that positive norms of national law might be inconsistent with the international law norms governing their application, he argued that such events are not necessarily anomalous. In fact, similar situations may occur with respect to unconstitutional domestic laws, which maintain their formal validity until their illegality is proclaimed by a competent authority.[316] So, until international law develops a positive rule mandating the invalidity of inconsistent domestic law, such normative conflicts ought to be resolved either through voluntary abrogation of the inconsistent norm by the state in question, or through application of international sanctions against the state.[317] While an individual might believe that she is subject to contradictory legal norms, Kelsen claimed that from a jurisprudential perspective, such a belief is logically erroneous.[318]

Applied to the topic at hand, Kelsenian monism would typically require courts—national and international law—to apply all the bodies of law relevant to the polity in which they operate or whose laws they apply. This means that a combination of national and international law should be applied by national courts (and by some international courts, such as ICSID tribunals, which are authorized to apply national law alongside international law). In consequence, the jurisdictions of national and international courts may always overlap—they have, at least in theory, parallel jurisdiction over claims grounded in international law and, in some cases, over those grounded in national law.

In addition, Kelsen's position on the hierarchical ordering of national and international law has significant implications for the jurisdictional relations between national and international courts: if the power of national courts to apply international law norms is delegated to them by the international legal system in order to fill normative and institutional gaps in the implementation of international law, then whenever sufficiently comprehensive international norms and reasonably effective international courts exist, the involvement of domestic courts becomes redundant. The superiority of international over national law, according to Kelsen, likewise lends support to the preferential status of international courts, which are

[314] Kelsen did not adequately explain, however, his empirical proposition that in the absence of a specific constitutional provision to the contrary, international law should be exempt from legal transformation. In fact, some common law countries (such as the UK or Israel) deny direct legal effect from international treaties, notwithstanding the lack of an explicit constitutional rule that mandates this outcome.

[315] Kelsen, above, n 305, at 194–5.

[316] Hence, Kelsen's theoretical construct should be distinguished from Kantian 'world government' political theories. See Immanuel Kant, 'To Eternal Peace', *The Philosophy of Kant* (Carl J Friedrich, ed, 1993) (1795) 475, 487–92. To Kelsen, the unity of legal systems is a logical, not a political construct.

[317] Kelsen, above, n 305, at 422.

[318] Ibid, at 427.

better situated to apply international law than are national courts, whose ability to apply international law may be circumscribed, inter alia, by reason of domestic law provisions (that is, until all incompatibilities between national and international law have been removed).

The EC legal system, perhaps, best illustrates the operation of the Kelsenian monist model, albeit with respect to a particular category of international norms—EC law: EC legislation and ECJ judgments enjoy direct effect and supremacy in the territory of all member states.[319] As a result, the jurisdictions of domestic courts and the ECJ may, and do, overlap in relation to matters governed by EC law; the vertical supervision exercised by the ECJ over the domestic courts of the member states also conforms to Kelsen's hierarchical model.[320]

Dédoublement Fonctionnel

The French jurist George Scelle accepted some of the basic premises of Kelsen's monism.[321] Yet, he also advocated some features that would be described today as pluralistic in nature.[322] To Scelle, law is comprised of one harmonious and hierarchically structured body of norms derived from numerous legal sources—including norms promulgated by statal, sub-statal, and supra-statal institutions.[323] While Scelle's broad anti-sovereignty monism[324] fell into disrepute over the years, his idea of *dédoublement fonctionnel* continues to appeal to some international lawyers.[325]

According to Scelle, the vacuum in international institutional structures is temporarily filled by national actors, acting in an international capacity.[326] His

319 See Case 26/62, *Van Gend & Loos v Netherlands Inland Revenue Administration*, [1963] ECR 1; *Amministrazione delle Finanze dello Stato v Simmenthal SpA*, [1978] ECR 629, 643–4. See also Joseph H H Welier, *The Constitution of Europe: 'Do the Clothes have an Emperor' and Other Essays* (1999) 189; Nikolaos Lavranos, 'The MOX Plant and IJzeren Rijn Disputes: Which Court Is the Supreme Arbiter?', 19 *Leiden J Int'l L* (2006) 223, 232–3.

320 One may note that this model may extend beyond matters directly governed by EC law. In fact, it has been argued that international law norms, including international judgments, are binding upon the EC, and therefore on the member states. Nikolaos Lavranos, *Decisions of International Organizations in the European and Domestic Legal Orders of Selected EU Member States* (2004) 142.

321 Georges Scelle, II *Précis de droit de gens* (1932) 11.

322 Scelle, above, n 303, at 338; Hubert Thierry, 'The European Tradition in International Law: Georges Scelle' 1 *EJIL* 193, 200 (1990); Antonio Cassese, 'Remarks on Scelle's Theory of "Role Splitting" (dédoublement fonctionnel) in International Law', 1 *EJIL* (1990) 210, 211.

323 Scelle also embraced a federalist vision of the international community. Scelle, above, n 303, at 330; Scelle, above, n 321, at vol I, 188–206; Georges Scelle, 'Quelques réflexions hétérodoxes sur la technique de l'ordre juridique interétatique', *Hommage d'un génération de juristes au Président Basdevant* (1960) 473, 477–81; Thierry, above, n 322, at 200. Indeed it is possible to view the *dédoublement fonctionnel* theory as a manifestation of federalism, on a normative (or functional), rather than an institutional level. Scelle, above, n 303, at 337; Thierry, above, n 322, at 203.

324 See eg, Scelle, above, n 303, at 334.

325 Richard A Falk, *The Role of Domestic Courts in the International Legal Order* (1964) 65, 76; Cassese, above, n 322, at 224 (citing numerous writers who support the *dédoublement fonctionnel* theory). See also ibid, at 225–31 (domestic courts play an increasingly important role as international-law applying agents); Schreuer, above, n 16, at 6–7.

326 Scelle, above, n 303, at 335, 341; Scelle, above, n 321, at vol II, 10–11; Cassese, above, n 322, at 215; Falk, above, n 325, at 93. The idea that the implementation of international functions is

dédoublement fonctionnel or 'role splitting' theory posits that in this context, national actors alternate between their positions under national and international law: when state representatives engage in treaty negotiations they serve as 'international law makers'; when national courts adjudicate claims relating to the international legal order (eg, when exercising universal jurisdiction) they comprise part of the international judiciary;[327] and when national authorities undertake self-help actions they act as international enforcement agents.[328] Significantly, the theory assumes that the transformation of national into international actors also results in a change in their institutional loyalties: as international actors they are committed to promote international—rather than national—values and interests.[329]

Applied to our topic, the *dédoublement fonctionnel* theory would have little difficulty in regarding national courts, whenever they apply norms reflective of international legal standards, as part of the international legal system. Hence, jurisdictional overlap between national and international courts is possible; its existence may depend on the actual role that national courts play vis-à-vis the dispute at hand—whether they purport to act as agencies applying national or international law.[330]

The Scelle theory, though essentially descriptive in nature, can also be understood to be making a normative claim regarding the delineation of international law's boundaries. Since the actual roles played by the institutions are considered more significant than their nominal institutional affiliations,[331] the theory might convey a preference for functionalism over formalism.[332] Still, the theory is open

decentralized and delegated to state organs was first expounded, however, by Hans Kelsen. Kelsen, above, n 305, at 325–7; Hans Kelsen, *Principles of International Law* (Robert W Tucker, ed, 2nd edn, 1966) 12–13, 20, 31, 552. See also *Banco Nacional De Cuba v Sabbatino*, 307 F 2d 845, 861 (1962) ('until the day of capable international adjudication among countries, the municipal courts must be the custodians of the concepts of international law, and they must expound, apply and develop that law whenever they are called upon to do so').

327 See eg, *Eichmann v Attorney-General*, 36 ILR 277, 304 (1962) (Supreme Court of Israel) (domestic court describing itself as a 'guardian of international law'); *US v Yunis*, 681 F Supp 896, 903 (DDC, 1988)('Not only is the United States acting on behalf of the world community to punish alleged offenders of crimes that threaten the very foundations of world order, but the United States has its own interest in protecting its nationals').

328 For a discussion, see Cassese, above, n 322, at 212–13.

329 Scelle (1956), above, n 303, at 339; Thierry, above, n 322, at 203.

330 Scelle (1932), above, n 321, at vol II, 10; Cassese, above, n 322, at 215.

331 The creation of hybrid criminal tribunals, comprising elements belonging to national and international law, should be seen, in part, as vindication of Scelle's ideas on the international capacity of domestic courts, and as signs of the erosion of the distinction between national and international institutions. Still, some recent decisions aiming to classify hybrid courts as either national or international courts stress the difficulty of applying Scelle's integrative vision in a world dominated by clear-cut binary rules. See *Prosecutor v Taylor*, decision of 31 May 2004, paras 37–42, <http://www.sc-sl.org/SCSL-03-01-I-059.pdf> (Special Court for Sierra Leone); *Stanković* (17 May 2005), above, n 37.

332 Cassese is probably correct, however, in observing that Scelle's approach suffers from certain rigidity: it does not permit for the possibility that national courts may perform simultaneously functions under national and international law; it also fails to explain the role of a-national judicial organs (such as arbitral tribunals). Cassese, above, n 322, at 213, 218–19.

to criticism for offering an unrealistic vision of national courts as donning at times the mantle of international institutions and as acting in disregard of national interests. The theory's inability to capture the potentially *simultaneous* dual roles of national courts in fulfilling both national and international functions, and the doctrinal complexities that ensue thereof, thus appears to detract from its explanatory power.[333]

The American School of Informal Socialization

A less dogmatic, more pragmatic approach characterizes the work of some leading American international law scholars who have addressed the interrelations between national and international courts whether directly or indirectly. According to writers such as Anne-Marie Slaughter, the penetration of international law into domestic law, and the authorization of international courts to apply domestic law,[334] has contributed to the erosion of the boundaries between the two sets of law and, consequently, between national and international courts.[335] The main task of all judicial bodies has thus become application of the rule of law, regardless of its institutional or normative source. While Slaughter hesitates to declare the existence of a 'global legal system', she regards the various national and international courts as comprising a 'community of courts'.[336]

The existence of this diverse judicial community is sustained by self-awareness, a sense of a common judicial enterprise and cross-fertilization of ideas through informal interaction, what may be considered an indirect judicial dialogue.[337] In other words, the community is built over time through informal epistemological links and socialization processes.[338] The establishment of transnational dialogue between domestic institutions, across national boundaries, goes hand in hand with the disaggregated vision of international relations advocated by Slaughter and other writers.[339]

Another American writer, Jenny Martinez, has recently made an even bolder claim: the common culture that characterizes national and international courts, the commitment to the same rule of law ideals,[340] the application of the same body of law, and the repeated interactions between the two groups of judicial fora, justify

333 See ibid, at 219.

334 See eg, ICSID Convention, art 42(1).

335 See Harold H Koh, 'Transnational Legal Process', 75 *Neb L Rev* (1994) 181, 184.

336 Slaughter, above, n 304, at 192. Cf Helfer and Slaughter, above, n 280, at 282 (1997) (discussing the emergence of a 'community of law'). For criticism of this approach, see Mills and Stephens, above, n 265.

337 Slaughter, above, n 304, at 192–3.

338 For an analysis of this process, see Harold H Koh, 'How is International Human Rights Law Enforced?', 74 *Ind LJ* (1999) 1397, 1408–11; Koh, above, n 335, at 184.

339 See eg, Helfer and Slaughter, above, n 280, at 289.

340 See also Mattias Kumm, 'International Law in National Courts: The International Rule of Law and the Limits of the Internationalist Model', 44 *Va J Int'l L* (2003) 19, 22–4. But see Michael K Addo, 'Interim Measures for Protection of Rights Under the Vienna Convention on Consular Relations', 10 *EJIL* (1999) 713, 730 (arguing that in *Breard* the US Supreme Court preferred national interests over the need to promote the international rule of law).

regarding them as an emerging judicial system,[341] a building block of the 'federalism of free nations'.[342] While referring to system theories, Martinez has contended that the international judiciary is 'an evolving, complex and self-organizing system'.[343] She has therefore asserted a normative position claiming that courts should introduce systemic considerations within all their activities.[344]

One may note that the differences between this and the more traditional monist theories of Kelsen's and Scelle's are striking. The American school of thought deliberately stays away from advocating a 'grand theory' on the relationship between national and international law and implicitly rejects the notion of hierarchy. Instead, it explores actual interactions between judges, emphasizes cultural, ideological and epistemological identities and focuses on the inherently persuasive power of legal reasoning as the main integrative vehicle of the emerging community or system.[345] In addition, it does not pretend to be comprehensive (it encompasses only courts that regard themselves as part of the emerging community of courts—that is, those courts of liberal democracies)[346]—and refrains from distinguishing between national-international judicial interactions on the one hand, and interactions between courts of different nations on the other.[347] Hence, the American School's emphasis on social processes replaces all pretense of doctrinal coherence. Instead, it offers a hollow vision of a judicial system—an assortment of elements and institutions betraying no overarching 'order' and no vision of 'unity'.[348]

At first glance, the informal socialization approach bodes ill for the jurisdictional organization project explored in the present book. Despite suggestions to the contrary, the American approach is anti-systemic (or, more precisely, defines a judicial system in an extremely loose manner, omitting any meaningful references to normative and institutional coherence as organizing principles) and even chaotic. It rejects strict jurisdiction-allocating rules while cherishing the informal dynamics of influence and overt displays of comity. As a result, the support it might lend to jurisdictional regulation is limited: it appears to encourage primarily reduction

341 Jenny S Martinez, 'Towards an International Judicial System', 56 *Stan L Rev* (2003) 429, 436.

342 Ibid, at 461. The term 'federalism of free nations' is of course borrowed from Immanuel Kant, 'Perpetual Peace', *Political Writings* (H Reiss, ed, H B Nisbet trans, 1995) 94, 104–5.

343 Martinez, above, n 341, at 443–4. At the same time, Martinez posited that the international judiciary was 'dancing on the edge of chaos'. She does not explicitly explain, however, what might be the destabilizing factors that would ultimately doom the international judicial system.

344 Ibid, at 447.

345 Slaughter, above, n 304, at 217 ('the community must accept the value of persuasive rather than coercive authority').

346 Slaughter, above, n 304, at 194; Anne-Marie Slaughter, 'International Law in a World of Liberal States', 6 *EJIL* (1995) 503, 509–10, 524–5; Helfer and Slaughter, above, n 280, at 335 (noting, however, the possibility, on occasion, of exceptional dynamics involving liberal and non-liberal legal systems). For a criticism, see Koh, above, n 335, at 201–3.

347 Slaughter, above, n 304, at 204; Martinez, above, n 341, at 436.

348 For a possible definition of a legal system, see Jean Combacau, 'Le droit international: Bric-a-brac ou systeme?', 31 *Archives de philosphie de droit* (1996) 85, 86.

of some of the practical hardships associated with multiple proceedings and the promotion of judicial economy. Alas, the loose nature of the 'community' or 'emerging system' of national and international courts, whose components relate to one another in ways not far from the a-systemic relations maintained between courts of different nations, implies that legal inconsistencies are to be tolerated, at least under the present configuration. In other words, the informal socialization approach can support a rudimentary level of jurisdictional coordination but not more explicit measures of harmonization.

Still, the informal socialization approach contains some important insights that can facilitate jurisdictional coordination across legal systems: the approach emphasizes links over barriers, integration over separation, and dialogue over disregard. In embracing an open vision of the relations between national and international courts and downplaying the significance of the doctrinal differences dividing the two groups of judicial fora and their laws, this approach indirectly supports the claim that domestic jurisdictions can interact with their international counterparts. In addition, the transnational interest in effectively managing multi-fora litigation through abatement of duplicate judicial efforts and the consequent harassment of litigants, aptly identified by Slaughter and others, supports the utility of jurisdiction-regulating norms.[349]

Pluralism

Another challenge to the traditional dichotomy between national and international law—and, as a result, to the deep chasm that dualism purports to introduce between national and international proceedings—comes from the growing literature on legal pluralism. According to writers such as the German scholar, Gunther Teubner,[350] globalization and deregulation have brought about a decline in the centrality of the state as the direct regulator of various aspects of life inside and outside national borders.[351] The state's near monopoly over domestic and international norm-promulgation has been replaced with a more heterogeneous

[349] Slaughter, above, n 304, at 207; Martinez, above, n 341, at 463.

[350] For a full exposition of pluralism, see Klaus Günther, *Legal Pluralism and the Universal Code of Legality: Globalisation as a Problem of Legal Theory* (2003), <http://www.law.nyu.edu/clppt/program2003/readings/gunther.pdf>; Teubner, above, n 306; Teubner, above, n 285; Bouventura de Sousa Santos, 'Law: A Map of Misreading—Toward a Postmodern Conception of Law', 14 *Journal of Law and Society* (1987) 279, 293–4; Andreas Fischer-Lescano and Gunther Teubner 'Regime-Collisions: the Vain Search for Legal Unity in the Fragmentation of Global Law', 25 *Mich J Int'l* (1999) 999; Simon Roberts, 'After Government? On Representing Law Without the State', 68 *Modern Law Review* (2005) 1.

[351] Martti Koskenniemi and Päivi Leino, 'Fragmentation of International Law? Postmodern Anxieties', 15 *Leiden Journal of International Law* (2002) 553, 557 ('the role of the state has been transformed from legislator to a facilitator of self-regulating systems'); Andreas L Paulus, 'Commentary to Andreas Fischer-Lescano and Gunther Teubner: The Legitimacy of International Law and the Role of the State', 25 *Mich J Int'l L* (2004) 1047, 1048 ('globalization appears indeed characterized by a shift from territorial borders to functional boundaries').

field of law makers—professional associations,[352] international bureaucracies,[353] multinational corporations[354] and local communities, to name just a sample—each endowed with distinctive 'self-legitimating' ancillary rules.[355]

This diversification in the sources of law-making has contributed to the evaporation of the bright line separating the national from the international.[356] As a result, legal phenomena such as *lex mercatoria*[357] or regulation of Internet site addresses by the Internet Corporation for Assigned Names and Numbers (ICANN)[358] are being developed outside statal frameworks. Yet, such 'private legislation' have normative implications, domestically and internationally, which may exceed in influence many state-created laws.[359]

In such a diverse and multi-sourced legal universe, insistence upon the organization of law in two polar 'legal systems'—national law and international law—may no longer be tenable. Significantly, it has been alleged that traditional non-pluralist discourses chronically overlook influential legal phenomena that have no statal origins.[360] Pluralism therefore appears to challenge the descriptive accuracy of dualism and its normative legitimacy.

Pluralism, in its application to the topic of this treatise, is not necessarily expected to lend support to the proposition that courts should apply all potentially relevant norms to the disputes pending before them, regardless of their normative origin, be it national, international or non-statal.[361] However, pluralism may countenance the need to regulate 'inter-systematic' conflicts[362]—conflicts involving the application of norms derived from different origins (treaty, national/international, private/public regimes)—and situated, according to Teubner, in heterarchical relations vis-à-vis one another.[363] We can thus appreciate that the move from the traditional

352 John Flood and Eleni Skordaki, 'Normative Bricolage: Informal Rule-making by Accountants and Lawyers in Mega-insolvencies', *Global Law Without a State* (Gunther Teubner, ed, 1997) 109; Brian Bercusson, 'Globalizing Labour Law: Transnational Private Regulation and Countervailing Actors in European Labour Law', above, at 133. See eg, International Chamber of Commerce Dispute Resolution Rules <http://www.iccwbo.org/court/arbitration/id4199/index.html>; International Chamber of Commerce Rules of Conduct and Recommendations on Combating Extortion and Bribery, <http://www.iccwbo.org/uploadedFiles/ICC/policy/anticorruption/Statements/ICC_Rules_of_Conduct_and_Recommendations%20_2005%20Revision.pdf>.

353 See eg, Michael Barnett and Martha Finnemore, *Rules for the World: International Organizations in Global Politics* (2004); Sean D Murphy, *Principles of International Law* (2006) 9.

354 Jean-Philippe Robé, 'Multinational Enterprises: The Constitution of a Pluralistic Legal Order', *Global Law Without a State* (Gunther Teubner, ed, 1997) 45, 52–6; Peter D Mulchinski, '"Global Bukowina" Examined: Viewing the Multinational Enterprise as a Transnational Law-making Community', above, at 79, 80–5.

355 Teubner, above, n 306, at 18. But see Paulus, above, n 351, at 1054–5.

356 Koskenniemi and Leino, above, n 351, at 557. In fact, Teubner emphasizes the invisibility of boundaries in the new global law. Teubner, above, n 306, at 7–8.

357 See Hans-Joachim Mertens, '*Lex Mercatoria:* A Self-applying System beyond National Law?', *Global Law Without a State* (Gunther Teubner, ed, 1997) 31, 33–43.

358 See Donna L Howard, 'Trademarks and Service Marks and Internet Domain Names: Giving ICANN Deference', 33 *Ariz St LJ* (2001) 637, 655–63; Susan P Crawford, 'The ICANN Experiment', 12 *Cardozo J Int'l & Comp L* (2004) 409.

359 Teubner, above, n 306, at 3–4.

360 Ibid, at 6.

361 See eg, Robé, above, n 354, at 55 ('the monist thesis in unconvincing').

362 Teubner, above, n 306, at 8 ('A new law of conflicts is emerging on the basis of intersystemic, rather than international, conflicts').

363 Ibid, at 14.

dichotomy between national and international law to a rich panoply of normative systems (otherwise known as the 'fragmented legal discourse') under pluralism[364] lends conceptual support to the analogy drawn in Chapter 3 between the regulation of conflicts among specific regimes of international law and between proceedings conducted under national and international legal systems.

In addition, pluralism would seem to view with suspicion some of the legal classifications introduced by national and international courts. For example, it is questionable whether the linkage offered by some ICSID tribunals between contract claims and national law is accurate or even necessary[365] since one may adopt a view of contracts as independent, self-referential instruments, having intrinsic sources of validity.[366] Similarly, pluralists may dispute the very need to classify unique phenomena, such as BIT umbrella clauses, as giving rise to either a contractual claim *or* a BIT claim.[367] These objections to artificial classifications should arguably have gathered exceptional force in litigation before ICSID arbitral tribunals as, it would seem, that ICSID was created to accommodate disputes primarily on the basis of a-national contractual norms selected by the parties (regardless of the formal status of the specific contractual undertakings in national or international law).[368] By downplaying the importance of normative sources, pluralists seem to encourage courts to employ pragmatic—not doctrinal—measures to address conflicts of laws.

Normative systemization

So, the rise of informal socialization and pluralism may be suggestive of the failure of structuralism *à la* Kelsen or Scelle to portray a plausible image of the relationship between national and international courts. Indeed, the disorganized state of relations among the various international law institutions,[369] and the lingering doubts concerning the nature of national courts' involvement in the operation of the international legal system, render it highly unlikely that a credible vision of institutional systemization, encompassing both court systems, can be offered at present[370] (possible exceptions being specific treaty regimes, such as the EC or the

[364] Ibid.

[365] See *Vivendi II*, 41 ILM at 1154–6; *El Paso*, above, n 195, at para 77; *Pan American*, above, n 220, at paras 108–10; *Joy Mining*, 44 ILM at 83–5.

[366] Teubner, above, n 306, at 15–19.

[367] See *Noble Ventures*, above, n 217, at para 55 ('umbrella clause, when included in a bilateral investment treaty, introduces an exception to the general separation of States obligations under municipal and under international law').

[368] ICSID Convention, art 42; Schreuer, above, n 16, at 558–66. Schreuer did question, however, the theoretical and practical feasibility of a *contrat sans loi*. Ibid, at 564–6. Instead, he advocated resort to residual application of national and international law, pursuant to art 42(2) of the ICSID Convention. See also ibid, at 632–3.

[369] See Georges Abi-Saab, 'Fragmentation or Unification: Some Concluding Remarks', 31 *NYU J Int'l L & Pol* (1999) 919, 921; Yuval Shany, *The Competing Jurisdictions of International Courts and Tribunals* (2003) 93–4.

[370] Cf Martti Koskenniemi, 'Repetition as Reform: Georges Abi-Saab Cours General de droit international public', 9 *EJIL* (1998) 405, 411; David Kennedy, 'The Disciplines of International Law and Policy', 12 *Leiden JIL* (2000) 9, 83.

ECHR, where such relations have been institutionalized). Better prospects for the development of a general theory of normative systemization may, however, be in the offing.

While national and international courts do not function as a unitary judicial system, they sometimes apply a common body of law—specifically, international law. The norms of international law do possess, arguably, coherence and organization-generating features: they derive their legitimacy from a common normative source,[371] they are identified by common rules of recognition,[372] they include certain hierarchical features,[373] they comprise primary and secondary norms linked through 'operative relations'[374] and they serve a common yet amorphic global constituency.[375] This configuration arguably reveals hidden systemic aspirations—the international normative system's marked inclination to maintain internal coherence and organization.

So, I argue that whenever international law is applied by either national or international courts, its systemic attributes and presumed ambitions should be taken into account. The jurisdiction-regulating international law norms or rules, to be discussed in Part II, constitute important building blocks needed to maintain and enhance the systemic nature of international law and to sustain the utility of having different courts speak a 'common language'.[376] As a result, strong policy considerations support incorporation of these rules into the applicable body of international law. In other words, jurisdiction-regulating rules represent part of the context for the application of international law, ie, background principles, which condition resort to international law norms. Their role in this respect is not dissimilar to other international background rules, such as the rules of treaty interpretation or state responsibility.

371 See Abi-Saab, above, n 369, at 920–1.

372 International law's central rule of recognition is found in the Statute of the International Court of Justice, 26 June 1945, art 38, XV UNCIO Doc 355 (hereinafter ICJ Statute). See Pierre-Marie Dupuy, 'The Danger of Fragmentation or Unification of the International Legal System and the International Court of Justice', 31 *NYU J Int'l L & Pol* (1999) 791, 793; Georges Abi-Saab, 'Cours général de droit international public', 207 *Recueil de cours* (1996) 9, 122. The seminal work on the systemic importance of rules of recognition is, of course, H L A Hart's *The Concept of Law* (2nd edn, 1984) 92.

373 See eg, VCLT, art 53. UN Charter, art 103. According to Kelsen, normative hierarchy is the organizing principle of all legal systems. Hans Kelsen, *Introduction to the Problems of Legal Theory* (1934) 55.

374 See eg, Draft Articles on State Responsibility, arts 1–3. For elaboration on the requirement that the norms of a legal system should be arranged in operative relations, see Joseph Raz, *A Concept of a Legal System* (2nd edn, 1980) 183–5; Michel van de Kerchove and Françoise Ost, *Legal System Between Order and Disorder* (Ian Stewart, trans, 1994) 38–45, 50–5. See also Hart, above, n 372, at 30.

375 Abi-Saab, above, n 369, at 921; Georges Abi-Saab, 'Whither the International Community?' 9 *EJIL* (1998) 248, 251–3; Philip Allot, *Eunomia: New Order for a New World* (1990) 396; Philip Allot, *The Emerging Universal Legal System*, presented in an Amsterdam Center for International Law seminar on Theoretical Approaches to the Relationship between International and National Law (2002) (copy with author); Andreas Paulus, 'The Influence of the United States on the Concept of the "International Community"', *United States Hegemony and the Foundations of International Law* (Michael Byers and Georg Nolte, eds, 2003) 57, 57–60. Cf Ryan Goodman and Derek Jinks, 'Toward an Institutional Theory of Sovereignty', 55 *Stan L Rev* (2003) 1749, 1758 (discussing the emergence of a 'world polity').

376 See Francioni, above, n 256.

It should be noted that the proposed notion of normative systemization assumes the possibility of distinguishing between the institutional and normative components of a legal system, a distinction I have developed elsewhere at some length.[377] It suffices to recall here that the formal discipline of conflict of laws (or private international law) is based on this distinction, meaning that it calls upon those courts institutionally belonging to one legal system to apply norms derived from a foreign legal system. A strong case can be made that when applying such foreign norms, domestic courts ought to construe them, inter alia, in light of the foreign system's organizing principles (eg, hierarchy of sources, rules of interpretation, etc).[378] The normative argument I am making is, therefore, different from Scelle's: when national courts directly and explicitly apply international law, they do not lose their institutional affiliation as part of a national legal system; instead, in this specific context, they simultaneously serve as instruments for the application of international norms. In this last capacity they ought to apply these norms, as far as possible, in a proper manner—that is, in accordance with the norms' systematic environment. This duty faithfully to apply international law can be derived either from international law itself, or from domestic law rules that refer national courts to apply international law.[379] Hence, support for the application of jurisdiction-regulating rules may transcend the classic monism/dualism debate to become linked to international law norms themselves—to the degree that they are applicable before the relevant national or international court.

2.2.3 Interim conclusions

The theoretic survey conducted in this section suggests that relations between national and international courts may be conceptualized in ways other than those offered by dualism. While Kelsenian monism and Scelle's *dédoublement fonctionnel* juxtapose dualism with integrative normative and institutional structures, the informal socialization and pluralist schools of thought advocate flexible links across legal regimes and downplay the salience of formal normative and institutional structures. In the same vein, these latter approaches also challenge the hierarchy promoted by monism, in both its Kelsenian and Scellian variations.

Normative systemization—ie, the acknowledgement that international law itself contains systemic features—might overcome some of the difficulties that the conflicting structural and anti-structuralist approaches raise. Hence, the proper field for exploring the relationship between national and international courts might be not the institutional field but, rather, the normative arena.

377 Shany, above, n 369, at 104–6.

378 See eg, Restatement of the Law (2nd), Conflict of Laws, §4 (1971) ('the "local law" of a state is the body of standards, principles and rules, exclusive of its rules of Conflict of Laws, which the courts of that state apply in the decision of controversies brought before them').

379 Less compelling policy arguments support the introduction of the full gamut of international jurisdiction-regulating rules in situations where the competing national and international courts apply the same body of *national* law. While many of the rationales for abating multiple proceedings and

At the end of the day, however, it seems fair to conclude that no single theory pretending to explain the institutional or normative relations maintained between national and international courts enjoys universal acceptance. Hence, the resort by certain courts to one theory—dualism, monism, or hierarchy—in the absence of clear jurisdictional signifiers installed within the relevant legal instruments governing the work of national and international courts may imply a political or ideological choice on the part of the relevant judges. While this preference may be well justified in many cases (and, as discussed above, different paradigms may be more suitable to one or another type of interaction over certain subjects) it is hardly ever inevitable.

inconsistent judgments discussed continue to apply (eg, inconvenience to the parties, judicial economy), the international interest in preserving the coherence of the domestic legal system is less apparent. Furthermore, domestic competition-regulating rules may also apply in the case (as background principles to the substantive norms), rendering resort to international standards in this area redundant. In any event, I would argue that the application of certain flexible international jurisdiction-regulating rules, such as comity and *abus de droit* could be supported in such cases, too.

3

The Fragmentation of International Law

3.1 Fragmentation and Jurisdictional Interaction

The controversy surrounding the jurisdictional relations between national and international courts could be considered against the background of the contemporary debate concerning the structure of international law, a debate encompassing descriptive and normative elements.[380] This broader debate's outcome may have indirect implications for understanding the relations holding between the national and international legal systems and, therefore, relations between national and international courts: if international law is comprised of distinct self-contained regimes that may govern—in parallel—the same issues, then national legal systems can likewise be conceptualized as just another set of self-contained regimes that also seek to regulate the same issues.[381] If, on the other hand, international law contains significant unifying features that render it a unique form of regulation, then the application of national law by national courts generates a qualitatively different legal effect, which can hardly be reconciled with international dispute settlement.

An interesting analogy between international/international and national/international jurisdictional interactions was recently offered by a PCA arbitral tribunal in the *Iron Rhine* case, a case dealing with a dispute between Belgium and the Netherlands over the restoration of an old railway line. In reviewing the jurisdictional relations in place between the treaty-based arbitral proceedings and the ECJ, the tribunal drew an analogy between the relations holding under the EC legal order between national courts—had they been requested to review the same dispute—and the ECJ. Hence, it justified its decision not to defer to the jurisdiction of the ECJ through reliance on the argument that in an analogous situation, a national court could also have refrained from invoking the preliminary ruling

380 See eg, International Law Commission, Report on the Work of the Fifty-Sixth Session, Ch X, UN GAOR, 59th Sess, Supp No 10 (A/59/10)(2004).

381 Martti Koskenniemi has made this analogy in his report on the fragmentation of international law, submitted to the ILC. International Law Commission Study Group, 'Fragmentation of International Law: Difficulties arising from the Diversification and Expansion of International Law', UN Doc A/CN.4/L.682 (2006), at 12 (prepared by Martti Koskenniemi) ('The fragmentation of the international legal system into technical "regimes" ... is not too different from its traditional fragmentation into more or less autonomous territorial regimes called "national legal systems"'). See also ibid, at 79.

procedure.[382] This analogy appears to convey the arbitral tribunal's belief that from an ECJ perspective, the same need to protect Community jurisdiction from unwarranted disruption by external legal systems arises whether the disruptive norms originate, say, in Dutch Law or an international law treaty between the Netherlands and Belgium. While the positive rules of regulation that currently govern the two types of jurisdictional interactions may differ,[383] the policy considerations requiring or militating against jurisdictional coordination might be similar.

If this is true, then general principles useful for coordinating jurisdictions in one context may have relevance in other contexts as well. Indeed, as I shall explain immediately, one may find in international/international as well as national/international interaction cases similar disintegrative or integrative strategies for tackling the theoretical and practical problems arising out of multiple litigation. Hence, it might be useful to apply the lessons to be learned from the debate over how to address the fragmentation of international law to the present discussion. The fact that some prominent individuals have played key roles in judicial or arbitral proceedings involving both types of interactions—they have sat as arbitrators in international arbitration proceedings that took place alongside national adjudication as well as in international arbitration proceedings that took place alongside international adjudication—and have embraced similar approaches to the problems arising under these two scenarios, further encourages development of the analogy.[384]

It seems as if courts involved in jurisdictional interactions across specific international regimes—litigation of disputes falling under the scope of more than one specific legal regime (eg, trade law and human rights; regional environmental treaty and UNCLOS)—are often faced with a methodological choice between (a) disintegrating the dispute into specific claims under different legal instruments and treating only these aspects of the dispute that directly arise under the legal regime in question; or b) integrating the different yet closely related claims into one inclusive dispute while taking into consideration the potential influence of other relevant legal regimes. Adjudication under choice (a) is conducted exclusively in accordance with the laws and procedures of the specific regime at hand (hereinafter 'disintegrationism'), whereas the adjudicative process under choice (b) attempts to resolve the dispute in a manner that coordinates, as far as possible, the laws and procedures applicable in all potential dispute settlement proceedings which might take place (hereinafter 'integrationism').

To my mind, these conflicting strategies ultimately derive from alternative narratives of international law. Disintegrationism accepts the fragmentation of

[382] *Iron Rhine* (Belgium/Netherlands), Award of 24 May 2005, at paras 100–6 (PCA).

[383] Most obviously, art 234 of the EC Treaty governs preliminary references from national courts and tribunals but not international arbitral tribunals such as the PCA.

[384] For example, James Crawford sat as an arbitrator in *SGS v Pakistan* (national/international jurisdictional interaction) and *UNCLOS MOX Plant* (interaction between two international courts), and embraced similar positions on regulating jurisdictional interactions in both settings.

international law into more or less self-contained regimes, whereas integrationism emphasizes the unifying features of the international legal system, which transcend all the different regimes. Moreover, the choice between disintegrationist and integrationist methodologies also implies a political choice: disintegrative methods may imply a preference for the well-being of specific legal regimes over the systemic welfare of the international legal system.[385] Because disintegrationism discourages courts operating in one specific regime from considering the effects of judicial proceedings and legal pronouncements originating in other legal regimes, it insulates the regime in question from outside influences that might undermine its internal coherence and disrupt the attainment of its specific goals.[386] This particular choice may stem from a bias in favour of the relevant regimes' political goals, but also from scepticism regarding the harmonization project, or even despair with respect to the feasibility of overcoming the fragmentation characterizing international law.[387]

At the same time, integrative coordination of parallel jurisdictions encourages normative reconciliation across legal regimes. Hence, it sacrifices the 'purity' of specific regimes for the advancement of systemic interests—the improved coherence, workability and, arguably, legitimacy of international law in its entirety.[388] This attitude may also be construed as expressing confidence in the possible existence of an 'international system'[389] and the desirability of the systemization project.[390]

One may also link the choice between disintegrative and integrative methodologies to a wider debate on the objectives of dispute settlement in general, and the role of judges in particular. Integrative methods are more pragmatic in orientation and are, as a rule, more sensitive to the concerns of some of the immediate parties to litigation, who might be loath to engage in 'piecemeal' litigation of the same basic dispute before a multiplicity of judicial fora and are likely to be interested in comprehensive resolution of the dispute. Integrationism thus encourages judges to act as problem solvers and to harnesses judicial power to the task of

[385] ILC Study Group, above, n 381, at 120 (there is a 'structural bias' that results in the interpretation of texts in accordance with the priorities of the law-applying body); Koskenniemi and Leino, above, n 351, at 561–2.

[386] For a general discussion of the advantages of closed social systems, see Gunther Teubner, *Law as an Autopoietic System* (1993) 15–16. Teubner also posited that 'the adoption of an alien code for operations which are unique to a particular system means the "disintegration" of that system.' Ibid, at 104. However, he, too, accepted that public order interests could override particular arrangements adopted by specific sub-systems. Ibid, at 114.

[387] See eg, Georges Abi-Saab, above, n 369, at 925–6 (describing the pressures on the general system created by specialized regimes); Teubner, above, n 386, at 106 ('calls for reintegration appear hopelessly out of step with reality').

[388] Gilbert Guillaume, 'The Future of International Judicial Institutions', 44 *ICLQ* (1995) 848, 862; Shany, above, n 369, at 117–20. On the link between normative coherence and legitimacy, see Thomas M Franck, *The Power of Legitimacy Among Nations* (1990) 147–8.

[389] See eg, Abi-Saab, above, n 369, at 926; Joost Pauwelyn, 'How to Win a World Trade Organization Dispute Based on Non-World Trade Organization Law?', 37 *Journal of World Trade* (2003) 997, 1001.

[390] For a discussion of international law's systemic features, see Lowe, above, n 311, at 209–10; Shany, above, n 369, at 93–4.

adapting law to the challenges of an increasingly complex legal landscape.[391] At the same time, disintegrative methods might involve, to some degree, preference for doctrine over pragmatism.[392] This is because it appears to protect the doctrinal integrity of the specific regimes under which international courts operate even at the price of complicating the legal situation of the parties to disputes pending before a multiplicity of judicial bodies.

Significantly, disintegrationism should not be automatically equated with hermetic closure of specific regimes from all outside influences. Such a position would clearly be untenable as it would divest the law from its important mission of mediating between social goals and changing realities and social environments. Still, disintegrationists tend to invest the task of harmonizing incompatible legal regimes with international law-makers—states, international organizations and the like (by means of the adoption of harmonious treaty norms by all relevant regimes)—and not with judges or arbitrators, who should merely act as 'law-appliers'. Here, as in other legal contexts, judicial legislation raises sensitive questions of judicial capabilities and political legitimacy.[393]

Finally, one may note that disintegrationism encourages judges to apply clear-cut choice of law rules, which exclude application of extra-regime norms. This solution leads to the conservation of the court's precious judicial time (as the application of clear-cut rules is less time-consuming than are complicated and discretionary balancing formulas) but also discourages judges from pronouncing on the application of legal norms that might fall outside the scope of their formal mandate and professional expertise.[394]

3.2 Disintegrationism and Integrationism in Practice

3.2.1 Disintegrationism in action

How do disintegrationist and integrationist methods of jurisdictional regulation actually work? A disintegrative approach to regulation of jurisdictional interaction

[391] See eg, Karin Oellers-Frahm, 'Multiplication of International Courts and Tribunals and Conflicting Jurisdiction—Problems and Possible Solutions' 5 *Max Planck YB of UN Law* (2001) 67, 72. Different legal traditions might also influence the role of judges and dispute settlement. See Benedict Kingsbury, 'The International Legal Order', IILJ Working Paper 2003/1 (History and Theory of International Law Series), at 12 <http://www.iilj.org> (Anglo-French influence has pushed international law to focus on solving bilateral problems at the expense of addressing community interests).

[392] See Kingsbury, above, n 391, at 12 ('pragmatic problem-solving has been used to prevent any system-threatening crisis of fragmentation—but the theoretical problems can be expected eventually to unsettle this temporizing resolution').

[393] See eg, Thomas W Merrill, 'Can Originalism be Reconciled with Precedent', 22 *Const Commentary* (2005) 271, 274–7.

[394] Under this worldview, judges should not step out of the scope of their mandate and expertise to resort to the active importation of 'foreign' norms into specific treaty regimes, as this might undermine the coherence and unity of the regimes in question. See eg, *Las Palmeras*, Inter-Am Ct HR (Ser C) No 67 (2000), at paras 32–4 (preliminary objections) (the I/A CtHR is incompetent to examine allegations of independent violations of the Geneva Convention).

stresses the distinct normative existence of the legal instruments that underlie the different regimes that purport to regulate a factual dispute, and reaches the conclusion that, from a legal point of view, separate disputes are attached to different legal issues.[395] In other words, a single dispute may be *disintegrated* into different legal claims whose number correlates with the number of legal regimes that apply to the facts of the case. Significantly, resort to a disintegration strategy does not depend on the establishment of actual differences in the way that the substantive norms of the respective legal instruments regulate the issue at hand. In the words of ITLOS in its decision on the request for provisional measures in the *MOX* case:

> Even if the [regional environmental] Convention, the EC Treaty and Euratom Treaty contain rights or obligations similar to or identical with the rights or obligations set out in the Convention [on the Law of the Sea], the rights and obligations under those agreements have a *separate existence* from those under the Convention[396] (emphasis added).

This decision largely mirrors a previous ITLOS decision in the *Bluefin Tuna* case, where it was held that a controversy that falls within the scope of a regional fisheries convention, having its own dispute-settlement procedures, may also give rise to a separate dispute under UNCLOS, which is not governed by any provisions of the regional convention.[397]

If the parallel claims before the different competent judicial fora are necessarily distinct, then incompatible judgments can never be rendered: violation of one set of 'separate norms', does not necessarily imply violation of a different set of 'separate norms'. Thus, under disintegrationism, jurisdictional conflicts may become normatively and descriptively impossible, and no doctrinal need to regulate the parallel jurisdictions of the various courts that address different aspects of the dispute will consequently arise. So, practical problems stemming from the fragmentation of general international law into multiple legal regimes, and the ensuing jurisdictional conflicts between the respective international courts, could be overcome through application of clear-cut choice of law rules. These rules would authorize judicial institutions to prefer intra-regime norms over norms derived from other sources.

Still, the utility of disintegrationism as a jurisdiction-regulating mechanism depends on the ability to maintain sharp divisions between the law applicable before each of the competing litigation fora: the separateness of the different litigation procedures needs to be maintained through confirmation of the separate existence

395 For a discussion of the 'same issues' test underlying the application of traditional jurisdiction-regulating rules, such as *res judicata* and *lis alibi pendens*, see below, Chapter 4.

396 *MOX Plant* (Ireland v UK), 41 ILM 405, 413 (2002) (hereinafter *MOX* (ITLOS)). For support of the proposition that specific regimes may develop specific principles of interpretation, see ILC Study Group (2006), above, n 381, at 77.

397 *Southern Bluefin Tuna* (Australia and New Zealand v Japan), 38 ILM 1624, 1632 (1999) ('the fact that the Convention of 1993 applies between the parties does not exclude their right to invoke the provisions of the Convention on the Law of the Sea in regard to the conservation and management of southern bluefin tuna').

of the related overarching legal regimes (eg, the separate nature of UNCLOS and EC law), but also through interpretive moves, meant to deny the competence of one judicial body to apply 'external' norms (norms originating in another regime). Otherwise, one might again encounter situations of jurisdictional overlap—different courts authorized to apply the same norms to the same issues contested by the same parties. Such situations may, in theory, compel the involved courts to address the consequences of inconsistent interpretations of the same body of law by different judicial bodies. This development would bring back—through the 'back door'—the need for jurisdiction-regulating measures. It could also undercut the attractiveness of the precise dichotomies provided by disintegrationism and deny some of the benefits that excluding external norms from judicial proceedings before a specific court may achieve (eg, simplifying procedures, discouraging judges from pronouncing on norms that fall outside their expertise). In short, the greater is the normative overlap between different international courts, the less effective are disintegrationist methods. As a result, supplementary interpretative strategies may be required to sustain disintegrationism.

This analysis might explain, for instance, some of the controversial interpretive moves adopted by the OSPAR arbitration tribunal in another phase of the life of the *MOX* case (OSPAR is a regional environmental treaty providing, inter alia, for disclosure of information on projects that could potentially harm the environment),[398] which involved a challenge by Ireland to the UK's refusal to provide it with comprehensive information on the operating plans of a processing facility for spent nuclear fuel in Sellafield, England.[399] Although article 32 of the OSPAR Convention authorizes arbitral tribunals to address any dispute over the interpretation and application of the Convention and to decide those disputes 'according to the rules of international law and, in particular, those of the Convention',[400] the majority view was that the tribunal's competence was limited to the application of OSPAR law:

> [T]he competence of a tribunal established under the OSPAR Convention was not intended to extend to obligations the Parties might have under other instruments (unless, of course, parts of the OSPAR Convention included a direct renvoi to such other instruments). Interpreting Article 32(6)(a) otherwise would transform it into an unqualified and comprehensive jurisdictional regime, in which there would be no limit ratione materiae to the jurisdiction of a tribunal established under the OSPAR Convention. Here, there is no indication that the Parties to the OSPAR Convention have, in their individual capacities, submitted themselves to such a comprehensive jurisdictional regime with respect to any other

[398] Convention for the Protection of the Marine Environment of the North-East Atlantic, 22 Sept 1992, 32 ILM 1069 (1992) (hereinafter OSPAR).

[399] *Access to Information under Article 9 of the OSPAR Convention* (Ireland v UK), 42 ILM 1118, 1136 (2003) (hereinafter *MOX* (OSPAR)). For a discussion, see Yuval Shany, 'The First MOX Plant Award: Coordinating between Competing Environmental Regimes and Dispute Settlement Procedures', 17 *Leiden JIL* (2004) 815.

[400] OSPAR, art 32(1), 32(6)(a).

international tribunal. Nor is it reasonable to suppose that they would have accepted such a jurisdictional regime through the vehicle of the OSPAR Convention.[401]

As a result, the tribunal held that no recourse ought to be made to the EC Directives that regulate environmental information disclosure. Configuration of the OSPAR dispute-settlement procedure as legally self-contained[402] facilitated the tribunal's determination of the lack of need to coordinate OSPAR proceedings with any prospective proceedings before the ECJ:

Each of the OSPAR Convention and Directive 90/313 is an independent legal source that establishes a distinct legal regime and provides for different legal remedies. The United Kingdom recognizes Ireland's right as an EU Member State to challenge the implementation of the Directive in the United Kingdom's domestic legal system before the ECJ. Similarly, a Contracting Party to the OSPAR Convention, with its elaborate dispute settlement mechanism, should be able to question the implementation of a distinct legal obligation imposed by the OSPAR Convention in the arbitral forum, namely this designated Tribunal... The similar language of the two legal instruments, as well as the fact that the 1992 Regulations are an implementing instrument for both Directive 90/313 and the OSPAR Convention, does not limit a Contracting Party's choice of a legal forum to only one of the two available, ie, either the ECJ or an OSPAR tribunal.[403]

In contrast, the dissenting arbitrator, Gavan Griffith, was of the view that '[t]he Tribunal cannot be confined to international conventional law or the language of the OSPAR Convention exclusively'.[404] Griffith went on to advocate reliance on EC law and the Aarhus Convention[405] as parts of the applicable law.[406] However, Griffith did not consider the possible implications of his position on the need to regulate the jurisdictional interaction between the OSPAR and ECJ proceedings.

Another example of disintegrationism at play in construing applicable law can be found in the aforementioned *Iron Rhine* arbitral award, issued by a PCA arbitral tribunal. In considering whether article 292 of the EC Treaty bars the exercise of jurisdiction by non-ECJ judicial fora,[407] the tribunal held that the application of EC law is not conclusive with respect to the issues at hand and that the dispute

[401] *MOX* (OSPAR), 42 ILM at 1136. The tribunal supported its conclusions on the proper interpretation of art 32(6) by invoking the *expressio unius est exclusio alterius* principle: since one particular OSPAR provision did contain explicit reference to non-OSPAR international law standards, a restrictive interpretation of all other provisions (in which no such mention was made) was required.

[402] See *MOX* (OSPAR), 42 ILM at 1144 ('the OSPAR Convention contains a particular and self-contained dispute resolution mechanism in Article 32, in accordance with which this Tribunal acts').

[403] Ibid. The OSPAR tribunal cited with approval the dicta employed by ITLOS regarding the separate existence of different treaty norms containing similar or identical language. *MOX* (ITLOS), 41 ILM at 413.

[404] *MOX* (OSPAR), 42 ILM at 1161 (dissenting opinion of Griffith).

[405] Convention on Access to Information, Public Participation in Decision-making and Access to Justice in Environmental Matters, 25 June 1998, 38 ILM 517 (1999).

[406] *MOX* (OSPAR), 42 ILM at 1162–5 (dissenting opinion of Griffith).

[407] EC Treaty, art 292 ('Member States undertake not to submit a dispute concerning the interpretation or application of this Treaty to any method of settlement other than those provided for therein').

can be decided exclusively on the basis of non-EC legal instruments.[408] Hence, the tribunal was of the view that the dispute could be resolved outside the scope of application of article 292.

The *Iron Rhine* decision demonstrates once more the possibility of circumventing the application of jurisdiction-regulating rules by excluding the law applicable in one set of potential proceedings (EC law) from the parallel set of proceedings (PCA arbitration). This legal manoeuvre leads first to the identification of two separate disputes, governed by two different bodies of law (EC law and non-EC law). Second, it results in the non-application of jurisdiction-regulating norms: since the two disputes are no longer 'the same', rules designed to curb multiple proceedings are no longer applicable. However, the tribunal's methodology is characterized by logical circularity: the conclusion that article 292 was irrelevant because EC law was not conclusive required in itself an interpretation of EC law by the tribunal; however, the consideration of EC law by a tribunal other than the ECJ seems to contradict the language and spirit of article 292.[409]

Arguably, the extensive literature on the 'open-ended' or 'self-contained' nature of applicable law provisions governing the work of specific international courts—most notably, the power of WTO panels and the Appellate Body to apply non-WTO law[410]—may have important implications for the need to coordinate adjudication before these bodies with other dispute settlement processes. Whereas application of external norms by such courts highlights the similarities of multi-faceted disputes—notwithstanding their pendency before different dispute settlement bodies—the exclusion of external norms underscores the uniqueness of the adjudicative process under the regime in question.

3.2.2 Integrationism in action

Despite the benefits of doctrinal clarity and practical ease that accompany disintegrationism, one can also identify alternative, integrative, methods of coordination between multiple proceedings in the practice of international courts. Such integrationist measures, which are, arguably, more nuanced and thus more difficult to apply, emphasize the pragmatic need to reconcile the various obligations of the parties and the multiple procedures that examine their activities. They strive, in effect, to acknowledge the real difficulties that complex legal situations entail. In the

[408] *Iron Rhine*, above, n 382, at paras 119–20, 137–41.

[409] See Lavranos, above, n 319, at 231.

[410] The WTO DSB has explicitly rejected its depiction as, 'self-contained'. *US–Standards for Reformulated and Conventional Gazoline*, 35 ILM 603, 621 (1996). However, the precise status of general international law under WTO law remains unclear. For a discussion, see Joost Pauwelyn, *Conflict of Norms in Public International Law: How WTO Law Relates to Other Rules of International Law* (2003) 478–86; Lorand Bartels, 'Applicable Law in WTO Dispute Settlement Proceedings', 35 *Journal of World Trade* (2001) 499, 512–18; Koskenniemi and Leino, above, n 351, at 571–4.

words of the UNCLOS arbitral tribunal in the *Southern Bluefin Tuna* case, a case demonstrating an instance of jurisdictional interplay between dispute-settlement arrangements under UNCLOS and a regional fisheries agreement:

[T]he Parties to this dispute—the real terms of which have been defined above—are the same Parties grappling not with two separate disputes but with what in fact is a single dispute arising under both Conventions. To find that, in this case, there is a dispute actually arising under UNCLOS which is distinct from the dispute that arose under the [1993 Convention for the Conservation of South Bluefin Tuna] would be *artificial*[411] (emphasis added).

As a result, the arbitral tribunal held that the dispute settlement procedures provided for in article 16 of the regional fisheries convention (the compromissory clause), also governed parallel disputes under UNCLOS:

The Tribunal accepts Article 16 of the 1993 Convention as an agreement by the Parties to seek settlement of the instant dispute by peaceful means of their own choice. It so concludes even though it has held that this dispute, while centered in the 1993 Convention, also implicates obligations under UNCLOS.[412]

Similarly, in the *MOX* (UNCLOS) case, an arbitral tribunal created pursuant to Part XV of UNCLOS was unwilling to embrace the distinction between UNCLOS law and non-UNCLOS law, which was suggested by ITLOS in an earlier stage of the proceedings.[413] Instead, it accepted that its jurisdiction was intimately linked to the way in which EC law governing the construction and operation of nuclear fuel processing plants was to be construed by the ECJ:

[T]here is a real possibility that the European Court of Justice may be seised of the question whether the provisions of the Convention on which Ireland relies are matters in relation to which competence has been transferred to the European Community and, indeed, whether the exclusive jurisdiction of the European Court of Justice, with regard to Ireland and the United Kingdom as Member States of the European Community, extends to the interpretation and application of the Convention as such and in its entirety... Until these issues are definitively resolved, there remain substantial doubts whether the jurisdiction of the Tribunal can be firmly established in respect of all or any of the claims in the dispute.[414]

Hence, the tribunal was of the view that article 292 of the EC Treaty might govern the proceedings, notwithstanding the fact they were brought under UNCLOS rather than EC law. Furthermore, in contradistinction to the *Iron Rhine* decision, the tribunal was of the view that ascertaining the relevance of EC law to the case at

[411] *Southern Bluefin Tuna* (Australia and NZ v Japan), 39 ILM 1359, 1388 (2000). See also *MOX Plant* (Ireland v UK), 42 ILM 1187 (2003) (hereinafter *MOX* (UNCLOS)); Case C-459/03, *Commission v Ireland* [2006] ECR I-04635, at para 120 (hereinafter *MOX* (ECJ)).

[412] *Southern Bluefin Tuna*, 39 ILM at 1388.

[413] *MOX* (UNCLOS), 42 ILM 1187.

[414] Ibid, at 1190–1.

hand ultimately fell within the jurisdiction of the ECJ and that it would be improper for the arbitral tribunal to rule on the matter (even as an ancillary issue).[415] This led the tribunal to stay the proceedings before it and defer to the ECJ's judgment on the applicability of article 292. The policy considerations underlying this last decision (which, arguably, supported other integrative moves adopted by the tribunal) were explained by the tribunal in the following terms:

> [A] procedure that might result in two conflicting decisions on the same issue would not be helpful to the resolution of the dispute between the Parties.[416]

Interestingly enough, in the 2006 *MOX* (ECJ) judgment on the compliance of Ireland with its obligations under article 292 of the EC Treaty, the ECJ has also adopted a broad view of the applicable law before it, effectively incorporating large parts of UNCLOS into EC law.[417] It also opined that, in principle, it might be possible for the UNCLOS arbitration tribunal to apply EC law to the dispute at hand:

> The act of submitting a dispute of this nature to a judicial forum such as the Arbitral Tribunal involves the risk that a judicial forum other than the Court will rule on the scope of obligations imposed on the Member States pursuant to Community law.[418]

The broad construction of the applicable law before the ECJ and the UNCLOS arbitral tribunal facilitated the ECJ in finding that overlapping jurisdictions exist, and that, as a result, the two relevant jurisdiction-regulating provisions—article 292 of the EC Treaty and article 282 of UNCLOS[419]—apply, with each of which confirming the exclusivity of ECJ jurisdiction over parallel disputes.

The *ECJ MOX* judgment can also be understood as critical of the approach taken by the *Iron Rhyne* tribunal.[420] This is because the ECJ objected to the competence of other international tribunals to render an interpretation of Community law regarding jurisdictional questions, even in ancillary matters:

> It is for the Court, should the need arise, to identify the elements of the dispute which relate to provisions of the international agreement in question which fall outside its jurisdiction.[421]

415 Ibid, at 1191. 416 Ibid. 417 *MOX* (ECJ), above, n 411, at para 121.

418 Ibid, at para 177. See also ibid, para 148 ('It is also common ground that those Community measures were invoked by Ireland pursuant to Article 293(1) of the Convention, which provides that a tribunal such as the Arbitral Tribunal is to "apply this Convention and other rules of international law not incompatible with this Convention"').

419 UNCLOS, art 282 provides that: 'If the States Parties which are parties to a dispute concerning the interpretation or application of this Convention have agreed, through a general, regional or bilateral agreement or otherwise, that such dispute shall, at the request of any party to the dispute, be submitted to a procedure that entails a binding decision, that procedure shall apply in lieu of the procedures provided for in this Part, unless the parties to the dispute otherwise agree.'

420 Since the arbitral award in *Iron Rhine* was issued only six days before the ECJ judgment, it is not clear to what degree the ECJ was even aware of it.

421 *MOX* (ECJ), above, n 411, at para 135.

3.3 Analogies to the National/International Relationship

3.3.1 The ICSID cases

A similar choice between disintegrative regulation and integrative coordination is available in the context of the relations between national and international courts. Indeed, dualism itself may be described as a disintegrative method of regulation, one that applies an exclusion rule emphasizing the formal sources of authority of the relevant norms—national or international law—in ways that obviate the doctrinal need for regulation of any jurisdictional interaction between national and international courts. So, application of a disintegrative methodology is expected to resist the direct normative relevance for international courts of judicial decisions formally grounded in domestic law (even if domestic law mirrors the contents of the international law norms applicable by international courts) and vice versa. At the same time, some of the more pragmatic or problem solving-oriented coordination strategies discussed herein—such as deference to decisions of other courts or broad interpretation of applicable law provisions—may be described as integrative in their orientation.

Review of the language and methodology employed in some of the jurisdictional interaction cases discussed in Chapter 1 highlights the linkage between the fragmentation and national/international courts debates. This relationship is, perhaps, most apparent in the ICSID cases on the relationship between contract claims and treaty claims, discussed below. However, a choice between disintegrationist and integrationist strategies may be available in other relevant contexts as well.

To my mind, the *Vivendi II* and *SGS v Pakistan* decisions can be analysed as disintegrationist in their orientation: first, they offer a disintegrative vision, with closely-related disputes neatly divided into separate analytic categories, based on different sources of applicable law. In the words of the ad hoc Committee in *Vivendi II*:

> [W]hether there has been a breach of the BIT and whether there has been a breach of contract are different questions. Each of these claims will be determined by reference to its own proper or applicable law—in the case of the BIT by international law; in the case of the Concession Contract, by the proper law of the contract, in other words, the law of Tucuman.[422]

Consequently, the arbitral tribunals in both cases were of the view that jurisdiction-regulating norms derived from one instrument (ie, the contractual forum-selection clause) do not apply with regard to the separate dispute existing under the other relevant legal instrument (the BIT)—a conclusion comparable to that reached by ITLOS in the *Bluefin Tuna* and *MOX* cases, as well as the arbitration tribunals in *MOX* (OSPAR) and *Iron Rhine*.

422 *Vivendi II*, 41 ILM at 1154. This conclusion was cited with approval by the *SGS v Pakistan* arbitral tribunal. *SGS v Pakistan*, 42 ILM at 1313–5.

Furthermore, *SGS v Pakistan* demonstrates the link between the resort to rules of exclusion and the need to apply restrictive rules of interpretation. Although the tribunal explicitly acknowledged the seemingly intertwined nature of contract and treaty claims,[423] it found a way to avoid the 'complexities' associated with overlapping jurisdictions: it construed both the scope of its subject matter jurisdiction and applicable law narrowly, to exclude contract claims. This was done notwithstanding the open-ended language of the relevant BIT clauses[424] (article 9 refers to ICSID 'disputes with respect to investments'; article 11—the umbrella clause—requires parties to 'constantly guarantee the observance of the commitments it has entered into with respect to the investments of the investors of the other Contracting Party').[425] In the same vein, the arbitral tribunal questioned the authority of the Pakistani arbitrator (invested, under the contract, with jurisdiction over contract claims) also to review BIT claims.[426] Hence, according to the tribunal, not only were the claims separable, but so also were the jurisdictions and laws applicable in the national and international fora.

The policy rationale underlying the narrow construction of jurisdiction and applicable law has been further elaborated in the recent *El Paso* ICSID case, where the arbitrators explained that the exclusion of contract claims from the relevant BIT umbrella clause was needed, inter alia, to avoid blurring the distinction between the national and international legal orders.[427] This line of reasoning seems to view preservation of the separate nature of national and international law as one objective of interpretation in international arbitration cases.

One can argue that the methodology employed in *SGS v Pakistan* resembles that used by the OSPAR arbitral tribunal in the *MOX* case:[428] narrow construction of jurisdiction in order to exclude claims grounded in external legal instruments, exclusion of external instruments from the applicable law governing the case and, as a result, refusal to consider the effect of a jurisdiction-regulating rule that might govern the parallel claims. Such disintegrative methodology has been

[423] *SGS v Pakistan*, 42 ILM at 1314 ('BIT claims and contract claims appear reasonably distinct in principle. Complexities, however, arise on the ground, as it were, particularly where, as in the present case, each party claims that one tribunal (this Tribunal or the PSI Agreement arbitrator) has jurisdiction over both types of claims which are alleged to co-exist').

[424] Ibid, at 1318 ('we do not see anything in Article 9 or in any other provision of the BIT that can be read as vesting this Tribunal with jurisdiction over claims resting ex hypothesi exclusively on contract'). It is perhaps interesting to note that the *SGS v Pakistan* arbitral tribunal suggested that a narrow reading of the umbrella clause would help protect host states from being dragged into international arbitration over contract claims in violation of contractual undertakings to litigate them before national fora. Ibid, at 1319. Yet, this position is somewhat odd given the tribunal's willingness to tolerate parallel contract and treaty claim proceedings over the same investment, arguably, in violation of the same contractual undertakings.

[425] Pakistan/Swiss BIT, above, n 198.

[426] *SGS v Pakistan*, 42 ILM at 1316 ('We are not persuaded that SGS's BIT claims against Pakistan are subject to the jurisdiction of the Islamabad arbitrator').

[427] *El Paso*, above, n 195, at para 77. See also *Pan American*, above, n 220, at para 111 ('These farreaching consequences of a broad interpretation of the so-called umbrella clauses [are] quite destructive of the distinction between the national legal orders and the international legal order').

[428] *MOX* (OSPAR), 42 ILM 1118.

applied by most investment arbitration tribunals that were called upon to determine the interplay between jurisdiction-regulating clauses in cases involving contract and treaty claims.[429] This is, perhaps, suggestive of the attractiveness of clear-cut and easy-to-apply disintegrationism.

At the same time, some of the ICSID decisions discussed in Chapter 1 reveal what appears to be integrationist thinking. In *Vivendi I*, the ICSID tribunal cited the practical impossibility of distinguishing between the investor's contract claims and its treaty claims as the reason for its decision to apply the contractual forum-selection clause vis-à-vis the treaty claims—ie, the tribunal chose to address the two claims under a single integrative legal framework:

> [T]he nature of the facts supporting most of the claims presented in this case make it impossible for the Tribunal to distinguish or separate violations of the BIT from breaches of the Concession Contract without first interpreting and applying the detailed provisions of that agreement.[430]

Such dicta come rather close to the language employed by the *Bluefin Tuna* UNCLOS arbitral tribunal regarding the 'artificiality' of identifying distinct disputes under UNCLOS and the regional fisheries treaty.[431] The result of the integrative approach employed in the two cases is also comparable: in both cases, the tribunals were willing to carry over the effect of a compromissory clause derived from one body of applicable law to proceedings based on another, yet closely related, body of law.

Parallels could also be drawn between the decision of the ICSID arbitral tribunal in *SGS v Philippines* and the decision of the UNCLOS arbitral tribunal in the *MOX* case.[432] As noted previously, the ICSID tribunal rejected the narrow interpretation of the analogous BIT provisions offered by its predecessor in *SGS v Pakistan*. Instead, it adopted a broad reading of the relevant BIT umbrella clause and the BIT jurisdictional clause, stating explicitly that:

> [D]rawing technical distinctions between causes of action arising under the BIT and those arising under the investment agreement is capable of giving rise to overlapping proceedings and jurisdictional uncertainty. It may be necessary to draw such distinctions in some cases, but it should be avoided to the extent possible, in the interests of the efficient resolution of investment disputes by the single chosen forum.[433]

The conclusion that both national and international tribunals may exercise concurrent jurisdiction over the investor's contract claims led the ICSID tribunal to apply a jurisdiction-regulating rule (the contractual forum-selection clause), resulting in its decline of jurisdiction over these claims; furthermore, the tribunal

[429] See eg, *Occidental*, above, n 179, at paras 50–2; *Wena*, 41 ILM at 940; *Azurix*, 43 ILM at 277; *Vivendi I*, 40 ILM at 438–9; *Loewen*, 42 ILM at 819, 833; *Anaconda*, 13 Iran–US CTR at 224; *Salini*, 44 ILM at 589.

[430] *Vivendi I*, 40 ILM at 428–9.

[431] *Southern Bluefin Tuna*, 39 ILM at 1388.

[432] *MOX* (UNCLOS), 42 ILM 1187.

[433] *SGS v Philippines*, above, n 208, at para 132(c).

opined that the (potentially) remaining treaty claims were intertwined with contractual claims and that as a result, resolution of the first in isolation of the latter was 'inappropriate'.[434] Since national courts had been invested with the sole authority to determine the contractual claims, the tribunal held that in the current circumstances, it would be 'premature' for it to address the treaty claims. It thus suspended the proceedings until local courts in the Philippines had decided that part of the case assigned to them by the parties.[435]

There are obvious similarities between the analysis employed in *SGS v Philippines* and in the UNCLOS *MOX* arbitral decision on jurisdiction: in both cases, the tribunal acknowledged the existence of a jurisdictional overlap between itself and another court; in both cases, the tribunal was willing to invoke a jurisdiction-regulating rule originating in an external instrument, foreign to the treaty establishing the arbitral tribunal (the commercial contract, not the BIT; the EC Treaty, not UNCLOS); and in both cases the tribunal accorded temporal priority to the parallel proceedings by reason of its preliminary nature, together with the overriding character of the relevant jurisdiction-regulating clause (in *SGS v Philippines*, the contractual clause was deemed *lex specialis* vis-à-vis the BIT; in *MOX* (UNCLOS), article 282 of UNCLOS itself accords priority to non-UNCLOS jurisdictional provisions). The link between the two decisions is further underscored by the explicit reference in *SGS v Philippines* to the UNCLOS arbitral decision, and by the two tribunals' choice of similar jurisdiction-regulating language.[436]

3.3.2 Other parallels

While less obvious, other decisions of national and international courts on the regulation of their jurisdictional interaction can be analysed in disintegrationist/integrationist terms. For example, the application of legal dualism so as to exclude the effect of legal proceedings taking place within the national legal system on proceedings taking place within the international legal system, and vice versa, has the effect of disaggregating a single dispute into two separate disputes under national as well as international law. Hence, the PCIJ cases on the irrelevance of proceedings before mixed arbitral tribunals or the US Supreme Court's position regarding the non-self-executing nature of ICJ decisions, discussed in Chapter 1, are comparable to the position taken by ITLOS with respect to the irrelevance of parallel proceedings, pursuant to non-UNCLOS law, and the position taken by the OSPAR

[434] Ibid, at para 162.

[435] Ibid. See also ibid, at para 174 ('the Philippines' responsibility under Article X(2) and IV of the BIT—a matter which does fall within its jurisdiction—is subject to "the factual predicate of a determination" by the Regional Trial Court of the total amount owing by the Respondent').

[436] See eg, *SGS v Philippines*, above, n 208, at para 162 ('there being an unresolved dispute as to the amount payable, for the Tribunal to decide on the claim in isolation from a decision by the chosen forum under the CISS Agreement is inappropriate and premature'); *MOX* (UNCLOS), 42 ILM at 1191 ('the Tribunal considers that it would be inappropriate for it to proceed further with hearing the Parties on the merits of the dispute in the absence of a resolution of the problems referred to').

arbitration tribunal relating to the lack of effect of potential ECJ proceedings, based on an EC Directive, on OSPAR arbitral proceedings.

At the same time, attempts by national courts to give effect to international judgments, either as independently binding sources of law or as persuasive authorities on the contents of international law norms (which are part of the law of the land) may be viewed as integrative in their orientation. This is because they strive to harmonize between the parties' rights and obligations under different legal orders.

3.3.3 Interim conclusions

In sum, one can draw analogies between the policy and methodological choices that govern the regulation of jurisdictional relations between different international courts and between national and international courts. Arguably, such choices are always influenced by visions of legal arrangements as comprising either closed or open legal systems whose interaction with their legal environment may be confined or intensive. In addition, such choices are influenced by conflicting positions on the role of courts and judges: whereas disintegration focuses on the norm-applying function of the judge and favours doctrinal clarity, integrationism stresses the pragmatic dispute-settling function of courts and attempts to tackle head-on the complexities of disputes subject to parallel jurisdictions.

The analogy between regulation of international/international jurisdictions and national/international jurisdictions may facilitate a better understanding of judicial interpretive strategies. By explaining dualism (and to a lesser degree, hierarchy) as a disintegrationist measure, the analysis exposes some of the policy considerations that support—or oppose—this jurisprudential position. Furthermore, by highlighting the link between disintegration/integration and specific interpretive manoeuvres—meaning a broad or narrow construction of what constitutes 'the same dispute' (a point further developed in Chapter 4), applicable law, and jurisdictional provisions—the analogy helps us appreciate the results of such interpretive moves, while it fosters debate over the desirability of their ultimate goals.

PART II

REGULATING RELATIONS BETWEEN NATIONAL AND INTERNATIONAL COURTS

4

The Feasibility of Regulation: Do National and International Proceedings Overlap?

Part I of this book established that there is some room for arguing that national courts might engage in jurisdictional interaction with international courts, and that a case could be made in favour of regulation of such interactions. Furthermore, it was shown that dualism and hierarchy do not always provide satisfactory or realistic answers to the problems associated with such jurisdictional interactions. While they can provide national and international courts with easy-to-apply rules of exclusion or jurisdictional primacy, such solutions are often artificial and incompatible with the problem-solving role of the judiciary, the interests of all parties participating in multiple litigation and general considerations of judicial economy and normative coherence. Hence, other regulatory solutions need to be explored.

Part II examines the possibility of applying to jurisdictional interactions between national and international courts jurisdiction-regulating rules originally developed, by and large, to regulate jurisdictional conflicts between different courts operating within the same legal system (a domestic legal system or the international legal system). While the application of most of these rules (particularly, those discussed in Chapter 5) depends on the way in which the relations between national and international courts are conceived, other regulatory solutions (discussed in Chapter 6) are more flexible in nature and thus more readily applicable, even to interactions occurring within dualistic or hierarchical paradigms. Given their discretionary nature, these solutions can be considered as 'soft harmonizing tools'.

Chapter 4 provides background to a discussion of the possibility of applying the rules offered in Chapters 5 and 6 to interactions between national and international courts. Since the application of jurisdiction-regulating rules to parallel proceedings normally depends on the fulfilment of several prerequisites—especially, the need for establishing the identical nature of the parties and issues at stake—it is sensible to explore the potential relevance of these prerequisites to the present context. If the prerequisites are transposable to the national/international context, then jurisdiction-regulating rules, such as forum selection undertakings, *lis alibi pendens* and *res judicata*, could conceivably apply to jurisdictional interactions between national and international courts. This conclusion would hold, however, provided that two additional prerequisites of a more preliminary nature are met: (1) the regulated interactions are not configured in a hierarchical manner; and

(2) the judicial bodies involved in jurisdictional interactions are authorized to apply international jurisdiction-regulating rules either by virtue of direct reliance on international law or on domestic law rules that mirror international law in their substance.

Given the preliminary nature of these last two conditions, the first two sections of Chapter 4 will briefly address their relevance to the topic at hand. The better part of the chapter will then address the potential applicability of 'same parties' and 'same issues' criteria, developed in national/national and international/international jurisdictional interaction contexts, to interactions between national and international courts.

4.1 Non-Hierarchical Context

From a pragmatic point of view, jurisdictional-regulation may be useful in either a vertical or horizontal jurisdictional setting—such as when one set of courts is deemed superior to the other or when the two sets of courts are viewed as more or less equal judicial alternatives to one another. Still, the contents of the regulatory scheme and its level of density may differ as a result of the shift in paradigms: this is because the principle of finality plays a radically different role under each paradigm (*res judicata* may apply in a horizontal context among parallel courts; whereas inferior court decisions can never bind superior courts in a vertical context). More generally, since hierarchy constitutes a jurisdiction-regulating regime in itself—it implies a division of competencies, certain procedural order, and regulation of the effects of the judgments rendered by the various courts—the application of most jurisdiction-regulating norms, designed primarily to govern the uncoordinated involvement of two or more courts or tribunals in the litigation of the same dispute becomes redundant. While some jurisdictional regulation may remain useful (eg, extension of some degree of comity to inferior courts),[1] the required intensity of regulation is much reduced. So, ascertaining the existence of a hierarchical or non-hierarchical context is crucial to the identification of a suitable regulatory scheme.

As mentioned in Chapter 2, jurisdictional hierarchy implies the following two principal features: (a) the permissibility of successive litigation of the same dispute before different courts, usually in a predetermined order (eg, recourse to national courts before recourse to international courts); (b) some, but not all, of the seized courts are authorized to resolve definitively the dispute or to issue an otherwise authoritative legal proclamation in a manner binding upon the other courts involved in litigating the same dispute. Hence, the principle of finality (or bindingness) applies in hierarchically configured jurisdictional relations in a unidirectional manner—the decisions of some designated courts are binding upon the other courts involved in

[1] See below, Chapter 6.

the litigation, but not vice versa. Ascertaining the hierarchical or non-hierarchical nature of the jurisdictional relations between national and international courts depends, by and large, on the existence of hierarchy or non-hierarchy signifiers that confirm or negate the existence of the aforementioned features.

4.1.1 Hierarchy signifiers

Perhaps the quintessential hierarchy signifier is the power of judicial review of one court over another court's decisions. A court's ability to examine the lawfulness of another's decision facilitates successive recourse to adjudication; it necessarily entails that pronouncements of the reviewed court do not bind the reviewing court; at the same time, it implies that the reviewing court's decisions are binding upon the parties. In other words, judicial review normally envisions a unidirectional application of the principle of finality. So, situations in which international courts are authorized to review the lawfulness of the decisions of national courts[2] or arbitral bodies[3] imply hierarchy and vice versa. This seems to be unremarkable when the power of review is grounded in specific provisions found in jurisdiction-conferring instruments (eg, ad hoc *compromis*). The situation becomes more controversial when courts (typically, national courts) assume the power of judicial review over other courts without explicit authorization.[4] In all events, it should be noted that when judicial review focuses not on the original dispute litigated by the first-seized court but on the propriety of that reviewed court's judicial conduct (eg, whether the judges or arbitrators acted in good faith or in excess of jurisdiction), the *issues* before the two courts cease to be identical.[5] Thus, due to the possible shift in the issues under consideration, jurisdictional-regulating rules precluding,

[2] See eg, *Arrest Warrant of 11 April 2000* (DRC v Belgium), 2002 ICJ 3; *Application of the Convention of 1902 Governing the Guardianship of Infants* (Netherlands v Sweden), 1958 ICJ 55; *'Camouco'* (Panama v France), 39 ILM 666 (2000); Agreement Establishing the Caribbean Court of Justice, 14 Feb 2001, art XXV <http://www.caribbeancourtofjustice.org/courtadministration/ccj_agreement.pdf> (hereinafter CCJ Agreement). See also *Duke Energy International Peru Investment No 1, Ltd v Peru*, decision on jurisdiction, 1 Feb 2006, at para 160 (ICSID), <http://www.investmentclaims.com/decisions/Duke-Peru-Jurisdiction.pdf> ('by agreeing to international arbitration in the DEI Bermuda LSA, Respondent affirmed Claimant's right to a review by an ICSID tribunal of the matters considered by the Peruvian administration and court system, to the extent those matters fall within the guarantees contained in the [agreement between the parties]').

[3] See eg, Agreement on Settlement of Questions Relating to the Agrarian Reforms and Mixed Arbitral Tribunals (Hungary–Czech.–Yugos.–Roumania), 28 April 1930, art X, 121 LNTS 81 (the parties agreed to 'a right of appeal to the [PCIJ] from all judgments on question of jurisdiction or merits which may be given henceforth by the Mixed Arbitral Tribunals'). This provision was relied upon before the PCIJ in *Appeal from a Judgment of the Hungaro–Czechoslovak Mixed Arbitral Tribunal (Peter Pázmány University v Czechoslovakia)*, (Czech v Hungary), 1933 PCIJ (Ser A/B), No 61.

[4] See eg, *Milošević v The Netherlands*, Hague District Court decision of 31 Aug 2001, summarized in XLVIII *Netherlands International Law Review* 357 (2001); *Iran Aircraft Industries v Avco Corp*, 980 F 2d 141 (1992) (reviewing the regularity of Iran–US Claims Tribunal proceedings); *Insas Bhd & Anor v Cumaraswamy*, 4 Mal LJ 727, 735–6 (2000) (examining the ICJ advisory opinion in the *Special Rapporteur* case).

[5] For a similar legal manoeuvre, see *Arbitral Award of 31 July 1989* (Guinea Bissau v Senegal), 1991 ICJ 53.

a priori, multiple litigation of the same dispute (raising the same issues) are inapplicable.

Another clear hierarchy signifier is the exhaustion of local remedies rule, applied in human rights litigation and in cases relating to the treatment of aliens.[6] This rule regulates the order of the national and international proceedings by channeling the unidirectional application of the finality principle—confirming thereby, by implication, the superior status of the decisions of international courts.[7] The same signalling effects may probably appertain to 'no U-turn' jurisdictional arrangements, such as article 1121(b) of NAFTA, which precludes resort to national courts after international proceedings have been initiated.[8] This is because such a rule tolerates multiple proceedings (the individual investor may seize a national court before invoking NAFTA Chapter 11) yet confers final status only on the decision of the international tribunal involved in the jurisdictional interaction.

A final example of a hierarchically configured regime is the preliminary ruling procedure created under EC law and various other regional trade arrangements.[9] Such procedures regulate the order of the proceedings—directing national courts to stay proceedings and to refer specific questions of law to international courts, with resumption of the proceedings possible only after issuance of the international court's preliminary ruling. The procedure also requires national courts to follow the rulings of international courts, thus conferring supremacy to its judicial pronouncements.[10]

[6] See generally, C F Amerasinghe, *Local Remedies in International Law* (2nd edn, 2004).

[7] See eg, Convention for the Protection of Human Rights and Fundamental Freedoms, 4 Nov 1950, art 35, ETS 5 (hereinafter ECHR); American Convention on Human Rights, 22 Nov 1969, art 46(a), OAS TS 36, 9 ILM 673 (1970) (hereinafter I/A CHR). See also Laurence R Helfer and Anne-Marie Slaughter, 'Towards a Theory of Effective Supranational Adjudication', 107 *Yale LJ* (1997) 282, 297.

[8] See North American Free Trade Agreement, 17 Dec 1992, art 1121(1)(b) 32 ILM 289 and 605 (1993) (hereinafter NAFTA) ('disputing investor may submit a claim under Article 1117 to arbitration only if both the investor and the enterprise... (b) waive their right to initiate or continue before any administrative tribunal or court under the law of any Party, or other dispute settlement procedures, any proceedings with respect to the measure of the disputing Party that is alleged to be a breach referred to in Article 1117, except for proceedings for injunctive, declaratory or other extraordinary relief, not involving the payment of damages, before an administrative tribunal or court under the law of the disputing Party.'). For a discussion, see *Waste Management Inc v Mexico*, 41 ILM 1315, 1320–1 (2002); William S Dodge, 'International Decision: Waste Management, Inc. v. Mexico', 95 *AJIL* (2001) 186, 190. For similar provisions, see eg, The Central America–Dominican Republic–United States Free Trade Agreement, 5 Aug 2004, art 10.18(2)(b) <http://www.ustr.gov/Trade_Agreements/Bilateral/CAFTA/CAFTA-DR_Final_Texts/Section_Index.html> (hereinafter CAFTA); Free Trade Agreement (US/Chile), 6 June 2003, art 10.17(2)(b) <http://www.ustr.gov/Trade_Agreements/Bilateral/Chile_FTA/Final_Texts/Section_Index.html> (hereinafter Chile/US FTA).

[9] See eg, Treaty Establishing the European Economic Community, 25 March 1957, art 234, 298 UNTS 3, as revised on 24 Dec 2002, 2002 OJ (C325) 33 (hereinafter EC Treaty); Treaty Creating the Court of Justice of the Cartagena Agreement, as amended by the Cochabamba Protocol, 10 March 1996, arts 32–6, <http://www.comunidadandina.org/ingles/normativa/ande_trie2.htm> (hereinafter Andean Court Treaty); CCJ Agreement, art XIV.

[10] For a discussion on the hierarchical nature of EC law, see Eric Stein, 'Lawyers Judges, and the Making of a Transnational Constitution', 75 *AJIL* (1981) 1. But see Helfer and Slaughter, above n 7, at 298 (ECJ and national courts have forged a partnership based on complementarity of jurisdiction).

4.1.2 Non-hierarchy signifiers

Of course, non-hierarchy signifiers can also be identified. Principal among these are *electa una via* (or 'fork in the road') provisions,[11] found in numerous BITs and comparable instruments, which enable the parties to a dispute to turn to either national or international courts. This arrangement is generally believed to reflect a horizontal configuration of relations between national and international courts as well as to introduce a bar against multiple proceedings.[12] Hence, it follows that the respective arrangements apply the finality principle in a bi-directional manner without conferring *a priori* hierarchy to one court or another.

One could also view the complementarity rule found in the Rome Statute[13] as a non-hierarchy signifier. This is because the rule rejects the possibility of initiating simultaneous or consecutive criminal proceedings before national and international courts (except in the case of patently inappropriate national proceedings) and applies the principle of finality (*ne bis in idem*) in a bi-directional manner. It therefore institutes what is largely a horizontal division of labour between national and international courts.

4.1.3 The uncertainty of the default rule

As discussed in Chapter 2, ascertainment of the nature of the relations between national and international courts in the absence of clear hierarchy signifiers remains controversial and dependant on how the relationship between national and international law is conceptualized (eg, monism v dualism, ascending v descending authority, centralized v decentralized international order).[14] The inconsistent practice of

[11] See eg, US Model Bilateral Investment Agreement, art VI, 1 *Basic Documents of International Economic Law* (Stephen Zamora and Ronald A Brand, eds, 1990) 655; Treaty Concerning the Encouragement and Reciprocal Protection of Investment (US–Jordan), 2 July 1997, art IX, 36 ILM 1498 (1997) ICSID Model Clauses, Clause 12, Doc ICSID/5/Rev. 2, <http://www.worldbank.org/icsid/model-clauses-en/main-eng.htm> (hereinafter ICSID Model Clauses) (facilitating choice of non-ICSID remedies); European Energy Charter, 12 Dec 1994, art 26, 33 ILM 360 (1995) (hereinafter Energy Charter) (choice between domestic courts and various international arbitration procedures).

[12] See eg, Christoph C Schreuer, *Commentary to the ICSID Convention* (2001) 364; Pamela B Gann, 'The US Bilateral Investment Treaty Program', 21 *Stan J Int'l L* (1985) 373, 437–8; K Scot Gudgeon, 'Arbitration Provisions of US Bilateral Investment Disputes', *International Investment Disputes: Avoidance and Settlement* (Seymor J Rubin and Richard W Nelson, eds, 1985) 41, 51; Jose Luis Siqueiros, 'Bilateral Treaties on the Reciprocal Protection of Foreign Investment', 24 *Cal W Int'l LJ* (1994) 255, 255–6; Antonio R Parra, 'Provisions on the Settlement of Investment Disputes in Modern Investment Laws, Bilateral Investment Treaties and Multilateral Instruments on Investment', 12 *ICSID Rev FILJ* (1997) 287, 334–5, 351–2.

[13] Statute of the International Criminal Court, 17 July 1998, art 17, 2187 UNTS 90 (hereinafter ICC Statute).

[14] J G Starke, 'Monism and Dualism in the Theory of International Law', 17 *Brit YB Int'l L* (1936) 75; Martti Koskenniemi, *From Apology to Utopia: The Structure of International Legal Argument* (1989) 40–2; Martti Koskenniemi, 'The Politics of International Law', 1 *EJIL* 4, 28–9 (1990); Hans Kelsen, *Principles of International Law* (1952) 437, 444–5.

national and international courts on the matter is indicative of the prevailing state of uncertainty in this regard.

In all events, the selection of either a pro- or non-hierarchy default rule inevitably affects the scope of the overlap between national and international courts: a pro-hierarchy presumption would minimize such an occurrence to situations governed by explicit non-hierarchy signifiers, while a non-hierarchy presumption would significantly increase the number and frequency of overlaps.

It is beyond the scope of the present treatise to settle the fundamental debate regarding the proper hierarchical configuration of national and international courts, which is ideological at its core. While it may be the case that one approach may dominate over time, it seems more probable that the choice of a default rule of configuration—whether vertical or horizontal—will gradually emerge on a regime-by-regime basis, as witnessed in the ECHR, EC, and ICC constitutive instruments. Such a gradual development has the benefit of tailoring the configuration selected to the needs of the specific regime and substantive subject matter: while those regimes and areas of law that place a high premium on legal certainty or view with suspicion the manner in which national courts apply international standards (eg, trade law or human rights law) could probably benefit from vertical jurisdictional structures; other regimes and substantive areas (eg, criminal law or investment law) may prefer a horizontal 'division of labour' approach. The institutional capabilities of the respective courts in handling large case loads might influence such a choice between horizontal and vertical jurisdictional arrangements or, perhaps, encourage lawmakers to create half-way regimes, combining elements from both paradigms.

4.2 Applicability of International Jurisdiction-regulating Rules

Another fundamental issue relates to the ability of those courts involved in a jurisdictional interaction—national courts in particular—to invoke the jurisdiction-regulating rules discussed in Chapters 5 and 6. The ability of courts to apply *international* jurisdiction-regulating rules necessarily assumes that they are in a position to invoke international law in the first place. In other words, international jurisdiction-regulating rules are applicable only to the degree that international law can be applied by the seized courts.

While this does not present a serious problem in relation to international courts—as the latter routinely apply general international law norms either directly (if they are invested, like the ICJ, with the power of invoking general international law) or indirectly (as a source for interpreting the specific treaty provisions they are expected to apply)[15]—the question of the applicability of international jurisdiction

[15] See eg, Understanding on the Rules and Procedures Governing the Settlement of Disputes (Annex 2 to the Agreement Establishing the World Trade Organization), 15 April 1994, art 3(2), 33 ILM 1226 (1994) (hereinafter DSU).

rules in domestic courts appears to turn on the doctrine governing incorporation of international law into domestic law in the particular jurisdiction. Here, too, the old dualistic/monistic quandary continues to exert its influence on the possibility of introducing coordination-enhancing measures.[16] Put differently, demarcation of the jurisdictional boundaries between national and international courts by way of international jurisdiction-regulating rules depends to a considerable degree on the internalization of these rules by the national legal system.[17]

Yet, it should be noted that even in the absence of explicit incorporation of international law into the domestic legal system, coordination may still transpire on the basis of national law doctrines such as *forum non conveniens*, comity, or *abus de droit*. In their content, such doctrines may mirror parallel international law rules, whose very development derives from the practice of national judicial institutions (either through qualifying as 'general principles of the law'[18] or by reflecting state practice underlying international customary law).[19] While such coordinating measures appear to be relevant here, other coordination techniques, developed only in domestic law, may be of too idiosyncratic a nature and thus irrelevant to the project of identifying *international* forms of regulation.

4.3 Conditions of Jurisdictional Competition

4.3.1 General considerations

Application of most international jurisdiction-regulating rules discussed in this Part depends on the existence of jurisdictional overlap between two judicial proceedings, each before different fora. For example, the application of rules designed to curb multiple proceedings—the *electa una via*, *lis alibi pendens*, and *res judicata* rules—presupposes that the regulated proceedings possess a significant degree of similarity.[20]

Conditioning the application of jurisdiction-regulating rules on a sufficient level of similarity between the parallel procedures derives from the main rationales for introducing those rules in the first place: it is redundant to litigate the *same* dispute in more than one set of proceedings (mainly for reasons of inconvenience to the parties and judicial economy); and it is undesirable that parties to a *single* dispute, through their own conduct, would generate inconsistent legal determinations of

[16] But see Andrew L Strauss, 'A Global Paradigm Shattered: The Jurisdictional Nihilism of the Supreme Court's Abduction Decision in Alvarez-Machain', 67 *Temple L Rev* (1994) 1209, 1232–8 (arguing that dualism cannot be applied to 'international jurisdictional law').

[17] Cf Gunther Teubner, 'Breaking Frames: The Global Interplay of Legal and Social Systems', 45 *Am J Comp L* (1997) 149, 156.

[18] See eg, Ian Brownlie, *Principles of Public International Law* (6th edn, 2003) 16 (general principle of law may derive from national jurisprudence).

[19] See eg, ibid, at 22 (national court decisions may be considered state practice).

[20] Yuval Shany, *The Competing Jurisdictions of International Courts and Tribunals* (2003) 24.

their rights and obligations.[21] While jurisdictional interactions can take place outside these constraints (eg, in related proceedings involving the same issue but different parties or the same parties and different issues), the policy considerations supporting regulation of such interactions are less compelling. The right of access to court, applied as a human right[22] and a general principle of justice,[23] militates against excessive restriction of party autonomy, that is, on the parties' freedom to control the conduct of litigation whenever there are genuine distinctions between the related procedures.[24] The involvement of different sets of parties and the raising of materially different issues in the course of litigation may, in effect, remove many of the objections to the conduct of multiple proceedings.

In the same vein, the application of forum selection rules—such as choice of forum or exclusive jurisdiction clauses that direct a specific dispute to a designated judicial forum—also depends largely on sufficient similarity between the competing procedures. A forum selection clause (or exclusive jurisdiction treaty provision), designating a specific dispute to the exclusive competence of a particular national or international court, would block the exercise of jurisdiction by courts other than those selected only if the two cases were effectively identical. Although the policy considerations involved here may be somewhat different—the principle of *pacta sunt servanda* governs obligations falling within the scope of forum selection clauses, but not matters falling beyond the scope of such clauses, the relevance of the 'sameness' criteria may be similar.

[21] Ibid, at 23–4. Note that the adverse doctrinal consequences of incompatible judgments construing norms derived from different legal systems (eg, the laws of two sovereign states) are smaller in comparison to incompatibilities pertaining arising under the same legal system: *inter*-systemic incompatibilities do not raise questions regarding the normative coherence of any distinct legal system that compromise its perceived fairness and legitimacy (most importantly, the notion that like cases are to be treated alike). Such normative conflicts can be easily resolved on the basis of inter-systemic choice of law rules. In contrast, *intra*-systemic conflicting judgments could raise serious coherency concerns. Hence, the classification of the jurisdictional interaction between national and international proceedings as intra- or inter-systemic (pursuant to the discussion of 'normative systemization' undertaken in Chapter 2) has important implications for the policy considerations supporting or opposing jurisdictional co-ordination. Ibid, at 120–2.

[22] See eg, ECHR, art 6; International Covenant on Civil and Political Rights, 16 Dec 1966, art 14, 999 UNTS 171.

[23] See eg, *Azinian v Mexico*, 39 ILM 537, 552 (2000) ('A denial of justice could be pleaded if the relevant courts refuse to entertain a suit'); *Restat. 3d of the Foreign Relations Law of the US*, § 711, cmt. a (1987) ('More commonly the phrase "denial of justice" is used narrowly, to refer only to injury consisting of, or resulting from, denial of access to court, or denial of procedural fairness and due process in relation to judicial proceedings, whether criminal or civil'); *National Iranian Oil Co (NIOC) v Israel*, decision of 1 Feb 2005 (Cour de Cassation, France), excerpts available through <http://www.kluwerarbitration.com> ('the impossibility for a party to access the court (or arbitral tribunal) entrusted with the settlement of that party's claim to the exclusion of all other state jurisdictions, and thus to exercise a right pertaining to international public policy, established by the principles of international arbitration and Art 6(1) of the European Convention on Human Rights, is a denial of justice').

[24] See Christoph C Schreuer, *Decisions of International Institutions before Domestic Courts* (1981) 329. See also Christoph H Schreuer, 'Concurrent Jurisdiction of National and International Tribunals', 13 *Hous L Rev* (1975–1976) 508, 526.

The balance between the conflicting factors underlying the application of jurisdiction-regulating norms is reflected in international law's definition of competing proceedings. Two tests have traditionally been offered in various international instruments and in the jurisprudence of national and international courts—the 'same parties' and the 'same issues' tests.[25] Policy choices regarding the application of jurisdiction-regulating rules (ie, generally parallel to the integrative or disintegrative methodologies discussed in Chapter 3) often boil down to a more or less flexible reading of these two sameness standards. However, even if one adopts a flexible reading of these tests, their application to cases of jurisdictional competition between national and international courts seems to be particularly challenging given the many intrinsic differences between the two groups of procedures.

4.3.2 Same parties

The unique challenge of applying the test in a national/international context

The first requirement of similitude—that the same parties would be involved in both sets of parallel proceeding—derives from the party autonomy considerations identified above. A legal undertaking governing proceedings between a particular set of disputing parties surely cannot bind a third party; in a similar vein, initiation of one set of proceedings by two parties to a conflict cannot debar a third from vindicating those of its rights stemming from the same transaction by means of another set of proceedings. However, as often is the case, 'third parties' may actually be closely related to one of the parties to the parallel case and their litigation interests; hence, third parties' independent rights to pursue the same set of legal interests may be open to question. The application of the 'same parties' test appears ultimately to hinge on the degree of formality applied in ascertaining 'sameness'—that is, whether one adopts a 'formal identity', 'essentially the same' standard, or any intermediate position.

The 'formal identity' test, focusing on the formally separate legal status of the potential parallel litigants, is particularly difficult to apply in cases of jurisdictional interaction between national and international courts. This is because the peculiar rules of standing before both national and international courts often require representation of specified legal interests by parties other than the original or direct

[25] *Certain German Interests in Polish Upper Silesia* (Germany v Poland), 1925 PCIJ (Ser A) No 6, at 20; *Benvenuti and Bonfat Srl v Congo*, 1 ICSID Rep 330, 340 (1980); *Amco Asia, Pan American Development Ltd v Indonesia*, 1 ICSID Rep 389, 409 (1983); *China Navigation Co Ltd (UK) v US (The 'Newchwang')*, 6 RIAA 64, 65 (1921); Cases 172, 228/83 *Hoogovens Greop v Commission* [1985] ECR 2831, 2846; *Waste Management*, 41 ILM at 1322; Convention on the Jurisdiction and the Enforcement of Judgments in Civil and Commercial Matters, 27 Sept 1968, art 27, 29 ILM (1990) 1413, as updated by Council Regulation 44/2001 of 22 December 2000 on Jurisdiction and the Recognition and Enforcement of Judgments in Civil and Commercial Matters, 2001 OJ (L 12) 1 (hereinafter Brussels Judgments Convention); Restatement of the Law (2nd), Judgments, §§ 17, 24.

right holder, or, at times, by selected right holders only. For example, international courts and tribunals often require that a contested set of private interests (which a private entity may have directly upheld before national courts) be brought before international fora through the medium of states, international organizations or other representative entities. Indeed, individual rights owed to alien nationals can only be vindicated before the ICJ if the aggrieved aliens' state of nationality decides to espouse their claims as if they were its own, through the exercise of diplomatic protection.[26] Similarly, some commercial claims of private corporations against their own 'state of nationality'[27] can only be submitted at the international level as international investment claims brought by the corporation's foreign shareholders, acting in their independent capacity.[28] At the same time, immunities accorded to foreign states and high-ranking state officials in domestic proceedings (eg, sovereign immunity, head of state immunity, diplomatic immunity) sometimes leads to the bringing of claims against persons or entities only partly responsible for the challenged state conduct (eg, private contractors or low-ranking foreign officials) that do not enjoy immunity before national courts. These non-immune actors serve, in effect, as substitutes to the primarily responsible yet immune persons or entities, which would have been the probable target of a suit brought before an international tribunal.[29]

These *locus standi* differences mean that instances of absolute identity of parties before national and international courts are bound to be rare. As a result, Christoph Schreuer has argued that the 'same parties' test, if applied to the relations holding

[26] See *Mavrommatis Palestine Concessions* (Greece v UK), 1924 PCIJ (Ser A), No 2, at 12 ('By taking up the case if one of its subjects and by resorting to diplomatic action or international judicial proceedings on his behalf, a State is in reality asserting its own rights'); Parra, above, n 12, at 335–6.

[27] For the international standard on determining the nationality of a corporation, see *Barcelona Traction, Light and Power Company, Ltd* (Belgium v Spain), 1970 ICJ 3.

[28] For example, the *Lauder/CME* cases involved domestic court proceedings in the Czech Republic between a local corporation and the local government, international arbitration proceedings between the Dutch corporation owning the Czech corporation and the Czech government (under the terms of the Dutch–Czech BIT), and arbitration proceedings between Mr Lauder, who owned the Dutch corporation and the Czech government (under the terms of the US–Czech BIT). *Lauder v Czech Republic*, Award of 3 Sept 2001, <http://www2004.mfcr.cz/static/Arbitraz/en/FinalAward.pdf>; *CME Czech Republic BV v Czech Republic*, Partial Award of 13 Sept 2001 <http://www.mfcr.cz/static/Arbitraz/en/PartialAward.pdf>.

[29] For example, Lord Hutton suggested that Pinochet does not enjoy immunity from criminal prosecution, notwithstanding the fact that he and Chile may invoke sovereign immunity in the context of civil proceedings brought against them. *R v Bow Street Metropolitan Stipendiary Magistrate and others, ex parte Pinochet Ugarte (No 3)*, [1999] 2 All ER 97, 158 (per Lord Hutton). Similarly, claims in the US under the Alien Tort Claims Act directed against former foreign officials or corporations could face fewer legal obstacles than claims lodged against foreign states. See eg, *Filartiga v Pena-Irala*, 630 F 2d 876 (1980); *John Doe I v Unocal Corp*, 395 F 3d 932 (2002). However, the civil immunity afforded to active diplomats under the 1961 Vienna Convention (Vienna Convention on Diplomatic Relations, 18 April 1961, art 31, 500 UNTS 95) appears to be broader in scope than that accorded to states under modern sovereign immunity doctrines (see eg, Draft United Nations Convention on Jurisdictional Immunities of States and Their Property, arts 10–14, GAOR 59th Sess, Supp No 22 (A/59/22, Annex I (2004)).

between national and international proceedings, should be construed liberally, so as to encompass parallel claims involving the same sets of interests.[30]

The 'same parties' test in practice

Some international law authorities may be cited in favour of a flexible or informal approach to the identification of similarities between parties involved in multi-fora litigation. For example, some international courts and tribunals have embraced 'essentially the same parties' or '*alter ego*' tests, thereby rejecting more formal formulations of party identity.[31] Flexible standards, implying a high degree of convergence of legal interests, have also been adopted in a few jurisdiction-creating instruments, especially in the field of international investment protection.[32]

Still, other authorities point to the opposite direction, and embrace a more formal 'identity of parties' test.[33] Furthermore, it has even been suggested in one ICSID case that a distinction should be made even between cases involving identical parties when at least one of these parties is acting in different capacities, such as a state acting in its sovereign or *jure imperii* capacity in one case and in its 'merchant' or *jure gestionis* capacity in another.[34] This amounts to adding an additional

[30] Schreuer (1981), above, n 24, at 331. See also Shany, above, n 20, at 24–5.

[31] See eg, Case 16358/90, *Martin v Spain*, Eur Comm'n HR Decision of 12 Oct 1992 (adopting an 'essentially the same parties' standard vis-à-vis competing ILO Committee on Freedom of Association proceedings brought by the labour union to which the applicants in the Strasbourg proceedings belonged); Comm 75/80 *Fanali v Italy*, UN Doc CCPR/C/18/D/75/1980 (1983), at para 7.2 (an *electa una via* rule covers claims by the same individual 'or someone else who has the standing to act on his behalf'); *Drouot Assurances SA v Consolidated Metallurgical Industries*, 1998 ECR I-3075, at para 23 (suggesting that the claim in question would have been blocked had the litigating interests of the related parties been identical and indissociable). See also August Reinisch, 'The Use and Limits of Res Judicata and Lis Pendens as Procedural Tools to Avoid Conflicting Dispute Settlement Outcomes', 3 *The Law and Practice of International Courts and Tribunals* (2004) 37, 57–60 (arguing that the 'economic approach' to investment disputes, which focuses on the economic realities and not on the formal identities of the parties, supports a flexible approach to the 'same parties' test).

[32] See eg, Canadian Model BIT 2004, art 26(1)(e), <http://ita.law.uvic.ca/documents/Canadian2004-FIPA-model-en.pdf> ('the investor and, where the claim is for loss or damage to an interest in an enterprise of the other Party that is a juridical person that the investor owns or controls directly or indirectly, the enterprise waive their right to initiate or continue before any administrative tribunal or court under the law of any Party, or other dispute settlement procedures, any proceedings with respect to the measure of the disputing Party that is alleged to be a breach referred to in Article 22'). See also CAFTA, art 10.18(2)(b)(ii).

[33] See the decisions in the Lauder/CME cases in which a 'formal identity' test was adopted. This approach was also upheld by a Swedish Court that reviewed a challenge to the CME proceedings. *Lauder*, above, n 28; *CME Czech*, above, n 28; *Czech Republic v CME Czech Republic BV*, 42 ILM 919 (2003). See also *Azurix Corp v Mexico*, 43 ILM 262, 280 (2004). See also Comm R.13/56, *Casariego v Uruguay*, UN GAOR, 37th Sess, Supp 40, at 185, 187 (Report of the HRC, 1981); Comm. R.2/10, *Altesor v Uruguay*, UN GAOR, 37th Sess, Supp 40, at 122, 125 (Report of the HRC, 1982); Comm 74/1980, *Estrella v Uruguay*, UN GAOR, 38th Sess, Supp 40, at 150, 156 (Report of the HRC, 1983) (in all three cases, the Committee held that parallel proceedings alleging violations of the applicants' rights cannot be blocked by a *lis alibi pendens* rule since they were filed by unrelated third parties).

[34] *El Paso Energy International Co v Argentina*, decision on jurisdiction of 27 April 2006, at paras 79–81, <http://www.investmentclaims.com/decisions/El_Paso_Energy-Argentina-Jurisdictional_Decision.pdf>; ILA International Commercial Arbitration Committee, Report on Res Judicata and

substantive requirement—identical capacities—to the formal identity test. In all events, it seems safe to assert that the *lex lata* on application of the 'same parties' test remains unsettled.

One especially problematic area of legal controversy involving conflicting authorities is application of the 'same parties' test in diplomatic protection cases. Earlier case law emphasized the differences in the nature of the individual and the espousing state's claims, implying that they should not be deemed the same. In the words of the PCIJ in *Mavrommatis*: 'By taking up the case of one of its subjects and by resorting to diplomatic action or international judicial proceedings on his behalf, a State is in reality asserting *its own rights*' (emphasis added).[35] However, it appears as if this distinction might no longer be plausible in contemporary international law. For example, in the field of international investment law, there appears to be a tendency to assimilate the rights of the foreign investor with her state of nationality for the purpose of applying jurisdiction-regulating rules. Indeed, article 27 of the ICSID Convention generally prohibits the initiation of state-to-state proceedings involving the investor's state of nationality and the host state in parallel to proceedings initiated by the foreign investor herself.[36] This rule appears to reflect a belief that the individual and state exercising diplomatic protection are the same parties for the purpose of applying jurisdiction-regulating rules designed to curb multiple proceedings.

In the light of the uncertainty of *lex lata*, it looks as if courts and other decision makers are faced with a policy choice not dissimilar to the choice between disintegrationism and intergrationism discussed in Chapter 3. They can either stress the distinctions between the two parallel proceedings—thereby evading the need for applying jurisdiction-regulation rules—or the common aspects of the two proceedings, for purposes of harmonization. While the first option has, like other disintegrationist techniques, the benefits of doctrinal clarity and ease of application, the second option, like other intergrationist measures, promotes court's ability to provide pragmatic problem solving but at the price of decreased legal certainty.

To my mind, excessive insistence on formal identity between the parties is unwarranted as, in most circumstances, this stance precludes the application of

Arbitration (2006), at para 46 (copy with author) (it is unclear whether the 'same parties' test contains a requirement that the parties act in the same capacity in two arbitration proceedings). But see Kelsen, above, n 14, at 429–30 (states only have one legal personality).

[35] *Mavrommatis*, 1924 PCIJ (Ser A), No 2, at 12.

[36] Convention on the Settlement of Disputes between States and Nationals of Other States, 18 March 1965, art 27(1), 575 UNTS 159 (hereinafter ICSID Convention) ('No Contracting State shall give diplomatic protection, or bring an international claim in respect of a dispute which one of its nationals and another Contracting State shall have consented to submit or shall have submitted to arbitration under this Convention ...'). See also *CMS Gas Transmission Co v Argentina*, 42 ILM 788, 795 (2003) (states no longer assert their independent interest in diplomatic protection claims); Report of the International Law Commission on the work of its fiftieth session, Ch 5, Diplomatic Protection, UN GAOR 53rd Sess, Supp No 10 (A/51/10 and Corr 1) (1998), at paras 76–82.

jurisdiction-regulating rules in the context of multiple litigation before national and international courts. Yet such preclusion undermines the main policy interests the rules were designed to serve—procedural justice, efficiency, and legal coherence. Excessively formal criteria also facilitate their abuse through deliberate recourse to multiple litigation by closely related entities. Such manipulation is particularly feasible in economic disputes, which tend to involve complex corporate structures and numerous potential litigants (eg, parent companies, subsidiaries, shareholders, indirect investors, etc.).[37] Hence, I believe that the common law's 'privity of interests' test, marking preference for substantive over formal identity, is more suitable for governing cases of competition between national and international courts.[38] Such a standard would support fulfilment of the 'same parties' test whenever the parties are formally identical or so closely related as to represent virtually identical sets of interests.[39] However, as already noted, excessive flexibility is also undesirable as it may result in oppressive incursions on party autonomy and unduly restrict access to court of parties with divergent sets of interests.[40] Here, as in other cases where flexible standards are employed, a fine line needs to be drawn between excessive formality and excessive flexibility.

[37] See Reinisch, above, n 31, at 56–7. This might be compounded by the multiple citizenship of the corporation and its shareholders. Cf *Olguín v Paraguay*, Award of 26 July, 2001 at paras 60–2, <http://www.worldbank.org/icsid/cases/Olgun-award-en.pdf>.

[38] *Gleeson v J Wippel & Co Ltd* [1977] 3 All ER 54, 60 (Ch Div) ('I do not say that one must be the alter ego of the other: but it does seem to me that, having due regard to the subject-matter of the dispute, there must be a *sufficient degree of identification* between the two to make it *just* to hold that the decision to which one was party should be binding in proceedings to which the other is party. It is in that sense that I would regard the phrase "privity of interest" ')(emphasis added); *Carl Zeiss Stiftung v Rayner & Keeler Ltd* [1967] 1 AC 853 (HL) ('There does, however, seem to me to be a possible extension of the doctrine of privity as commonly understood. A party against whom a previous decision was pronounced may employ a servant or engage a third party to do something which infringes the right established in the earlier litigation and so raise the whole matter again in his interest. Then, if the other party to the earlier litigation brings an action against the servant or agent, the real defendant could be said to be the employer, who alone has the real interest, and it might well be thought unjust if he could vex his opponent by relitigating the original question by means of the device of putting forward his servant'). See also Restatement of the Law (2nd), Judgments, § 39 ('A person who is not a party to an action but who controls or substantially participates in the control of the presentation on behalf of a party is bound by the determination of issues decided as though he were a party'); ibid, at § 41 (illustration no 2) (assignor and assignee are normally viewed as the same party in litigation with the other contractual party). For additional support for the suitability of the 'privity of interests' standard, see Joost Pauwelyn, 'How to Win a World Trade Organization Dispute Based on Non-World Trade Organization Law?', 37 *Journal of World Trade* (2003) 997, 1018.

[39] Arguably, this standard is not met in cases involving concurrent claims by corporations and their shareholders when the two entities have divergent interests (eg, if the corporation needs to accommodate the interests of other shareholders as well). See eg, *Genin v Estonia*, Award of 25 June 2001, at para 332 <http://www.worldbank.org/icsid/cases/genin.pdf> (majority shareholder investor's claim is not the same as the owned corporation's claim); *Enron Corp v Argentina*, decision on jurisdiction of 14 Jan 2004, at para 98, <http://www.asil.org/ilib/Enron.pdf> (ICSID).

[40] See eg, *National Grid Plc v Argentina*, decision of 20 June 2006, at para 169, <http://ita.law.uvic.ca/documents/NationalGrid-Jurisdiction-En.pdf> (UNCITRAL). ('The Tribunal recalls the fact that National Grid is not a party to the Concession Contracts, in which the Concessionaires agreed to the exclusive jurisdiction of the federal courts in Argentina's federal capital').

4.3.3 Same issues

Treaty law

Even more difficult questions of law and policy are presented by the second condition underlying jurisdictional competition—the 'same issues' test. This test can be broken down into sub-tests: the same fact pattern and the same legal claims[41] (or 'same object' (*petitum*), 'same legal grounds' (*causa petendi*) and 'same remedy'[42] criteria).[43] Here too, considerations of party autonomy militate against extending the blocking effect of jurisdictional agreements and multiple proceedings beyond the scope of issues actually regulated or litigated.

The jurisdiction-regulating treaty norms mentioned in Chapter 1 provide limited guidance concerning the application of the 'same issues' test. Indeed, some regulatory norms make no specification of the conditions for material overlap that underlie their invocation. For example, the principle of complementarity, introduced by the Rome Statute,[44] fails to delineate explicitly the required substantive degree of similarity that parallel national proceedings should meet in order to prevent the ICC from exercising its own jurisdiction in the case: particularly, it does not clarify whether national proceedings based on ordinary criminal law offences under domestic law would give rise to complementarity.[45]

Furthermore, even when specific jurisdiction-regulating norms delineate the scope of overlap they govern, this choice may be dictated by unique policy considerations that are not easily transposable beyond the purview of the relevant regime. So, for example, the exhaustion of local remedies rule under the ECHR,[46] which clearly favours an informal approach to inter-fora competition (as it does not limit its application to local proceedings based on international rules),[47] may be

41 Shany, above, n 20, at 25.

42 See eg, *Factory at Chorzów* (Poland v Germany), 1927 PCIJ (Ser A) No 9, at 29–30 (jurisdiction).

43 See eg, *Trail Smelter* (US v Canada), 3 RIAA 1907, 1952 (1941); *A v B*, excerpts in Collection of ICC Arbitral Awards 1974–1985 (1990) 11, 13.

44 ICC Statute, art 17.

45 For a discussion, see Jann K Kleffner, *The Impact of Complementarity on National Implementation of Substantive International Criminal Law*, 1 JICJ 86, 95–9 (2003) (Kleffner leans to the position that domestic crime definitions could satisfy the test of complementarity). But note that the ICTY, ICTR, and Sierra Leone Special Court may re-litigate criminal cases adjudicated by national courts if the latter had characterized the acts in question as ordinary crimes. This seems to suggest that only proceedings grounded in *international* criminal law could enjoy a *ne bis in idem* effect. See Statute of the International Criminal Tribunal for the Former Yugoslavia, 25 May 1993, art 10(2)(a), 32 ILM 1192 (1993)(most recently updated version available at <http://www.un.org/icty/legaldoc-e/basic/statut/statuteindex.htm>) (hereinafter ICTY Statute); Statute of the International Tribunal for Rwanda, art 9(2)(a), SC Res 955, UN SCOR, 49th Sess, 3453d mtg at 3, 33 ILM 1600 (1994) (hereinafter ICTR Statute); Statute for the Special Court in Sierra Leone, 16 Jan 2002, art 9(2)(a), <http://www.pict-pcti.org/courts/pdf/SL/SpecialCourtStatute2002.pdf> (hereinafter SCSL Statute). For a discussion, see *Prosecutor v Bagaragaza*, decision on Rule 11*bis* appeal of 30 Aug 2006 (ICTR Appeals Chamber).

46 ECHR, art 32.

47 See eg, *Guzzardi v Italy*, 39 Eur Ct HR (Ser A), at 26 (application of the exhaustion of local remedies rules undertaken 'with a certain degree of flexibility and without excessive regard for matters of form'); *Akdivar v Turkey*, 1996-IV EHRR 1210, 1211.

explained in light of the vertical institutional balance between the ECtHR and national courts, the need to control the ECtHR's case load and the close interplay between human rights law and national law. Such considerations may be inappropriate however, in trade or investment cases or, more generally, in horizontal jurisdictional interactions.

Case law

The case law regarding the application of the 'same issues' test is also far from settled. While a number of international judicial bodies have expressed preference for a flexible approach toward the issue—an 'essentially the same issue' standard[48]—other authorities pointing to a formal 'identity of issues' test exist as well.[49] The conflicting positions of the *Vivendi I* and *SGS v Pakistan* arbitral tribunals on whether related contract and treaty claims can be deemed the same claims for jurisdictional-regulation purposes are indicative of this state of uncertainty.[50]

In addition, it may be noted that here, too, ascertaining the 'sameness' or 'separateness' of the issues raised in situations involving diplomatic protection claims presents a particularly difficult challenge: the protection of alien nationals may

[48] See eg, *Elettronica Sicula SpA (ELSI)* (US v Italy), 1989 ICJ 15, 45–6; Case 144/86, *Gubisch Maschinenfabrik v Palumbo* [1987] ECJ 4861, 4876 (competing claims need not be entirely identical); *Delgado* (US v Spain), 3 *International Arbitrations to which the United States has been a Party* (John Bassett Moore ed, 1881) 2196, 2199; App 16717/90, *Pauger v Austria*, 80 D & R 24 (1995); Comm 452/1991, *Glaziou v France*, UNGAOR, 51st Sess, Supp 40(II), at 277, 281 (adopting a 'substantially the same issues' standard); *Methanex Corp v US*, Determination of 30 June 2000, Doc A/14/SEM/99-001/06/14 (3), at 5–7 (CEC Secretariat), <http://www.cec.org/files/pdf/sem/99-1-DET-E1.pdf>; *SGS Société Générale de Surveillance SA v Philippines*, decision of 29 Jan 2004, at para 128 <http://www.worldbank.org/icsid/cases/SGSvPhil-final.pdf> ('drawing technical distinctions between causes of action arising under the BIT and those arising under the investment agreement is capable of giving rise to overlapping proceedings and jurisdictional uncertainty'). Cf *Fisheries Jurisdiction* (Spain v Canada), 1998 ICJ 437, 467 (Canada's reservation with relation to disputes over conservation measures cannot be bypassed by way of presenting the dispute as a dispute over enforcement measures); *Commission v Ireland*, [2006] ECR I-4635, at para 120 ('the Convention provisions on the prevention of marine pollution relied on by Ireland, which clearly cover a *significant part of the dispute* relating to the MOX plant, come within the scope of Community competence which the Community has elected to exercise by becoming a party to the Convention') (emphasis added). Restatement of the Law (2nd), Judgments, §24 ('What factual grouping constitutes a "transaction", and what groupings constitute a "series" [covered by the *res judicata* rule], are to be determined pragmatically, giving weight to such considerations as whether the facts are related in time, space, origin, or motivation, whether they form a convenient trial unit, and whether their treatment as a unit conforms to the parties' expectations or business understanding or usage'). See also Reinisch, above, n 31, at 62–3 (arguing that there are strong policy arguments objecting to 'claim splitting); Pauwelyn, above, n 38, at 1017.

[49] See eg, *Lauder*, above, n 28, at para 165, 173–5; *CME Czech*, above n 28, at para 412 (the two arbitral tribunal were of the opinion that claims under separate yet virtually identical BITs do not raise the same issues). See also *Cesar Fierro v United States*, Report No 99/03, Inter-Am CHR, OEA/Ser./L/V/II.114 Doc. 70 rev. 1 at 769, at para 57 (2003) (a claim under the Vienna Convention on Consular Relations is distinct from a claim under human rights instruments).

[50] *Compania de Aquas del Aconquija, SA v Argentina*, 40 ILM 426, 428–9 (2001) (hereinafter *Vivendi I*); *Société Générale de Surveillance SA (SGS) v Pakistan*, 42 ILM 1290, 1298 (2003). For a discussion, see above, Chapter 1.

sometimes be achieved through the cumulative imposition upon the host state of international law obligations owed directly to the alien individual (which her state of nationality may also espouse) and obligations directly due to her state of nationality.[51] A thorny question that arises in such cases is how, if at all, one can distinguish between the state of nationality's diplomatic protection claims and its own direct claims. In practical terms, the question often arising is whether the exhaustion of local remedies requirement, which appertains to the diplomatic protection claims, also extends to the independent claims of the state of nationality, or whether the two claims are of a sufficiently separate character so as the limit the scope of exhaustion requirement to the diplomatic protection claim exclusively.

The relationship between diplomatic protection claims and the state of nationality's direct claims is addressed in the new ILC Draft Articles on Diplomatic Protection. According to article 14(3) of the Draft Articles, '[l]ocal remedies shall be exhausted where an international claim, or request for a declaratory judgment related to the claim, is brought preponderantly on the basis of an injury to a national or other person referred to in article 8.'[52] This formulation is largely consistent with the refusal of the ICJ in *ELSI* to acknowledge the independent nature of US investment protection direct claims under the Italy–US Friendship, Navigation and Commerce (FCN) treaty and to exempt such claims from the exhaustion of local remedies rule that had governed the diplomatic protection claims brought by the US on behalf of investing US companies.[53] Applied to the topic at hand, this approach probably means that an inter-state claim could be subsumed in a more dominant, yet related, diplomatic protection claim.[54] This outcome appears to be consistent with the *Vivendi I* tribunal's decision to extend the choice of forum clause governing the investor's contractual claim to the less dominant yet closely related treaty claims.[55]

Still, several authorities may be cited in favour of the diametric proposition that a single set of circumstances relating to the interests of alien nationals may generate analytically distinct inter-state treaty claims and diplomatic protection claims—with each set of claims subject to a separate jurisdictional regime. Hence, jurisdictional regulations governing diplomatic protection should not necessarily carry over to the state of nationality's direct claims. This was essentially the position taken by

[51] See eg, Vienna Convention on Consular Relations, 24 April 1963, art 36, 596 UNTS 261.

[52] International Law Commission Draft Article on Diplomatic Protection, Report of the International Law Commission, GAOR 61st Sess, Supp No 10 (A/61/10)(2006).

[53] *ELSI*, 1989 ICJ at 42–3 ('The Chamber, however, has not found it possible in the present case to find a dispute over alleged violation of the FCN Treaty resulting in direct injury to the United States, that is both distinct from, and independent of, the dispute over the alleged violation in respect of Raytheon and Machlett').

[54] For support of this formulation, see *Avena* (Mexico v US), 43 ILM 581, 636 (Separate Opinion of Judge Parra-Aranguren); ibid, at 630 (Separate Opinion of Judge Vereshchetin).

[55] See also *Mexican Union Railway (Ltd)* (GB v Mexico), 5 RIAA 115, 120 (1930) (a Calvo Clause governs the separate claim of the foreign state against the host state if the foreign state's interest in the claim is limited to representation of its national).

the PCIJ in the *Chorzów Factory* and *Serbian Loans* case,[56] the ICJ in the *Avena* case,[57] and ITLOS in the merits phase of the *M/V Saiga* case.[58] In the same vein, the UK Court of Appeals suggested in the recent *Occidental* case that the right to bring suit, which investment treaties confer upon private investors, is independent from the right conferred by the same treaties upon their state of nationality.[59]

The impact of applicable law

The identification of jurisdictional overlap between national and international courts might depend, at the end of the day, on acceptance of the proposition that two claims formally grounded in different legal systems can nonetheless be viewed as 'essentially the same'.[60] This position can be maintained through two potential methods of reasoning, each of which entails different delineations of the potential scope of competition:

a) *Application of the same body of law*—When national courts directly and explicitly apply international law to the disputes before them,[61] they become engaged in a dispute resolution or law application project of a comparable nature to the process of resolution or application that could have or has taken place before international courts. This is because all relevant courts perform essentially the same task within the context of the same normative system.[62] The claims before the two sets of judicial bodies can thus be viewed as 'essentially the same' despite their different institutional underpinnings. Virtually the same argument governs instances where international courts and tribunals apply national law in parallel to national courts (eg, ICSID or NAFTA Chapter 19);

b) *Application of the same substantive normative standards and remedies*—when national courts apply a body of law that prescribes essentially the same rules of

[56] *Chorzów Factory*, 1927 PCIJ (Ser A), No 13, at p 28 ('Rights or interests of an individual the violation of which rights causes damage are always in a different plane than rights belonging to a State, which rights may also be infringed by the same act'); *Payment of Various Serbian Loans Issued in France* (France v Serb–Croat–Slovene), 1929 PCIJ (Ser A), No, 20/21, at 18 ('there exists between the two Governments a difference of opinion which, though fundamentally identical with the controversy already existing between the Serb-Croat-Slovene Government and its creditors, is distinct therefrom'). See also *Certain German Interests*, 1925 PCIJ (Ser A), No 6, at 20.

[57] *Avena*, 43 ILM at 599. See also *Fierro*, above, n 49, at para 56 (inter-state proceedings before the ICJ and individual human rights complaint proceedings before the I/A Commission on Human Rights do not involve the 'same parties').

[58] *'M/V Saiga'* (Saint Vincent and the Grenadines v Guinea), judgment of 1 July 1999, at para 98 (merits), <www.itlos.org/case_documents/2001/document_en_68.doc>. But see ibid, at para 49–52 of the dissenting opinion of Judge Wolfrum (available at <www.itlos.org/case_documents/2000/document_en_97.doc>); ibid, at para 13–16 of the dissenting opinion of Judge Rao (available at <www.itlos.org/case_documents/2000/document_en_95.doc>); ibid, at para 61 of the dissenting opinion of Judge Warioba (available at <www.itlos.org/case_documents/2001/document_en_66.doc>).

[59] *Occidental Exploration and Production Co v Ecuador*, 45 ILM 249, 255–6 (2006). See also Zachary Douglas, 'The Hybrid Foundations of Investment Treaty Arbitrations', (2003) *BYIL* 151, 182.

[60] See *The Loewen Group, Inc v US*, 42 ILM 811, 848–9 (2003).

[61] The question of what constitutes 'direct and explicit application' of international standards might become more complicated when national law incorporated, by way of specific legislation, international law standards.

[62] For a discussion, see above, Chapter 2.

conduct as the applicable norms of international law (or other bodies of law) that bind the competing international procedure and entails essentially the same remedies, one should regard the two proceedings as addressing 'essentially the same claims'.[63] Obviously, this second method of reasoning is more controversial as it advocates a much more informal and flexible approach to application of the 'same issues' test.

It is perhaps interesting to note that both of the aforementioned methodological alternatives facilitate competition between different national courts operating in separate national legal systems. Under alternative (a), national courts that apply international law can compete with other national courts (of different countries) that also apply international law—international law being a 'common language', facilitating the interaction.[64] One may argue that international law's competition-regulating rules can govern such interactions when transpiring between international law-applying bodies.

Under alternative (b), national courts can compete with one another if the applicable laws before them offer essentially identical protections and remedies. However, as already noted, the potential application of the international jurisdiction-regulating norms (as discussed below) to such interactions usually depends on the scope of incorporation of international law into the respective national systems.

It is in relation to the first alternative assertion—that competition between national courts and international courts applying the same body of law is possible—that monists and dualists are likely to part ways: monism and other theories of normative systemization view international and national legal systems as parts of a single normative enterprise, whereas dualism insists on their separation. Hence, while the same legal claim could conceivably be addressed by international and national courts under monism, dualists would probably reject that possibility altogether and regard the law-applying roles of national and international courts as conceptually discrete. In fact, dualists may further posit that even when domestic courts explicitly apply international law, they do so through the prism of national law, an event that prevents the transposition of their jurisprudence to the international level.[65]

[63] See eg, *Waste Management*, 40 ILM 56, 67–8 (2001) (NAFTA, art 1121 requires claimants to waive all proceedings relating to the same measures, including any challenge based on a different law). But see ibid, at 78–9 (dissenting opinion of Highet). For a discussion, see Dodge, above n 8, at 189–90; William S Dodge, 'National Courts and International Arbitration: Exhaustion of Remedies and Res Judicata under Chapter Eleven of NAFTA', 23 *Hastings Int'l & Comp L Rev* (2000) 357, 371.

[64] See Francesco Francioni, 'International Law as a Common Language for National Courts', 36 *Tex Int'l LJ* (2001) 587.

[65] See eg, Rett R Ludwikowski, 'Supreme Law or Basic Law? The Decline of the Concept of Constitutional Supremacy' 9 *Cardozo J Int'l & Comp L* (2001) 253, 255; Cyril M. Picciotto, *Relation of International Law to the Law of England and the United States* (1915) 10 (Introduction by Lassa Oppenheim); George Slyz, 'International Law in National Courts', 28 *NYU J Int'l L & Pol* (1996) 65, 67. See also Hans Kelsen, *Principles of International Law* (Robert W Tucker, ed, 2nd edn, 1966) 293–4; Gunther Teubner, 'Global Bukowina: Legal Pluralism in the World Society', *Global Law Without a State* (Gunther Teubner, ed, 1997) 3, 13 ('It is the phenomenological world constructions

The second alternative assertion—that the substance of the rights and remedies, and not their source of validity, is the overriding criterion—circumvents the monism/dualism debate. Still, this position does invite consideration of policy alternatives, ie, a choice between disintegrative and integrative methods of addressing formally separate yet substantively similar legal claims. Here, too, I would prefer a flexible methodology that examines the entire gamut of the rights, obligations and potential remedies under all relevant legal orders and discourages 'claim splitting'. Such a methodology is more attuned to the aforementioned rationales inherent in the major competition-regulating norms—mitigation of practical inconvenience to the parties and abatement of the risk of inconsistent judgments.[66] Still, I must acknowledge that this approach cannot be said to represent current *lex lata*.

Furthermore, the application of jurisdiction-regulating rules that curb multiple proceedings can be justified, to a large extent, by the need for protecting the *perceived* coherency and legitimacy of the international legal system.[67] However, this policy consideration supports the introduction of such rules only where international law is explicitly invoked in the different courts. Hence, the policy arguments for mitigating substantive overlap, which arise under a flexible paradigm, may be supportable from a pragmatic point of view but less compellingly from a doctrinal perspective.

In all events, even according to a loose definition of the 'same legal claims' sub-test (alternative (b)), most domestic proceedings would fail to overlap international proceedings. This is because the residual application of domestic law by domestic courts is expected to introduce new rights, obligations or remedies, or bar reliance on the international rights, obligations and remedies available in international judicial fora.[68] In consequence, national and international fora may, at times, inevitably reach divergent conclusions on the legality of the same transaction and its repercussions.[69] In short, even when international law norms can be invoked before domestic courts, the domestic law prism under which they are applied is likely to have a distorting effect on their contents. Full-scale competition between national and international courts operating in a non-hierarchical context is thus expected to take place in a limited number of cases: for example, if international law has been fully incorporated into domestic law and there are no additional domestic norms of relevance, or where international courts are directed to apply primarily domestic law.[70] While these scenarios are not unimaginable, they are expected to

within a discourse that determine the globality of the discourse, and not the fact that the source of the use of [legally coercive] force is local').

[66] See also Reinisch, above, n 31, at 64–5.

[67] Shany, above, n 20, at 117–19.

[68] For example, if the *SGS v Pakistan* tribunal was correct in believing that the Pakistani arbitrator was unable to address the BIT claims (*SGS v Pakistan*, 42 ILM at 1316) and that the BIT did not encompass contract claims, then its conclusion that the two proceedings were never in genuine competition to one another (*SGS v Pakistan*, 42 ILM at 1322) appears plausible. See also *Joy Mining Machinery Ltd. v Egypt*, 44 ILM 73, 84 (2005).

[69] See eg, *Compania de Aquas del Aconquija, S.A. v. Argentina*, 41 ILM 1135, 1154 (2002) (hereinafter *Vivendi II*) ('A State may breach a treaty without breaching a contract and vice versa').

[70] See eg, ICSID Convention, art 42(1).

be quite rare.[71] Still, as I argue below, resort to flexible principles discussed in Chapter 6, which govern cases of competing proceedings and related proceedings will always be desirable.

4.4 Interim Conclusions

The application of jurisdiction-regulating norms to jurisdictional interactions between national and international courts depends on the theoretic characterization of that relationship and on the ability of the involved courts to invoke, directly or indirectly, international law standards. Hence, before exploring the application of any particular jurisdiction-regulating norm, one has to examine the hierarchical (or non-hierarchical) configuration of the courts involved in the jurisdictional interaction and to explore the permissibility of domestic courts reliance on international law (or, in some cases, on identical domestic standards). While this examination may lead to decisive answers in some instances—especially, when clear hierarchy or non-hierarchy signifiers are available—its outcome may turn on a variety of policy and ideological considerations in other cases.

Still, even if regulation is conceivable, one has to confront the difficult challenge of ascertaining the identicalness of the disputes that are amenable to the concurrent jurisdiction of national and international courts. The application of the traditional 'same parties' and 'same issues' tests to the interaction between national and international judicial bodies is acutely problematic since differences in the rules of personal standing as well as the actual and conceptual distinctions between domestic and international law add several layers of complexity to the tests. At the end of the day, it would seem as if a policy choice between flexibility and inflexibility—not dissimilar to the choice expounded in Chapter 3 between disintegrationist and integrationist approaches—is required. A flexible approach would seek to harmonize between the various proceedings and their potential outcomes by inclining toward application of jurisdiction-regulating rules; at the same time, an inflexible approach would narrowly construe the prerequisites and often deny the very existence of jurisdictional competition. While this last strategy is vulnerable to the criticism that it perpetuates rather than resolves jurisdictional problems,[72] it cannot be denied that it offers a clear and simple way out of many of the legal conundrums invited by jurisdictional coordination through judicial means.

[71] ILA Committee on International Commercial Arbitration, Final Report on *Lis Pendens* and Arbitration (2006) 4 (copy with author). Cf Dan Ciobanu, 'Litispendence between the International Court of Justice and the Political Organs of the United Nations', 1 *The Future of the International Court of Justice* (Leo Gross, ed, 1977) 209, 216 ('because of the peculiar nature of inter-State relations, one could hardly find a single case in which at least one of the three conditions of litispendence, mentioned above, would not be absent').

[72] See also Schreuer (1981), above, n 24, at 331–2.

5

Application of Jurisdictional-regulating Norms

The discussion conducted in Chapter 4 provides, as I see it, a sufficient basis for the proposition that domestic and international proceedings can be viewed as concurrent proceedings in need of jurisdictional regulation if certain prerequisites are met. This is particularly the case when national and international courts apply international law (including international jurisdiction-regulating rules) to the same dispute yet do not consider themselves jurisdictionally superior to one another. Even then, a policy choice might still be available to courts and other policy makers when evaluating the scope and applicability of international law's jurisdiction-regulating rules to the said interaction. From another perspective, this choice is, arguably, comparable to that to be made between the disintegrationist and integrationist methodologies discussed in Chapter 3 above.

This chapter describes the key international jurisdiction-regulating rules that govern competing proceedings. Such rules can be divided into two principal and subsequent sub-categories: a) choice of forum rules—ie, general freedom of choice principles and specific forum selection arrangements, ranging from exclusive jurisdiction to residual jurisdiction clauses; and b) multiple proceedings-regulating norms, comprised of the principles of election (*electa una via* or 'fork in the road'), *lis alibi pendens*, and *res judicata*. A third group of overarching principles—comity and abuse of right—can also be identified. However, their application does not necessarily hinge on the existence of full jurisdictional overlap between national and international proceedings; furthermore, they may encompass related proceedings (including proceedings taking place in the context of vertical jurisdictional interaction). Hence, they will be discussed separately in Chapter 6.

Given the sparse and haphazard nature of existing rules regulating jurisdictional interaction between national and international courts, it is often difficult if not outright impossible to identify treaty law or customary law on the matter. Recourse to domestic law and, in particular, to the practice of national courts involved in jurisdictional competition cases (involving, inter alia, foreign national courts), in the hope of identifying general principles of law, may thus be necessary.[73]

[73] Such an analogy must, however, be undertaken with proper caution, while bearing in mind the differences between foreign and international adjudication. Cf Schreuer (1981), above, n 24, at 15.

5.1 Choice of Forum Rules

International law does not normally limit the parties' freedom to choose whether to litigate their disputes before national or international judicial fora in clear and explicit language. As the next segment illustrates, the parties are free to choose a forum together: Forum selection agreements are generally enforceable; in the absence of a joint choice of forum, applicants normally retain the freedom to 'forum shop', ie, choose which amenable jurisdiction to invoke. Hence, international law seems to embrace a liberal jurisdiction-regulating regime that values party autonomy and freedom of choice. At the same time, this regime assigns relatively little weight to objective considerations such as judicial efficiency.

5.1.1 Forum-selection agreements

Contractual clauses

The first question to be addressed is what effect is to be given by national courts to agreements in which parties to a dispute accept the jurisdiction of an international court and vice versa, specifically, what effect should international courts grant an agreement to refer the dispute to a national court? Such acceptance of jurisdiction or reference is expressed, inter alia, in the form of binding forum selection clauses found in contracts or through exclusive jurisdiction clauses found in the constitutive instruments of the relevant international courts.

There is little question nowadays that agreements representing a choice of jurisdiction, as concluded by the parties to a dispute, should be generally enforced—an outcome that stems directly from the *pacta sunt servanda* principle, which constitutes a general principle of law.[74] Indeed, it is the virtually uniform practice of national courts to enforce exclusive choice of forum agreements (including agreements referring disputes to foreign courts), unless they are unfair or unreasonable, or contravene important public policies.[75] Such a rule of enforceability has been prescribed as well by the Brussels Judgments Convention and the Hague Choice of Court Convention (with relation to choice of foreign courts),[76] and the New York Convention (with regard to choice of arbitral fora).[77] It can therefore be asserted

[74] See Bin Cheng, *General Principles of Law as Applied by International Courts and Tribunals* (1987) 112–14.

[75] See eg, *Breman v Zapata Offshore Co*, 1407 US 1 (1972); *The 'Eleftheria'*, [1969] All ER 641 (P); *Oceanic Sun Line Special Shipping Co Inc v Fay*, 165 CLR 197 (1998) (High Court of Australia); CA 25/63 *Oneon Insurance Co Ltd v Moshe*, 17 PD 646 (Supreme Court of Israel); ZPO § 38 (German Civil Code); Civil Procedure Law § 24 (China); Code of Civil Procedure, art 25 (Japan); *Harvest Trader*, 28 Oct 1988, [1988] NJ 765 (Supreme Court of the Netherlands).

[76] Brussels Judgments Convention, art 13, 17, 21; Convention on the Choice of Court Agreements, 30 June 2005, art 5–6, 44 ILM 1294 (hereinafter Choice of Court Convention).

[77] Convention on the Recognition and Enforcement of Foreign Arbitral Awards, 10 June 1958, art II(3), 330 UNTS 38 (hereinafter New York Convention). See also ILA Committee Report, above, n 71, at 19.

that the presumptive validity of choice of forum agreements constitutes a general principle of law.[78]

Similarly, international court practice supports the conclusion that choice of forum arrangements directing disputes to the jurisdiction of national courts ought, as a rule, to be respected. For example, the practice of the mixed claims commissions on the effects of contractual Calvo Clauses, which confer to national courts exclusive jurisdiction over contractual claims, leans towards the position that such clauses are enforceable and so divest claims commissions of jurisdiction over claims relating to contracts.[79] In the same vein, the PCIJ held in several cases that competent international courts should exercise their jurisdiction if seized by the parties, unless faced with a sufficiently clear exclusive jurisdiction arrangement directing another court to exercise jurisdiction over the same case.[80] Significantly, at least one of these cases—the *Chorzów Factory* case—involved alleged jurisdiction competition between domestic and international procedures.

Even the inconsistent ICSID case law on the jurisdictional interaction between contract and treaty claims, discussed in Chapter 1, generally supports the enforceability of contractual choice of forum agreements. While the tribunals differed in their positions regarding the effect of the contractual clause vis-à-vis the related treaty claims, they all seem to have accepted that ICSID was divested of jurisdiction over contract claims by virtue of the contractual forum selection clause.[81]

Interpretive challenges to the enforcement of choice of forum provisions

While there are some precedents where international courts refused to give effect to forum-selection instruments referring disputes to domestic judicial fora, such decisions usually presented interpretive challenges to the reach of the forum-selection instruments rather than to the notion of their enforceability.

One issue that has arisen in this context is whether the parties to the forum-selection agreement intended the choice to be preclusive of other fora. For example, in *Lanco*—an ICSID case relating to foreign investment in Argentina—the tribunal held that the contractual clause by which the parties undertook to 'agree to the jurisdiction' of domestic Argentinean administrative tribunals was not designed to constitute an *exclusive* jurisdiction clause, meant to divest ICSID of its jurisdiction.[82]

78 See Shany, above, n 20, at 153.

79 *Woodruff* (US v Venezuela), 9 RIAA 213 (1903); *North American Dredging Company of Texas* (US v Mexico), 4 RIAA 26 (1926); *El Oro Mining and Railway Co (Ltd)* (GB v Mexico), 5 RIAA 191 (1931); *Mexican Union Railway*, 5 RIAA 115 (1930).

80 See *Rights of Minorities in Upper Silesia (Minority Schools)* (Germany v Poland), 1928 PCIJ (Ser A), No 15, at 23; *Chorzów Factory*, 1927 PCIJ (Ser A), No 9, at 30; *Mavrommatis*, 1924 PCIJ (Ser A), No 2, at 31. For a discussion of these cases, see Shany, above, n 20, at 230–4.

81 *SGS v Philippines*, above, n 48, at para 138 ('The basic principle in each case is that a binding exclusive jurisdiction clause in a contract should be respected unless overridden by another valid provision'). See also *Vivendi I*, 40 ILM at 443. These decisions appear to be consistent with *Vivendi II*, which suggested that an exclusive jurisdiction arrangement found in a contract should bar international tribunals from addressing disputes which are predominantly of a contractual nature. *Vivendi II*, 41 ILM at 1155. See also *SGS v Pakistan*, 42 ILM at 1318.

82 *Lanco International Inc v Argentina*, 40 ILM 457, 466 (2001).

This is because under Argentinean law, the jurisdiction assigned to administrative tribunals is mandatory, not consent-based. Hence, the said contractual clause merely acknowledged an already existing legal situation. However, this position was criticized by the ICSID tribunal in *SGS v Philippines*. The latter tribunal remarked that the mandatory nature of the jurisdiction of the domestic court selected by a contractual clause does not imply that the parties could not have agreed, through conclusion of a forum-selection clause, to block other avenues for dispute settlement.[83]

Here, as in other situations involving the interpretation of the preclusive effect of one jurisdictional instrument vis-à-vis the other,[84] one's views on the feasibility and appropriateness of adjudication before the competing forum influence the interpretive process.[85] This last proposition receives some support in the *Chorzów Factory* case, where the PCIJ held that differences in the remedies available to the applicant under domestic and international law would create a presumption against attributing to the parties the intent to designate exclusivity to the domestic procedure.[86] Hence, policy considerations relating to the need to protect effectively the entire gamut of rights owed to the disputing parties might militate in favour of permitting multiple litigation of related claims. At the same time, fairness considerations might pull in the other direction, Indeed, in the early 20th century, mixed claims commission opined in a number of cases that it would be unjust and inequitable to construe inter-state agreements establishing their jurisdiction in a way that would effectively nullify contractual choice of forum provisions freely negotiated between the parties to the investment.[87]

Another interpretive question that affects the impact of contractual choice of forum provisions is directed at the actual interplay between different jurisdiction-conferring instruments—especially to the relations between the *lex specialis* and *lex posteriori* principles. While most of the international judicial decisions in which contractual clauses were given effect were based on the notion that such clauses represent *lex specialis* norms that override general provisions conferring jurisdiction

[83] *SGS v Philippines*, above, n 48, at para 138, n 68.

[84] See eg, *SGS v Philippines*, above, n 48, at para 138; *Vivendi II*, 41 ILM at 1151. An analogous question of interpretation may arise in the case of treaty provisions purporting to deviate from pre-existing forum clauses. See eg, Declaration of the Government of the Democratic and Popular Republic of Algeria concerning the Settlement of Claims by Iran and the United States, 19 Jan 1981, art VII(2), 20 ILM 230 (1981)(hereinafter Settlement of Claims Declaration); *North American Dredging Co*, 4 RIAA at 32.

[85] For a discussion of conflicting decisions on the implied exclusivity of international dispute settlement arrangements, see Schreuer (1981), above, n 24, at 338–9. Schreuer argued that there should exist a presumption that some international procedures, such as the employment-related claim procedures for employees of IGOs, were designed to be exclusive. Ibid, at 339–40.

[86] *Chorzów Factory*, 1927 PCIJ (Ser A), No 9, at 30. Some support to this proposition is also found in *Klöckner Industrie-Angalen GmbH v Cameroon*, 2 ICSID Rep 3, 115 (1985)(ad hoc annulment committee) (parties should be presumed not to have waived through later-in-time agreements the protections afforded to them by the ICSID Convention).

[87] See eg, *Woodruff*, 9 RIAA at 222; *North American Dredging Co*, 4 RIAA at 33; *Mexican Union Railway*, 5 RIAA at 120. But see Ted L Stein, 'Jurisprudence and Jurists' Prudence: The Iranian-Forum Clause Decisions of the Iran-U.S. Claims Tribunal', 78 *AJIL* (1984) 1, 25.

on international courts,[88] some judges have stressed the *lex posteriori* nature of the latter provisions. For example, Antonio Crivellaro, the dissenting arbitrator in *SGS v Philippines*, took the position that the Swiss-Philippine BIT, which was concluded after the entry into force of the initial contract between the investor and the host state, conferred new benefits upon investors.[89] Hence, the BIT effectively altered the jurisdictional provisions of the contract and provided the investor with the right to refer the dispute to ICSID—notwithstanding its earlier commitment to limit itself to adjudication before domestic courts.[90]

It may be interesting to note that a comparable holding was adopted in *Martini*—an early 20th century decision issued by the Italian–Venezuelan Mixed Claims Commission—where it was held that a contractual exclusive jurisdiction provision between the parties to the dispute is overridden by a subsequent inter-state agreement referring to the commission all outstanding disputes between Venezuela and Italian investors relating to the political unrest in Venezuela. Still, the commission based its conclusion not on the *lex posteriori* principle but on the perceived supremacy of public inter-state arrangements over private contractual undertakings.[91]

Note, however, that the positions of Prof. Crivellaro in *SGS v Philippines* and the commission in *Martini* ultimately depend on a broad understanding of the intended effect of inter-state agreements on the parallel contractual choice of forum provisions—an interpretative position that may be open to challenge in some cases. Indeed, the majority in *SGS v Philippines* disputed the proposition that the BIT intended to interfere with the specific contractual undertaking entered into by the parties to the investment and held that the BIT was designed merely to provide a public international law framework for the investment.[92]

Finally, another interpretive challenge often raised relates to the material scope of forum-selection norms. As discussed in Chapter 4, different approaches exist as to whether potential proceedings before different courts pertain to 'the same dispute'—that is, whether they involve the same parties and raise the same issues. Hence, a question may arise as to whether competing sets of proceedings brought pursuant to different forum-selection clauses (eg, a contractual forum-selection

[88] See eg, *SGS v Philippines*, above, n 48, at para 141; *Mavrommatis*, 1924 PCIJ (Ser A), No 2, at 31–2; *Southern Pacific Properties (Middle East)(SPP) v Egypt* (jurisdiction), 3 ICSID Rep 131, 150 (1988). See also Ian Sinclair, *The Vienna Convention on the Law of Treaties* (2nd edn, 1984) 96–8; Vaughan Lowe, 'Overlapping Jurisdiction in International Tribunals', 20 *Australian YB International Law* (1999) 191, 195.

[89] *SGS v Philippines*, above, n 48, at para 10 of Crivellaro's declaration (available at, <http://www.worldbank.org/icsid/cases/SGSvPhil-declaration.pdf>) ('thanks to a subsequent treaty, the investor has become the beneficiary of a more favorable treatment, including the privilege to chose [sic] other forums'). The majority, however, questioned the validity of this characterization, noting that both the contract and the BIT were renewed on several occasions—making it virtually impossible to establish an anterior-posterior relationship. *SGS v Philippines*, above, n 48, at para 142.

[90] Ibid, Crivellaro's Declaration, at paras 9–10.

[91] *Martini & Co v Venezuela* (Italy v Venezuela), 10 RIAA 644, 663 (1903).

[92] *SGS v Philippines*, above, n 48, at para 142. The majority also disputed the applicability of the *lex posteriori* rule to instruments of a different nature, such as a treaty and a contract (but failed to explain its own willingness to apply the *lex specialis* rule to these same instruments). Ibid, at para 141.

clause regulating disputes over the interpretation or application of a contract, and a treaty-based clause governing disputes over the interpretation and application of a treaty) actually meet the said 'sameness' criteria. If not, then each of these forum-selection clauses cannot aspire to govern the conduct of the other set of proceedings.

Once again, the case law on the matter is inconsistent. For example, cases submitted to the mixed claims commissions and the PCIJ in the early 20th century demonstrate differences in approach as to whether Calvo Clauses and other exclusive jurisdiction-selection provisions governing relations between foreign nationals and host states preclude litigation between host states and the foreigners' states of nationality (in the exercise of diplomatic protection over their individual claims).[93] In the same vein, the conflicting ICSID decisions on the effects of a contractual choice of forum clause on BIT claims, discussed in Chapter 1, well demonstrate the interpretative tension existing with respect to the classification of similar claims presented under different legal instruments.[94] These interpretative questions depend, arguably, on the general policy choices between flexible and inflexible readings of jurisdictional clauses, discussed in Chapters 3 and 4.

5.1.2 Treaty provisions on choice of forum

Exclusive jurisdiction clauses

Another potential source for valid choice of forum norms are exclusive jurisdiction provisions found among the constitutive instruments of several international courts. Such provisions preclude the disputing parties from litigating disputes falling under their jurisdiction before any other judicial forum. While exclusive jurisdiction provisions were designed mainly to regulate jurisdictional relations between different international courts,[95] the language of some provisions can lend itself to cases of competition between national and international courts. In fact, there is clear evidence that the drafters of article 23 of the WTO Dispute Settlement Understanding (DSU)—an exclusive jurisdiction clause—were primarily preoccupied with preventing national courts from determining violations of GATT law (fearing that such determinations would weaken the authority of the DSB); their intent was to achieve this effect through the language of article 23.[96] It would seem that national courts that fail to uphold such choice of forum provisions may implicate the international responsibility of their countries.[97]

[93] See eg, *Woodruff*, 9 RIAA at 222; *Mexican Union Railway*, 5 RIAA at 120; *Chorzów Factory*, 1927 PCIJ (Ser A) No 9, at 26.

[94] See *SGS v Pakistan*, 42 ILM at 1318; *SGS v Philippines*, above, n 48, at paras 141–3; *Vivendi I*, 40 ILM at 443; *Vivendi II*, 41 ILM at 1154.

[95] For a discussion, see Shany, above, n 20, at 180–95.

[96] See Raj Bhala and Kevin Kennedy, *World Trade Law* (1998) 43; Terrence P Stewart (ed), II *The GATT/Uruguay Round: A Negotiating History* (1986–1992) (1993) 2777.

[97] See eg, *Lanco*, 40 ILM at 470 ('if a local court does not apply the norm, it may expose its own State to an international claim . . .').

Still, most exclusive jurisdiction clauses applied through the constitutive instruments of international courts may be inappropriate or ineffective in regulating jurisdictional competition between national and international courts. Exclusive jurisdictional arrangements under economic integration regimes, such as article 292 of the EC Treaty,[98] or article 55 of the European Human Rights Convention, are largely irrelevant for national courts. This is because the EC and ECHR treaty regimes, by creating a system of vertical supervision of national courts, negate one of the principal prerequisites for the existence of jurisdictional competition—non-hierarchical configuration. Another exclusive jurisdiction provision—article 26 of the ICSID Convention[99]—is ineffective because while confirming the freedom of the parties to select a forum, it only provides that ICSID will enjoy exclusive jurisdiction, *if selected by the parties*.[100] The main utility of such a provision is, therefore, to provide an interpretive presumption in favour of the exclusivity of forum-selection provisions covering ICSID and to clarify that there is normally no need to exhaust local remedies before invoking ICSID's jurisdiction.[101] One should note, however, that in practice, this provision was used to block national courts from issuing provisional relief while ICSID proceedings were still pending.[102]

In any event, the same line of legal reasoning underlying the recognition and enforcement of exclusive jurisdiction clauses designed to protect the jurisdiction of international courts vis-à-vis national courts can also support opposing jurisdictional arrangements, providing for the exclusive jurisdiction of national courts in contradistinction to international courts. Indeed, the Iran–US Claims Tribunal respected, by and large, article II(1) of the Algiers Declaration on the Settlement of Claims between Iran and US that excluded from its jurisdiction disputes that the parties agreed to refer to the exclusive jurisdiction of the domestic Iranian courts.[103]

Other international law restrictions on forum shopping

Some contractual forum-selection clauses and exclusive jurisdiction provisions found in the constitutive instruments of international courts limit the parties' right

98 See also Andean Court Treaty, art 42; Protocol of Tegucigalpa of Reforms of the Charter of the Organization of the Central American States, 13 Dec 1991, art 3, <http://www.ccj.org.ni/CCJsite/doc_base/normjurd/prottegu.htm> (in Spanish); Treaty Instituting the Benelux Economic Union, 3 Feb 1958, art 51(1), 381 UNTS 165.

99 ICSID Convention, art 26 ('Consent of the parties to arbitration under this Convention shall, unless otherwise stated, be deemed consent to such arbitration to the exclusion of any other remedy. A Contracting State may require the exhaustion of local administrative or judicial remedies as a condition of its consent to arbitration under this Convention').

100 See Shany, above, n 20, at 194–5.

101 See *SGS v Philippines*, above, n 48, at paras 146–7 ('Article 26 was intended as a rule of interpretation, not a mandatory rule'); *Lanco*, 40 ILM at 469; Schreuer, above, n 12, at 368.

102 See eg, *Marine International Nominees Establishment (MINE) v Guinea*, 3 ICSID Rep 13, 35 (1983) (ICSID Panel); *Guinea v Marine International Nominees Establishment (MINE)*, 4 ICSID Rep 32, 33–4 (1985) (Court of First Instance, Belgium); *Guinea v Marine International Nominees Establishment (MINE)*, 4 ICSID Rep 39, 40 (1985) (Tribunal Fédéral, Switz); *Guinea v Atlantic Triton Co*, 3 ICSID Rep 7, 11 (1986) (Cour de Cassation, France). See also Dodge, above, n 63, at 371. But see, *Atlantic Triton Co v Guinea*, 3 ICSID Rep 13, 35 (1983) (ICSID panel).

103 This provision has been, however, narrowly construed by the Tribunal. Charles N Brower and Jason D. Brueschks, *The Iran-United State Claims Tribunal* (1998) 60–72; Mohsen Mohebi, *The International Law Character of the Iran-United States Claims Tribunal* (1999) 142.

to initiate litigation before a national or international court that would otherwise have been competent to address the case. These are, however, not the only sources that set limitations on the freedom to 'forum shop', ie, the parties' right to choose among the different available fora. Several international rules may be mentioned in this regard.

First, it has already been observed that some international treaties create hierarchical relations between national and international courts. These instruments often provide that international courts may be seized only after domestic courts have addressed the same matter, either partially or fully; they thus regulate the order of the proceedings and necessarily circumscribe the applicant's ability to seize an international forum directly. However, as noted above, these jurisdictional arrangements are largely irrelevant for the subject of the present chapter, which focuses on *horizontal* and not vertical interaction between national and international courts.

Another, perhaps more relevant, horizontal jurisdiction-regulating regime is found in the field of international criminal law, where some choice between national and international courts is available in the sense that prosecuting authorities can decide whether to pursue a criminal case before national or international judicial fora.[104] However, this choice is normally governed by rules assigning preference to one forum over the other: the constitutive instruments of most international and hybrid criminal courts include jurisdiction-allocation provisions that accord primacy to international courts when they deem it necessary,[105] or give right of way to national courts willing and able to prosecute the case (under a rule of complementarity).[106] Interestingly enough, no uniformity of approach as to the preferential status of national or international courts can be identified even in this narrow field of international law.

Some other legal instruments—such as BITs—often provide parties to specific transactions with a limited choice of procedure, which may include a choice between specific international and national courts.[107] Such arrangements necessarily limit the exercise of choice by the parties between specified and non-specified courts: it would seem that the listing of a few specified courts bars the parties from choosing

[104] It should be noted that although criminal proceedings in different jurisdictions do not technically involve the same parties, given the differences in the identities of the prosecuting authorities, one can maintain that the prosecution of violations of international criminal law before national courts is executed, in fact, on behalf of the international community and that such proceedings advance the same set of interests to those pursued in international proceedings. See eg, *Eichmann v Attorney-General*, 36 ILR 277, 304 (1962) (Supreme Court, Israel). Consequently, it is arguable that the parties are 'essentially the same' and that primacy, concurrency or complementarity rules govern forum selection between competing national and international procedures. Indeed, several instances of application of jurisdiction-regulating rules, designed to divide labour between national and international criminal proceedings, can be identified. See eg, *In re Tadić*, I ICTY Judicial Reports 3, 19 (1994) (application for deferral of case pending before the German courts to the ICTY); *Bagaragaza*, above, n 45 (application for transfer of case from ICTR to Norway).

[105] A rule of supremacy was introduced in the ICTY, ICTR, and SCSL Statute. ICTY Statute, art 9; ICTR Statute, art 8; SCSL Statute, art 8. The jurisdictional regime adopted by other hybrid tribunals is less clear. See above, Chapter 1 at n 36.

[106] ICC Statute, art 17.

[107] See above, n 11.

non-specified courts. And, as the discussion in the next section on the application of the *electa una via* rule will demonstrate, once a certain court has been selected by an applicant party, it may not invoke the jurisdiction of another court.[108]

Finally, residual jurisdiction arrangements, such as article 282 of UNCLOS, may also limit choice of fora since they confer primacy on jurisdictional arrangements concluded outside the legal regime in question.[109] Hence, an agreement to litigate a marine dispute before a national court of one of the states involved in the dispute may arguably bar the same parties from invoking dispute settlement procedures under article 287 of UNCLOS[110] (but not matters governed by specific UNCLOS procedures such as seabed area disputes).[111]

5.1.3 The general permissibility of forum shopping

So, various instruments—contracts, treaties and the like—introduce limitations on the parties' freedom to choose between national and international courts. The question remaining to be decided, however, is whether there exists a general principle of law that supplements the specific contractual or treaty arrangements and

[108] The 'no U-turn' rule found in Chapter 11 of NAFTA and several other investment protection instruments applies the restriction on the choice of more than one forum in a more nuanced manner so as to block invocation of national courts only after international arbitration had been selected. See eg, NAFTA, art 1121; CAFTA, art 10.18(2)(b); Treaty Concerning the Encouragement and Reciprocal Protection of Investment (US/Uruguay), 25 Oct 2004, art 26(2)(b) <http://www.ustr.gov/assets/World_Regions/Americas/South_America/Uruguay_BIT/asset_upload_file582_6728.pdf> (hereinafter Uruguay/US BIT); Chile/US FTA, art 10.17(2)(b).

[109] For a discussion, see Shany, above, n 20, at 201–8.

[110] The language of the United Nations Convention on the Law of the Sea, 10 Dec 1982, art 282, UN Doc A/CONF.62/122 (1982), 21 ILM 1261 (1982) (hereinafter UNCLOS), is arguably broad enough to encompass selection of domestic courts: 'If the States Parties which are parties to a dispute concerning the interpretation or application of this Convention have agreed, through a general, regional or bilateral agreement or otherwise, that such dispute shall, at the request of any party to the dispute, be submitted to a *procedure that entails a binding decision*, that procedure shall apply in lieu of the procedures provided for in this Part, unless the parties to the dispute otherwise agree'(emphasis added).

[111] Recourse to domestic courts appears to be barred in disputes relating to the seabed area involving private entities, because these disputes are governed by the choice of forum provisions of article 188 of UNCLOS (which directs the parties to international commercial arbitration). Furthermore, article 188 (which belongs to Part XI of UNCLOS) appears to fall outside the residual jurisdiction arrangement found in article 282 of the Convention that applies to the dispute settlement bodies mentioned in Part XV of UNCLOS. The situation is less clear with respect to prompt release of vessel situations. Here, too, the language of UNCLOS implies that an agreement to resort to domestic adjudication might divest ITLOS of jurisdiction over the case. UNCLOS, art 292(1) ('... the question of release from detention may be submitted to *any court* or tribunal agreed upon by the parties...') (emphasis added). However, the provision also envisions that the jurisdiction of ITLOS (or any other competent international court) would be invoked while domestic proceedings relating to the offence underlying the vessel's detention are still pending. UNCLOS, art 292(3) ('The court or tribunal shall deal without delay with the application for release and shall deal only with the question of release, without prejudice to the merits of any case before the appropriate domestic forum against the vessel, its owner or its crew.'). In practice, ITLOS has rejected arguments claiming that invocation of the jurisdiction of domestic courts by the vessel's owner implies a waiver of ITLOS jurisdiction. See *Camouco*, 39 ILM at 678.

restricts forum shopping among judicial fora on the basis of their suitability to adjudicate the case. In other words, is there a general *forum non conveniens* principle under international law that would restrict the applicant party's freedom of choice?

International law has yet to develop a general *forum non conveniens* theory (although some jurisdictional rules, such as the rules of primacy and complementarity governing the work of international criminal tribunals, reflect prioritization of jurisdictions in specific legal contexts on the basis of their suitability to address certain types of disputes).[112] In the same vein, examination of analogous practices of domestic courts in regulating their jurisdictional relations vis-à-vis competing courts sitting in foreign jurisdictions (which could indicate the existence of a general principle of law or state practice from which customary law may be derived) reveals inconsistencies in the application of the *forum non conveniens* principle: while common law courts increasingly apply the *forum non conveniens* doctrine, which restricts the ability of applicant parties to select a local forum when a more-appropriate foreign forum is available,[113] this doctrine is not generally applied by civil law courts.[114] Furthermore, even common law courts often do not proscribe 'forum shopping' among judicial fora operating within the same legal system.[115] Hence, there appears to be no general principle of law or rule of custom that would preclude parties from choosing the proper forum before which to institute their claims in the absence of specific regulation on the matter.

Application of the *Lotus* principle—that states (and presumably other international actors) retain freedom of action in areas not covered by positive norms[116]—to choice of forum tactics would also support the conclusion that forum shopping between national and international judicial fora is generally permissible from

[112] For a discussion, see Shany, above, n 20, at 139–48. For a recent affirmation of this proposition in the context of competition between two international courts, see *Mexico—Tax Measures on Soft Drinks and Other Beverages*, WTO Doc WT/DS308/AB/R (2006), at para 44–57 (AB Report) (DSB panels do not have general discretion to dismiss claims just because NAFTA proceedings may be more appropriate).

[113] See eg, *Gulf Oil Corp v Gilbert*, 330 US 501 (1947); *Spiliada Maritime Corp v Cansulex Ltd*, [1987] AC 460; *Regie National des Usines Renault SA v Zhang*, [2002] HCA 10 (High Court of Australia); *Amchem Products Inc v British Columbia (Workers' Compensation Board)*, 102 DLR (4th) 96 (Supreme Court of Canada); *McDonnel Dowell Constructors Ltd v Lloyd's Syndicate 396* [1988] 2 NZLR 257 (New Zealand Court of Appeal).

[114] See eg, Haimo Schack, 'Report on Germany', *Declining Jurisdiction in Private International Law* (J J Fawcett, ed, 1995) 189. 195; J J Fawcett, 'General Report', ibid, at 1, 20–2.

[115] For example, the US Supreme Court generally tolerates forum shopping between state courts. See eg, *Allstate Insurance Co v Hague*, 449 US 302 (1981); *Sun Oil Co v Wortman*, 486 US 717 (1988). A similar approach has been adopted by Australian courts with regard to forum shopping between courts of the different Australian States or Territories. *McKain v R W Miller & Co (S Austl) Pty Ltd*, 175 CLR 1 (1991): *Stevens v Head*, 176 CLR 433 (1993). Moreover, civil law courts do not generally consider forum shopping to be a problem. Markus Lenenbach, 'Antisuit Injunctions in England, Germany and the United States: Their Treatment under European Civil Procedure and the Hague Convention', 20 *Loy LA Int'l & Comp LJ* (1998) 257, 297.

[116] *Lotus* (France v Turkey), 1927 PCIJ (Ser A), No 10, at 18–19.

an international law perspective.[117] This conclusion can be buttressed by several policy considerations: in general, the autonomy of the parties to make decisions regarding the dispute at hand ought to be respected; excessive rigidity in the allocation of jurisdiction may result in negative conflicts of jurisdiction (situations where all potential courts may refuse to adjudicate the case);[118] freedom of choice usually encourages litigation (as it increases the likelihood that the applicant will identify a competent and convenient forum) and this, in turn, promotes enforcement of the rule of law in general and international norms in particular;[119] finally, competition between courts over cases encourages them to improve the quality of their work and procedures in order to attract business.[120]

Still, the general right to forum shop ought to be qualified by one important condition: courts should not entertain claims brought before them through an abusive process. This qualification—which enjoys considerable support in the literature as well as international and domestic case law and is reflected in a number of international instruments—means that while some forms of forum shopping should be tolerated, abusive forum shopping is prohibited under international law as it conflicts, by definition, with the general principle of law prohibiting abuse of rights (*abus de droit*).[121] The scope and implications of this qualifying principle will be further discussed in Chapter 6.

5.2 Multiple Proceedings

Whereas the first part of this chapter addressed the parties' initial choice of forum, prior to the initiation of any court proceedings, this second half addresses situations in which one or more sets of proceedings have already been initiated. The question explored in this context is whether either general or specific rules limiting the parties' right to engage in multiple litigation can be identified.

There are, of course, cogent policy reasons that could justify, in principle, aversion of multiple proceedings relating to the same dispute. Multiple litigation draws heavily on scarce judicial resources, overburdens some of the litigants (typically the respondent party in the second set of proceedings)[122] and introduces the risk of inconsistent decisions, with all the ensuing legal uncertainty and practical difficulties. As a result, most domestic legal systems contain rules designed either to

[117] Joost Pauwelyn, 'Going Global, Regional, or Both? Dispute Settlement in the Southern African Development Community (SADC) and Overlaps with the WTO and Other Jurisdictions', 13 *Minn J Global Trade* (2004) 231, 290–1.

[118] See eg, Schreuer (1981), above, n 24, at 336; *Waste Management*, 41 ILM at 1321; *Chorzów Factory*, 1927 PCIJ (ser A) No 9, at 30.

[119] Shany, above, n 20, at 144–5.

[120] For a discussion, see Ibid, at 144.

[121] Ibid, at 137.

[122] Cf *SGS v Pakistan*, procedural order no 2, 16 Oct 2002, <http://www.worldbank.org/icsid/cases/SGS-order.pdf> ('The Tribunal, however, also believes that normally it would be wasteful of resources for two proceedings relating to the same or substantially the same matter to unfold separately while the jurisdiction of one tribunal awaits determination').

restrict the potential for multiple proceedings or mitigate their effects. The same can be said with respect to the manner in which international law regulates jurisdictional relations between different international courts. Here too, the dominant trend appears to be restriction of parallel or successive litigation of the same dispute.[123]

There is little reason to believe that similar policy considerations should not apply to the relations maintained between national and international proceedings. In fact, it would seem as if considerations of judicial economy, overall convenience and the need to reduce legal inconsistencies[124] would support regulation of multiple proceedings before national and international courts (provided that they operate in a non-hierarchical context). Given that, the applicability of the three most relevant jurisdiction-regulating rules found in the purely domestic or purely international context—*electa una via*, *lis alibi pendens*, and *res judicata*—to jurisdictional interactions between national and international courts ought to be explored.

5.2.1 *Electa una via*

The *electa una via* (the principle of election) reflects, essentially, an estoppel rule that bars a party that selected a specific forum for litigating a dispute from referring the same dispute to a different litigation forum.[125] In the field of international dispute resolution, it applies particularly in reference to the choice among various international human rights enforcement procedures,[126] and between NAFTA and WTO panels.[127] Still, the *electa una via* rule does not seem to reflect a general rule of international law;[128] it does not apply in the absence of an explicit treaty provision.[129]

[123] For a discussion, see Shany, above, n 20, at 175, 228, 270–1.

[124] This is especially so because of international law's notorious enforcement deficiencies, which complicate the prospects of resolving problems of conflicting judgments at the enforcement stage. See Schreuer (1981), above, n 24, at 328.

[125] For a discussion of the status of the estoppel rule, see Cheng, above, n 74, at 141–9.

[126] See ECHR, art 35(2); Convention against Torture and Other Cruel, Inhuman or Degrading Treatment or Punishment, 10 Dec 1984, art 22(5), GA res 39/46, annex, 39 UN GAOR Supp (No 51) at 197, UN Doc A/39/51 (1984); Optional Protocol to the Convention on the Elimination of All Forms of Discrimination against Women, 6 Oct 1999, art 4(2)(I), UN Doc A/54/49 (vol 1) (2000), 39 ILM 281 (2000); International Convention on the Protection of the Rights of All Migrant Workers and Members of Their Families, 18 Dec 1990, art 77(3), GA res 45/158, annex, 45 UN GAOR Supp (No 49A) at 262, UN Doc A/45/49 (1990).

[127] NAFTA, art 2005. A similar provision has been introduced into the MERCOSUR Protocol of Olivos. Olivos Protocol, 18 Feb 2002, art 1(2), 42 ILM 2 (2003).

[128] See Shany, above, n 20, at 229.

[129] This is demonstrated most clearly in the case law of the Human Rights Committee which accepts complaints after they have been addressed by other human rights mechanisms, See P R Ghandi, *The Human Rights Committee and the Right of Individual Communications: Law and Practice* (1988) 221–2. Confirmation of the position that the *electa una via* is not part of positive international law (in the absence of explicit provision to that effect) can be found in *Argentina—Definitive Anti-dumping Duties on Poultry from Brazil*, WTO Doc WT/DS241/R (2003), at para 7.38 (Panel Report) (rejecting an argument that litigation before MERCOSUR dispute settlement panels bars subsequent proceedings before the DSB).

Given its weak status under international law, it is rather difficult to maintain that the principle of election should govern relations between national and international courts as a default jurisdiction-regulating rule. Nevertheless, the comity and *abus de droit* principles discussed in Chapter 6 could place analogous limitations on improper forum-selection practices, as will be shown.

Some international legal instruments, especially in the field of international investment law, have adopted an *electa una via* rule (or 'fork in the road' provision) with respect to relations between national and international courts. For example, as previously indicated, several BITs and comparable instruments invite investors to choose whether to initiate proceedings before national courts or international arbitration tribunals.[130] A strong argument has been made that choice of one of the enumerated alternatives should necessarily bar, as a matter of treaty interpretation, the investor's ability to select all other dispute settlement alternatives[131] (at least when the choice of the domestic forum was freely undertaken).[132] Acceptance of this argument causes the rule to operate like an *electa una via* clause governing jurisdictional relations between different international courts.

As was already noted, article 1121 of NAFTA does not constitute an ordinary *electa una via* clause but, rather, a 'no U-turn provision', which bars domestic litigation after Chapter 11 arbitral proceedings have been initiated, but not vice versa—that is, invocation of domestic proceedings does not bar subsequent litigation before NAFTA.[133] Still, it is interesting to note that some recent investment protection instruments, such as CAFTA, have supplemented this rule by introducing an *electa una via* provision that would bar American investors from successively seizing domestic courts and international arbitration proceedings.[134] An *electa una via* rule has thus been established for US investors whereas a 'no U-turn' rule continues to apply for non-US investors.

130 See eg, Energy Charter, art 26(3)(b); CAFTA, Annex 10-E(2); US/Uruguay BIT, Annex C(2); Chile/U.S. FTA, Annex 10-E(2). Another *electa una via* rule can be found in art VII(2) of the 1981 Algiers Settlement of Claims Declaration ('Claims referred to the Arbitral Tribunal shall, as of the date of filing of such claims with the Tribunal, be considered excluded from the jurisdiction of the courts of Iran, or of the United States, or of any other court'). However, the Tribunal held that this provision does not necessarily bar arbitration proceedings. Case 333, *Flour Corp v Iran*, 11 Iran–US Cl Trib Rep 296 (1986) (interim award).

131 Schreuer, above, n 12, at 364; Gann, above, n 12, at 437–8; Gudgeon, above, n 12, at 51; Siqueiros, above, n 12, at 255–6; Parra, above, n 12, at 334–5, 351–2 (1997); Declaration of Prof Andreas Lowenfeld of 10 Nov 1999 (expert opinion submitted to ICSID in *Genin v Estonia*), at 6–7, available at <http://www.transnational-dispute-management.com>. See also *CMS*, 42 ILM at 800 ('Had the Claimant renounced recourse to arbitration, for example by resorting to the courts of Argentina, this would have been a binding selection under the BIT'); *Lanco*, 40 ILM at 468, 470. However, in investment disputes, there may be a need to distinguish between forum selection undertaken by the investor and the local corporation in which it invests. See eg, *CMS*, 42 ILM at 800; *Genin*, above, n 39, at para 332.

132 See *Genin*, above, n 39, at para 333; *Enron*, above, n 39, at para 98; *Occidental Exploration and Production Co v Ecuador*, Award of 1 July 2004, at para 60, <http://www.asil.org/ilib/OEPC-Ecuador.pdf> (UNCITRAL) (in all three cases, the tribunals held that the local company had no choice but to challenge the lawfulness of the adverse legal measure in domestic courts).

133 See *Waste Management*, 41 ILM at 1320–1.

134 See eg, CAFTA, Annex 10-E(2); US/Uruguay BIT, Annex C(2); Chile/US FTA, Annex 10-E(2).

5.2.2 *Lis alibi pendens*

The *lis alibi pendens* rule (or litispendence rule) is applied by the majority of national legal systems in order to prevent the parallel pendency of the same dispute before more than one court operating within the same legal system.[135] Much less certain is the principle's application in parallel proceedings before courts operating in different legal systems. While some national legal systems apply the rule in cross-border competition cases,[136] others do not.[137] A third group of national legal systems apply discretionary *forum non conveniens* doctrines to address multiple proceedings involving foreign courts.[138] One can therefore maintain that the *lis alibi pendens* rule applies as a general principle of law only in cases of intra-systemic jurisdictional competition.[139]

This conclusion on the intra-systemic field of application of the *lis alibi pendens* rule means that further conceptualization of the relations between national and international courts is required before application of the rule can be considered. Arguably, application of the rule is justified only if domestic courts are viewed as integral to the international legal system (at least when they apply international law). Even then, a question may arise as to whether the application of international law norms in domestic courts constitutes an intra-systemic form of interaction if the said norms are formally grounded in different legal regimes.[140]

The practice of applying the *lis alibi pendens* rule by international courts vis-à-vis domestic court proceedings is too sparse to be conclusive.[141] In the *Certain German Interests* case, the PCIJ opined that mixed arbitral tribunals operating on the basis of national law cannot generate genuine jurisdictional competition with the PCIJ. It therefore rejected a *lis alibi pendens* argument based on the parallel pendency of arbitration proceedings.[142] In the same vein, a 1985 ICSID arbitral panel decision disputed the very relevance of the rule to international adjudication (in a case involving, inter alia, competition between national and international procedures).[143]

135 See eg, Supreme Court Act 1981, s 49(2)(UK); Am Jur 2nd, Courts § 91; New Code of Civil Procedure, art 100 (France); Code of Civil Procedure, art 231 (Japan); Code of Civil Procedure, art 222 (Greece).

136 See eg, ZPO § 261(3); Private International Law Statute, art 9(1)(Switzerland); Brussels Judgments Convention, art 27. See also Henry Donnedieu de Vabres, 'Le conflit des lois de compétence judicaire dans les actions personnelles', 26 *Recueil des cours* (1929) 207, 262.

137 A most obvious example for the lack of applicability of the doctrine in competition across legal systems may be found in the US—under US law, parallel proceedings before state and federal courts are generally permissible. *Colorado River Water Conservation District v US* 424 US 800 (1976). Some other countries refuse to apply the *lis alibi pendens* rule to foreign proceedings. See eg, ILA Committee Report, above n 71, at 8.

138 See eg, *The 'Abidin Daver'*, [1984] AC 398; Restatement of the Law (2nd), Conflict of Laws, § 84 comment e (1971); *Sentry Corp v Peat Marwick Mitchell & Co*, 95 Aust LR 11 (1990) (Federal Court of Australia—General Div).

139 Reinisch, above, n 31, at 48; Shany, above, n 20, at 162.

140 For a parallel debate on the application of the *lis alibi pendens* to relations between different international courts, see Shany, above, n 20, at 239–45.

141 See eg, Karin Oellers-Frahm, 'Multiplication of International Courts and Tribunals and Conflicting Jurisdiction—Problems and Possible Solutions', 5 *Max Planck Yearbook of United Nations Law* (2001) 67, 77–8.

142 *Certain German Interests*, 1925 PCIJ (Ser A), No 6, at 19–20.

143 *SPP*, 3 ICSID Rep at 112, 129 (1985) (jurisdiction).

However, other authorities can also be invoked: a 1980 ICSID panel, when confronting a *lis alibi pendens* objection to jurisdiction, did not rule out possible application of the rule (although it found that the two parallel proceedings did not involve the same parties);[144] Clause 12 of ICSID Model Clauses also embraces a *lis alibi pendens* rule.[145] Furthermore, the UN Compensation Commission, responsible for indemnifying victims of Iraq's war in Kuwait, adopted a policy of suspending its proceedings upon initiation of proceedings before domestic courts.[146] Finally, it can be noted that Judge Vukas, in his dissent in the ITLOS *Camouco* case, was of the view that Panama's application to ITLOS while the same dispute was pending before local French courts was barred by reason of *lis alibi pendens*.[147] This view was not, however, accepted by the majority in the Tribunal.

The inconclusive nature of the theory and practice underlying the application of the *lis alibi pendens* rule to parallel national and international proceedings invites the conclusion that no hard and fast rule of international law on the matter appears to exist.[148] One should note in this regard that no substantial practice regarding application of the *lis alibi pendens* rule at the international level has evolved in relations between various international courts.[149] As a result, it would seem more prudent to address coordination issues between simultaneous proceedings from the perspective of the more general principles of comity and *abus de droit*, discussed in Chapter 6. This method of analysis represents a pragmatic way of bypassing the conceptual problems associated with the current state of legal uncertainty regarding *lis alibi pendens*.

5.2.3 *Res judicata*

There is little question that *res judicata* currently constitutes a general principle of law, applied in tandem by national and international courts.[150] *Res judicata*

144 *Benvenuti*, 3 ICSID Rep at 129.

145 ICSID Model Clauses, clause 12 ('The consent to the jurisdiction of the Centre recorded in [citation of basic clause above] shall not preclude either party hereto from resorting to the following alternative remedy: [identification of other type of proceeding]. While such other proceeding is pending, no arbitration proceeding pursuant to the Convention shall be instituted').

146 Norbert Wühler, 'The United Nations Compensation Commission: A New Contribution to the Process of International Claims Resolution', 2 *J Int'l Eco L* (1999) 249, 260.

147 *Camouco*, 39 ILM at 696 (dissenting opinion of Judge Vukas). Judge Vukas did however suggest that the *lis alibi pendens* rule might be derogated from by way of agreement or upon showing of vital reasons that justify derogation.

148 See ILA Committee Report, above, n 71, at 14 (*lis pendens* does not apply between supra-national and domestic courts).

149 See Shany, above, n 20, at 241–2. For example, the I/A CtHR suggested that the general interest of state parties to the I/A CHR in obtaining guidance from the court concerning their human rights obligations could mean that it should assume jurisdiction even if other international courts exercise parallel jurisdiction. Advisory Opinion OC-16/99, *The Right to Information on Consular Assistance in the Framework of Guarantees of the Due Process of Law*, Opinion of 1 Oct 1999, at paras 54–65, <http://www.corteidh.or.cr/docs/opiniones/seriea_16_ing.pdf>.

150 See eg, *Application of the Convention of the Crime of Genocide* (Bosnia v Serbia) Judgment of 26 Feb 2007, at paras 115–16; *Effects of Awards of the UN Administrative Tribunal*, 1954 ICJ 47, 53; *Chorzów Factory*, 1927 PCIJ (Ser A), No 13, at 27 (dissenting opinion of Judge Anzilotti); *Amco Asia*,

can likewise be regarded as part of customary international law.[151] However, this rule's scope of application to interactions between national and international courts depends upon the degree of flexibility associated with the definition of jurisdictional competition (ie, 'same parties' and 'same issues') adopted, and on the specific theory of relations between national and international courts applied.[152] Certainly, parties to litigation—even proceedings involving domestic and international courts—should be entitled to obtain closure, ie, a final decision upon which they can rely,[153] meaning release from continual harassment by endless legal proceedings.[154] Yet, irrespective of their validity, these interests ought sometimes to be balanced against the institutional interest of different courts in applying the normative prescriptions of their respective legal order to the dispute at hand—an institutional interest sometimes reflected in the court's constitutive instrument or the national constitution.

Although domestic courts often accord *res judicata* to domestic and international arbitral awards,[155] a number of countries do not apply the *res judicata* rule or its correlative in criminal cases—the *ne bis in idem* rule—to foreign judgments.[156] Rules of finality are sometimes inapplicable even across federal borders within the same country.[157] The application of *res judicata* across international regimes has also been questioned on occasion.[158] Such variety is indicative of less-than-universal acceptance of the flexible approach to jurisdictional competition presented in Chapter 4. As a result, it is perhaps not surprising that some international courts

1 ICSID Rep, at 549; *Trail Smelter*, 3 RIAA at 1950; *Waste Management*, 41 ILM at 1322; Cheng, above, n 74, at 336; Vaughan Lowe, 'Res Judicata and the Rule of Law in International Arbitration', 8 *African Journal of International and Comparative Law* (1996) 38, 39; Schreuer, above, n 12, at 1079–80; John Collier and Vaughan Lowe, *The Settlement of Disputes in International Law* (1999) 261; Reinisch, above, n 31, at 44. Most legal systems accept that the *res judicata* rule encompasses both claim-estoppel and issue-estoppel. Shany, above, n 20, at 165; Dodge, above, n 63, at 366; ILA Committee Report, above, n 34, at paras 51–64.

151 See Shany, above, n 20, at 245; Reinisch, above, n 31, at 44.

152 See Christoph H Schreuer, 'The Authority of International Practice in Domestic Courts', 23 *ICLQ* (1974) 681, 684.

153 Note, however, that jurisdictional decisions do not create, as a rule, a *res judicata* effect. *Waste Management*, 41 ILM 1315 (decisions on jurisdiction do not create *res judicata* with respect to proceedings on the merits). But see *Application of the Genocide Convention*, above, n 150, at para 138 (judments on jurisdiction create *res judicata* effect).

154 Cf *The Ampthill Peerage Case* [1977] AC 547, 575–6; Restatement of the Law (2nd), Conflict of Laws, § 98, comment b (1971); Neil Andrews, *Principles of Civil Procedure* (1994) 503.

155 See eg, Arbitration Act, 1996, s 58 (UK); 9 USC § 13; New York Convention, art III; ICSID Convention, art 54.

156 See eg, the practice of Sweden and Finland with regard to foreign judgments. Fawcett, above, n 166, at 67. Refusal to enforce foreign criminal judgments is perhaps even more common. See eg, Christine Van den Wyngaert and Guy Stessens, 'The International Non Bis in Idem Principle: Resolving Some of the Unanswered Questions', 48 *ICLQ* 779, 781–90 (1999). But Cf Brussels Judgments Convention, arts 32–7 (recognition of foreign civil and commercial judgments); Choice of Court Convention, art 8; Penal Code, Art 68 (Netherlands); Preliminary Title to Criminal Procedure Code, Art 13 (Belgium); 11(1) Halsbury's Laws of England 473 (4th edn, 1990).

157 See eg, *US v Lanza*, 260 US 227 (1922); *US v Wheeler, Arizona*, 435 US 313 (1978).

158 See eg, *Hornsby*, 1998 (II) Eur Ct HR at 738; *SPP*, 3 ICSID Rep at 162–3; *Poultry*, above, n 129, at para 7.41.

and prominent authors have claimed that the *res judicata* rule does not even apply to regulation of competition between national and international courts.[159] Still, here, too, there are a few authorities that point to a diametrically opposite direction (both in the case law of national and international courts).[160]

In addition, some courts have resorted to interpretive methodologies that perhaps circumvent the need for pronouncing upon the formal application of the *res judicata* rule. One particularly interesting method for recognizing the legal validity of international judgments has been suggested by some judges in the US. They suggest to deduce the conclusive effect of such judgments from those international treaties that the international courts have been empowered to construe (rather than on the basis of an intrinsic effect attributed to that international judicial decision). If such treaties are 'part of the law of the land', then judgments regarding those treaties, procured through procedures mandated by the respective treaties enjoy a similar status.[161] For example, in the *Medellin* case—one of the Consular Notification cases brought before the US Supreme Court in the aftermath of the *Avena* case—Justice Breyer suggested that ICJ judgments may be binding upon US courts by virtue of article 94 of the UN Charter, which requires the US to comply with ICJ judgments.[162] Moreover, in *Torres*—another *Avena*-related case—an Oklahoma Appeals Court judge held that acceptance of ICJ compulsory jurisdiction over disputes relating to the Vienna Convention on Consular Relations necessitates granting 'full faith and credit' to ICJ judgments.[163]

Of course, the question of the reciprocal legal effects of national and international court judgments does not arise when interactions between those courts have been explicitly or implicitly regulated in ways that confer *res judicata* status on those judgments or deprives them of a preclusive effect. For example, the Rome Statute clearly applies the *ne bis in idem* principle in relations between the ICC and national courts, in a bi-directional manner (subject to the qualification that improper or ineffective national proceedings would not bar the ICC from re-litigating the case).[164]

159 See *Amco Asia*, 1 ICSID Rep, at 413, 460 (1984); Brownlie, above, n 18, at 50–1; Dodge, above, n 63, at 367; Schreuer, above, n 153, at 683. For a similar position, which rejects the direct effect of ICJ/PCIJ judgments in domestic legal systems, see *Socobel v Greece*, 18 ILR 3, 4–5 (Belg, Trib Civ de Bruxelles 1951). For a discussion of other instance of refusal by domestic courts to implement international judgments, see A Mark Weisburd, 'International Courts and American Courts', 21 *Mich J Int'l L* (2000) 877, 886–7.

160 *Cysne* (Portugal v Germany), II RIAA 1035 (1930); Agreement between Costa Rica and the Inter-American Court of Human Rights, 16 Oct 1982, art 27, OAS Doc, OEA Ser.L/III.6 doc 13 (decisions of the I/A CtHR are granted in Costa Rica the same effect given to domestic court decisions).

161 See eg, Aparna Sridhar, 'Creating Judicial Remedies for Violations of the Vienna Convention on Consular Relations: A Proposed Resolution to Medellin v. Dretke', 2 *Stan JCR & CL* (2006) 333, 356.

162 See eg, *Medellin v Dretke*, 544 US 660, 693–4 (2005) (dissenting opinion of Justice Breyer).

163 *Torres v State*, order granting stay of execution and remanding case for evidentiary hearing of 13 May 2004, (concurring opinion of Judge Chapel) <http://www.debevoise.com/publications/pdf/StayofExecutionandRemandingCase.PDF>.

164 ICC Statute, art 20. See also ICTY Statute, art 10 (applying the *ne bis in idem* principle to relations between national and international courts, but excluding criminal judgments of national courts that have characterized the acts in question as ordinary crimes or judgments procured through proceedings that

The same rule applies, *mutatis mutandis*, with respect to relations holding between judgments issued by mixed criminal tribunals and national courts.[165] Furthermore, the ICSID Convention provides that ICSID awards will enjoy the status of domestic court judgments in the territories of all its members.[166] At the same time, human rights treaties, which explicitly or implicitly authorize international courts to review the conformity of domestic court decisions with international human rights standards (thereby instituting vertical jurisdictional relations), implicitly deprive these latter decisions of *res judicata* vis-à-vis the international courts specified in those treaties.[167]

Ways to circumvent the rule of finality

Even if one were to recognize that national and international court decisions could, in theory, generate final decisions that are binding upon one another as a matter of law, such decisions would not necessarily be enforced. This is because there are ways available for courts to circumvent the *res judicata* rule.

One method used by national courts to avoid giving effect to international judgments has been to link the status of international court decisions to the non-self-executing status of international law in the relevant polity—an approach taken by some US courts in several cases involving the effects of ICJ and WTO DSB decisions.[168] This means that even if the international judgments were binding as a matter of international law, they are non-enforceable in domestic law.

Another circumvention tactic has been to regard the second-in-time set of proceedings, which reviews the decision issued by the first-in-time court, as proceedings that raise issues analytically distinct from the substantive issues addressed in the first-in-time proceedings. To illustrate, denial of justice cases are typically presented as cases arising outside the scope of the finality principle: since international courts only examine processual issues regarding the litigation by the first-seized

were not impartial or independent or were designed to shield the accused from international criminal responsibility, or if the case was not diligently pursued). But see ICTY Rules of Procedure and Evidence (revised version), 30 May 2006, Rule 12, UN Doc. IT/32/Rev 38 (2006) ('Subject to Article 10, paragraph 2, of the Statute, determinations of courts of any State are not binding on the Tribunal').

165 Regulation No 2000/15 on the Establishment of Panels with Exclusive Jurisdiction over Serious Criminal Offences, s 11, UN Doc. UNTAET/REG/2000/15 (2000) (East Timor); SCSL Statute, art 9. It may be noted that the Sierra Leone Special Court was granted broader authority to reject national court judgments than the ICC (including characterization of the offence as an ordinary crime). For a discussion, see Jann K Kleffner and André Nollkaemper 'The Relationship Between Internationalized Courts and National Courts', *Internationalized Criminal Courts—Sierra Leone, East Timor, Kosovo, and Cambodia* (Cesare P R Romano et al, eds, 2004) 359, 374. Relations between the mixed criminal tribunals and national courts in Kosovo and Cambodia are, however, less than clear. Kleffner and Nollkaemper, above, at 374–376.

166 ICSID Convention, art 54(1). See also Schreuer, above, n 12, at 1100–34. For a comparable rule governing judgments of the ECJ, see EC Treaty, art 256.

167 See eg, ECHR, art 35; I/A CHR, art 46(a).

168 See eg, *Sanchez-Llamas v Oregon*, 126 S Ct 2669, 2684 (2006); *Corus Staal BV v Dept of Commerce*, 395 F 3d 1343, 1348–49 (2005).

national courts (whether the process amounted to an independent breach of international standards; not how the original dispute should have been decided by the first-in-time court), the two proceedings do not raise the 'same issues'.[169] In the same vein, instances of judicial review by national courts over the work of international courts, especially in the sphere of criminal law, may be analysed as raising due process issues separate from the substantive claims adjudicated before the international courts.[170]

Whether or not one accepts this (rather strained) construction, I argue in Chapter 6 that national and international courts should always exercise comity vis-à-vis the findings of law and facts made by their counterpart courts.[171] Similar manifestations of comity should be afforded to decisions of international quasi-judicial bodies (such as the Human Rights Committee), which cannot create a *res judicata* effect as their decisions are of a non-binding nature.[172]

5.3 Interim Conclusions

Some traditional jurisdiction-regulating rules governing forum-selection and multiple proceedings may be relevant to regulation of the relations holding between national and international courts. In particular, choice-of-forum agreements excluding the jurisdiction of other courts should be respected (including, *electa*

[169] See eg, *North American Dredging Co*, 4 RIAA at 32 (resubmission of case litigated before national courts to arbitration on denial of justice grounds is permissible); Christopher Greenwood, State Responsibility for the Decisions of National Courts, *Issues of State Responsibility before International Judicial Institutions* (Malgosia Fitzmaurice and Danesh Sarooshi, eds, 2004) 55, 60 (distinguishing domestic court decisions that independently violate international law from decisions that merely review violations by other state actors); Jan Paulsson, *Denial of Justice in International Law* (2005) 71. Cf *Arbitral Award of 1989*, 1991 ICJ 53.

The ICJ cases involving a review of the propriety of criminal proceedings conducted before national courts may also raise distinct issues than the substantive claims adjudicated before national fora. See eg, *Arrest Warrant* (Congo v Belgium), 2002 ICJ 3.

[170] See eg, *Milošević*, above, n 4. This decision, which presented a challenge to the ICTY authority to try *Milošević*, reaffirmed the legal propriety of the creation of the ICTY and relied heavily, to this effect, on the 1995 *Tadić* case. *Prosecutor v Tadić*, Decision of 2 Oct 1995, (ICTY Appeals Chamber), <http://www.un.org/icty/tadic/appeal/decision-e/51002.htm>. The Dutch court also rejected arguments that the ICTY lacks the necessary guarantees of independence and impartiality, relying this time on the ECtHR *Naletilić* case. *Naletilić v Croatia*, 2000-V Eur Ct HR 489.

[171] Cf *1989 Arbitral Award*, 1991 ICJ at 69; Shany, above, n 20, at 251. This approach is consistent with the margin of appreciation doctrine, which some international courts apply vis-à-vis national courts. See also Case 589/1994 *Tomlin v Jamaica*, UN Doc CCPR/C/57/D/589/1994, at para 6.3 (Report of the HRC, 1996) ('it is generally for the appellate courts of States parties to the Covenant to evaluate the facts and evidence in a particular case; similarly, it is for the appellate courts and not for the Committee to review specific instructions to the jury by the judge in a trial by jury...').

[172] Cf *Azurix*, 43 ILM at 280 (a regulatory authority cannot be deemed as a court for the purpose of applying competition-regulating rules). But see J. Scott Davidson, 'Intention and Effect: The Legal Status of the Final Views of the Human Rights Committee', 2001 *NZ Law Review* 125, 131 et seq (discussing arguments that HRC views could be viewed as binding under certain international law constructions).

una via clauses); otherwise, the parties retain their freedom to forum shop (in a non-abusive manner).

However, the scope of application of such forum-selection arrangements, as well as the very applicability of rules designed to govern multiple proceedings—especially, *lis alibi pendens* and *res judicata*—appears to be mired in conceptual confusion. The application of some rules depends on a conceptualization of national and international courts as judicial bodies operating within the legal system; application of other rules depend on conceptualization of proceedings before national and international courts as addressing the 'same issues'. Since it might be impossible, at present, to identify consensus on these difficult problems, the emphasis should, arguably, shift to the general principles discussed in Chapter 6 that represent a more flexible methodology of coordination, which is less dependant on a 'grand theory' of the relations holding between national and international courts.

6

Flexible Jurisdiction-regulating Rules

Whereas Chapter 5 covered jurisdiction-regulating rules designed to govern interactions between national and international courts involved in litigation of the 'same dispute' the present chapter discusses two broader legal principles—comity and *abus de droit*—which govern these as well as additional types of jurisdictional interactions: interactions between related proceedings (ie, proceedings involving related parties and/or issues that do not meet 'sameness' criteria) and vertical jurisdictional interactions. Hence, their application could circumvent some of the doctrinal as well as practical uncertainty over the nature of the relations between national and international courts and the controversial definition of the 'same dispute'. If these principles can likewise apply to identical proceedings, related proceedings or vertical interactions, there may be no urgent need for classifying such interactions.

Still, resort to the jurisdiction-regulating principles discussed in the chapter is not immune to criticism. First, both principles, particularly judicial comity, ultimately serve a pro-coordination agenda. While the present author believes that improvement of coordination between national and international courts is generally laudable, such an agenda may be criticized for empowering the judicial status of national or international courts, an act whose legitimacy and propriety may be open to question (eg, from a national law perspective, the empowerment of less-accountable international courts might be problematic; similarly, from an international law perspective, the empowerment of less-credible national courts might be deemed undesirable).[173]

Second, unlike the rather clear binary rules of coordination discussed in Chapter 5, which stipulate whether jurisdiction should be exercised, the coordinative principles discussed here confer a wide measure of discretion on the courts applying them. The unpredictable nature of the exercise of such discretionary powers may, in turn, compromise certainty and further complicate the already difficult task of navigating between the competing judicial procedures.

[173] See Yuval Shany, 'Toward a General Margin of Appreciation Doctrine', 16 *EJIL* (2005) 907, 908–9.

6.1 Comity

6.1.1 Policy underpinnings

The principle of judicial comity, which calls on courts to defer, when appropriate, to other courts and to treat their procedures and decisions with courtesy and respect, is accepted in the practice of many national courts and applied vis-à-vis both foreign courts and international courts.[174] It is also increasingly applied by international courts to regulate jurisdictional relations between their own jurisdictions and those of other courts—national and international.[175]

The benefits of judicial comity

To my mind, the principle of comity has considerable potential for alleviating some of the more difficult aspects of jurisdictional competition. This is because comity encourages courts to accommodate related procedures and to consider the decisions such procedures produce in a favourable manner. In other words, this principle represents a strategy for soft coordination and harmonization between the entire gamut of jurisdictional configurations. This coverage, in turn, increases prospects of smooth, rational and effective cumulative operation of the different dispute settlement systems involved. Furthermore, to the degree that international law is applied through domestic and international procedures, comity may contribute to its consistent application and to international law's coherence.[176] The principle

[174] See eg, *Hilton v Guyot*, 159 US 113, 163–4 (1895); *Thirty Hogsheads of Sugar v Boyle*, 13 US (9 Cranch) 191, 198 (1815); *Dallal v Bank Mellat* [1986] 1 QB 441, 461–2 (Hobhouse J); Anne-Marie Slaughter, 'A Global Community of Courts', 44 *Harv Int'l LJ* (2003) 191, 206–10. For a comprehensive survey of domestic cases that discussed the status and application of the principle of *comitas gentium*, see Lambertus Erades, *Interactions between International and Municipal Law: A Comparative Case Law Study* (Malgosia Fitzmaurice and Cees Flinterman, eds., 1993) 17–40.

[175] See eg, *SPP*, 3 ICSID Rep at 129; *SGS v Philippines*, above, above, n 48, at para 162, 175; Brussels Judgments Convention, art 28; Allan Rosas, 'With a Little Help from My Friends: International Case—Law as a Source of Reference for the EU Courts', 5 *The Global Community: Yearbook of International Law and Jurisprudence* (2005) 203, 230; Robert B Ahdieh, 'Between Dialogue and Decree: International Review of National Courts', 79 *NYU L Rev* (2004) 2029, 2051–52. But see *Ahlström Osakeytiön v Commission* [1988] ECR 5193, 5244 (comity cannot deprive the EC of jurisdiction to apply its competition rules).

[176] See International Law Commission Study Group, 'Fragmentation of International Law: Difficulties arising from the Diversification and Expansion of International Law', UN Doc A/CN.4/L.682 (2006), at 20 (prepared by Martti Koskenniemi) ('Legal interpretation, and thus legal reasoning, builds systematic relationships between rules and principles by envisaging them as parts of some human effort or purpose... [I]t may also be rationalized in terms of a *political obligation* on law appliers to make their decisions cohere with the preferences and expectations of the community whose law they administer'). Cf *Prosecutor v Semanza*, Case ICTR-97-20-A, decision of 31 May 2000, at 10–12 (ICTR Appeal Chamber) (Separate Opinion of Judge Shahabuddeen) (international courts have a legal duty to consider the need for coherence in the whole field of international law); Restatement of the Law (2nd), Conflict of Laws, § 6, cmt d (1971) ('Probably the most important function of choice-of-law rules is to make the interstate and international systems work well'); *Sanchez-Llamas*, 126 S. Ct. at 2700 (dissenting opinion of Justice Breyer) ('"respectful consideration" reflects the

of judicial comity can also be supported by other policy considerations—eg, the value of inter-forum courtesy, the economics of improved coordination and cooperation, and the enriching and educational potential of normative cross-fertilization between courts.[177] Simply put, the inter-judicial dialogue facilitated by judicial comity is likely to improve the quality of judicial outcomes, and, in consequence, increase their legitimacy.[178]

Furthermore, the discretionary nature of judicial comity is consistent with the view that states ought to preserve some latitude in deciding how to implement their international law obligations, including international judgments. And, in some specific domestic legal contexts, resort to comity with respect to international law decisions conforms to the non-self-executing nature of many relevant international law norms.[179]

Flexibility v rigidity

In effect, the flexibility afforded to courts as a result of the discretionary nature of judicial comity has several notable advantages over the rigidity of traditional jurisdiction-regulating rules such as *lis alibi pendens* or *res judicata*. Hence, in the current state of international affairs, one can argue that a comity framework for addressing jurisdictional interactions between national and international courts may provide a method more suitable than rigid jurisdiction-regulating rules for balancing the competing interests of the two legal systems.

The dialogue between national and international courts, as facilitated by the jurisdiction-regulating rules discussed in this book, is bound to increase the salience and influence of international case law in national law.[180] Although from an

understanding that uniformity is an important goal of treaty interpretation . . . the ICJ's position as an international court specifically charged with the duty to interpret numerous international treaties . . . provides a natural point of reference for national courts seeking that uniformity'). See also Pauwelyn, above, n 38, at 1011. But see, Martti Koskenniemi and Päivi Leino, 'Fragmentation of International Law? Postmodern Anxieties', 15 *Leiden Journal of International Law* (2002) 553, 556–62 (postmodernity is inevitably characterized by normative lack of coherence).

[177] See Richard A Falk, *The Role of Domestic Courts in the International Legal Order* (1964) 106.

[178] See Helfer and Slaughter, above, n 7, at 320 (improved reasoning might also strengthen the 'compliance pull' of international judgments). On the link between legitimacy and compliance, see Thomas M Franck, *The Power of Legitimacy Among Nations* (1990) 24.

[179] See eg, *Medellin*, brief submitted by the US to the Supreme Court, sec III(B)(1) <http://www.usdoj.gov/osg/briefs/2004/3mer/1ami/2004-5928.mer.ami.html> ('because Article 94(1) [of the UN Charter] does not detail the means of compliance with an ICJ decision, it necessarily contemplates that the political branches of member Nations would have discretion to choose how to comply. If an ICJ decision were subject to immediate private enforcement in the courts of member Nations, it would rob the political branches of that discretion'). Cf Jacques H J Bourgeois, 'The European Court of Justice and the WTO: Problems and Challenges', *The EU, The WTO, and NAFTA: Towards a Common Law of International Trade?* (J H H Weiler ed, 2000) 71, 115.

[180] Such influence might often operate by indirect means—for example, through encouraging domestic courts to redefine the national interests of the polity as including compliance with international norms. Jenny S Martinez, 'Towards an International Judicial System', 56 *Stan L Rev* (2003) 429, 471; Harold H Koh, 'Bringing Human Rights Home', 35 *Hous L Rev* (1998) 623, 632 et seq; Harold H Koh, 'Transnational Legal Process', 75 *Neb L Rev* (1994) 181, 203–4; Abram Chayes and Antonia H Chayes, *The New Sovereignty: Compliance with International Regulatory Agreements* (1995) 25–8.

international law perspective this may be a desirable development, it has been argued that empowerment of international courts merits our support only if the procedures and decisions adopted by these courts by and large meet procedural and substantive justice requirements.[181] Given the democratic deficit of many international institutions, and most international courts—being far removed from electoral accountability[182]—and in light of the chronic problems hindering the satisfactory operation of certain international adjudicative procedures,[183] some degree of prudence on the part of domestic courts when deferring to international courts appears advisable.[184] The discretionary nature of judicial comity could thus serve as an important check on the operation of international courts by enabling national courts to mitigate the effects of improper or illegitimate international adjudication. This filtering process ensures that international procedures and decisions conform to basic local principles of justice and confers at the same time some domestic legitimacy on international adjudication.

Were national courts unable to exercise some discretion as to how and to what degree to give effect to international procedures, they might be inclined to resist consideration of the procedural and normative effects of international adjudication altogether (inter alia, through the adoption of dualist and other disintegrative and avoidance strategies). Hence, insistence on total deference by national courts to international judgments could lead to inferior coordination; furthermore, excessive deference can deter states from acceptance of international court jurisdiction in some cases.[185]

In the same vein, depriving international courts of their own powers of discretion as to the effect to be given to national court decisions can also be counter-productive.

[181] For example, Slaughter maintains that transnational comity analysis should be based on recognition of minimum standards of international justice and on willingness to evaluate foreign courts on the basis of the same criteria under which domestic courts are evaluated. Slaughter, above, n 174, at 211. See generally Schreuer, above, n 153, at 704.

[182] See eg, Martinez, above, n 180, at 461–2.

[183] See eg, Adam M Smith, '"Judicial Nationalism" in International Law: National Identity and Judicial Autonomy at the ICJ' 40 *Tex Int'l LJ* (2005) 197; Eric A Posner and Miguel FP de Figueiredo, 'Is the International Court of Justice Biased?', 34 *J Legal Stud* (2005) 599; Eric A Posner and John C Yoo, 'Judicial Independence in International Tribunals', 93 *Calif L Rev* (2005) 1. But see Laurence R Helfer and Anne-Marie Slaughter, 'Why States Create International Tribunals: A Response to Professors Posner and Yoo', 93 *Calif L Rev* (2005) 899 (and see Eric A Posner and John C Yoo, 'Reply to Helfer and Slaughter', 93 *Calif L Rev* (2005) 957).

[184] Cf Johan G Lammers, 'Challenging the Establishment of the ICTY before the Dutch Courts: The Case of Slobodan Milosevic v The Netherlands', *Review of the Security Council by Member States* (Erika de Wet and Andre Nollkaemper, eds, 2003) 107, 110 (domestic courts find it difficult blindly to abide by the decision of international institutions in areas related to human rights protection).

[185] See eg, Mari Presley, 'Sovereignty and Delegation Issues Regarding US Commitment to the World Trade Organization's Dispute Settlement Process', 8 *J Transnat'l L & Pol'y* (1998) 173, 196 (accepting the rule-making authority of international courts will constrain the US from joining such institutions). Note, however, that some lawyers have taken a more radical position, suggesting that exercise of any degree of comity might deter countries from accepting the jurisdiction of international tribunals. *Sanchez-Llamas, amicus curiae* (Professors of International Law, Federal Law, Federal Jurisdiction and the Foreign Relations Law of the US), at 20–2, <http://www.debevoise.com/publications/pdf/RespondentsLawProfessorsAmicus.pdf>.

Given the problems associated with national adjudication of matters of international concern, international courts might justifiably be reluctant to grant 'full faith and credit'[186] to domestic judgments for varied reasons. Judicial proceedings before some national courts fall short of minimal standards of fairness, as perceived by international courts.[187] Furthermore, even when national courts do apply international law, such applications may be distorted by the effect of national law on the legal analysis as well as by the mixed political loyalties of national courts (vis-à-vis their national and international constituencies) that colour domestic judgments. Given the likelihood that international courts will resist application of non-discretionary jurisdiction-regulating rules requiring them to defer automatically to domestic judicial procedures, the attractiveness of comity increases. Comity, in its simplest sense, provides international courts, too, with a 'safety valve' that enables them to give some effect only to those national procedures that they deem proper (eg, conducted in an orderly manner and resulting in a persuasive decision).

From a different perspective, one may note that some legal contexts, such as human rights law, do attach high value to the synergetic effect of dialogue between national and international courts. In these contexts, encouragement of consecutive judicial proceedings can militate against application of rigid choice of forum rules or multiple proceedings-regulating rules, which curb possibilities for multiple adjudication of the same dispute and undercut percolation of the best available decisions through inter-judicial dialogue.[188]

Criticisms of judicial comity

Of course, the application of judicial comity is also open to criticism. First of all, discretionary rules are always open to abuse.[189] Review of the comity-inspired 'respectful consideration' offered by the US Supreme Court vis-à-vis the ICJ in the Consular Notification cases[190] and the 'appropriate weight' granted by Israel's Supreme Court to the ICJ advisory opinion on the *Wall* in *Mara'abe*[191] indeed

[186] Cf US Constitution, art 4(1).

[187] See Dodge, above, n 63, at 369; Brent Wible, '"De-Jeopardizing Justice": Domestic Prosecutions for International Crimes and the Need for Transnational Convergence', 31 *Denv J Int'l L & Pol'y* 265, 270–7. See also *Loewen*, 42 ILM at 825 (holding that proceedings in Mississippi fell short of international due process standards).

[188] See *Azinian*, 39 ILM at 550 ('it would be unfortunate if potential claimants under NAFTA were dissuaded from seeking relief under domestic law from national courts, because such actions might have the salutary effect of resolving the dispute without resorting to investor-state arbitration under NAFTA'); Dodge, above, n 63, at 382 (arguing that it is important to protect the 'two bites at the apple' regime of NAFTA Chapter 11).

[189] See eg, Frederick Schauer, *Playing by the Rules: A Philosophical Examination of Rule-Based Decision-Making in Law and in Life* (1991) 149–155; Pierre Schlag, 'Rules and Standards', 33 *UCLA L Rev* (1985) 379, 381–3; Kathleen M Sullivan, 'The Justices of Rules and Standards', 106 *Harvard L Rev* (1992) 22, 57–9.

[190] *Breard v Greene*, 523 US 371, 375 (1998); *Sanchez-Llamas*, 126 S Ct at 2683. But see ibid, at 2702–3 (dissenting opinion of Justice Breyer).

[191] HCJ 7957/04 *Mara'abe v Prime Minister of Israel*, Judgment of 15 Sept 2005 (an English translation is available at ILDC 157 (IL 2005)).

suggests that only token deference may have been afforded to the ICJ in those cases. It appears that no real effort was expended on the part of these national courts to harmonize their decisions with the parallel ICJ jurisprudence (this criticism applies with particular force to the US decisions, which were based on different interpretations of treaty law than the one offered by the ICJ; in contrast, the Israeli court decision disputed the ICJ mainly on factual grounds). One can even maintain that the display of comity by these national courts was merely designed to improve the domestic and international legitimacy of their own decisions, or to undermine the legitimacy of the relevant ICJ decisions.

While such criticism is valid—discretionary standards are, in fact, more susceptible to abuse than are norms[192]—the question remains as to whether an alternative rule prohibiting any deference or requiring automatic compliance would produce better judicial decisions or greater compliance. To my mind, the modest degree of mutual influence facilitated by comity is preferable to the total normative detachment that a bar on comity, or an excessively rigid jurisdiction-regulation rule, would entail (this is because such imposition will likely be bypassed). Under present conditions, judicial comity might also represent the most far-reaching yet still politically palatable framework for cooperation just because it balances mutual respect with distrust. Any alteration of the relationship holding between national and international courts that goes beyond discretionary weighing of the effects of the competing procedure would probably require a special legal instrument (such as the ECHR or the Rome Statute) for its legitimization.

Another criticism of judicial comity pertains to its selective nature that suggests lack of courtesy. It is sometime argued that rejection of a judicial decision issued by a different court or refusal to accommodate its overlapping proceedings, by virtue of the other court's untrustworthiness, inadequate procedures or unpersuasive nature, denotes an extreme lack of courtesy. Hence, across-the-board abstention from consideration of the effects of competing proceedings may be, on the whole, more consistent with the rationale of comity than is the condescension embodied in review of the propriety of these proceedings.[193]

I believe this objection to be unconvincing: first, the utter disregard solution undercuts the coordination and harmonization functions of comity, meant to address the interests of the disputing parties; it therefore throws out, in effect, the baby with the bath water. In other words, judicial comity promotes a variety of interests—not only does it convey respect and courtesy towards foreign institutions, it

192 For a different view, see Schlag, above, n 189, at 412–13.

193 See eg, *Medellin*, 544 US at 670 (concurring opinion of Justice Ginsburg) ('when a judgment binds or is respected as a matter of comity, a "let's see if we agree" approach is out of order'); *Argentina v Mellino*, 80 AR 1, 25 (Supreme Court of Canada) ('the assumption by a Canadian court of responsibility for supervising the conduct of the diplomatic and prosecutorial officials of a foreign state strikes me as being in fundamental conflict with the principle of comity on which extradition is based').

also operates as a tool to help courts to manage efficiently multi-fora disputes. The latter role may be completely eliminated if comity were to be systematically denied. Second, one may question whether the insult associated with complete disregard of a foreign court's judicial procedures does not actually exceed the occasional lack of courtesy generated by the selective approach. Third, the selective approach might encourage national and international courts to upgrade their procedures and reasoning, so as to attract greater respect from other judicial bodies. This incentive disappears when no comity can be exercised. Fourth, similar arguments against the selective approach have been raised and dismissed in common law jurisdictions with respect to the exercise of judicial comity vis-à-vis foreign proceedings and judgments;[194] the same pragmatic arguments that support the application of comity towards foreign judicial procedures should equally apply in the context of the relations between national and international courts.

Finally, it has been alleged that comity has no place in the relations between national and international bodies.[195] This is because historically, the principle of comity was developed in order to regulate, on a reciprocal basis,[196] relations between sovereign nations. Yet, it can be argued that such rationales do not justify the granting of comity by national courts to international courts: the latter do not, after all, represent any sovereign power nor do they appear inclined to reciprocate and treat national courts with deference.

This objection is also unconvincing. As already noted, deference to other judgments and procedures can be justified by considerations of international courtesy but also by the parties' overall interest in coordinated dispute settlement procedures. In addition, disrespect of international courts may imply disrespect of their sponsoring organizations and their member states. It is difficult to accept an attitude of discourtesy toward all of these international actors (some of which may play important roles in the international arena). Moreover, the contention that international courts do not reciprocate with comity toward national courts is inaccurate. As the ensuing discussion demonstrates, the application of margin of appreciation by the ECtHR towards ECHR member states and the ICJ's position in the consular notification cases (which confirmed the US legal system's freedom of choice of the means of implementing the judgment), could be regarded as displays of judicial comity, inviting reciprocal deference.[197]

194 See eg, *Kindler v Canada*, [1991] 2 SCR 779, 850 ('At the end of the day, the question is whether the provision or action in question offends the Canadian sense of what is fair, right and just, bearing in mind the nature of the offence and the penalty, the foreign justice system and considerations of comity and security, and according due latitude to the Minister to balance the conflicting considerations'); Adrian Briggs, 'Crossing the River by Feeling the Stones: Rethinking the Law on Foreign Judgments', 8 *Singapore YBIL* (2004) 1, 18–19.

195 *Sanchez-Llamas, amicus curiae*, above, n 185, at 17–18.

196 Cf *Hilton v Guyot*, 159 US at 227–8.

197 *LaGrand* (Germany v US), 2001 ICJ 466, 514; *Avena*, 43 ILM at 619–20.

6.1.2 The principle's legal basis

Inherent powers

While the status of judicial comity under positive international law (custom or general principle of law) is somewhat unclear,[198] it may derive its legal effect from courts' inherent authority to manage their proceedings in accordance with principles of justice and efficiency.[199] Such inherent powers are sometimes reflected in 'general powers' provisions, found in the constitutive instruments of national and international courts and tribunals.[200] At other times, the exercise of comity can be viewed as intimately linked to the inherent judicial discretion possessed by courts in determining an effective timetable for their proceedings and in considering the persuasive weight of the authorities submitted by the parties.[201]

International judgments and the incorporation of international law into domestic law

Specific manifestations of judicial comity can be supported by way of national and international legal doctrines. For example, the decision by national courts to accord some degree of deference to international judgments may be theoretically

[198] See Shany, above, n 20, at 261–3. But see *SGS v Pakistan*, 42 ILM at 1323 (holding that once jurisdiction is established, no stay of proceedings can be considered).

[199] *Legality of use of Force* (Serbia and Montenegro v Belgium), 44 ILM 299, 342–3 (2005) (separate opinion of Judge Higgins) ('The Court's inherent jurisdiction derives from its judicial character and the need for powers to regulate matters connected with the administration of justice, not every aspect of which may have been foreseen in the Rules'). *SPP*, 3 ICSID Rep at 129; *SGS v Philippines*, above, n 48, at para 171 ('international tribunals have a certain flexibility in dealing with questions of competing forums'); *Questions of Interpretation and Application of the 1971 Montreal Convention Arising from the Aerial Incident at Lockerbie* (Libya v US), 1992 ICJ 3, at 113 (order of 14 April 1992) (dissenting opinion of Judge El-Kosheri) (courts have inherent power to ensure the proper administration of justice); *Prosecutor v Bobetko*, decision of 29 Nov 2002, at para 15, <http://www.un.org/icty/bobetko/appeal/decision-e/bob-dec29nov2002.htm> (ICTY Appeals Chamber). See also eg, ICSID Convention, art 44. Cf *Degan v US*, 517 US 820, 823 (1996). But see ECJ's *Wood Pulp* judgment. *Ahlström* [1988] ECR 5193, at para 22 ('As regards the argument relating to disregard of international comity, it suffices to observe that it amounts to calling in question the Community's jurisdiction to apply its competition rules to conduct such as that found to exist in this case and that, as such, that argument has already been rejected.'); *Soft Drinks*, above, n 112, at paras 44–57.

[200] See eg, ICSID Rules of Procedure for Arbitration Proceedings (as amended on 29 Sept 2002), art 19, <http://www.worldbank.org/icsid/basicdoc/partF.htm> (hereinafter ICSID Rules); UNCLOS, annex VII, art 5 (Arbitration Rules); DSU, art 12.1; 24 Am Jur 2d Dismissal, Discontinuance, and Nonsuit § 63.

[201] See eg, International Court of Justice Rules of Court 1978, as amended on 5 Dec 2000, art 58(2), <http://www.icj-cij.org/icjwww/ibasicdocuments/ibasictext/ibasicrulesofcourt_20001205.html>; International Criminal Court Rules of Procedure and Evidence, 10 Sept 2002, art 63(2), ICC Off Rec ICC/ASP/1/3 (2002); DSU, art 11. The ability to deduce rules of evidence from the inherent powers of the international judiciary has been confirmed by the ICTY. *Prosecutor v Jelisić*, decision of 15 Nov 2000, <http://www.un.org/icty/jelisic/appeal/decision-e/01115AE314047.htm> (ICTY Appeals Chamber). For example, courts may sometimes consult informal sources. Vaughan Lowe, 'The Politics of Law-making: Are the Method and Character of Norm Creation Changing?', *The Role of Law in International Politics: Essays in International Relations and International Law* (Michael Byers, ed, 2000) 200, 219–20.

linked to the status of international law in the domestic legal system: if international courts interpret international norms that are relevant to the dispute at hand, then it is the duty incumbent upon national courts to consider the relevant international law norms (either as a binding source of law or as an interpretive tool), a duty that arguably extends to a consideration of the interpretation of such norms by international courts.[202] Failure on the part of national courts to comply with the interpretive decisions of international courts may, at times, entail international responsibility.[203]

This type of analysis was offered by Israel's Supreme Court in its *Mara'abe* judgment. In considering whether the opinion of the ICJ in the *Wall* case was relevant to the determination of international law norms applicable to the case at hand, the Supreme Court held:

> [T]he opinion of the International Court of Justice is an interpretation of international law, performed by the highest judicial body in international law. The ICJ's interpretation of international law should be given its full appropriate weight.[204]

While the Supreme Court accepted, by and large, the legal framework offered by the ICJ,[205] it eventually rejected its factual findings and thus reached a different conclusion on the very lawfulness of the decision to construct a separation barrier in the occupied territories. The different treatment of the ICJ's legal and factual findings illustrates the link between judicial comity and incorporation doctrines. While there appears to be a presumptive incorporation of international law as identified and interpreted by the ICJ into domestic law, there is no similar presumption in favour of the ICJ's factual holdings. In the latter case, Israel's Supreme Court disapproval of the fact-finding process employed by the ICJ served to counter any notion of judicial deference that such factual findings might otherwise have attracted.[206]

202 See eg, *Hyundai Elecs Co, Ltd v US*, 53 F Supp 2d 1334, 1343–4 (1999)(US CIT). For a discussion, see James Thuo Gathii, 'Foreign Precedents in the Federal Judiciary: The Case of the World Trade Organization's DSB Decisions', 34 *Ga J Int'l & Comp L* (2005) 1, 20–1.

203 The obligation to implement internatonal judgments may be particularly strong when international instruments explicitly endow international court judgments with a 'final and binding' status. See eg, UN Charter, art 94; Statute of the International Court of Justice, 26 June 1945, arts 59–60, XV UNCIO Doc 355; The Hague Convention for the Pacific Settlement of International Disputes, 18 Oct 1907, art 81 in *The Hague Conventions and Declarations of 1899 and 1907* (James Brown Scott, ed, 2nd edn, 1915) 41; UNCLOS, art 256; ECHR, art 44, 46(1); I/A CHR, art 67; ICSID Convention, art 53(1); Rules of Procedure of the Court of Justice of the European Communities, art 65, 1991 OJ (L176) 7.

204 *Mara'abe*, above, n 191, at para 56. See also *Medellin*, 544 US at 692 (dissenting opinion of Justice Souter) ('Medellin's case now presents a Vienna Convention claim in the shadow of a final ICJ judgment that may be entitled to considerable weight, if not preclusive effect').

205 *Mara'abe*, above, n 191, at para 57.

206 The Israeli court noted the following deficiencies in the fact-finding process before the ICJ: lack of information on Israel's security needs that prompted the construction of the barrier; reliance on imprecise data concerning the barrier's effects on the lives of the affected Palestinians; the non-adversarial nature of the ICJ proceedings; the failure to distinguish between the various considerations underlying the routing of different barrier segments. Ibid, at paras 61–72. For a discussion, see Yuval Shany

A similar linkage between the effects of international judgments and the doctrine of incorporation of international law into domestic law was offered by a NAFTA Chapter 19 binational panel in its 2005 decision on the lawfulness of US zeroing practices. In examining the impact of a WTO DSB rulings on the incompatibility of zeroing with US obligations under the WTO Anti-Dumping Agreement, the bi-national panel held that while DSB holdings are not directly applicable in the US legal system,[207] they serve to clarify US obligations under the WTO. These obligations are, in turn, relevant for statutory construction (under the *Charming Betsy* canon of interpretation,[208] which requires statutes to be construed when possible, in accordance with 'the law of nations'):

> DSB decisions are not directly binding on US Courts, nor—by Implication—on NAFTA Chapter 19 binational panels... The [Uruguay Round Agreements Act] does not render *Charming Betsy* unavailable as a rule of statutory construction. The obligations of the WTO Antidumping Agreement have been clarified in the WTO *Softwood Lumber* Decision, and that clarification was accepted by the United States in the Final Section 129 Determination.[209]

Hence, the panel held that the DSB reports render past determinations of the US trade authorities on zeroing unlawful.[210]

The linkage created between international judicial decisions and the need to apply international law domestically can justify, in general, the consideration of international judgments by national courts (even if those judgments were rendered in the context of different disputes).[211] Still, the need to consider such judgments applies *a fortiori* where the cases before the two courts are indistinguishable. This is because of the absence of distinguishing factors allowing for variations in legal interpretation between the judgments in addition to the disputing parties' legitimate expectations that the same 'international law' would be applied by the different litigation fora.

Another way to conceptualize the linkage between the granting of comity to court decisions and the binding or otherwise influential status of the international norms they expound may be found in article 38(1)(d) of the ICJ Statute (which

'Capacities and Inadequacies: A Look at the Two Separation Barrier Cases' 38 *Isr L Rev* (2005) 230, 240–2. Of course, this pick-and -choose methodology can be easily manipulated; still, it at least requires national courts to enter into some form of judicial dialogue with their international counterparts and engage in comparison of the relative strengths and weaknesses of the respective adjudicative processes.

207 See Uruguay Round Trade Agreements Act of 1994 § 102(a), 19 USC § 3512(c) (2000). Cf Council Decision 94/800, 1994 OJ (L 336) 1 (EU).

208 *Murray v The Schooner Charming Betsy*, 6 US 64 (1804).

209 *Certain Softwood Lumber Products from Canada: Final Affirmative Antidumping Determination*, decision of 9 June 2005, at 42–3 (NAFTA Chapter 19 bi-national panel).

210 The conclusion on the retroactive influence of DSB reports conforms to the proposition that US courts may revisit their own decisions if new rules of international law emerge. See *Medellin*, 544 US at 689–90 (dissenting opinion of Justice O'Connor); *Sanchez-Llamas*, 126 S Ct, at 2704 (dissenting opinion of Justice Breyer).

211 See eg, *Jogi v Voges*, 425 F 3d 367, 383 (2005) (relying on *Avena* in a case involving a non-Mexican national).

contains a list of international law sources). The article directs international law-applying bodies to rely on the decisions of other courts as subsidiary means for identifying the rules of international law.[212] Although the article does not distinguish between the authority of national and international decisions, international court decisions are more likely to be invoked as evidence of the content of international law:[213] international courts possess, as a rule, greater international law expertise, they typically transcend narrow national interests and escape the potentially distorting national law prism through which national courts perceive international law. Hence, international courts' pronouncements on the contents of international law are likely to attract more comity-inspired compliance.[214]

Uniform interpretation of international law

A related legal consideration supporting the extension of judicial comity is the need to promote uniform interpretation of international treaties for the purpose of increasing their effectiveness as coordinative measures. Courts should consequently strive to avoid deviating from past decisions that have already construed the treaty in question (even if those decisions were issued by different national courts). Indeed, national courts have been willing, on some occasions, to attribute significant weight to foreign court decisions that interpreted the same treaty provisions under consideration, citing the need for promoting interpretive uniformity.[215] It would seem that this line of argumentation would apply with greater

[212] For a survey of national and international court decisions citing international law precedents from the practice of domestic, foreign and international courts, see Erades, above, n 174, at 206–39.

[213] Teubnar has referred to an analogous ranking of influence in the field of arbitration as 'reputational hierarchy'. Teubner, above, n 65, at 21.

[214] See eg, *Prosecutor v Kupreškić*, Judgment of 14 Jan 2000, at para 542, <http://www.un.org/icty/kupreskic/trialc2/judgement/index.htm> (ICTY Trial Chamber) ('international criminal courts such as the International Tribunal must always carefully appraise decisions of other courts before relying on their persuasive authority as to existing law. Moreover, they should apply a stricter level of scrutiny to national decisions than to international judgments, as the latter are at least based on the same *corpus* of law as that applied by international courts, whereas the former tend to apply national law, or primarily that law, or else interpret international rules through the prism of national legislation'); Andre Nollkaemper, 'Decisions of National Courts as Sources of International Law: An Analysis of the Practice of the ICTY', *International Criminal Law Developments in the Case Law of the ICTY* (Gideon Boas & William A Schabas, eds, 2003) 277, 291–2. Indeed, Rosas observes that the ECJ has only exceptionally referred to legal decisions issued by the national courts of EU members. Rosas, above, n 175.

[215] See eg, *Air France v Saks*, 470 US 392, 404 (1985)('In determining precisely what causes can be considered accidents [under the Warsaw Convention on the Unification of Certain Rules Relating to International Transportation by Air], we "find the opinions of our sister signatories to be entitled to considerable weight" ') (cite omitted); A H 36/84, *Teichner v Air-France*, 41(1) PD 589, 635 (foreign decisions that can contribute to a uniform interpretation of a convention should be preferred over foreign decisions couched in specific domestic law doctrines). See also Vienna Convention on the Law of Treaties, 23 May 1969, art 31(3)(b), 1155 UNTS 311 (hereinafter VCLT). But see *Teichner*, above, at 612 (dissenting opinion of Justice Barak) ('Once a "uniform" norm of an international background is adopted into national law . . . it becomes part of domestic law . . . Throughout the process of adoption it transforms its nature and adapts itself to its national environment') (unofficial translation).

force to international judgments since international courts are particularly well placed to influence treaty interpretation. This they do by virtue of their international law expertise, their detachment from any particular national agenda and the considerable publicity that their decisions typically receive.

Analogy to comity vis-à-vis foreign procedures

Another possible source for the application of judicial comity is the perception that international court judgments are entitled to no less deferential treatment than judgments of foreign courts and arbitral tribunals.[216] If courtesy and respect are due to individual foreign sovereigns and their judicial organs, then international political entities and their judicial organs, which represent the rights and interests of numerous foreign sovereigns (and possibly the forum state itself), should be entitled, *a fortiori*, to comity. Hence, the traditional notions of inter-state comity (*comitas gentium*) that underlie inter-judicial comity may be extended by way of analogy, to encompass comity directed to international organizations in general, and international courts in particular.[217]

6.1.3 Modalities for application of judicial comity

The analogy to strict jurisdiction-regulating rules

Comity analysis is resorted to at three different stages of the multi-fora litigation process: (1) after the first-in-time court was seized but before initiation of the alternative set of proceedings; (2) when two or more sets of proceedings are simultaneously pending; and (3) after conclusion of the case before the competing court. Application of comity in such circumstances is thus roughly comparable to a finding of no jurisdiction and the application of *lis alibi pendens* and *res judicata* rules.

A crucial difference exists, however, between the resort to strict jurisdiction-regulating rules and the application of judicial comity in their stead. Whereas the application of strict jurisdiction-regulating rules normally results in the termination of the proceedings before one or more of the judicial bodies involved, application of comity normally cannot justify total abdication of jurisdiction by the comity-affording court because such an act would exceed that court's scope of authority.[218] Instead, application of comity is more circumscribed, meaning it may result merely in the postponement of court hearings and/or the granting of due consideration to the decisions of other courts. Still, a different effect may be attributed to comity in cases of discretionary jurisdiction exercised by a seized court (eg, when national court proceedings are governed by the *forum non conveniens*

[216] See eg, *Medellin*, 544 US at 670 (opinion of Justice Ginsburg).

[217] It might be difficult, however, to apply this sort of justification to *a-national* dispute settlement bodies, such as private international arbitration. See eg, Teubner, above, n 65, at 18.

[218] See eg, *Soft Drinks*, above, n 112, at paras 44–57; *SPP*, 3 ICSID Rep at 128 (claimant is 'entitled' to pursue the case if consent to jurisdiction is established); *Vivendi II*, 41 ILM at 1152 (failure on the part of an arbitral tribunal to exercise jurisdiction is ground for annulment); *SGS v Pakistan*, 42 ILM at 1323 ('This Tribunal is ***bound*** to exercise its jurisdiction') (emphasis added).

rule). The court may decide here that considerations of comity support a decline of jurisdiction on its part, in whole or in part.[219]

Encouraging litigation before more suitable fora

So, a comity-type analysis may be relevant whenever a court is seized with a case whereas other courts—national or international—appear better situated to address some or all of the issues brought before them. The breadth or narrowness of the respective competencies of the involved courts, ie, which court can address a greater number of aspects of the dispute, should impact on the assessment of their suitability to address the case. Such assessments are also bound to be influenced by the comparative institutional advantages and disadvantages of the courts involved. For example, national courts typically have better fact-finding and enforceability capabilities than do international courts;[220] still, the latter courts have better international law-pronouncing expertise than do their domestic counterparts.[221] In circumstances where multiple proceedings are foreseeable and a more-suitable forum is available, it may be advisable for the first-seized court to consider a stay of its proceedings until the other court handles the same case (or a closely related case).[222]

The decision of the UNCLOS *MOX Plant* arbitral panel to stay proceedings in the face of likely parallel proceedings before the ECJ—a manifestation of comity towards another international court—is instructive:

> In the circumstances, and bearing in mind considerations of *mutual respect and comity which should prevail between judicial institutions* both of which may be called upon to determine rights and obligations as between two States, the Tribunal considers that it would be inappropriate for it to proceed further with hearing the Parties on the merits of the dispute in the absence of a resolution of the problems referred to. Moreover, a procedure that might result in two conflicting decisions on the same issue would not be helpful to the resolution of the dispute between the Parties[223] (emphasis added).

There is no reason why similar respect and comity considerations should not be applied regularly by international courts in situations where national courts are deemed to be more appropriate fora for addressing the same dispute. In fact, such an approach was taken by the *SGS v Philippines* tribunal:

> [F]or the Tribunal to decide on the [BIT] claim in isolation from a decision by the chosen forum under the CISS agreement is *inappropriate and premature*...[224]

[219] See eg, *Joseph Muller Corp Zurich v Société Anonyme de Gérance et d'Armement*, 451 F. 2d 727, 729 (1971) ('considerations of international comity would suggest that—given the policy expressed in the Franco-Swiss treaty—United States courts should decline to exercise jurisdiction over a purely private action such as the contract suit here at issue').

[220] See eg, Richard B Lillich, 'Preface', *Fact-Finding before International Tribunals* (1992) x–xi.

[221] See eg, Martinez, above, n 180, at 493; *Sanchez-Llamas*, 126 S Ct, at 1700 (dissenting opinion of Justice Breyer) ('"respectful consideration" also reflects an understanding of the ICJ's expertise in matters of treaty interpretation, a branch of international law'). Cf Rosas, above, n 175, at 230.

[222] Cf Pauwelyn, above, n 38, at 1027.

[223] *MOX Plant* (Ireland v UK), 42 ILM 1187, 1191 (2003) (hereinafter *MOX* (UNCLOS).

[224] *SGS v Philippines*, above, n 48, at para 162.

As a result, the tribunal held that:

> [J]ustice would be best served if the Tribunal were to stay the present proceedings pending determination of the amount payable, either by agreement by the parties or by the Philippine courts in accordance with Article 12 of the CISS Agreement.[225]

This decision largely mirrors the approach of an earlier ICSID arbitral tribunal that, in the face of parallel arbitration proceedings, had decided to stay its proceedings until the domestic court of the *situs* sorted out the challenge to the jurisdiction of the parallel procedure.[226] These cases suggest that international courts may, when appropriate, allow national courts to 'take the first bite of the apple' with respect to the dispute at hand.

The exhaustion of local remedies rule, which directs parties to adjudicate claims before national courts prior to the seizing of international courts (unless such proceedings are deemed futile)[227] demonstrates the practical advantages that international courts can obtain from having before them the conclusions reached by those national courts that reviewed the same case.[228] While the local remedies rule generally stems from a hierarchical jurisdictional paradigm entailing international judicial superiority over national courts, it nonetheless confirms the position that, in some situations, domestic courts ought to be viewed as more appropriate fora for taking a first look at certain types of international law violations.[229]

One could thus argue that international courts should entertain the option of allowing national courts to proceed with parallel or related claims (including resort to domestic appellate procedures)[230] before addressing the same issues (or related issues). This proposition finds support in the dicta of the PCIJ in *Prince von Pless*, which suggested that the PCIJ might be required to arrange its proceedings so as to facilitate the prior consideration by a national court of the issues presented before the international court.[231]

It should be noted, however, that a stay of proceedings may not be feasible for international courts whose operations are governed by strict timetables[232] or when

[225] Ibid, at para 175. [226] *SPP*, 3 ICSID Rep at 129–30.

[227] See eg, Malcolm N Shaw, *International Law* (5th edn, 2003) 255; J G Merrills and A H Robertson, *Human Rights in Europe: A Study of the European Convention for Human Rights* (4th edn, 2001) 304–5; Amerasinghe, above, n 6, at 204–10.

[228] Cf *Occidental*, above, n 132, at para 58 ('the decisions adopted thus far by Ecuadorian courts on matters of interpretation of Ecuadorian Tax Law have been of great help to this Tribunal in its own interpretation of both the Treaty and the relevant provisions of Ecuadorian law').

[229] See Shany, above, n 20, at 142–3; Greenwood, above, n 169, at 64 (international courts should not intervene before the local system's checks and balances are exhausted).

[230] Cf ILA Committee Report, above, n 71, at 21–4 (arbitral tribunals may in some cases stay proceedings in the face of parallel court litigation).

[231] *Prince von Pless Administration* (Germany v Poland), PCIJ (Ser A/B), No 52, at 16 (1933) (interim order) ('it will certainly be an advantage to the Court... to be acquainted with the final decisions of the Supreme Polish Administrative Tribunal upon the appeals brought by Prince von Pless and now pending before that Tribunal... the Court must therefore arrange its procedure so as to ensure that this will be possible').

[232] See eg, DSU, art 20.

urgent actions on behalf of the court are highly valued.[233] Under such circumstances, the procedural straitjacket governing the work of the courts can be considered as *lex specialis* or a consideration overriding any general notion of judicial comity.

Similar powers to stay proceedings can of course be invested with domestic courts faced with related international proceedings.[234] Some domestic decisions favourable to this stance can be cited.[235] Here, too, considerations of procedural expediency and the anticipated utility of the guidance to be offered by the international court in question should be weighed.[236]

In any event, there ought to be, to my mind, no *a priori* preference for either course in the assignment of the jurisdictional right of way, with discretion on forum propriety to be exercised on a case-by-case (or regime-by-regime) basis. Such discretionary weighing should reflect the nature of the case and the capabilities and jurisdictional powers of the respective competing courts, among other factors (respective caseloads, convenience and preferences of the parties, etc). Still, judicial economy considerations usually support retention of jurisdiction by the first-seized court—unless overwhelming considerations lean toward the contrary. In addition, respect for party autonomy normally requires that deference be given to the forum explicitly selected by the parties to the dispute even if the relevant forum-selection instrument is not directly enforceable before the seized court (for reasons of non-incorporation of international instruments into the domestic legal system, etc).[237]

Mitigating the effects of parallel proceedings

The second situation in which comity may be appropriate occurs when the proceedings before national and international courts are indeed pending in parallel. A discretionary stay of proceedings by one court will ease the difficulties encountered by the parties to the parallel litigation at the same time that it may enable the staying court to enjoy the aforesaid benefit of recourse to the parallel court's decisions.[238]

[233] See eg, GA Res A/RES/ES-10/14 (A/ES-10/L.16) (2003) (the General Assembly decides to request the ICJ to issue *urgently* an advisory opinion on the legal consequences of the construction of a wall in the Occupied Palestinian Territory).

[234] See Schreuer (1981), above, n 24, at 332, 343; ILA Committee Report, above, n 71, at 7 (common law courts can stay proceedings in order to accommodate parallel proceedings).

[235] *Mexico v Metalclad Corp* [2001] BCD Civ J, 2581 (British Columbia Supreme Court, Canada); *Cumaraswamy v Insas Bhd & Anor*, decision of 1 Oct 1998 (Court of Appeals, Malaysia), discussed in *Cumaraswamy*, 4 Mal LJ, at 734. Other such cases are discussed in Schreuer (1981), above, n 24, at 332–3, 335, 341.

[236] See Schreuer (1981), above, n 24, at 333–4. Such influence may depend, in part, on the domestic forum's ability subsequently to rely on an international court decision under the prevailing rules of incorporation of international law into domestic law.

[237] *Mitsubishi Motors Corp v Soler Chrysler-Plymouth Inc*, 473 US 614, 629 (1985) ('concerns of international comity, respect for the capacities of foreign and transnational tribunals, and sensitivity to the need of the international commercial system for predictability in the resolution of disputes require that we enforce the parties' agreement, even assuming that a contrary result would be forthcoming in a domestic context').

[238] Cf *Laker Airways Ltd v Sabena, Belgian World Airlines*, 731 F 2d 909, 939 (1984) ('Comity ordinarily requires that courts of a separate sovereign not interfere with concurrent proceedings based on the same transitory claim, at least until a judgment is reached in one action').

Hence, the same considerations that support giving the right of way to the better-situated tribunal in situations of jurisdictional interaction apply with even greater force when the other set of proceedings cease to be speculative.[239]

Some support for the application of judicial comity in concurrent proceedings can also be found in judicial practice.[240] For example, Judge Anderson opined in his dissent in *Camouco* that 'judicial caution' warranted stay of ITLOS proceedings until the conclusion of parallel proceedings before the French courts.[241] However, the tribunal's majority was of the view that the UNCLOS prompt release of vessel provisions require quick action on the tribunal's part irrespective of the domestic proceedings' progress. One can construe this latter position as implying that the Convention's call for urgent action constituted *lex specialis*, a condition that overrides any comity-type discretion that the tribunal might wish to exercise.

Another example of a discretionary stay of proceedings in the face of parallel quasi-judicial and judicial proceedings can be found in the Privy Council decision in the *Thomas and Hilaire* case.[242] In this case, it was held that a constitutional right to due process would be violated if the two respective criminals convicted by the courts of Trinidad and Tobago were to be executed in contravention of the provisional measures order issued by the Inter-American Court of Human Rights (I/A CtHR) for the purpose of facilitating the Commission on Human Rights' consideration of Thomas and Hilaire's petitions. While the idea of judicial comity was not explicitly mentioned in the decision, the Privy Council supported its decision to stay the execution by reference to the expectation that the local authorities in Trinidad and Tobago would, in due time, consider the Commission's report (or, if the case were to be referred by the Commission to the I/A CtHR—the latter court's judgment). This decision illustrates the possibility of scheduling procedures so as to facilitate cross-fertilization between courts—a notion that sits well with some of the fundamental rationales of judicial comity.

In any event, it seems that resort to inter-jurisdictional battles between parallel national and international proceedings, captured in the issuance of anti-suit (or anti-anti-suit) injunction-type remedies does not sit well with the pro-comity stance advocated here.[243] On the contrary, comity considerations can support a wide variety of

239 For example, order no 4 issued by the *MOX Plant* (UNCLOS) arbitration tribunal after the parallel ECJ proceedings commenced, confirmed the stay of proceedings already ordered before initiation of the ECJ proceedings. *MOX Plant* (Ireland v UK), Order No 4 of 14 Nov 2003, <http://www.pca-cpa.org/ENGLISH/RPC/MOX/MOX%20Order%20No4.pdf>.

240 For an example derived from treaty law, not judicial practice, see Treaty Concerning the Establishment and the Statute of a Benelux Court of Justice, 31 March 1965, art 10(3), 924 UNTS 1 (establishing the authority of the Benelux Court to stay proceedings in the face of parallel or related proceedings before another competent forum).

241 *Camouco*, 39 ILM at 690 (dissenting opinion of Judge Anderson).

242 *Thomas v Baptiste* [1999] 3 WLR 249 (PC). For a discussion, see Natasha Parassram Concepcion, 'The Legal Implications of Trinidad & Tobago's Withdrawal From the American Convention on Human Rights', 16 *Am U Int'l L Rev* (2001) 847, 867–8.

243 For example, in *SGS v Pakistan*, the Pakistani courts issued an injunction against the pursuit of the ICSID arbitration. At the same time, the ICSID panel recommended a stay of arbitral proceedings

judicial cooperation measures, including transfer of testaments, sharing of evidence and enforcement of interim decisions.[244]

Considering the effects of previous decisions on the same matter

A third possible sphere for application of judicial comity appears in situations where one court has already decided the case in full or in part. The pertinent question here is what—if any—effect should be granted to such a decision by the other courts reviewing the same or a related case. The systemic and pragmatic considerations discussed above—particularly the need for consistency in dispute settlement and institutional judicial economy considerations—appear to support the normative proposition that courts should follow decisions issued by other national or international courts or apply a rebuttable presumption in their favour in the absence of strong reasons to the contrary.[245] When both proceedings are rooted in international law, the normative systemization considerations discussed in Chapters 2 and 4 lend additional support to this position.[246] So, in any event, the notions of respect and courtesy represented by judicial comity imply that at a very bare minimum, courts should accord due consideration to the previous decisions of other national or international court on the same issues and articulate reasons for deviating from those past decisions.[247]

The German Constitutional Court decisions on the status of EC law in Germany (the Maastricht and Bananas decisions)[248] seem to represent, by and large, a particularly

in Pakistan, pending determination of its scope of jurisdiction. *SGS v Pakistan* (order no. 2), above, n 122, at 296, 304. The recommendation was eventually accepted by the Pakistani arbitrator. *SGS v Pakistan*, 42 ILM at 1298. For another example of issuance of an anti-suit injunction (this time directed by an international tribunal at a domestic court), see *Tokios Tokeles v Ukraine*, decision on jurisdiction of 29 April 2004, at para 12 <http://www.worldbank.org/icsid/cases/tokios-decision.pdf> (noting previous decision by the arbitral tribunal to order the suspension of local court proceedings in the Ukraine). In any event, it seems that *in personam* injunctions that are designed to prevent double recovery by the same plaintiff before international and national judicial mechanisms may be more justified than 'ordinary' jurisdiction-protecting injunctions. See eg, *Occidental*, above, n 132, at para 209. Cf *Mareva Compania Naviera SA v International Bulkcarriers SA*, [1975] 2 Lloyd's Rep 509 (CA). But see *Waste Management*, 40 ILM at 63 ('This Tribunal . . . lacks the necessary authority to bar the Claimant from initiating other proceedings in fora other than the present one').

[244] See eg, Ahdieh, above, n 175, at 121–33.

[245] See eg, *The Janko (The Nordsktank)*, 54 F Supp 241, 244 (1944) ('Comity would not permit in the present cause an exploration as to whether the seizure of the Janko by the Dutch Prize Court was lawful'); *Quintette Coal Limited v Nippon Steel Corporation* [1991] 1 WWR 219, at para 37 (British Columbia Court of Appeal, Canada) ('[It is] a matter of policy, to adopt a standard which seeks to preserve the autonomy of the forum selected by the parties and to minimize judicial intervention when reviewing international commercial arbitral awards in British Columbia').

[246] See eg, *Camouco*, 39 ILM at 699 (dissenting opinion of Judge Wolfrum) ('These discretionary powers or margin of appreciation on the side of the coastal State limit the powers of the Tribunal on deciding whether a bond set by national authorities was reasonable or not'). Cf Martinez, above, n 180, at 487.

[247] Martinez, above, n 180, at 495. Cf Michael D Ramsey, 'Escaping "International Comity"', 83 *Iowa LR* (1998) 257, 295.

[248] *Brunner v European Union Treaty*, 89 BverfGE 155, 12 Oct. 1993, translated in [1994] 1 CMLR 57, 89; Order on the Constitutionality of the Application of the European Union's Common

strong presumption in favour of compliance with international decisions: EC norms, including ECJ decisions, are given effect by German courts subject to their consistency with fundamental German constitutional principles—a consistency that is normally presumed.[249] This position seems to be compatible with some of the comity rationales previously discussed. Other domestic courts have taken similar positions, applying a presumption in favour of following international court decisions, especially in the field of human rights and economic integration.[250]

Still, domestic practice in this area is hardly consistent. One can identify incidences in which national courts have outright rejected international decisions rendered with respect to the same dispute (deemed not to be formally binding).[251] Notable examples are the refusals by US courts to respect the ICJ's provisional measures orders in the *Breard* and *LaGrand* cases,[252] or follow WTO DSB decisions on zeroing, discussed in Part 1.[253]

While international practice of granting deference to national court decisions is somewhat less conspicuous, some notable examples can be identified. In *Brazilian Loans*, the PCIJ refused to ignore municipal court decisions regarding the contents

Market for Bananas in Germany, 102 BverfGE 147, 7 June 2000, excerpts translated in George A. Bermann et al, Cases and Materials on European Union Law (2002) 321. According to the German Constitutional Court, EC law would be denied of effect only if shown to fall short of guaranteeing an absolute minimum of protection of fundamental rights. For a discussion, see Carl Lebeck, 'National Constitutionalism, Openness to International Law and the Pragmatic Limits of European Integration—European Law in the German Constitutional Court from EEC to the PJCC', 7 *German Law Journal* (2006) 907, 914–26; Norbert Reich, 'Judge-made "Europe à la carte": Some Remarks on Recent Conflicts between European and German Constitutional Law Provoked by the Banana Litigation', 7 *EJIL* (1996) 1, 9–10. See also *Internationale Handelsgesellschaft mbH v Einfuhr- und Vorratsstelle für Getreide und Futtermittel*, 37 BVerfGE 271 (1974), translated in [1974] 2 CMLR 540, 552–4 (1974); *Frontini v Ministero Delle Finanze*, Judgment of 27 Dec 1973 (Constitutional Court, Italy), translated in [1974] 2 CMLR 372, 389 (1974). Cf *Traité portant statut de la Cour pénale internationale*, decision of the 22 Jan 1999 (Conseil Constitutionnel, France), <http://www.conseil-constitutionnel.fr/decision/1998/98408/98408dc.htm> (certain ICC decisions might be incompatible with essential guarantees of national sovereignty under the French Constitution).

249 *In re Wunsche Handelsgesellschaft (Solange II)* [1987] 3 CMLR 225, 265; *Brunner* [1994] 1 CMLR, at 79. See also the public policy exception in the New York Convention. New York Convention, art 5(2).

250 See Human Rights Act, 1998, s 2(1) (UK); *R v Secretary of State for Transport, ex parte Factortame Ltd*, [1999] 4 All ER 906 (HL); Holly D Jarmul, 'The Effects of Decisions of Regional Human Rights Tribunals on National Courts', 28 *NYU J Int'l L & Pol* 311, 334–61 (1996); Helfer and Slaughter, above, n 7, at 296; Schreuer (1981), above, n 24, at 33–4.

251 See eg, 19 USC § 3512 (b)(2)(B)(i) ('a report of a dispute settlement panel or the Appellate Body convened under the Dispute Settlement Understanding regarding the State law, or the law of any political subdivision thereof, shall not be considered as binding or otherwise accorded deference').

252 See *Breard*, 523 US 371; *Federal Republic of Germany v US*, 526 US 111 (1999). For a discussion, see Sanja Djajic, 'The Effect of International Court of Justice Decisions on Municipal Courts in the United States: Breard v Greene', 23 *Hastings Int'l & Comp L Rev* 27, 94–100 (1999) (arguing that the Supreme Court failed to exercise comity toward the ICJ); Curtis Bradley, 'Breard, Our Dualist Constitution, and the Internationalist Conception', 51 *Stan L Rev* 529 (1999) (describing the claims for enforcement of ICJ decisions as 'unrealistic').

253 See *Corus Staal*, 395 F 3d 1343; *Timken Co v US*, 354 F 3d 1334 (2004). See also Gathii, above, n 202, at 20–1.

of the relevant municipal laws, notwithstanding the parties' agreement that it may do so. Instead, the Court stated that it must 'pay the utmost regard to the decisions of the municipal courts of a country'.[254] Although this decision clearly stems from the unique circumstances of the case, in which an international court was requested to identify those contents of domestic law that govern the matter at hand, it can lend support to a more general proposition, encouraging international courts to defer to national court decisions concerning matters over which the latter courts enjoy greater expertise (eg, fact-analysis and appreciation of local conditions).

Indeed, in *Camouco*, one of the dissenting judges, Judge Anderson, opined that French courts are better situated than ITLOS to determine the bond that should be deposited in order to facilitate the prompt release of a detained vessel. Hence, their decisions should be followed as a rule:

> The work of the national court, however, is an indispensable part of the factual background and there is a need for judicial restraint at the international level. It should be recognised that the local courts are best placed to appreciate all the relevant considerations of fact and law in the State concerned. In a matter such as this, concerning as it does procedure in a current criminal case, the local court should be accorded a wide discretion in fixing the amount of the security for release pending trial. In other words, national courts should be accorded a broad 'margin of appreciation' ... In my view, it follows that an Applicant has to show very strong grounds for reducing the amount of the security fixed by a national court under local law in order to succeed under article 292.[255]

Judge Wolfrum also suggested in his dissent in the same case that national court decisions on bond setting should attract considerable deference:

> [T]he power of the Tribunal to challenge decisions taken, namely the decision on the amount of the bond, is restricted. The Tribunal is in a situation which is not dissimilar to that faced by international human rights courts which, in general, have to verify whether national decisions or measures are in conformity with an international human rights agreement. They restrict themselves, generally speaking, to ascertaining whether such a decision or measure was unlawful under international law, or was arbitrary, or constituted an abuse of authority, or was made in bad faith, or was disproportionate.[256]

Another example of judicial comity exercised by an international court towards a national court is found in *Azinian*. In this case, a NAFTA Chapter 11 arbitral tribunal held that at least for the purpose of Chapter 11, national court decisions, even

254 *Payment in Gold of the Brazilian Federal Loans Issued in France* (France v Brazil), 1929 PCIJ Ser A, No 20/21, at 124.

255 *Camouco*, 39 ILM at 689–90 (dissenting opinion of Judge Anderson). See also *'Monte Confurco'* (Seychelles v France), Judgment of 18 Dec 2000 (declaration of Judge Mensah), available at <http://www.itlos.org/cgi-bin/cases/case_detail.pl?id=5&lang=en> ('the Tribunal should exercise utmost restraint in making statements that might plausibly imply criticism of the procedures and decisions of the domestic courts').

256 *Camouco*, 39 ILM at 700 (dissenting opinion of Judge Wolfrum).

if erroneous, should be followed unless those decisions reveal denial of justice[257] or demonstrate bad faith.[258] Indeed, as the next section illustrates, international courts engaged in vertical review of national court decisions (as Chapter 11 tribunals arguably do) often treat their domestic counterparts with some degree of deference. Such deference sometimes leads to the extension of non-intrusive standards of review or to the issuance of flexible remedies that entrust national courts with discretion as to the manner of implementation of those same remedies.

Of course, here, too, some contrary examples can be noted. For example, the ICJ Advisory Opinion on the *Wall* did not assign any weight to the previous decision of Israel's Supreme Court on the legality of the separation barrier,[259] nor did it envision any role for the Israeli courts in implementing the ICJ opinion.[260] Similarly, the ITLOS prompt release of vessel decisions discussed in Chapter 1 generally refrain from assigning significant weight to domestic court determinations on the proper level of release bonds.[261]

Deferential review

Judicial review constitutes a special context for application of judicial comity. Although courts exercising vertical control over other court decisions certainly need not follow the latter's decisions (that would, of course, defeat the object of the review process), it is interesting to note a general tendency by reviewing courts to embrace non-intrusive or deferential standards of review. Although such a tendency can be explained by reference to notions of courtesy and respect—which might be weaker in situations of vertical supervision than in horizontal interaction between 'equal' courts—reliance on deferential standards does seem to make a positive contribution to cooperation between national and international institutions maintaining hierarchical relationships. The deferential treatment of reviewed courts may also reflect the perception that the norms in question are of an open-ended nature and that certain policy considerations (eg, judicial economy, liberalism) militate against strict scrutiny of their implementation by the first-seized courts. In addition, unique considerations relating to the subsidiary nature of international law (that is, a decentralized vision of international governance)[262] also appear to support deference by international courts toward their domestic counterparts.

[257] However, denial of justice standards remain elusive. See eg, Paulsson, above, n 169, at 57–9; Andrea K Bjorklund, 'Reconciling State Sovereignty and Investor Protection in Denial of Justice Claims', 45 *Va J Int'l L* (2005) 809, 867–8.

[258] *Azinian*, 39 ILM at 551–2 ('Even if the Claimants were to convince this Arbitral Tribunal that the Mexican courts were wrong with respect to the invalidity of the Concession Contract, this would not per se be conclusive as to a violation of NAFTA. More is required; the Claimants must show either a denial of justice, or a pretence of form to achieve an internationally unlawful end').

[259] HCJ 2056/04, *Beit Sourik Village Council v Gov't of Israel*, 58 PD 806 (an English translation is available at ILDC 16 (IL 2004)). One possible explanation for this omission is the short time between the Israeli Supreme Court's decision and the date of the advisory opinion's publication.

[260] For a criticism, see Shany, above, n 206, at 206; Shany, above, n 173, at 938–9.

[261] *Saiga* (merits), above, n 58; *Camouco*, 39 ILM 666; *Monte Confurco*, above, n 257.

[262] Cf *EC–Measures Concerning Meat and Meat Products (Hormones)*, WTO Doc WT/DS26/AB/R (1998), at para 115 (AB report) ('The standard of review... must reflect the *balance* established in

The margin of appreciation doctrine, in one version or the other, is perhaps the most well-known and well-developed vehicle for promoting the aforementioned considerations in vertical contexts. This doctrine, which has already been applied by a fair number of international courts, is constructed of two core elements:

a) *Judicial deference*—International courts should grant national authorities, including domestic courts,[263] a certain degree of deference and respect their discretion regarding how to execute their international law obligations. This means that international courts ought to refrain from substituting their own discretion and evaluation of facts for those exercised by national authorities[264] or from reviewing national decisions *de novo*. In other words, international judicial bodies should exercise judicial restraint.[265]

b) *Normative flexibility*—Those international norms subject to this doctrine can be characterized as open-ended or unsettled.[266] Such norms provide states with limited guidance and establish a broad 'zone of legality' within which they are free to operate.[267] In consequence, different national authorities in each state can conceivably reach diverse yet lawful decisions regarding the application of the same international norm.[268]

Although these two elements are analytically separate—the first element, which is more relevant to our topic, relates to norm-application, whereas the second element pertains to norm-interpretation (even outside the context of jurisdictional

that [SPS] Agreement between the jurisdictional competences conceded by the Members to the WTO and the jurisdictional competences retained by the Members for themselves'); Claus-Dieter Ehlermann and Nicolas Lockhart, 'Standard of Review in WTO Law', 7 *J Int'l Eco L* (2004) 491, 493. One can also link the debate over the status of the margin of appreciation doctrine to debates over the constitutionalization of international law. Stefan Zleptnig, 'The Standard of Review in WTO Law: An Analysis of Law, Legitimacy and the Distribution of Legal and Political Authority', 6 *European Integration online Papers (EIoP)*, N° 17 (2002), at 9–10, <http://eiop.or.at/eiop/texte/2002-017a.htm>, at 9–10.

263 But see Shany, above, n 173, at 918–19 (judicial decision-making at the national and international level suffer from chronic deficiencies that support the delegation of decision-making powers to non-judicial decision-makers).

264 *Ireland v UK*, Eur Ct HR (Ser A), No 25, at 82 (1978); Ehlermann and Lockhart, above, n 262, at 502.

265 *James v UK*, 1986 Eur Ct HR (Ser A), No 98, at 32 ('the Court cannot substitute its own assessment for that of the national authorities'); *Karataş v Turkey*, 1999-IV Eur Ct HR 81, at 120 (joint partly dissenting opinion of Judges Wildhaber, Pastor Ridruejo, Costa, and Baka) ('In the assessment of whether restrictive measures are necessary in a democratic society, due deference will be accorded to the State's margin of appreciation; the democratic legitimacy of measures taken by democratically elected governments commands a degree of judicial self-restraint.'); *Hormones* (AB), above, n 262, at para 117 ('the applicable standard is neither *de novo* review as such, nor "total deference", but rather the "objective assessment of the facts" '); *Argentina–Safeguard Measure on Imports of Footwear (Footwear)*, WTO Doc WT/DS121/AB/R (2000), at para 121 (AB Report); *EC–Measures Affecting Asbestos and Asbestos-Containing Products*, WTO Doc WT/DS135/AB/R (2001), at para 168 (AB report).

266 See eg, *Sheffield v UK*, 1998-V Eur Ct HR 2011, at 2028; *Odièvre v France*, [2003] Eur Ct HR 86, at para 40.

267 See eg, *VO v France* [2004] ECHR 326, at para 82.

268 See eg, Final Report to the Prosecutor by the Committee Established to Review the NATO Bombing Campaign against the Federal Republic of Yugoslavia (2000), at para 50, <http://www.un.org/icty/pressreal/nato061300.htm>. See also Douglas Lee Donoho, 'Autonomy, Self-Government, and the Margin of Appreciation: Developing a Jurisprudence of Diversity within Universal Human Rights', 15 *Emory Int'l L Rev* (2001) 391, 457; Steven Greer, 'Constitutionalising Adjudication under the European Convention on Human Rights', 23 *Oxford Journal of Legal Studies* (2003) 405, 409.

interaction)—international courts have not always distinguished between them in practice. Furthermore, the two elements enmesh: the construction of international norms as ambiguous facilitates the exercise of judicial deference and vice versa. In any event, one must stress that the margin of appreciation afforded under the doctrine is never unlimited.[269] Hence, international courts are ultimately responsible for the review of national decisions' lawfulness. The scope of review can include, inter alia, assessment of the decision-making process (eg, whether all pertinent considerations were taken into account) and substantive outcomes (eg, whether the decision promoted attainment of normative goals).[270]

Arguably, this combination of discretion on the part of national authorities and non-intrusive review by international courts can produce the proper mix between deference and supervision given the respective advantages of the two sets of actors.[271] Furthermore, it looks as if the division of labour between national authorities and international courts institutionalized by the margin of appreciation doctrine nurtures a sense of partnership between national and international courts.[272] The shared decision-making and joint responsibility for the final outcome, which the doctrine entails, also accelerate internalization of international law norms by domestic institutions.[273]

In practice, the ECtHR's extensive application of the margin of appreciation doctrine is, perhaps, the most conspicuous example of its use.[274] For example, in the

[269] See *Hormones* (AB), above, n 262, at para 117; Eyal Benvenisti, 'Margin of Appreciation, Consensus and Universal Values', 31 *NYU J Int'l L & Pol* (1999) 843, 844.

[270] See *Rekvényi v Hungary*, 1999-III Eur Ct HR 423, 443–4 ('the court has to satisfy itself that the national authorities applied standards which were in conformity with the principles embodied in art. 10 and, moreover, that they based their decisions on an acceptable assessment of the relevant facts'); *US–Restrictions on Imports of Cotton and Man-Made Fiber Underwear*, WTO Doc WT/DS24/R (1996), at para 7.13 (Panel Report) ('an objective assessment would entail an examination of whether the [US Committee for the Implementation of Textiles Agreements] had examined all relevant facts before it..., whether adequate explanation had been provided of how the facts as a whole supported the determination made, and, consequently, whether the determination made was consistent with the international obligations of the United States'); *Footwear*, above, n 265, at para 121.

[271] Cf Paolo G. Carozza, 'Subsidiarity as a Structural Principle of International Human Rights Law', 97 *AJIL* (2003) 38, 67.

[272] Ibid, at 74–5; Helfer and Slaughter, above, n 7, at 310–12; Paul Mahoney, 'Judicial Activism and Judicial Self-restraint in the European Court of Human Rights: Two Sides of the Same Coin', 11 *Hum Rts LJ* (1990) 57, 81.

[273] Koh, above, n 180, at 648–50. In addition, the margin of appreciation doctrine can provide international courts with a flexible tool for the long-term monitoring of national actors: it enables international courts to criticize states without explicitly pronouncing their conduct illegal, and to prod national actors to gradually improve their performance. Such incremental approach could weaken resistance to judicial supervision and facilitate the long-term internalization of international norms and values. Ronald St J MacDonald, 'The Margin of Appreciation', *The European System for the Protection of Human Rights* (R St J MacDonald et al, eds, 1993), 83, 123 ('The margin of appreciation gives the flexibility needed to avoid damaging confrontations between the Court and the Contracting States'); Ahdieh, above, n 175, at 2051–2 (discussing the focus on prospective change in the dialogue between international and domestic courts).

[274] See eg, *Engel v Netherlands* 1 EHRR 647 (1979); *Golder*, 1975 Eur Ct HR (Ser A), No 18; *De Wilde v Belgium* 1 EHRR 373 (1979); *Mellacher v Austria*, 12 EHRR 391 (1990); *Goodwin v UK* 22 EHRR 123 (1996); *Smith v UK* 29 EHRR 493 (2000); *Pretty v UK* 2002-III Eur Ct HR 155; *Dudgeon v UK* 4 EHRR 149 (1982); *Lehideux v France*, 38 ILM (1999) 30.

1976 *Handyside* case, the Court reviewed the lawfulness of a prohibition imposed by UK officials and approved by the local courts upon the distribution of a teenage guidebook alleged to affect public morals adversely. In accepting the government's position that the measure in question was a legitimate restriction on freedom of expression, the Court elaborated the main parameters of the margin of appreciation doctrine:

Article 10(2) leaves to the Contracting States a margin of appreciation. This margin is given both to the domestic legislator ('prescribed by law') and *to the bodies, judicial amongst others, that are called upon to interpret and apply the laws in force* [cites omitted]. Nevertheless, Article 10(2) does not give the Contracting States an unlimited power of appreciation. The Court, which, with the Commission, is responsible for ensuring the observance of those States' engagements (art. 19), is empowered to give the final ruling on whether a 'restriction' or 'penalty' is reconcilable with freedom of expression as protected by Article 10. The domestic margin of appreciation thus goes hand in hand with a European supervision[275] (emphasis added).

In other words, the ECtHR does not purport to sit as a 'fourth court of appeal' over domestic courts but, rather, serves as a less-than-intrusive supervisory mechanism.

Significantly, application of the margin of appreciation doctrine by the ECtHR depends on a variety of factors:[276] (a) *the comparative advantage of local authorities*—broader margins are afforded to local authorities with respect to questions they are better situated to assess (eg, local moral sensitivities);[277] (b) *the indeterminacy of the applicable standard*—broader margins are granted over issues lacking a European consensus;[278] and (c) *the nature of the contested interests*—broader margins are granted when more important national interests are at stake and the alleged violation appears less fundamental.[279] This last condition has received legislative endorsement in Protocol 14 to the ECHR, which authorizes the ECtHR to dismiss cases

[275] *Handyside v UK*, 1976 Eur Ct HR (Ser A), No 24, at 22–3.

[276] See Eva Brems, 'The Margin of Appreciation Doctrine in the Case Law of the European Court of Human Rights', 56 *Heidelberg J Int'l L* (1996) 240, 256; Howard C Yourow, *The Margin of Appreciation Doctrine in the Dynamics of European Human Rights Jurisprudence* (1996) 186–96.

[277] See *Sunday Times v UK*, 2 EHRR 245 (1980), at para 59.

[278] See *Rees v United Kingdom*, 106 Eur Ct HR (Ser A) (1986) No 106; Yourow, above, n 276, at 54. For criticism of the Court's emphasis on consensus, see Benvenisti, above, n 271, at 851–2; Laurence R Helfer, 'Consensus, Coherence and the European Convention on Human Rights', 26 *Cornell Int'l LJ* (1993) 133, 141–2; MacDonald, above, n 273, at 124; Paulo G Carozza, 'Uses and Misuses of Comparative Law in International Human Rights: Some Reflections on the Jurisprudence of the European Court of Justice', 73 *Notre Dame L Rev* (1998) 1217; Yutaka Arai-Takahashi, *The Margin of Appreciation Doctrine and the Principle of Proportionality in the Jurisprudence of the ECHR* (2002) 195–6; Mahoney, above, n 272, at 74.

[279] For example, see *Leander v Sweden* 116 Eur Ct HR (Ser A) (1987) at para 59; *Rekvényi*, 1999-III Eur Ct HR, at para 57; *Çakici v Turkey*, 1999-IV Eur Ct HR 583, 617. But see, *Rotaru v Romania*, 2000-V Eur Ct HR 61, 134–5; *Smith v UK*, 1999-VI Eur Ct HR 45, 82; *Tinnelly & Sons v UK*, 1998-IV Eur Ct HR 1633, 1661–3; *Chahal v UK*, 1996-V Eur Ct HR 1831, 1870–1.

that raise less serious violations of the Convention—provided that they were previously handled by domestic courts.[280]

Similar manifestations of margin of appreciation or analogous principles of deference to national authorities can be found in the practice of the ECJ,[281] WTO DSB,[282] certain human rights courts and quasi-judicial bodies,[283] as well as some arbitral awards.[284] In the same vein, many national courts reviewing motions to recognize and enforce international arbitral awards—in effect exercising vertical control over their implementation—have also applied a deferential standard.[285]

280 Protocol No 14 to the Convention for the Protection of Human Rights and Fundamental Freedoms, 13 May 2004, art 12, ETS 194.

281 See eg, Case C-83/94, *Germany v Leifer* 1995 ECR I-3231, 3250; Case 273/97, *Sirdar v Army Bd*, 1999 ECR 7403, at para 27; Case C-368/95, *Vereinigte Familiapress Zeitungsverlags- und vertriebs GmbH v Heinrich Bauer Verlag*, 1997 ECR I-3689, 3716; Case C-260/89, *Elliniki Radiophonia Tileorassi AE (ERT) v Dimotiki Etairia Pliroforissis (DEP)*, 1991 ECR I-2925, 2960; *Dory v Bundesrepublik Deutschland*, 2003 ECJ CELEX LEXIS 99, at para 36; *Kreil v Bundesrepublik Deutschland*, 2000 ECR I-69, 105; Case 131/79, *R v Secretary of State for Home Affairs, ex parte Santillo*, 1980 ECR 1585, 1600–1; Case 34/79, *R v Henn*, 1979 ECR 3795, 3818–814. Carozza maintains that the ECJ's traditional deference to human rights decisions taken at the national level is indicative of its recognition of the comparative advantage of national institutions. Carozza, above, n 271, at 55.

282 See eg, *EC–Measures Concerning Meat and Meat Products (Hormones)*, WTO Doc WT/DS26/15 (1998) (arbitration under Article 21.3 (c) of the DSU) ('An implementing Member, therefore, has a measure of discretion in choosing the means of implementation'); *Underwear*, above, n 272, para 7.13; *Footwear*, above, n 265, at para 121; *Asbestos*, above, n 265, at para 168; *US–Tax Treatment of 'Foreign Sales Corp'*, WTO Doc WT/DS108/ARB (2002), at para 5 (art 22.6 arbitration); *EC–Regime for the Importation, Sale and Distribution of Bananas*, WTO Doc WT/DS27/ARB/ECU (2000), at para 52 (art 22.6 arbitration) ('these subparagraphs leave a certain margin of appreciation to the complaining party concerned in arriving at its conclusions in respect of an evaluation of certain factual elements'). This approach is generally consistent with the decision taken by a GATT panel in the 1994 *Tuna* case (*US–Restrictions on Imports of Tuna*, 33 ILM 839 (1994)) and with the explicit standard of review provided for in art 17.6 of the Anti-Dumping Agreement. Agreement on the Implementation of Article VI of the General Agreement on Tariff and Trade 1994, Annex 1A to the Agreement Establishing the World Trade Organization, 15 Apr 1994, 33 ILM 1144 (1994) ('(i) in its assessment of the facts of the matter, the panel shall determine whether the authorities' establishment of the facts was proper and whether their evaluation of those facts was unbiased and objective. If the establishment of the facts was proper and the evaluation was unbiased and objective, even though the panel might have reached a different conclusion, the evaluation shall not be overturned; (ii) the panel shall interpret the relevant provisions of the Agreement in accordance with customary rules of interpretation of public international law. Where the panel finds that a relevant provision of the Agreement admits of more than one permissible interpretation, the panel shall find the authorities' measure to be in conformity with the Agreement if it rests upon one of those permissible interpretations').

283 See eg, *Proposed Amendments to the Naturalization Provision of the Constitution of Costa Rica*, 1984 Inter-Am Ct HR (Ser A), No 4. Many other decisions reveal methodological choices that are consistent with the doctrine—that is, they provide domestic institutions with latitude in the implementation of the relevant treaty norms—without explicitly invoking the margin of appreciation doctrine. See eg, Comm 547/1993 *Mahuika v New Zealand*, UN Doc CCPR/C/70/D/547/1993 (2000), para 9.10–9.11; Comm 35/1978, *Aumeeruddy-Cziffra v Mauritius*, UN Doc A/36/40 (1981), at para 9.2(b)(2)(ii). Benvenisti, above, n 271, at 844–5.

284 *Heathrow Airport User Charges* (US/UK), Award of 30 Nov 1992, ch 5, at 84 (first question), *cited in* Samuel W Witten 'The US-UK Arbitration Award concerning Heathrow Airport User Charges' 89 *AJIL* (1995) 174, 187; *D Myers, Inc v Canada*, 40 ILM 1408, 1438 (2001).

285 See eg, *Mexico v Kapra*, 136 ACWS (3d) 200, at LEXIS 20–1 (Ontario Court of Appeal, Canada) ('Quite apart from principles of international comity domestic law in Canada dictates a high degree of deference for decisions of specialized tribunals generally and for awards of consensual

This accumulation of decisions has led one ITLOS judge to declare that the margin of appreciation principle is a well-known principle of international law.[286] Still, one should note that the ICJ's position on the matter is less than clear. Whereas some ICJ decisions have implicitly accepted that states enjoy some latitude in applying legal standards (while noting that the ICJ retains the ultimate authority to review the legality of the conduct in question),[287] it seems to have rejected the margin of appreciation doctrine in the recent *Oil Platforms* case, at least in relation to cases involving the use of force.[288]

All told, the copious examples of the doctrine's use suggest that judicial deference can be applied and may in fact be imbued in the interaction between national and international courts, regardless of the paradigm—vertical or horizontal—governing their relations. In fact, considerations relating to the comparative advantage of one court over the other,[289] together with notions of judicial economy[290] that militate in favour of granting courts a margin of appreciation in a vertical context, can apply *a fortiori* in a horizontal context. Whereas all parties to vertical interactions typically agree to multi-fora adjudication and to the attendant risk of inconsistent findings, most horizontal interaction cases do not involve such agreements. Hence, a higher premium should be placed on the prevention of impositions that seriously inconvenience the parties to proceedings conducted within the latter context. Alternatively, it may be expected that courts of equal status will be more inclined

arbitration tribunals in particular'); *Karaha Bodas Co, LLC, v Perusahaan Pertambangan Minyak Dan Gas Bumi Negara*, 364 F 3d 274 , 290 (2004) ('Under the New York Convention, the rulings of the Tribunal interpreting the parties' contract are entitled to deference'). But see *Ministry of Defense of Islamic Republic v Gould, Inc*, 969 F 2d 764 (1992) (partially vacating an award of the Iran–US Claims Tribunal).

286 *The Volga* Case (Russia v Australia), 42 ILM (2003) 159, 183–6 (separate opinion of Judge Cot). For application of the principle by other ITLOS judges, see *Camouco*, 39 ILM at 690, 699 (dissenting opinions of Judges Anderson and Wolfrum)

287 See *Military and Paramilitary Activities in and Against Nicaragua* (Nicaragua v US), 1986 ICJ 14, 141; *Gabcikovo/Nagymaros* (Hungary/Slovakia), 1997 ICJ 7, 40; *Legality of the Threat or Use of Nuclear Weapons*, 1996 ICJ 226, at Part III, sec 2 of the separate opinion of Judge Shahabuddeen.

288 *Oil Platforms* (Iran v US), 42 ILM 1334, 1361 (2003). For a discussion, see Shany, above, n 173, at 931–4; David Kaye, 'Adjudicating Self-Defense: Discretion, Perception, and the Resort to Force in International Law', 44 *Colum J Transnat'l L* (2005) 134. Two individual ICJ judges—judges Koojimans and Buergenthal—were of the view that some margin of discretion was due, in the circumstances of the case, to the positions taken by the US authorities. *Oil Platforms*, 42 ILM at 1400–1 (separate opinion of Judge Koojimans); ibid, at 1414 (separate opinion of Judge Buergenthal).

289 For example, national courts may be more familiar with local conditions and more likely to compel submission of evidence than their international counterparts; domestic courts are more democratically accountable; international courts may be more experienced in applying international law and less susceptible to political bias than domestic courts. See eg, *Handyside* (1976) Eur Ct HR (Ser A), No 24, at para 48; *Ireland v UK*, Eur Ct HR (Ser A), No 25, at 82; Shany, above, n 173, at 918–23.

290 For example, international courts facing heavy case loads might be inclined to exercise less intrusive supervision over their domestic counterparts. See eg, Council of Europe, Explanatory Report to Protocol No 14 to the Convention for the Protection of Human Rights and Fundamental Freedoms, amending the control system of the Convention (CETS No 194), at para 77–9, <http://conventions.coe.int/Treaty/EN/Reports/Html/194.htm> (because of excessive workload ECtHR may decline to review some cases raising minor violations).

to treat one another with respect and courtesy than will courts operating under a vertical paradigm.

Discretion in implementation

Although, the ICJ has been in a few recent cases reluctant to apply the margin of appreciation doctrine while reviewing decisions adopted at the national level, it has displayed more willingness to defer to national court discretion in questions relating to judgment implementation. In two cases concerning the US failure to provide timely consular notification—*LaGrand* and *Avena*—the Court refrained from spelling out any specific remedial obligations (including the review of past convictions of foreign defendants who should have been notified of their right to consular assistance). Instead, the Court held in *LaGrand* that:

> [I]t would be incumbent upon the United States to allow the review and reconsideration of the conviction and sentence by taking account of the violation of the rights set forth in the Convention. This obligation can be carried out in various ways. The choice of means must be left to the United States.[291]

In the same vein, it held in *Avena* that:

> The question . . . is an integral part of criminal proceedings before the courts of the United States and it is for them to determine the process of review and reconsideration.[292]

The deference afforded to US courts in selecting the appropriate remedies, an acknowledgement of their comparative institutional advantage in such matters, and the ICJ's refusal to assume bad faith on their part[293]—which denoted some degree of inter-judicial courtesy—generated a legal discourse that mirrors the traditional justifications for the margin of appreciation doctrine. Significantly, the degree of control over the application of remedies as retained by domestic courts invested with the respective discretion helps sustain their confidence in the international adjudicative process and provides states with face-saving leeway.[294] Such a mechanism may, arguably, improve the prospects of domestic enforcement of international judgments.[295] Of course, discretion in implementation can also be conferred by national courts to those international courts whose decisions are subject to vertical judicial review. For example, one may cite a recent decision of a

[291] *LaGrand*, 2001 ICJ at 514. For a generally similar position, see *Haya de la Torre* (Colom v Peru), 1951 ICJ 71, 83 ('Having thus defined in accordance with the Havana Convention, the legal relations between the Parties with regard to the matters referred to it, the Court has completed its task. It is unable to give any practical advice as to the various courses which might be followed with a view toward terminating the asylum, since, by doing so, it would depart from its judicial function').

[292] *Avena*, 2004 ICJ at 615. For a criticism, see *Avena*, 2004 ICJ at 643 (separate opinion of Judge ad hoc Sepúlveda). The Court noted, however, that the margin of discretion afforded to US authorities is not unlimited. Ibid, at 617.

[293] *LaGrand*, 2001 ICJ at 513.

[294] See Benvenisti, above, n 271, at 849.

[295] This consideration is of particular importance given the under-enforcement of many international judgments. Steven P Croley and John H Jackson, 'WTO Procedures, Standard of Review, and Deference to National Governments', 90 *AJIL* (1996) 193, 212.

local Canadian court to remit some issues for reconsideration to an ICSID arbitration panel, in order to evade the need for setting aside the award in full.[296]

More generally, one can argue that it would be wise for courts entertaining a reasonable expectation that other national and international courts will be called upon to apply their decisions in the future to construct those decisions in a comity-inspiring manner:[297] given the discretionary nature of comity, the first-in-time court should strive to persuade subsequent courts of the correctness and reasonableness of its decisions.[298] Unarticulated judgments cannot be expected to invite automatic compliance.[299] The first-in-time court would also do well to consider utilizing the institutional advantages (eg, greater enforceability of domestic court decisions) of the other courts expected to be involved in the case and to acknowledge their structural sensitivities (eg, respect for national sovereignty, aversion to infringement of institutional independence of courts) by leaving some margin of appreciation in the implementation of its decision.[300]

6.2. *Abus de droit*

The *abus de droit* (abuse of right) doctrine constitutes, in some form or the other, part of the law of the land in most domestic legal systems[301] and has been applied in numerous judicial pronouncements of international courts and tribunals.[302]

[296] *Metalclad* [2001] BCD Civ J, 2581 (note that the case was arbitration held under the ICSID Additional Facility, whose enforcement mechanisms are less robust than those of ICSID).

[297] See Helfer and Slaughter, above, n 7, at 308 (describing the determination of the ECJ to woo national courts through deference to their decisions).

[298] See Schreuer, above, n 153, at 707.

[299] See Philippe Sands, 'After Pinochet: The Proper Relationship between National and International Courts', *The International Legal System in Quest of Equity and Universality—Liber Amicorum Georges Abi-Saab*, (Laurence Boisson de Chazournes and Vera Gowland-Debbas, eds, 2001) 699, 715 (international courts must apply appropriate standards if they wish to be taken seriously at the national level); Schreuer (1981), above, n 24, at 16–17.

[300] See eg, *James*, 98 Eur Ct HR (Ser A) at 44. On the advantages of forming such partnerships between international and national courts, see Helfer and Slaughter, above, n 7, at 309–10. Indeed, the US argued in *Avena* that: 'When the Court fashions remedies for breaches of international law, it does not attempt to penetrate the sovereignty of a State and itself reconfigure State systems to meet the international obligation. Instead, it assumes that States, having voluntarily undertaken the obligations contained in the treaty, may be counted on to carry them out. The assumption concerning the bona fides of a sovereign State and its elected or appointed public officials is, indeed, essential to the Court's authority and the Court's effectiveness.' *Avena*, verbatim record of oral pleadings of 16 Dec 2003, ICJ Doc CR 2003/26, at para 1.11, <http://www.icj-cij.org/icjwww/idocket/imus/imuscr/imus_icr2003-26_20031216.PDF>.

[301] See eg, New Civil Code (NBW), arts 1–2 (Netherlands); Civil Code, art 2 (Switzerland); Civil Procedure Rules, Rule 3.4(2)(b)(England); Cour d'Appel, Colmar, 2 May 1985, DP II 1856, at 9 (France).

[302] *Fisheries* (UK/Norway), 1951 ICJ 116, 142; *Corfu Channel* (UK v Albania), 1949 ICJ 4, 46 (separate opinion of Judge Alvarez); *Certain German Interests*, 1926 PCIJ (Ser A), No 7, at 30; *Free Zones of Upper Savoy and the District of Gex* (France/Switz), 1932 PCIJ (Ser A/B), No 46, at 167; *Oscar Chinn* (UK/Belgium), 934 PCIJ (Ser A/B), No 63, at 86; *Fur Sea Deal* (GB v US), 1 *History and Digest of International Arbitrations* (Moore, ed, 1898) 755, 889–90.

A sound basis therefore exists to view the doctrine as a general principle of law[303] and as part of customary international law (either as an independent principle or an element of the good faith requirement).[304] It is also sometimes grounded in specific treaty language.[305]

The *abus de droit* principle provides that rights cannot be applied in a malicious manner with the sole intent of causing harm to others, in a fictitious manner (for a purpose totally different to that which the right was created), in a wholly unreasonable manner causing harm disproportionate to the interests of the right-holder,[306] or in disregard of the rights and obligations of other parties.[307] There is little question that the *abus de droit* rule governs the exercise of rights during the litigation process, ie, abuse of process.[308] For example, under this principle, attempts to circumvent forum-selection clauses by introducing fictitious new parties or new issues would be viewed as abusive.[309] In the same vein, the initiation of multiple proceedings to escape the application of the *lis alibi pendens* or *res judicata* rules may be deemed abusive if the initiating party is unable to identify a legitimate interest in multiple court review of the case.

Similar considerations should apply, in my view, to cases of competition between national and international courts. Hence, national or international decisions reached through fraudulent proceedings are devoid of any form of judicial deference.[310] Furthermore, here too, creation of fictitious distinctions between the parties to the proceedings or the litigated issues for the purpose of circumventing the preclusive rules barring multiple proceedings[311] may represent yet another form of abuse of right. It may also be alleged that reference to one court, when a clearly more appropriate national or international court is available may be deemed abusive.[312] This is because reference to the less-appropriate court might suggest

[303] Cheng, above, n 74, at 121; Lowe, above, n 88, at 202–3.

[304] See *US–Import Prohibition of Certain Shrimp and Shrimp Products*, 38 ILM 118, 165 (1998) (AB Report).

[305] See eg, UNCLOS, art 294, 300.

[306] Cheng, above, n 74, at 121–3; *US–Standards for Reformulated and Conventional Gazoline*, 35 ILM 603, 626 (1996).

[307] *Reformulated Gasoline*, 35 ILM at 626; *Import of Shrimp*, 38 ILM at 164–5; *Trail Smelter*, 3 RIAA at 1965; *North Atlantic Coast Fisheries* (GB/US), 1 Hague Court Reports 141, 171 (1910).

[308] Shany, above, n 20, at 258.

[309] Analogous considerations seem to govern the doctrine of piercing the corporate veil. See eg, *Barcelona Traction*, 1970 ICJ at 39.

[310] See eg, *'Grand Prince'* (Belize v France), Judgment of 20 April 2001, at para 8 of the declaration of Judge ad hoc Cot (available at <http://www.itlos.org/cgi-bin/cases/case_detail.pl?id=7&lang=en#judgement>) ('In order to speak of "fraud against the Convention" or of "prompt confiscation", it would be necessary to establish that the criminal prosecution was prompted by an intention of evading the provisions of article 292 of the Convention. In such a case, the Tribunal would then be entitled to proceed to recharacterize the national proceedings and to declare itself as having jurisdiction. That is obviously not so in the present case').

[311] In the *Lauder/CME* cases, it was questioned whether the distinction between the American shareholder (Ronald Lauder) and one of his Dutch subsidiary companies (CME), which enabled the presentation of two separate claims arising from the same investment, had been genuine. *Lauder*, above, n 28; *CME*, above, n 28.

[312] See ALI/UNIDROUT Principles of Transnational Civil Procedure, art 2.5, <http://www.unidroit.org/english/principles/civilprocedure/ali-unidroitprinciples-e.pdf> ('Jurisdiction may be

improper motives. Such an impropriety clearly occurs when a claimant seizes one judicial body in violation of a contractual or treaty obligation to refer the dispute to another court or tribunal. While the seized tribunal may be formally unable to apply the contract or treaty in question due to the applicable law governing its proceedings, it may still resort to the *abus de droit* rule in order to prevent violation of the said forum-selection obligation.

Indeed, one of the underlying motivations for the decision of the mixed claims commission in *North American Dredging* to uphold the contractual Calvo Clause[313] and decline jurisdiction was the commission's perception of the impropriety of the investor's conduct:

> The claimant, after having solemnly promised in writing that it would not ignore the local laws, remedies and authorities, behaved from the very beginning as if article 18 of its contract had no existence in fact... The record before this Commission strongly suggests that the claimant used article 18 to procure this contract with no intention of ever observing its provisions.[314]

In the same vein, the Umpire in *Woodruff*—another early 20th century case, discussed in Chapter 1—cited considerations of equity that militate in favour of considering a contractual exclusive jurisdiction clause in international proceedings involving rights and duties governed by the same contract.

Another situation where the *abus de droit* rule may be relevant is seizure of a national court while the same or a related case is pending before an international court, or vice versa. As previously explained, the *lis alibi pendens* rule is inapplicable in many of these cases even though the legitimacy of invocating multiple proceedings simultaneously may still be open to challenge on grounds of good faith.[315] Indeed, in his dissent to the *Camouco* judgment, Judge Anderson expressed strong objections to the propriety of seizing ITLOS parallel to the French courts that had already been seized by the same claimant party.[316] Another dissenting judge, Judge Vukas, opined that given the circumstances of the case, there were no 'vital reasons' for engaging in parallel proceedings.[317]

declined or the proceeding suspended when the court is manifestly inappropriate relative to another more appropriate court that could exercise jurisdiction'). See also August Reinisch, *International Organizations before National Courts* (2000) 326 (reference of employees of international organizations to national courts when international administrative courts are available is illegitimate).

313 For a discussion of Calvo Clauses, see F V García-Amador, 'Calvo Doctrine, Calvo Clause', I *Encyclopedia of Public International Law* (Rudholf Bernhardt, ed, 1997) 521.

314 *North American Dredging Co*, 4 RIAA at 31–2.

315 For an analogous situation involving the improper invocation of the jurisdiction of one national court in order to vex the claimant in proceedings before another court, see *Turner v Grovit* [1999] 3 All ER 616 (CA). The decision was reversed by the House of Lords following a preliminary reference to the ECJ. *Turner v Grovit* [2002] 1 All ER 960; Case C-159/02, *Turner v Grovit* [2004] All ER 485.

316 *Camouco*, 39 ILM at 690 (dissenting opinion of Judge Anderson) ('It must be unprecedented for the same issue to be submitted in quick succession first to a national court of appeal and then to an international tribunal, and for the issue to be actually pending before the two instances at the same time. This situation is surely undesirable and not to be encouraged. It smacks of "forum hopping" and hardly makes for the efficient administration of justice').

317 Ibid, at 696 (dissenting opinion of Judge Vukas).

It should be noted that both arbitral tribunals in the *Lauder/CME v Czech Republic* case embraced a much narrower view of the *abus de droit* principle and held that initiation of similar claims by related but non-identical parties cannot be deemed abusive. By doing so, they essentially adopted the same rigid standards for abuse of right and *lis alibi pendens*.[318] While such an approach may be vulnerable to the criticism of logical inconsistency (if the exercise of an available right can never be deemed abusive, then there is no room for the application of the *abus de droit* rule), it appears to indicate that the dynamic application of the abuse of right principle as advocated by the present writer is far from being settled law.

6.3 Interim Conclusions

While the application of the strict jurisdiction-regulating rules discussed in Chapter 5 to situations of jurisdictional competition between national and international courts appears to be marred by serious doctrinal uncertainties, the general principles discussed in this chapter seem to offer a pragmatic approach to resolving these problems. Indeed, I believe that flexible jurisdiction-regulating principles—comity and *abus de droit*—are applicable in *all* cases of jurisdictional interaction and *all* related proceedings that do not meet the strict conditions for jurisdictional overlap.

Hence, I propose that courts faced with potential jurisdictional overlap first examine whether there are real similarities between the relevant national and international proceedings, assuming *arguendo* that they function in the same legal system (ie, that they potentially involve the same issues). In the second stage of the analysis, I propose that judges consider application of the two aforementioned flexible jurisdiction-regulating rules. The degree of similarity between the competing procedures at the first stage of the analysis would influence the application of comity and *abus de droit* in the second stage of the analysis: thus, the closer the proceedings are to one another the less inclined would the courts be to disregard problematic exercises of forum selection or multiple proceedings. As a result, domestic court decisions based on the same international law norms that apply in the parallel international proceedings should attract, as a rule, greater deference than would domestic decisions based on national law. Willingness would also increase to

318 *Lauder*, above, n 28, at para 174; *CME*, above, n 28, at para 412. See also *Azurix*, 43 ILM at 281; *SGS v Pakistan*, 42 ILM at 1321; *Poultry*, above, n 129, at para 7.36 ('we consider that two conditions must be satisfied before a Member may be found to have failed to act in good faith. First, the Member must have violated a substantive provision of the WTO agreements. Second, there must be something "more than mere violation". With regard to the first condition, Argentina has not alleged that Brazil violated any substantive provision of the WTO agreements in bringing the present case. Thus, even without examining the second condition, there is no basis for us to find that Brazil violated the principle of good faith in bringing the present proceedings before the WTO').

stay proceedings in favour of a competing set of proceedings involving essentially the same parties (in contradistinction to situations involving different sets of parties).

The proposed methodology is supportable by valid policy considerations. It facilitates legitimate competition between domestic and international courts while it curbs bad faith jurisdictional choices and unwarranted invocation of multiple proceedings. It is also dictated by the indeterminacy of traditional jurisdiction-regulating rules that could, in theory, apply to such interactions as well as by the gap between the feasibility of applying traditional jurisdiction-regulating rules and the undesirability of uncritical recognition of the effects of competing proceedings. This last argument applies, of course, as long as the organization of the international community remains at its present stage.

Conclusions

The number and frequency of interactions between national and international courts seems to be on the rise, a phenomenon corresponding to the expanding reach of international law into matters previously regulated only by national law, together with the increased invocation of international norms by national courts. As a result, parties to a growing number of disputes now possess rights under national and international law that can be upheld in a variety of national and international fora. Questions relating to the coordination of such proceedings and harmonizing their outcomes are thus increasingly coming to the fore. Whereas some international legal regimes contain rules that regulate some jurisdictional interactions (eg, the exhaustion of local remedies rules under the ECHR, the preliminary ruling procedure under the EC Treaty, the complementarity and *ne bis in idem* rules under the Rome Statute), other interactions are unsatisfactorily regulated or not regulated at all.

Chapter 1 of the book surveyed several categories of these inadequately regulated interactions between national and international courts that appear in widely varied litigation contexts (application of Calvo Clauses to alien protection cases, remedial obligations deriving from a failure to provide timely consular notification, permissibility of constructing a security barrier in occupied territories, lawfulness of certain trade-restricting measures, prompt release of detained vessels and investment disputes governed by contractual and BIT jurisdictional clauses). Despite the different factual circumstances and institutional settings that characterize these cases, some common strategies for handling jurisdictional interactions have emerged.

Many courts, national and international, solve jurisdictional conflicts through resort to legal dualism, ie, by stressing the different normative foundations of national as opposed to international proceedings. If national court decisions are 'mere facts' incapable of impacting on the rights and obligations of the parties at the international level, then no meaningful degree of coordination between the two levels is warranted.[319] In the same vein, if international judgments are 'non-self-executing' or otherwise devoid of domestic legal effect, national courts need not expend any effort to reconcile their procedures and decisions with international procedures.[320]

As Chapters 3 and 4 demonstrate, dualism is often sustained by acts of interpretation: courts applying dualism sometimes construe their jurisdictions and applicable law narrowly, so as to avoid any overlap with other courts adjudicating

[319] See eg, *Certain German Interests*, 1925 PCIJ (Ser A), No 7; *Monte Confurco*, above, n 257.
[320] See eg, *Breard*, 523 US 371; *Corus Staal*, 395 F 3d 1343.

the same transaction on the basis of another body of law;[321] in addition, they often contest that the respective disputes before the parallel courts are 'the *same* disputes'.[322]

Another often-resorted-to strategy for avoiding the need to coordinate between national and international proceedings is the invocation of jurisdictional hierarchy. If national courts have supreme authority over the law applicable within their sovereign territory, it follows that the positions taken by international courts have limited influence on national proceedings; similarly, if international courts have the authority to supervise the work of national courts, there is little need to harmonize national and international proceedings and decisions.[323]

I have tried to argue that resort to dualism and hierarchy is open to criticism on a number of grounds. First, from a theoretical point of view, as Chapter 2 establishes, the legal dualism based on a deep chasm that separated the national from the international has lost much of its explanatory power. Instead, explanations of the relations holding between national and international courts are increasingly formulated in more functional terms (as courts engage in the common project of resolving disputes and upholding the rule of law), substantive theories of normative systemization are evolving that focus on the common international law-applying role of national and international courts, or embrace a pluralist perspective. The latter approach challenges the doctrinal and functional need for categorization of norms into national or international 'legal systems' as a precondition for their judicial application. In a similar vein, the assumed hierarchical configuration of national and international courts has come to represent simply one methodological alternative to the conceptualization of court relations.[324] National and international courts can also be viewed at times as dispute-settlement bodies, constituting alternatives to one another. Hence, the decision to portray national and international courts as institutions operating in different legal universes or as exercising vertical power one over the other, may ultimately have derived from specific policy choices.

However, when policy considerations are analysed, the case in favour of dualism and hierarchy loses its decisiveness. True, resort to dualism and hierarchy has its advantages: they offer judges clear cut rules for resolving jurisdictional conflicts and refer them primarily to the familiar body of law propounded by the polity they serve. However, from the perspective of the parties' interests, dualism and hierarchy fail to address many of the practical difficulties arising from multi-fora litigation: unnecessary expenses, misuse of scarce judicial resources, conflicting injunctions and incompatible judgments, to name the dominant ones. Just as importantly, dualism and hierarchy may encourage judges to disregard litigation taking place before other fora—a problem exacerbated if all the courts involved

[321] See eg, *Vivendi II*, 41 ILM 1135; *SGS v Pakistan*, 42 ILM 1290.

[322] See eg, *Chorzów Factory*, 1927 PCIJ (Ser A), No 13, at 29–30.

[323] See eg, *Sanchez-Llamas*, 126 S Ct 2669; *Chorzów Factory*, 1927 PCIJ (Ser A), No 12, at 33.

[324] Such possible conceptualization may be premised on ascending or descending authority theories. See Koskenniemi (1989), above, n 14, at 40–2.

adopt such an attitude (reciprocal disregard or conflicting claims of supremacy) towards their counterparts.

In Chapter 3, I argued that the policy choices faced by judges adjudicating multiple proceedings before national and international fora are not fundamentally different from the choices available in cases of jurisdictional interaction between different international courts. There, too, it is possible either to disaggregate a single dispute into several separate claims, each arising under different legal regimes,[325] or to view the dispute in a more integrative manner, as a whole comprised of essentially indissociable claims.[326] This analogy is perhaps most apparent when international multi-fora disputes such as the *MOX* cases[327] are contrasted with ICSID cases on the jurisdictional relations between contract and treaty claims.[328] In all cases, it would seem that judges ought to consider three main sets of interests: the interests of the legal regime under which their court operates, the interests of the overarching international legal system in maintaining consistency and averting conflicts as well as the interests of the disputing parties in efficient resolution of the dispute. The choice between disintegrative and integrative strategies is informed by these considerations, together with the dominant perceptions of the judge's role. Whereas disintegrationism underscores the law-applying role of the judge (and delegates the resolution of systemic problems to the legislature), integrationism invests judges with more active problem-solving powers, including the power to coordinate and harmonize parallel proceedings.

The choice between dualism, hierarchy and other, more integrative approaches to jurisdictional interactions ultimately boils down to specific legal questions—do proceedings before national and international courts involve the *same dispute* (entailing the same parties and issues)? Should jurisdiction-regulating rules be applied? In Chapter 4, I argued that jurisdictional overlap between national and international courts is conceivable (but quite rare), given three conditions: when their jurisdictions are not hierarchically configured, when the parallel sets of parties are sufficiently related, so as to represent the same sets of interests and when the same facts, norms, and remedies are invoked in both fora. Even then, the application of jurisdiction-regulating rules depends on the applicability of international law before national as well as international courts, or on the existence of common jurisdiction-regulating rules under national law.

In Chapter 5, I examined the applicability of strict jurisdiction-regulating rules that accord preference to one set of proceedings over the other. I suggested that parties generally enjoy unlimited freedom to choose a proper forum for litigation

[325] See eg, *MOX Plant* (Ireland v UK), 41 ILM 405 (2002) (hereinafter *MOX* (ITLOS)).

[326] See eg, *Southern Bluefin Tuna* (Australia and NZ v Japan), 39 ILM 1359 (2000). See also *MOX Plant* (UNCLOS), 42 ILM 1187.

[327] *MOX* (ITLOS), 41 ILM 405; *MOX* (UNCLOS), 42 ILM 1187; *Access to Information under Article 9 of the OSPAR Convention* (Ireland v UK), 42 ILM 1118 (2003); *Commission v Ireland* [2006] ECR I-4635.

[328] *Vivendi I*, 40 ILM 426; *Vivendi II*, 41 ILM 1135; *SGS v Pakistan*, 42 ILM 1290; *SGS v Philippines*, above, n 48.

but that once selected, all other courts should respect this choice and decline to adjudicate the same dispute. It is here that forum-selection clauses apply. In addition, one can identify some jurisdiction-regulating rules that govern multiple proceedings. Besides the *lis alibi pendens* and *res judicata* rules, which prohibit simultaneous or consecutive litigation of the same dispute, various treaty clauses introduce either *electa una via* ('fork in the road') or 'no U-turn' provisions that restrict multiple proceedings. Still, the doctrinal uncertainties surrounding the application of such rules to disputes pending before national and international courts has led to limited practice, an effect complicating identification of the general legal standard applicable in this sphere.

At the same time, the application of two flexible jurisdiction-regulating principles—comity and *abus de droit*—can be considered, I would argue, even in cases of related proceedings that fail to meet the strict conditions for jurisdictional competition. By providing a pragmatic avenue for consideration, in good faith, of the effects of the proceedings conducted and decisions rendered by different courts, these principles offer a framework of analysis that circumvents many of the aforementioned vexing doctrinal issues. Chapter 6 indeed provided demonstrations of the application of these principles (focusing especially on the broader notion of judicial comity) in horizontal as well as vertical contexts. To my mind, comity and *abus de droit* capture some of the integrative and pro-systemic impulses required by the growing interaction between national and international courts, and do so in a practical matter. At the same time, they possess sufficient flexibility to accommodate legitimate concerns about the trustworthiness of specific national and international judicial proceedings. They also refrain from challenging the constitutional principles governing the application of national and international law. Hence, at this point in time, they appear to represent the most promising mechanisms for regulating jurisdictional interactions between national and international courts.

Bibliography

BOOKS

Philip Allot, *Eunomia: New Order for a New World* (1990)
C. F. Amerasinghe, *Local Remedies in International Law* (2nd edn, 2004)
Neil Andrews, *Principles of Civil Procedure* (1994)
Yutaka Arai-Takahashi, *The Margin of Appreciation Doctrine and the Principle of Proportionality in the Jurisprudence of the ECHR* (2002)
Anthony Arnull, *The European Union and its Court of Justice* (2nd edn, 2006)
Michael Barnett and Martha Finnemore, *Rules for the World: International Organizations in Global Politics* (2004)
Albert Jan van den Berg, *The New York Arbitration Convention of 1958: Towards a Uniform Judicial Interpretation* (1981) (reprinted in 1994)
George A Bermann et al, Cases and Materials on European Union Law (2002)
Raj Bhala and Kevin Kennedy, *World Trade Law* (1998)
Edwin M Borchard, *The Diplomatic Protection of Citizens Abroad: The Law of International Claims* (1915)
Gary B. Born, *International Arbitration and Forum selection Agreements: Drafting and Enforcing* (3rd edn, 2006)
Charles N. Brower and Jason D. Brueschks, *The Iran–United State Claims Tribunal* (1998)
Ian Brownlie, *Principles of Public International Law* (6th edn 2003)
Abram Chayes and Antonia H. Chayes, *The New Sovereignty: Compliance with International Regulatory Agreements* (1995)
Bin Cheng, *General Principles of Law as Applied by International Courts and Tribunals* (1987)
John Collier and Vaughan Lowe, *The Settlement of Disputes in International Law: Institutions and Procedures* (1999)
Benedetto Conforti, *International Law and the Role of Domestic Legal Systems*, (1993)
Richard A. Falk, *The Role of Domestic Courts in the International Legal Order* (1964)
J. J. Fawcett, 'General Report', *Declining Jurisdiction in Private International Law* (1995) 1
Thomas M. Franck, *The Power of Legitimacy Among Nations* (1990)
Emmanuel Gaillard (ed), *Anti-Suit Injunctions in International Arbitration* (2005)
P. R. Ghandi, *The Human Rights Committee and the Right of Individual Communications: Law and Practice* (1988)
H. L. A. Hart, *The Concept of Law* (2nd edn, 1984)
Robert Jennings and Arthur Watts, *Oppenheim's International Law* (9th edn, 1992)
Hans Kelsen, *General Theory of Law and State* (Anders Wedberg trans, 1999) (1945)
——, *Introduction to the Problems of Legal Theory* (1934)
——, *Principles of International Law* (1952)
Michel van de Kerchove and Françoise Ost, *Legal System Between Order and Disorder* (Ian Stewart, trans, 1994)
Martti Koskenniemi, *From Apology to Utopia: The Structure of International Legal Argument* (1989)
Nikolaos Lavranos, *Decisions of International Organizations in the European and Domestic Legal Orders of Selected EU Member States* (2004)

Richard B. Lillich, 'Preface', *Fact-Finding before International Tribunals* (1992)
Myres S. McDougal, Harold D. Lasswell, and James C. Miller, *The Interpretation of International Agreements and World Public Order: Principles of Content and Procedure* (1994)
J. G. Merrills and A. H. Robertson, *Human Rights in Europe: A Study of the European Convention for Human Rights* (4th edn, 2001)
Hans-Joachim Mertens, '*Lex Mercatoria:* A Self-applying System beyond National Law?', *Global Law Without a State* (Gunther Teubner, ed, 1997)
Mohsen Mohebi, *The International Law Character of the Iran-United States Claims Tribunal* (1999)
Sean D. Murphy, *Principles of International Law* (2006)
Myron H. Nordquist *et al* (ed), V *United Nations Convention on the Law of the Sea 1982: A Commentary* (1989)
Clare Ovey and Robin White, *European Convention on Human Rights* (3rd edn, 2002)
Jan Paulsson, *Denial of Justice in International Law* (2005)
Joost Pauwelyn, *Conflict of Norms in Public International Law: How WTO Law Relates to Other Rules of International Law* (2003)
Cyril M. Picciotto *Relation of International Law to the Law of England and the United States* (1915) (Introduction by Lassa Oppenheim)
Joseph Raz, *A Concept of a Legal System* (2nd edn, 1980)
August Reinisch, *International Organizations before National Courts* (2000)
Shabtai Rosenne *The Perplexities of Modern International Law* 122 (2002)
Georges Scelle, II *Précis de droit de gens* (1932)
Frederick Schauer, *Playing by the Rules: A Philosophical Examination of Rule-Based Decision-Making in Law and in Life* (1991)
Christoph C. Schreuer, *Commentary to the ICSID Convention* (2001)
——, *Decisions of International Institutions before Domestic Courts* (1981)
Christoph H. Schreuer, *The ICSID Convention: A Commentary* (2001)
Yuval Shany, *The Competing Jurisdictions of International Courts and Tribunals* (2003)
Malcolm N. Shaw, *International Law* (5th edn, 2003)
Ian Sinclair, *The Vienna Convention on the Law of Treaties* (2nd edn, 1984)
Terrence P. Stewart (ed), II *The GATT/Uruguay Round: A Negotiating History* (1986–1992) (1993)
Gunther Teubner, *Law as an Autopoietic System* (1993)
A. Cancado Trindade, *Exhaustion of Local Remedies in International Law* (1983)
St George Tucker, 1 *Blackstone's Commentaries: With Notes of Reference, to the Constitution and Laws, of the Federal Government of the United States; and of the Commonwealth of Virginia* (1803)
Joseph H. H. Welier, *The Constitution of Europe: 'Do the Clothes have an Emperor' and Other Essays* (1999)
Howard C. Yourow, *The Margin of Appreciation Doctrine in the Dynamics of European Human Rights Jurisprudence* (1996)

ARTICLES

Georges Abi-Saab, 'Cours général de droit international public', 207 Recueil de cours (1996) 9

Georges Abi-Saab, 'Fragmentation or Unification: Some Concluding Remarks', 31 *NYU J Int'l L & Pol* (1999) 919

——, 'Wither the International Community?' 9 *EJIL* (1998) 248

Michael K. Addo, 'Interim Measures for Protection of Rights Under the Vienna Convention on Consular Relations', 10 *EJIL* (1999) 713

Robert B. Ahdieh, 'Between Dialogue and Decree: International Review of National Courts', 79 *NYU L Rev* (2004) 2029

Alberto Alemanno, 'Judicial Enforcement of the WTO Hormones Ruling Within the European Community: Toward EC Liability for the Non-Implementation of WTO Dispute Settlement Decisions?', 45 *Harv Int'l LJ* (2004)

Philip Allot, *The Emerging Universal Legal System*, presented in an Amsterdam Center for International Law seminar on Theoretical Approaches to the Relationship between International and National Law (2002)

Philip Alston & Joseph H. H. Weiler, 'An 'Ever Closer Union' in Need of a Human Rights Policy: The European Union and Human Rights', *The EU and Human Rights* (Philip Alston ed, 1999)

Eduardo Junenez de Aréchaga, 'International Law in the Past Third of a Century', 159 *Recueil des cours* (1978) 1

Lorand Bartels, 'Applicable Law in WTO Dispute Settlement Proceedings', 35 *Journal of World Trade* (2001) 499

Judith H. Bello, 'The WTO Dispute Settlement Understanding: Less Is More', 90 *AJIL* (1996) 416

Ariel L. Bendor, 'Are There Any Limits to Justiciability? The Jurisprudential and Constitutional Controversy in Light of the Israeli and American Experience', 7 *Ind Int'l & Comp L Rev* (1997)

Eyal Benvenisti, 'Judicial Misgivings Regarding the Application of International Law: An Analysis of Attitudes of National Courts', 4 *EJIL* (1993) 159

——, 'Margin of Appreciation, Consensus and Universal Values', 31 *NYU J Int'l L & Pol* (1999) 843

Brian Bercusson, 'Globalizing Labour Law: Transnational Private Regulation and Countervailing Actors in European Labour Law', *Global Law Without a State* (Gunther Teubner, ed, 1997) 45

Andrea K. Bjorklund, 'Reconciling State Sovereignty and Investor Protection in Denial of Justice Claims', 45 *Va J Int'l L* (2005) 809

——, 'Waiver and the Exhaustion of Local Remedies Rule in NAFTA Jurisprudence', *NAFTA Investment Law and Arbitration: Past Issues, Current Practice, Future Prospects* (Todd Weiler, ed, 2004) 253

Rudolf Blühdorn, 'Le fonctionnement et la jurisprudence des tribunaux arbitraux mixtes créés par les traités de paris' 41 *Recueil des cours* (1932-III) 141

Daniel Bodansky, 'The Legitimacy of International Governance: A Coming Challenge for International Environmental Law?', 93 *AJIL* (1999) 596

Jacques H. J. Bourgeois, 'The European Court of Justice and the WTO: Problems and Challenges', *The EU, The WTO, and NAFTA: Towards a Common Law of International Trade?* (J H H Weiler ed, 2000) 71

Curtis Bradley, 'Breard, Our Dualist Constitution, and the Internationalist Conception', 51 *Stan L Rev* 529 (1999)

Eva Brems, 'The Margin of Appreciation Doctrine in the Case Law of the European Court of Human Rights', 56 *Heidelberg J Int'l L* (1996) 240

Gerard Brennan, 'The Rule and Role of Domestic Law in International Relations', Singapore Academy of Law Annual Lecture 1998

Adrian Briggs, 'Crossing the River by Feeling the Stones: Rethinking the Law on Foreign Judgments', 8 *Singapore YBIL* (2004) 1

Aron Broches, 'Observations on the Finality of ICSID Awards', 6 *ICSID Rev FILJ* (1991) 321

Aron Broches, 'On the Finality of Awards: A Reply to Michael Reisman', 8 *ICSID Rev FILJ* (1993) 92

Thomas Buergenthal, 'Self-Executing and Non-Self-Executing treaties in National and International Law', 235 *Recueil des cours* 303 (1992-IV)

William Burke-White 'A Community of Courts: Towards a System of International Criminal Law Enforcement', 24 *Mich J Int'l L* (2002) 1

Hannah L. Buxbaum, 'Transnational Regulatory Litigation', 46 *Virginia J Int'l L* (2006) 251

David D. Caron, 'The Nature of the Iran-United States Claims Tribunal and the Evolving Structure of International Dispute Resolution', 84 *AJIL* (1990) 104

——, 'Reputation and Reality in the ICSID Annulment Process: Understanding the Distinction Between Annulment and Appeal', 7 *ICSID Rev FILJ* (1992) 21

Paulo G. Carozza, 'Subsidiarity as a Structural Principle of International Human Rights Law', 97 *AJIL* (2003) 38

——, 'Uses and Misuses of Comparative Law in International Human Rights: Some Reflections on the Jurisprudence of the European Court of Justice', 73 *Notre Dame L Rev* (1998) 1217

Antonio Cassese, 'Remarks on Scelle's Theory of 'Role Splitting' (dédoublement fonctionnel) in International Law', 1 *EJIL* (1990) 210

Christine Chinkin, 'A Critique of the Public/Private Dimension', 10 *EJIL* 387, 389 (1999)

Dan Ciobanu, 'Litispendence between the International Court of Justice and the Political Organs of the United Nations', 1 *The Future of the International Court of Justice* (Leo Gross, ed, 1977) 209

Alan W. Clarke, 'Procedural Labyrinths and the Injustice of Death: A Critique of Death Penalty Habeas Corpus (Part Two)', 30 *U Rich L Rev* (1996) 303

Mark Clodfelter, 'US State Department Participation in International Economic Dispute Resolution', 42 S *Tex L Rev* (2001) 1273

Jack J. Coe, Jr, 'Toward a Complementary Use of Conciliation in Investor-State Disputes—A Preliminary Sketch', 12 *UC Davis J Int'l L & Pol'y* (2005) 7

Amichai Cohen, 'Administrating the Territories: An Inquiry into the Application of International Humanitarian Law by the IDF in the Occupied Territories', 38 *Isr L Rev* (2005) 24

Juscelino F. Colares, 'Alternative Methods of Appellate Review in Trade Remedy Cases: Examining Results of US Judicial and NAFTA Binational Review of US Agency Decisions from 1989 to 2005' (2006)

Jean Combacau, 'Le droit international: Bric-a-brac ou systeme?', 31 *Archives de philosphie de droit* (1996) 85

Natasha Parassram Concepcion, 'The Legal Implications of Trinidad & Tobago's Withdrawal From the American Convention on Human Rights', 16 *Am U Int'l L Rev* (2001) 847

Carole C. Cooke, 'Procedural Defaults at the Appellate Stage and Federal Habeas Corpus Review', 38 *Stan L Rev* (1986) 463

Andrew P. Cortell and James W. Davis, 'When Norms Clash: International Norms, Domestic Practices, and Japan's Internalisation of the GATT/WTO', 31 *Rev Int'l Studies* (2005) 3

Susan P. Crawford, 'The ICANN Experiment', 12 *Cardozo J Int'l & Comp L* (2004) 409

Steven P. Croley and John H. Jackson, 'WTO Procedures, Standard of Review, and Deference to National Governments', 90 *AJIL* (1996) 193

J. Scott Davidson, 'Intention and Effect: The Legal Status of the Final Views of the Human Rights Committee', 2001 *NZ Law Review* 125

Sanja Djajic, 'The Effect of International Court of Justice Decisions on Municipal Courts in the United States: Breard v Greene', 23 *Hastings Int'l & Comp L Rev* 27

William S. Dodge, 'International Decision: Waste Management, Inc v Mexico', 95 *AJIL* (2001) 186

——, 'Loewen v United States: Trials and Errors Under NAFTA Chapter Eleven', 52 *DePaul L Rev* (2002) 563

——, 'National Courts and International Arbitration: Exhaustion of Remedies and Res Judicata under Chapter Eleven of NAFTA', 23 *Hastings Int'l & Comp L Rev* (2000) 357

—— and David D. Caron, 'Loewen Group, Inc v United States', 98 *AJIL* (2004) 155

Douglas Lee Donoho, 'Autonomy, Self-Government, and the Margin of Appreciation: Developing a Jurisprudence of Diversity within Universal Human Rights', 15 *Emory Int'l L Rev* (2001) 391

Zachary Douglas, 'The Hybrid Foundations of Investment Treaty Arbitrations, (2003) *BYIL* 151

Pierre-Marie Dupuy, 'The Danger of Fragmentation or Unification of the International Legal System and the International Court of Justice', 31 *NYU J Int'l L & Pol* (1999) 791

Claus-Dieter Ehlermann and Nicolas Lockhart, 'Standard of Review in WTO Law', 7 *J Int'l Eco L* (2004) 491

Lambertus Erades, *Interactions between International and Municipal Law: A Comparative Case Law Study* (Malgosia Fitzmaurice and Cees Flinterman, eds, 1993) 17

Richard A. Falk, 'Toward Authoritativeness: The ICJ Ruling on Israel's Security Wall', 99 *AJIL* (2005) 42

Andreas Fischer-Lescano and Gunther Teubner 'Regime-Collisions: the Vain Search for Legal Unity in the Fragmentation of Global Law', 25 *Mich J Int'l* (1999) 999

Gerald Fitzmaurice, 'The General Principles of International Law Considered from the Standpoint of the Rule of Law', 92 *Recueil des cours* (1957-II) 68

John Flood and Eleni Skordaki, 'Normative Bricolage: Informal Rule-making by Accountants and Lawyers in Mega-insolvencies', *Global Law Without a State* (Gunther Teubner, ed, 1997) 109

Erik Franckx, ' "Reasonable Bond" in the Practice of the International Tribunal for the Law of the Sea', 32 *Cal W Int'l LJ* (2002) 303

Francesco Francioni, 'International Law as a Common Language for National Courts', 36 *Tex Int'l LJ* (2001) 587

Giorgio Gaja, *Dualism—A Review*, a paper presented in an Amsterdam Center for International Law Seminar on Theoretical Approaches to the Relationship between International and National Law (2003) 2 (copy with author)

Pamela B. Gann, 'The US Bilateral Investment Treaty Program', 21 *Stan J Int'l L* (1985) 373

David A. Gantz, 'The Evolution of FTA Investment Provisions: From NAFTA to the United States–Chile Free Trade Agreement', 19 *Am U Int'l L Rev* (2004) 679

——, 'A Post-Uruguay Round Introduction to International Trade Law in the United States', 12 *Ariz J Int'l & Comp Law* (1995) 7

F. V. García-Amador, 'Calvo Doctrine, Calvo Clause', I *Encyclopedia of Public International Law* (Rudholf Bernhardt, ed, 1997) 521

James Thuo Gathii, 'Foreign Precedents in the Federal Judiciary: The Case of the World Trade Organization's DSB Decisions', 34 *Ga J Int'l & Comp L* (2005) 1

Bradford K. Gathright, 'A Step in the Wrong Direction: The Loewen Finality Requirement and the Local Remedies Rule in NAFTA Chapter Eleven', 54 *Emory LJ* (2005) 1093

Yvonne N. Gierczyk, 'The Evolution of the European Legal System: The European Court of Justice's Role in the Harmonization of Laws', 12 *ILSA J Int'l & Comp L* (2005) 153

Ryan Goodman and Derek Jinks, 'Toward an Institutional Theory of Sovereignty', 55 *Stan L Rev* (2003) 1749

Christopher Greenwood, 'State Responsibility for the Decisions of National Courts', *Issues of State Responsibility before International Judicial Institutions* (Malgosia Fitzmaurice and Danesh Sarooshi, eds, 2004) 55

Steven Greer, 'Constitutionalising Adjudication under the European Convention on Human Rights', 23 *Oxford Journal of Legal Studies* (2003) 405

K. Scot Gudgeon, 'Arbitration Provisions of US Bilateral Investment Disputes', *International Investment Disputes: Avoidance and Settlement* (Seymor J Rubin and Richard W Nelson, eds, 1985) 41

Gilbert Guillaume, 'The Future of International Judicial Institutions', 44 *ICLQ* (1995) 848

Klaus Günther, 'Legal Pluralism and the Universal Code of Legality: Globalisation as a Problem of Legal Theory' (2003)

Gerard Hafner, 'Pros and Cons Ensuing from Fragmentation of International Law', 25 *Mich J Int'l L* (2004) 849

Zaha Hassan, 'Building Walls and Burning Bridges: Legal Obligations of the United States with respect to Israel's Construction of the Wall of Separation in Occupied Palestinian Territory', 13 *Willamette J Int'l L & Dispute Res* (2005) 197

Laurence R. Helfer, 'Consensus, Coherence and the European Convention on Human Rights', 26 *Cornell Int'l LJ* (1993) 133

—— and Anne-Marie Slaughter, 'Towards a Theory of Effective Supranational Adjudication', 107 *Yale LJ* (1997) 273

—— and ——, 'Why States Create International Tribunals: A Response to Professors Posner and Yoo', 93 *Calif L Rev* (2005) 899

Donna L. Howard, 'Trademarks and Service Marks and Internet Domain Names: Giving ICANN Deference', 33 *Ariz St LJ* (2001) 637

Francis G. Jacobs 'Judicial Dialogue and the Cross-Fertilization of Legal Systems: The European Court of Justice', 38 *Tex Int'l LJ* (2003) 547

John H. Jackson, 'The WTO Dispute Settlement Understanding-Misunderstandings on the Nature of Legal Obligation', 91 *AJIL* (1997) 60

Holly D. Jarmul, 'The Effects of Decisions of Regional Human Rights Tribunals on National Courts', 28 *NYU J Int'l L & Pol* 311

Immanuel Kant, 'To Eternal Peace' *The Philosophy of Kant* (Carl J Friedrich, ed, 1993) (1795) 475
——, 'Perpetual Peace', *Political Writings* (H Reiss, ed, HB Nisbet trans, 1995) 94
Suzanne Katzenstein, 'Hybrid Tribunals: Searching for Justice in East Timor', 16 *Harv Hum Rts J* (2003) 245
David Kaye, 'Adjudicating Self-Defense: Discretion, Perception, and the Resort to Force in International Law', 44 *Colum J Transnat'l L* (2005) 134
Patricia Kelmar, 'Binational Panels of the Canada–United States Free Trade Agreement in Action: The Constitutional Challenge Continues', 27 *GW J Int'l L & Econ* (1993) 173
David Kennedy, 'The Disciplines of International Law and Policy', 12 *Leiden JIL* (2000) 9
——, 'When Renewal Repeats: Thinking Against the Box', 32 *NYU J Int'l L & Pol* 335
Benedict Kingsbury, 'The International Legal Order', IILJ Working Paper 2003/1 (History and Theory of International Law Series)
——, 'Is the Proliferation of International Courts and Tribunals a Systematic Problem?', 31 *NYU JILP* (1999) 679
——, Nico Krisch and Richard B. Stewart, 'The Emergence of Global Administrative Law', 68 *Law & Contemp Prob* (2005) 15
Frederic L. Kirgis, 'President Bush's Determination Regarding Mexican Nationals and Consular Convention Rights', *ASIL Insights* (March 2005)
Benjamin Klafter, 'International Commercial Arbitration as Appellate Review: NAFTA's Chapter 11, Exhaustion of Local Remedies and Res Judicata', 12 *UC Davis J Int'l L & Pol'y* (2005) 409
Hannu Klami, 'Monism and Dualism in Law: National Versus International or Supranational Law', *Coherence and Conflict in Law* (Bob Brouwer et al eds 1992) 139
Jann K. Kleffner, 'The Impact of Complementarity on National Implementation of Substantive International Criminal Law', 1 *J Int'l Crim J* (2003) 86
—— and André Nollkaemper, 'The Relationship Between Internationalized Courts and National Courts', *Internationalized Criminal Courts—Sierra Leone, East Timor, Kosovo, and Cambodia* (Cesare PR Romano *et al*, eds, 2004) 359
Hannu Klami, 'Monism and Dualism in Law: National Versus International or Supranational Law', *Coherence and Conflict in Law* (Bob Brouwer et al eds 1992) 139
Harold H. Koh, 'Bringing Human Rights Home', 35 *Hous L Rev* (1998) 623
——, 'How is International Human Rights Law Enforced?', 74 *Ind LJ* (1999) 1397
——, 'Transnational Legal Process', 75 *Neb L Rev* (1994) 181
Martti Koskenniemi, 'The Politics of International Law', 1 *EJIL* 4 (1990)
—— and Päivi Leino, 'Fragmentation of International Law? Postmodern Anxieties', 15 *Leiden Journal of International Law* (2002) 553
——, 'Repetition as Reform: Georges Abi-Saab Cours General de droit international public', 9 *EJIL* (1998) 405
Mattias Kumm, 'International Law in National Courts: The International Rule of Law and the Limits of the Internationalist Model', 44 *Va J Int'l L* (2003) 19
Pierre Lalive, 'The First 'World Bank' Arbitration (Holiday Inns v Morocco)—Some Legal Problems', 1 ICSID Rep 645 (1980)
Carolyn B. Lamm, 'Jurisdiction of the International Centre for Settlement of Investment Disputes', 6 *ICSID Rev FILJ* (1991) 462
Johan G. Lammers, 'Challenging the Establishment of the ICTY before the Dutch Courts: The Case of Slobodan Milosevic v The Netherlands', *Review of the Security Council by Member States* (Erika de Wet and Andre Nollkaemper, eds, 2003) 107

Nikolaos Lavranos, 'The MOX Plant and IJzeren Rijn Disputes: Which Court Is the Supreme Arbiter?', 19 *Leiden J Int'l L* (2006) 223

Carl Lebeck, 'National Constitutionalism, Openness to International Law and the Pragmatic Limits of European Integration—European Law in the German Constitutional Court from EEC to the PJCC', 7 *German Law Journal* (2006) 907

Markus Lenenbach, 'Antisuit Injunctions in England, Germany and the United States: Their Treatment under European Civil Procedure and the Hague Convention', 20 *Loy LA Int'l & Comp LJ* (1998) 257

Vaughan Lowe, 'Overlapping Jurisdiction in International Tribunals', 20 *Australian YB International Law* (1999) 191

——, 'Res Judicata and the Rule of Law in International Arbitration', 8 *African Journal of International and Comparative Law* (1996) 38

——, 'The Politics of Law-making: Are the Method and Character of Norm Creation Changing?', *The Role of Law in International Politics: Essays in International Relations and International Law* (Michael Byers, ed, 2000) 200

Rett R. Ludwikowski, 'Supreme Law or Basic Law? The Decline of the Concept of Constitutional Supremacy', 9 *Cardozo J Int'l & Comp L* (2001) 253

Ronald St. J. MacDonald, 'The Margin of Appreciation', *The European System for the Protection of Human Rights* (R St J MacDonald *et al*, eds, 1993), 83

Paul Mahoney, 'Judicial Activism and Judicial Self-restraint in the European Court of Human Rights: Two Sides of the Same Coin', 11 *Hum Rts LJ* (1990) 57

Jenny S. Martinez, 'Towards an International Judicial System', 56 *Stan L Rev* (2003) 429

Chris McGreal, 'Israelis Hasten Land Grab in Shadow of Wall', *Guardian*, Dec 14, 2004

Thomas W. Merrill, 'Can Originalism be Reconciled with Precedent', 22 *Const Commentary* (2005) 271

Alex Mills and Tim Stephens, 'Challenging the Role of Judges in Slaughter's Liberal Theory of International Law', 18 *Leiden Journal of International Law* (2005) 1

Laura Moranchek, 'Protecting National Security Evidence While Prosecuting War Crimes: Problems and Lessons for International Justice from the ICTY', 31 *Yale J Int'l L* (2006)

Peter D. Mulchinski, ' "Global Bukowina" Examined: Viewing the Multinational Enterprise as a Transnational Law-making Community', *Global Law Without a State* (Gunther Teubner, ed, 1997) 79

Andre Nollkaemper, 'Decisions of National Courts as Sources of International Law: An Analysis of the Practice of the ICTY', *International criminal law developments in the case law of the ICTY* (Gideon Boas and William A Schabas, eds, 2003) 277

Karin Oellers-Frahm, 'Multiplication of International Courts and Tribunals and Conflicting Jurisdiction—Problems and Possible Solutions', 5 *Max Planck Yearbook of United Nations Law* (2001) 67

Antonio R. Parra, 'Provisions on the Settlement of Investment Disputes in Modern Investment Laws, Bilateral Investment Treaties and Multilateral Instruments on Investment', 12 *ICSID Rev FILJ* (1997) 287

Colter Paulson, 'Compliance with Final Judgments of the International Court of Justice since 1987', 98 *AJIL* (2004) 434

Andreas L. Paulus, 'Commentary to Andreas Fischer-Lescano and Gunther Teubner: The Legitimacy of International Law and the Role of the State', 25 *Mich J Int'l L* (2004) 1047

——, 'The Influence of the United States on the Concept of the 'International Community'', *United States Hegemony and the Foundations of International Law* (Michael Byers and Georg Nolte, eds, 2003) 57

Joost Pauwelyn, 'Going Global, Regional, or Both? Dispute Settlement in the Southern African Development Community (SADC) and Overlaps with the WTO and Other Jurisdictions', 13 *Minn J Global Trade* (2004) 231

——, 'Bridging Fragmentation and Unity: International Law as a Universe of Inter-Connected Islands', 25 *Mich J Int'l L* (2004) 903

——, 'How to Win a World Trade Organization Dispute Based on Non-World Trade Organization Law?', 37 *Journal of World Trade* (2003) 997

Ernst-Ulrich Petersmann, 'Justice as Conflict Resolution: Proliferation, Fragmentation and Decentralization of Dispute Settlement in International Trade, 27 U *Pa J Int'l Econ L* (2006) 273

Eric A. Posner and Miguel F. P. de Figueiredo, 'Is the International Court of Justice Biased?', 34 *J Legal Stud* (2005) 599

—— and John C. Yoo, 'Judicial Independence in International Tribunals', 93 *Calif L Rev* (2005) 1

—— and ——, 'Reply to Helfer and Slaughter', 93 *Calif L Rev* (2005) 957

Mari Presley, 'Sovereignty and Delegation Issues Regarding US Commitment to the World Trade Organization's Dispute Settlement Process', 8 J *Transnat'l L & Pol'y* (1998) 173

Michael D. Ramsey, 'Escaping "International Comity"', 83 *Iowa LR* (1998) 257

Norbert Reich, 'Judge-made "Europe à la carte": Some Remarks on Recent Conflicts between European and German Constitutional Law Provoked by the Banana Litigation', 7 *EJIL* (1996) 1

August Reinisch, 'The Use and Limits of Res Judicata and Lis Pendens as Procedural Tools to Avoid Conflicting Dispute Settlement Outcomes', 3 *The Law and Practice of International Courts and Tribunals* (2004)

Michael W. Reisman, 'The Breakdown of the Control Mechanism in ICSID Arbitration', [1989] *Duke LJ* 739

Jean-Philippe Robé, 'Multinational Enterprises: The Constitution of a Pluralistic Legal Order', *Global Law Without a State* (Gunther Teubner, ed, 1997) 45

Simon Roberts, 'After Government? On Representing Law Without the State', 68 *Modern Law Review* (2005)1

Allan Rosas, 'With a Little Help from My Friends: International Case—Law as a Source of Reference for the EU Courts', 5 *The Global Community: Yearbook of International Law and Jurisprudence* (2005) 203

Philippe Sands, 'After Pinochet: The Proper Relationship between National and International Courts', *The International Legal System in Quest of Equity and Universality—Liber Amicorum Georges Abi-Saab*, (Laurence Boisson de Chazournes and Vera Gowland-Debbas, eds, 2001)

Georges Scelle, 'La phénomène juridique du dédoublement fonctionnel', *Rechtsfragen der Intenationalen Organisation: Festschrift für Hans Wehberg* (1956) 324

—, 'Quelques réflexions hétérodoxes sur la technique de l'ordre juridique interétatique', *Hommage d'un generation de juristes au Président Basdevant* (1960) 473

Haimo Schack, 'Report on Germany', *Declining Jurisdiction in Private International Law* (JJ Fawcett, ed, 1995) 189

Pierre Schlag, 'Rules and Standards', 33 *UCLA L Rev* (1985) 379, 381–383

Christoph H. Schreuer, 'The Authority of International Practice in Domestic Courts', 23 *ICLQ* (1974) 681
——, 'Concurrent Jurisdiction of National and International Tribunals', 13 *Hous L Rev* (1975–1976) 508
——, 'Traveling the BIT Route: of Waiting Periods, Umbrella clauses and Forks in The Road', 5 *J World Inv* (2004)
Jillaine Seymour, 'The International Tribunal for the Law of the Sea: A Great Mistake?', 13 *Ind J Global Leg Stud* (2006) 1
Yuval Shany, 'Capacities and Inadequacies: A Look at the Two Separation Barrier Case', 38 *Isr L Rev* (2005) 230
——, 'The First MOX Plant Award: Coordinating between Competing Environmental Regimes and Dispute Settlement Procedures', 17 *Leiden JIL* (2004) 815
——, 'How Supreme is the Supreme Law of the Land? A Comparative Analysis of the Influence of International Human Rights Conventions upon the Interpretation of Constitutional Texts by Domestic Courts', 31 *Brooklyn J Int'l L* (2006) 341
——, 'Toward a General Margin of Appreciation Doctrine', 16 EJIL (2005) 907
Ibrahim F. I. Shihata & Antonio R. Parra, 'The Experience of the International Centre for Settlement of Investment Disputes', 14 *ICSID Rev- FI L J* (1999) 299
Bruno Simma *et al*, 'The Role of German Courts in the Enforcement of International Human Rights', *Enforcing International Human Rights in Domestic Courts* (Benedetto Conforti and Francesco Francioni, eds, 1997) 71
—— and Dirk Pulkowski, 'Of Planets and the Universe: Self-contained Regimes in International Law', 17 *EJIL* (2006) 483
——, 'Self-Contained Regimes', XVI *NYBIL* (1985) 111
Anthony C. Sinclair, 'The Origins of the Umbrella Clause in the International Law of Investment Protection', 20 *Arb Int'l* (2004) 41
Jose Luis Siqueiros, 'Bilateral Treaties on the Reciprocal Protection of Foreign Investment', 24 *Cal W Int'l LJ* (1994) 255
Anne-Marie Slaughter, 'A Global Community of Courts', 44 *Harv Int'l LJ* (2003) 191
——, 'International Law in a World of Liberal States', 6 *EJIL* (1995) 503
——, 'Judicial Globalization', 40 *Virginia J Int'l L* (2000) 1103
George Slyz, 'International Law in National Courts', 28 *NYU J Int'l L & Pol* 65, 67 (1996)
Bouventura de Sousa Santos, 'Law: A Map of Misreading—Toward a Postmodern Conception of Law', 14 *Journal of Law and Society* (1987) 279
Adam M. Smith, ' "Judicial Nationalism" in International Law: National Identity and Judicial Autonomy at the ICJ' 40 *Tex Int'l LJ* (2005) 197
Shane Spelliscy, 'The Proliferation of International Tribunals: A Chink in the Armor', 40 *Colum J Transnat'l L* (2001) 143
Aparna Sridhar, 'Creating Judicial Remedies for Violations of the Vienna Convention on Consular Relations: A Proposed Resolution to Medellin v Dretke', 2 *Stan JCR & CL* (2006) 333
J. G. Starke, 'Monism and Dualism in the Theory of International Law', 17 *Brit YB Int'l L* (1936) 66
Eric Stein, 'Lawyers Judges, and the Making of a Transnational Constitution', 75 *AJIL* (1981) 1
Ted L. Stein, 'Jurisprudence and Jurists' Prudence: The Iranian-Forum Clause Decisions of the Iran-US Claims Tribunal', 78 *AJIL* (1984) 1

Andrew L. Strauss, 'A Global Paradigm Shattered: The Jurisdictional Nihilism of the Supreme Court's Abduction Decision in Alvarez-Machain', 67 *Temple L Rev* (1994) 1209

Kathleen M. Sullivan, 'The Justices of Rules and Standards', 106 *Harvard L Rev* (1992) 22

Bert Swart, 'Internationalized Courts and Substantive Criminal Law', *Internationalized Criminal Courts—Sierra Leone, East Timor, Kosovo, and Cambodia* (Cesare PR Romano *et al*, eds, 2004) 291

Kevin Andrew Swartz, 'Powerful, Unique, and Anonymous: The European Court of Justice and Its Continuing Impact on the Formation of the European Community', 3 S *Cal Interdisc LJ* (1994) 687

Gunther Teubner, 'Breaking Frames: The Global Interplay of Legal and Social Systems', 45 *Am J Comp L* (1997)

——, 'Global Bukowina: Legal Pluralism in the World Society', *Global Law Without a State* (Gunther Teubner, ed, 1997)

Hubert Thierry, 'The European Tradition in International Law: Georges Scelle' 1 *EJIL* 193, 200 (1990)

Jenia I. Turner, '*Nationalizing International Criminal Law*', 41 *Stan J Int'l L* (2005) 1

Mark Tushnet, 'Transnational/Domestic Constitutional Law', 37 *Loy LA L Rev* (2003) 239

Henry Donnedieu de Vabres, 'Le conflit des lois de compétence judicaire dans les actions personnelles', 26 *Recueil des cours* (1929) 207

Carlos Manuel Vazquez, 'The Four Doctrines of Self-Executing Treaties', 89 *AJIL* 695 (1995)

Thomas Wälde, 'The Umbrella Clause in Investment Arbitration—A Comment on Original Intentions and Recent Cases', 6 *J World Invest & Trade* (2005) 183

Lawrence R. Walders, 'Citation by US Courts to Decisions of International Tribunals in International Trade Cases', 69 *Alb L Rev* (2006) 817

—— and Neil C. Pratt, 'Trade Remedy Litigation—Choice of Forum and Choice of Law', 18 *St John's JL Comm* (2003) 51

A. Mark Weisburd, 'International Courts and American Courts', 21 *Mich J Int'l L* (2000) 877

——, 'International Judicial Decisions, Domestic Courts, and the Foreign Affairs Power', *CATO Supreme Court Review 2004–2005* (Mark K Moller, ed, 2005) 287

Joseph R. Wetzel, 'Improving Fundamental Rights Protection in the European Union: Resolving the Conflict and Confusion Between the Luxemburg and Strasbourg Courts', 71 *Fordham L Rev* (2003) 2823

Brent Wible, ' "De-Jeopardizing Justice": Domestic Prosecutions for International Crimes and the Need for Transnational Convergence', 31 *Denv J Int'l L & Pol'y* 265

Andrew Williams, 'Enlargement of the Union and Human Rights Conditionality: A Policy of Distinction?', 25 *Eur L Rev* (2000) 601

Samuel W. Witten, "The US–UK Arbitration Award concerning Heathrow Airport User Charges" 89 *AJIL* (1995) 174

Norbert Wühler, 'Mixed Arbitral Tribunals', III *Encyclopedia of Public International Law* (Rudholf Bernhardt, ed, 1997)

——, 'The United Nations Compensation Commission: A New Contribution to the Process of International Claims Resolution', 2 *J Int'l Eco L* (1999) 249

Christine Van den Wyngaert and Guy Stessents, 'The International Non Bis in Idem Principle: Resolving Some of the Unanswered Questions', 48 *ICLQ* 779 (1999)
Ernest A. Young, 'Institutional Settlement in a Globalization Judicial System', 54 *Duke LJ* (2005) 1143
Stefan Zleptnig, 'The Standard of Review in WTO Law: An Analysis of Law, Legitimacy and the Distribution of Legal and Political Authority', 6 *European Integration online Papers* (*EIoP*), N° 17 (2002)

Index

The manufacturer's authorised representative in the EU for product safety is Oxford University Press España S.A. of el Parque Empresarial San Fernando de Henares, Avenida de Castilla, 2 – 28830 Madrid (www.oup.es/en or product.safety@oup.com). OUP España S.A. also acts as importer into Spain of products made by the manufacturer.

www.ingramcontent.com/pod-product-compliance
Ingram Content Group UK Ltd.
Pitfield, Milton Keynes, MK11 3LW, UK
UKHW020923170926
475595UK00031B/49
* 9 7 8 0 1 9 9 2 1 1 7 9 1 *